SECRET SERVICES

Your very own pocket concierge

Also by Cary Whitley
theweddingfile

SECRET SERVICES

Your very own pocket concierge

Cary Whitley

Fab Publishing Limited 2007

First published in Great Britain in 2007 by Fab Publishing Limited
1 Evesden House, The Forest, London E11 1PJ

www.fabpublishing.co.uk

A CIP catalogue record for this book is available from the British Library

ISBN 978-0-9556481-0-6

Disclaimer
We have taken all steps possible to ensure the accuracy of the information in this guide,
nevertheless, the publishers can accept no responsibility for errors or changes in or omissions
from the details given.
If any information is incorrect please send an email with updated details to
corrections@fabpublishing.co.uk

All trademarks are acknowledged

Printed and bound in Slovenia
Typeset • Special Edition Pre-Press Services, London

A NOTE FROM CARY

This book has been a labour of love and it combines some of my greatest pleasures in life. I confess – I love shopping (my friends claim I'm addicted!), but I also love discovering new, unusual and useful products and wonderfully creative people.

I'm always excited to hear about the many talented craftsmen and women in this country who have the passion to survive and succeed by offering bespoke products and fantastic customer service. So, as our world becomes more impersonal and automated, I feel we need more than ever to support brilliant ideas, excellent small businesses and individuals, and I have therefore tried to include as many brave young enterprises as possible. Of course I have also included some of the 'big boys' who still offer a wonderful personal service and remain great British institutions.

I wrote this book for many reasons. It was definitely a good use for my thirty well-worn notebooks and six bulging filing cabinets, which contain information on fabulous shops I have visited, quirky products, must-visit places, fantastic services and solutions to every problem and so much more. I have personally selected every entry in this book and have tried and tested a great many (some I couldn't for logistical or financial reasons – I am saving… hard!). I have visited the shops, used the services and paid my own bills to ensure you have a genuinely independent and impartial guide to the very best on offer. And yes, it was also a great excuse to enjoy beauty treatments, try services and buy products without feeling guilty because 'it's all in the name of research!'

I'm sure you'd agree that for most people today, time is a most precious gift. In the end, I think that is the real reason I wrote this book, because surely one of the greatest pleasures in life is finding the time to enjoy the things and people you love.

It's great to know there are companies or individuals who will do all those jobs you haven't got time to do, hate doing, don't know how to do or just simply can't be bothered to do! And I hope that in spreading the word about these services and people who can make your life easier, you too will find more time to enjoy life.

A BIG THANK YOU

Researching and writing this book has been a much bigger project than I initially anticipated and I would like to thank several people who have helped me.

Firstly a very big thank you to:
> Vicki Newell for sub-editing and writing some very witty headings.
> Ian Findlay for the original design ideas, and for being one of the most talented designers I've ever had the pleasure to work with.
> Romilly Hambling and Corinne Orde from Special Edition Pre-Press Services, for their

patience, support and skilful typesetting.

> To my dear mother, Kate Whitley, who cast her sharp eye over the text and made suggestions and corrected mistakes!
> Ruth Burns, Romilly Hambling and Corinne Orde for copy editing.
> Julie Martin for cover layout.
> Michéle Clarke for the index.

I would also like to thank my husband Marcus and my son Finn for their enormous patience and love, especially over the last frantic six months when I was chained to my desk and couldn't come out to play.

Thanks to all my dear friends who have stopped saying 'Is it finished yet?'

And a special thanks to Lottie Johansson and Kathy Rudd for their immense support and help over the years.

But most of all, I want to say thank you to all the entrepreneurs in the book who have had the courage and conviction to start their own businesses – I salute your determination and passion and hope your ventures continue to go from strength to strength.

A FEW NOTES ON THE ENTRIES

Some shops have many stores nation- and worldwide and there were far too many to list. Where shops have several branches, the address and telephone number listed often refer to the main branch or flagship store, so I make reference to checking online, for which I offer no apologies. This is often the best way to check for other branches, new addresses or any updated information.

All phone numbers and addresses were updated three weeks prior to print, but as I learnt the hard way… these do change! Please do check before visiting.

I would be very grateful for any information that will help me to update future editions. If you discover that any entry details have changed please email me at:

corrections@fabpublishing.co.uk

And don't forget to check our website for any news and updates:

www.fabpublishing.co.uk

CONTENTS

HOME   64-103

TRAVEL

FASHION

SHOPPING & PRESENTS 182-211

BEAUTY & PAMPERING 212-242

EAT

FAMILY (Pregnancy, Babies, Children ... And Pets) 266–306

INDEX 308–333

CELEBRATE AND ENTERTAIN
DINNERPARTIES
PROPS
PARTYPLANNERS
BARSERVICE
DRESSES FABFLORISTS
BUTLER
CATERERS CANDLES
DECORATIONS FOOD
WEDDINGS
STATIONERY ENTERTAINMENT

DINNER PARTIES

DINNER PARTY PREPARATION

LAY YOUR TALENTS ON THE TABLE

> If you love hosting dinner parties or lunches, but fear that your food-laden dining room table doesn't quite cut the dash you desire, then book yourself onto a course with the charming and entertaining Jan and Sherrie from Dare To Do It.

> Hosted at Sherrie's wonderful home, you'll have a fun-filled day learning practical, inspiring and money-saving ideas for creating 'ta-da' table settings and making shop-bought food look like a visually delightful 'here's one I made earlier'.

> Jan and Sherrie show you inspiring ways to use things you may already have in your home, from giving a new lease of life to old candlesticks, to raiding the fruit and vegetable baskets, to making attractive table decorations. They also take you through a couple of real TV makeover show moments, as they spray-paint fans with wonderful pearly paint or use old records as table mats.

> Throughout the day you'll be shown six to eight different table themes. You'll have a delicious two-course lunch, meet some very interesting people and go away with a head full of inspiring ideas to make your next dinner party the talk of the town.

> This course would make a great gift for a close friend and would be a fabulous thing to do for a hen party or girlie get-together, as they also cater to private parties. (£95.00 for the one-day course).

> During November and December they offer a three-hour workshop in Kensington, specialising in Christmas table decoration. At just £45.00, it will set you back less than a box of fancy crackers!

> If it is something you'd rather leave to the experts, you can also book them privately to style your dinner party or wedding.

> **Dare To Do It, 27 Danes Court, St Edmund's Terrace, London NW8 7QR
T·Sherrie Bodie 020 7586 0300 / 07989 402 259; Jan Grinling 07836 689 603**

SHOPPING TO DINE FOR

> I really should leave my credit cards at home when I visit this store as I cannot restrain myself from wanting to buy, buy and then buy some more. They sell everything you could want for your dining room, from candles and antique chandeliers, to vintage cocktail shakers and china. Unsurprisingly, their customers flock from all over the world. They can source hard-to-find items including silver, and make bespoke furniture and glass items. I always like to add to my vintage cake-stand collection.

> The shop is brimming with ideas for gorgeous presents – how about a vintage tea cup hand-painted with soft pink roses, a beautiful antique lace-edged tablecloth, or a Victorian monogrammed napkin ring – a charming christening present.

> They also specialise in made-to-order table linen, which can be monogrammed. I love their Christmas shopping day, usually held in November in conjunction with the wonderful shop Tobias and the Angel (*see page* 190). You can find all sorts of goodies for the Christmas table, but you will have to get there early to nab the best stuff.

> **The Dining Room Shop, 62-64 White Hart Lane, Barnes, London SW13 0PZ
T·020 8878 1020
W·thediningroomshop.co.uk**

To add a truly personal touch, get a recent individual picture of all your guests (or you could use photos of them as children) and pop along to your local print shop who will transfer their photo onto a placemat. You will surprise all your guests with their bespoke table setting and it makes a nice gift for them to take away. Or you could do as I did when I had a Blue Peter moment: I scanned in their photos, printed them onto transfer paper, then ironed them onto vintage linen napkins – great alternative place cards!

PRIVATE CHEFS

According to those in the know, the most commonly commented-on aspect of a party is always the food, followed by the drink, then the music. I was under the impression it was gossip and who was there, but what do I know? Don't be alarmed if food preparation doesn't top the list of your talents, all you need is a little bit of help. First choice for me, naturally, is the chef who comes to your home to cook up a feast for you and your guests.

COOK BY NAME, CHEF BY NATURE

> You've probably heard about Serena Cook, known as the Ibiza fixer – the foremost concierge and catering company on the island. However, from September to June she is available as a private chef (with A-list clients) in London and will gladly cook a dinner for two or 200. She says, 'no request is too ordinary or extraordinary'. Having opened her first restaurant in Colombia at the age of 20, she has subsequently worked with Oliver Peyton and also opened Deli Organic with Sheherazade Goldsmith.
> She loves cooking different ethnic cuisines

but particularly enjoys Japanese food – gets round all that no-dairy, no-wheat and no-more-than-two-bites-or-I'll-put-on-weight kind of thing.
> She can also provide additional waiting staff, decorations and flowers. In fact, there's not much she can't help you with, but since she runs Deliciously Sorted, you'd expect no less. Oh yes, did I mention that she speaks Spanish, French, Italian and English? Speed dial entry, for sure.
> **Serena Cook T·07780 633 225
W·deliciouslysortedibiza.com**

SIX HUNDRED SAVOUR STEFANIA'S SPAGHETTI!

> Anyone who meets the lovely Stefania will realise that cooking is not her job, it's her passion. Stefania and her husband Giacomo are highly sought after for their wonderful Italian cooking – what she would call 'real family food'. She has cooked for private clients from London to New York to the Bahamas, including rustling up a little home made Potato Gnocchi with Vongole for her favourite leading men (she is known as the 'Queen of Pasta'.)
> Stefania can cook anything for any occasion, from an intimate dinner party for eight, to pasta for 600. Happy to put her clients' needs first, she recently pulled together a very impromptu dinner party (having already cooked all day at another function) for a celebrity who had called in a last-minute panic and begged and pleaded!
> Enough Stefania anecdotes from me – having cooked professionally for over 20 years, she has many a tale to tell, so why don't you hear them first hand?
> **Stefania Lussco T·07961 877 234**

*See also **Iona Grant** (page 15), who will cook up a treat. **Sophie Douglas-Bate** (page 13) offers a fabulous private-chef service.*

Also see pages 11-16 for caterers who offer this service.

GLAD YOU COULD MAKE IT!
DINNER PARTY DELIVERIES

Need to rustle up dinner for eight but you're too exhausted or can't find the time? Don't fret, there are now a number of companies that will take that strain away from you – all you have to do is decide whether you're going to own up to it!

MARIA MAKES ENTERTAINING FUN

> Maria Balfour is someone you must have in your speed dial. Her company, Effortless Eating, offers home-cooked British food delivered straight to our homes. The meal arrives in elegant white ovenproof china dishes (which are yours to keep) that can go straight from the oven to the table. All the dishes are made using the freshest seasonal ingredients, with no added colours, preservatives or stabilisers. You can order freshly-prepared starters, mains, side dishes, puddings and tea-time treats. You also have a choice of two types of food – meals that are fully cooked and just need you to re-heat, or the fully prepared dishes that need to be cooked, but come with a full set of instructions. All you need decide is whether you are going to own up to your guests to having had more than a little professional help!

> Weekday orders are required two days before delivery date and weekend orders must be in by Tuesday for delivery on Friday. Orders must be for a minimum of four people having the same menu (from £90.00). Delivery is free within certain London post-codes (for other addresses there will be an extra delivery charge-unless your order value is over £200.00).

> Now my favourite bit ... Maria creates some great gift boxes. The Baby Box will give a welcome respite to the new parents and bulges with soup, a main meal for two,

and goodies such as chocolate brownies and cupcakes – all beautifully wrapped and tied up with a blue or pink ribbon. Or why not help your stress-ridden friends when they move home by giving them the Moving Home Box as a lovely house-warming present – it even includes the cutlery and napkins! The range includes the Baby Box (£95.00), Moving Home Box (£95.00), Bachelor Box (priced on request), and Sweet & Savoury Tooth Box (£70.00). Of course, Maria can also create bespoke boxes for you.

> **Effortless Eating Ltd (Head Office), 32 Roland Gardens, London SW7 3PL T·07766 285 711 W·effortless-eating.com**

IF YOU CAN'T BEAT IT, EAT IT

> I insist that you visit this shop, or at least visit them online. I spent hours salivating at their wonderful selection of divine starters, soups, mains, desserts and treats, and then spent a fortune buying lots and lots. I really recommend their meals when you need to dish up a quick posh dinner. Phone the very charming and helpful staff at 6 Elgin Crescent (not during the busy lunch hour), who will gladly go through suggestions with you. You can pick up your order from their shops or they can send it to you in a taxi

> The packaging is so simple and elegant, it seems a shame to hide it in the bin when you're trying to bluff it! The food is mouth-watering and there are no artificial 'anythings' added. The company was established by the owners of the Sugar Club, so it comes with a great reputation already attached.

> **The Grocer on Elgin, 6 Elgin Crescent, London W11 2HX T·020 7221 3844**
> **The Grocer on King's, 184 King's Road, London SW3 5XP T·020 7351 5544**
> **W·thegroceron.com**

THERE'S NOTHING STAID ABOUT READY-MADE

> Winners of many accolades for their meat, with a reputation built up over 17 years of business, Swaddles are no secret among top chefs. They are unique in that you can choose exactly the size of the joint, the thickness and even how you would like it packed. If any of your guests are vegetarian, they can also offer tasty alternatives to the main meat dish.

> Dedicated to taking 'the pain out of entertaining', you won't go wrong ordering from their à la carte section offering your favourite cuts combined with their range of sauces, marinades or butters. They also offer frozen ready meals, so stock up and you need never again fear that unexpected visitor. It's reassuring to know that everything is organic, from their meat to their children's meals, sauces and dairy products.

> There's a £35.00 minimum charge, and if you place your order by 11.00 a.m. you can receive it the next day. If you do a lot of entertaining, get on their VIP list and they will call you to go through your order.

> Make sure you check out their website at Christmas as they offer a fantastic range, including ready-made Christmas hampers and fabulous gift selections.

> **Swaddles Organic T·0845 456 1768 / 01460 234 387 W·swaddles.co.uk**

PARTY PARTY!
BAR SERVICES
& MIXOLOGISTS

When it comes to cocktails, I remember the exact moment I realised it pays to go professional. Having rented a big house in Scotland to see in the New Year with 20 of our closest friends, we wanted to make it a night to remember. We foolishly decided to name a cocktail after each guest like, 'Annie Thing'll Do After This' (Vodka, Kahlua, Baileys Irish Cream and vanilla ice-cream) and 'Alma Eggs in One Basket' (fresh banana, rum, lime juice, papaya and orange juice), and consequently spent the whole evening slaving over the cocktail bar trying to keep up with demand and remember what went in whose drink. We were so busy we almost missed the big countdown!

MIX IT UP A LITTLE

> Booked for film premières and all the hot parties for their great attitude, experience and innovative drinks, Bamboo are known for their cocktail mixologists. Try their Envy or Grand Passion cocktail and you'll never want your 'usual' again. They also have fantastic Flair bartenders who offer cocktail theatre by juggling, sleight of hand, hurling bottles into the air and balancing glasses on the end of bar spoons. Guaranteed to get your guests in the party mood.

> They can provide the bar (see their website for the amazing ice-bar filled with roses) along with lighting, DJ and props if needed. *See page* 25 for their sister company At Your Service if you'd like catering or party staff. Prices: from £100.00 per bartender for four hours, plus around £3.25 per cocktail

> **Bamboo, Unit 12, The Talina Centre, Bagley's Lane, London SW6 2BW T·020 7610 8606 W·eventmixology.com**

WHO NEEDS TOM CRUISE?

> Everything you ever wanted to know about the cocktail but were too afraid to ask. Cocktail.com's mission is 'to bring the drink aficionados and bartenders of the world the best cocktail recipes and advice'. Miss Cocktail is ready and waiting to answer any of your questions and the fabulous recipes, including the intriguing Maiden's Blush and Little Green Fairy, are guaranteed to knock you off your feet. I was particularly

impressed by the $650.00 cocktail currently popular with those out to impress at the Starlight Rooms in San Francisco. I now know exactly how to make it and the DIY version is a bit cheaper!

> Other highlights of this website are the month's top drinks, the top-10 classic cocktails list and a great section on ingredients. I just hope I can find something to use up that alarming bottle my friend brought me back from Greece in 1998...

> **W·cocktail.com**

THE COOLEST CLUBBERS STAY HOME

> When Alex Carlton, owner of Funkin, supplier of fresh fruit juices and purées to the bar world, wanted to wow his party-goers with club-quality cocktails at his home, a whole new genre was born.

> Party in a Box offers a completely portable, contemporary bar, complete with internationally-acclaimed bartenders and a cocktail menu of over 500 drinks — with room for a couple of your own concoctions!

> They can also provide stylish waiting staff, gourmet nibbles, DJ, photographer and — if you can't quite face the morning after — a cleaner.

> The service is available throughout the South East (extra charge for outside the M25) for a minimum of 50 guests. Prices start from £1,000.00.

> If you still fancy being behind the bar yourself, you can buy their fruit juices and purées to make your own cocktails, smoothies or desserts. I love their liquid dark chocolate. Of course, they are all made from 100 per cent fruit, free from any artificial flavourings. Buy online from **W·thedrinkshop.com** or from Harvey Nichols, Selfridges and Waitrose.

> **Funkin At Home, 33 Londsdale Road, London NW6 6RA**
> **T·020 7328 4440 W·funkin.co.uk**

DON'T BE SQUARE, BUY THE CUBES

> Forget the spiky cocktail umbrellas and the wilting slices of banana, the cocktails at a recent fashion party I attended were lit up with fantastic LED ice cubes. The divine metallic silver number that the size 0 model was wearing went unnoticed by the Beautiful People in attendance and I knew I simply had to get some of these glittery cubes for our next drinks party.

> Filled with a special non-toxic gel, they freeze like any other ice cube; just press the button to activate the light, which can flash or remain static. You can buy them in individual colours (from £1.72) or in packs of mixed colours. You can purchase them from the Lite Factory, who offer a great selection including the cubes, slices, wedges, dice, footballs, rugby balls and golf balls, and I also happened to notice you could hire their three- to five-metre-high lit coconut trees if you fancy!

> **Litefactory Ltd, PO Box 2570, Ascot SL5 8XN**
> **T·Ascot: 0870 770 2993 / Brighton: 0870 770 3178 W·litefactory.co.uk**

NOT A DRY GLASS IN THE HOUSE

> No party host/ess should be without the number of Lock-In, a late-night drinks service that will deliver chilled wine, beer, spirits, soft drinks and tobacco in around 30 minutes. The Lock-In delivers to all London SW postcodes, nearly all W codes and to most NW, SE, E, EC and WC areas. Many of the SW codes include free delivery, otherwise expect to pay £2-£15.00 delivery charge. There is no minimum order, but orders of less than £50.00 value incur a £5.95 delivery charge. Red wines are priced from £6.75, white wines from £6.95. When I logged on, they had 20 per cent off any 12 bottles of wine purchased. So if you find your last bottle of Veuve Clicquot (£33.85) or Bollinger (£39.95) finished, and your party still has many

hours to go, you know whom to call. Open from 6.00 p.m., last orders 6.00 a.m.
> **The Lock-In T · 020 7350 2424 or Text 07781 472 084 W · latelondon.co.uk**

SAY CHIN CHIN TO THE PERFECT PARTY

> With over 12 years' experience working in some of the top bars and private clubs, there's not much Chin Nicholson doesn't know about cocktails. We're prepared to bet that you'll never taste a better Margarita, which is why he's been re-booked by clients more times than you've had one-too-many-brightly-coloured drinks. All you have to do is supply the sink and he'll supply the rest. One client said, 'It's the first time I've had a party that I've actually enjoyed.'
Prices: from £20 to 27.00 per head for approximately 40 guests.
> **Chin Nicholson T · 07946 373 956**

For some rather novel paper party cups and ice cubes see page 286

BIG HOUSES FOR HIRE

SIZE IS EVERYTHING!

> The Big Domain's properties include Chateau de Marouatte, a stunning 14th-century fortified castle set in a 240-acre estate in the Dordogne region of Perigord. Twelve bedrooms sleep up to 23 guests in five different areas, so you can always sneak away into the Garden Tower for a little lie-down... Hold a banquet night, browse the shelves of the library, take a stroll in the formal gardens, or just sit and admire the antique furnishings, tapestries and oil paintings. Children are very welcome, with babysitting by arrangement. In fact, you won't be able to keep them out of the heated pool, set against the backdrop of towers and pointy castle spires. Prices are from £2,990 to £5,990.00 per week (up to

16 guests – additional guests extra), with shorter stay rates available.
> If a castle isn't your scene, The Big Domain have over 170 fantastic properties in the UK and abroad, from ski chalets and luxury islands to villas and boats, which all sleep more than 12 people. If you have a big group to house, look up Villa Lucia, Vorno, Tuscany, and take over the three fabulous villas which would sleep up to 42.
> And for all you romantics out there, they have just launched **W · thelittledomain.com** which is full of romantic properties for two – not always easy to find.
> All of the properties featured on The Big Domain are rented directly from the owners.
> **The Big Domain T · 01326 240 028 W · thebigdomain.com**

IS YOUR LIFE LACKING A LITTLE LUXURY?

> If you want a taste of the life we all wish we could become accustomed to, think big... The Big House offers exclusive hire of two sumptuous houses in the Somerset country-side for birthdays, anniversaries, reunion parties, weddings or just a big family get-together. All you have to do is set the date and you'll arrive to a wonderfully warm, spotlessly clean house full of character and atmosphere.
> Tone Dale House is an 18th-century Georgian Palladian villa set in four acres of landscaped grounds, centring on the mill stream. It sleeps 21, but if you also hire the Stables you will have accommodation for up to 31 people. A great games room with roulette, table tennis and pool ensures fun tournaments, and you can even try a spot of croquet on the lawn outside. If you've had a long drive down, they can have a hot tub (for hire, pre-book) ready for you to have a leisurely soak on arrival. Filled with antiques, family portraits and a roaring cosy fire, it's like a (big) home away from home. (From £2,175.00 midweek for two nights.)

> The other house, Widcombe Grange, was built in the late 1800s and is set in 22 acres of landscaped woodland on the Blackdown Hills. It can sleep 24. Widcombe has a natural pond with its own island gazebo and a two acre spring-fed fishing lake with lovely woodland walks. There is so much to do in the area... if you fancy a spot of clay pigeon shooting, horse riding, fly fishing tuition or golf, then it can be arranged in advance. Or why not just stick around the house and after a swim have a massage, which they can also arrange for you. In fact, as long as it's legal, they can arrange anything! Nothing is too much trouble, and although the staff live off the premises they're on hand to provide help and guidance if needed. Bring your own food, or for a little extra have the lovely staff come over and dish up gourmet dinners and scrummy breakfasts. They can even fill your fridge with home-made meals that only need re-heating. Bliss! (From £2,250.00 midweek for two nights.)

> If you log on to their website and check for any late availability, you may get one of the houses at a real steal or have a special offer thrown in – I was offered £1,000.00 off!

> **The Big House, Tone Dale House, Wellington, Somerset TA21 OEZ**
> **T·01823 662 673 W·thebighouseco.com**

TOGETHERNESS WITH TIME OUT

> If the idea of spending a week with your entire extended family under one roof is not an appealing one, I suggest hiring all of these seven self-catering luxury cottages instead. Together they can sleep up to 32, but you keep a little personal space. Of course, you could just hire one and leave all your friends and family behind!

> I wanted to include this delightful set of holiday cottages owned by Sarah Callander Beckett, a former PR of Laura Ashley, as they have all been tastefully restored with Jane Churchill, Nina Campbell and Designer Guild interiors, following themes ranging from African, Indian and Medieval, to Austrian and French. Naturally the cottages have all mod cons and there is a shop where you can buy wonderful estate products along with seasonal home-made dishes which you can serve in your own cottage.

> The seven cottages are set beside England's largest private lake and 1,000 acres of woodlands, and have been skilfully integrated into a Grade II stable block built in 1837. There are 15 acres of walled garden, pleasure gardens and garden woods which are great for walking and picnics, and you can enjoy cycling, fishing, lake swimming, tennis, croquet, bird-watching and painting. The area is also renowned for fantastic antique hunting (their website offers a pop-down menu listing all the nearby antique shops and markets).

> They have great facilities for children, and babysitters can be booked in advance. You can also book a relaxing treatment with their holistic therapists in the privacy of your cottage, or take advantage of the half-day pamper session at a nearby health and beauty spa.
> Prices: (weekly) from £557.00 for a cottage sleeping four; £794.00 for cottages sleeping six.

> **Combermere Abbey Cottages, Combermere Abbey, Whitchurch, Shropshire SY13 4AJ**
> **T·01948 662 876**
> **W·combermereabbey.co.uk**

HUNDREDS OF GOOD REASONS TO TAKE A BREAK

> With over 520 holiday cottages and houses in the West Country, the lovely family-run business Helpful Holidays inspect all their properties personally and offer a frank and objective description so you know exactly what you're renting.

> Their wonderful brochure clearly categorises all the properties into sections such as:

4+ bedrooms; five-star; detached; dogs welcome; on farms where you can help; with a tennis court; good for honeymooners; with wheel-chair facilities; with outstanding sea or estuary views; with pool or near a beach – the list is endless.

> With 30 properties sleeping 12 or more, you can have a wonderful party, reunion or wedding reception, set within the most spectacular countryside or beach locations. Whilst some of the bigger properties are very modestly furnished and not the sort of rooms you'd see gracing glossy interior magazines, the location and sheer atmosphere of these unique homes cannot be beaten.

> On their books they have what is probably the largest individual self-catering property in the UK: Colehayes Park, a Grade II-listed country house in 20 acres of parkland, streams and gardens, sleeps up to 70 in 21 bedrooms with nine showers, two baths and 14 loos! The accommodation is very modest and geared to stays free from the worry of damaging priceless antiques. This amazing holiday opportunity is priced at £3,400.00 for 40 people with extra people charged pro rata.

> Or you could try to hire all 14 apartments on Burgh Island Causeway with its spectacular sea views, sandy beach, private leisure centre and balconies to sit and enjoy breakfast in the sunshine. They can sleep up to 65 if you manage to book them all – you'll have to try well in advance. Prices vary depending on the size of the apartment.

> Technically these next mentions aren't 'big houses', but I couldn't resist telling you about them, so take a look. You can hire the thatched, hexagonal, Grade II-listed 'Gingerbread House' (sleeps six), a Tower Apartment in a castle with outstanding sea views (sleeps eight), a boathouse built in 1760 in the most secluded, romantic setting in South Devon (sleeps four), or Casa Del Rio, a house modelled on Pickfair – Douglas Fairbanks and Mary Pickford's home in Beverley Hills (sleeps 20).

> **Helpful Holidays T · 01647 433 593 W · helpfulholidays.com**

THROW A SAFARI DINNER

A great evening's entertainment if you hire a group of cottages with friends.

1 Number all the cottages (after a few drinks, remembering the cottages' names may prove too challenging)

2 Start at cottage 1 and have pre-dinner cocktails

3 Move to cottage 2 and have the starter

4 Move to cottage 3 and have the main course

5 Move to cottage 4 and have dessert

6 Move to cottage 5 and have coffee and petit fours

7 Move to cottage 6 for dancing

8 Move to cottage 7 for those who want an early night

9 Stay away from cottage 3 – it has the most washing up

10 Put all the children in cottage 8 with a babysitter

11 Cottage 9 can make breakfast in the morning

12 Cottage 10 can remain a quiet zone for those with hangovers or those who just want a lie-in

HIDEAWAY HEAVEN OVER THE WATER

> Despite Moongate being perched on Mount Leinster with stunning views over the countryside, the medieval city of Kilkenny nearby, and only two hours drive from Dublin Airport, the amazing location is not this property's biggest attraction. As you sweep through the 18th-century oak door you'll be arguing over who is going to have the Venetian master bedroom with the brass roll-top bath – but don't worry if you lose out, the other eight themed bedrooms have their own uniqueness with an eclectic mix of elegant styles from across the globe.

> Salvaged goodies from all over the world mix beautifully with 21st-century convenience. As you wander through the delightful rooms look out for the 200-year-old doors from a maharajah's palace, the Art Nouveau chandelier made by Asprey, a 300-year-old wardrobe, Afghani doors, and a stunningly crafted gate from a French church. With wonders like this, be prepared to feel a little dissatisfied with your faithful Ikea flat-pack furniture on your return home!

> The main house has a grand entrance hall, music room with walnut baby grand piano and galleried library, billiard room, dining room, study, six bedrooms, three bathrooms, steam room, kitchen and pantry, and there is also a guest cottage with two bedrooms and a bathroom. Naturally there are a raft of things to do during your stay: from billiards, to lazy hours catching up on all the films you've missed, board games, books, watching satellite TV, relaxing with holistic treatments and, for the more energetic, mountain walking, horse riding and quad biking.

> Hire just the house or talk to them about bespoke services and functions – they will help you host your own murder mystery weekend, an Irish evening with ceilidh, or even a wedding party. Gourmet breakfasts and afternoon teas are also available as optional extras and catering can be arranged.

Moongate sleeps up to 15.
Prices: one night €1,850; two nights €2,450; one week €4,200

> **Moongate, Tom Duff, Borris, County Carlow, Ireland**
  Bookings: contact Jasmine Crilly
  T·07956 509 028 W·moongatesite.com

DON'T BE A BIG SOUK

> If you want a fantastic house for a party, take a look at Villa Ezzahra. A Moroccan walled villa 15 minutes from the medina of Marrakech, this beautiful home has a dining terrace, five luxurious bedrooms, roof terrace, paddle rackets court, gym, hammam, treatment room and cinema. All you have to decide is whether to lie by the pool, nap in the Berber tent, bargain in the souk, or trek in the Atlas range, before enjoying a relaxing massage. The rental includes a resident house manager, cook and masseuse, all meals and non-alcoholic drinks. Rates are £200.00 – £260.00 per person per day for a minimum of eight persons (maximum 14) and a minimum let of five nights.

> Should you prefer the South of France, rent the luxury villa Domaine St Jacques with spectacular views, a divine swimming pool, water garden, tennis court, orangerie and a state of the art kitchen.
  Prices: From £5,000.00 per week sleeping 12 adults (2 young) in high season, 20 adults in low-mid season.

> PPA handpick their luxurious, diverse, charming or scenic properties with great care and all houses are staffed. Some even have a chef for the ultimate pampered holiday experience.

> **Private Properties Abroad**
  T·01423 330 533 W·ppaproperties.com

OTHER OPTIONS FOR LARGE GROUPS

> **Abercrombie & Kent** – expensive, exclusive but unsurpassed. A chateau, farmhouse, beach retreat or private island – whichever

one you choose it will be spectacular. (*Also see page* 136)

> T · 0845 070 0618
> W · abercrombiekent.co.uk

> **The Owners' Syndicate** has an excellent reputation for quality villa holidays. Take a look at Il Palazzo in Tuscany: it sleeps 18 in 9 bedrooms – a poolside paradise.
> T · 020 7381 7492 W · ownerssyndicate.com

> **Rentvillas.com** offer some fantastic properties throughout Europe. They have a great section, 'Fit For Friends', which ensures that everyone sleeps in equitable quarters – don't want to be stuck in the box room do you? Or try their 'Group Getaways' to find properties that sleep from 12 to 36. Prices are quoted in US dollars.
> T · +1 805 641 1650 W · rentvillas.com

> **tuscanynow.com** list 200 hand-picked Italian villas, farmhouses, apartments and castles. Individual comments by previous holiday-makers are very helpful.
> T · 020 7684 8884 W · tuscanynow.com

CAKES

For party, birthday and celebration cakes see pages 251-255

For wedding cakes see page 55

For couture cupcakes see pages 252-254

CATERERS & PARTY PLANNERS

PLAN ON DELEGATING

If you just want to make one phone call and have a dedicated party-planner or designer, caterer or party organiser take over, then here are some of the best in the business.

MORE THAN YOU COULD EVER DREAM OF

> There is nothing these guys won't do. I once saw their semi-clad hunky waiters wearing only round tables filled with the most delectable canapés walking amongst the guests who devoured the tasty morsels – a completely refreshing idea.

> The Admiral Crichton team of designers create amazing themed parties, produce spectacular sets for everything from product launches to film premières, book the very best entertainment and work with the world's leading suppliers to deliver magical events. Established in 1981, they have got creative in the most extraordinary places – up snow-covered mountains, on tropical islands, in museums and palaces, on yachts and in aeroplanes.

> If you've booked a venue where you have to use in-house caterers, then book AC to do the decorations. You will have access to their wonderful warehouse – an Aladdin's cave of silks from Samarkand and velvets from St Petersburg, twisted Italian glasses in shades from mulberry to absinthe, giant lanterns, engraved glass and plates in the finest china. Each year they travel the world in search of the latest, most ravishing, beautiful and fun additions to their private collection which you can choose from.

> In one year they organised 452 parties for 82,530 guests, serving a total of 387,000 canapés and 25,576 dinners. No need to

mention who they've worked for – it's all the well-known names!

> In their own words, they 'take their client's idea of the dream party and make the reality even better'. Minimum spend £5,000.00.

> **The Admirable Crichton, Unit 5, Camberwell Trading Estate, Denmark Road, London SE5 9LB**
T · 020 7326 3800
W · admirable-crichton.co.uk

DELICIOUS THROUGH AND THROUGH

> If you think going to a barbeque means suspect sausages in buns dripping tomato ketchup, what about trying shark cooked in banana leaves, or pineapple soaked in vodka with cracked pepper and maple syrup! The food just melted on my tongue – absolutely scrummy! And I can't stand doing barbeques myself, so having it all prepared definitely gets my vote.

> Blistering Barbeques have cooked at weddings, film premières and festivals, and they not only offer the traditional bangers and burgers but can do plated three-course meals, with all the food being cooked on wood-fired ovens and barbeques.

> They brought out a book full of wonderful recipes last summer. It's available in specialist bookshops – grab a copy now.

> **Blistering Barbeques, Unit 2, Imex Business Centre, Ingate Place, London SW8 3NS**
T · 020 7720 7678 W · blistering.co.uk

FOLLOW THAT WAITER!

> Speak to those in the know on party planning and the name on their lips for slick design and presentation is Blue Strawberry. Founders Molly Ronan and James Macdonald-Buchanan believe 'their food is the most delicious in London, and their decoration and presentation unique and imaginative'; their impressive list of clients would seem to agree. They have been called on to provide a

luncheon for 150 including royalty, a cocktail reception for 400 and a plated picnic for 800 guests.

> Of course, they will also cater for small dinners and receptions. Their canapés are mouth-watering and moreish – this is my choice for my next party: grilled swordfish skewers glazed with a pomegranate syrup and served with aioli sauce; char-grilled polenta squares topped with Marsala chicken pieces, basil and deep-fried leek; bacon and egg toasted croustade with soft quails egg and maple bacon finished with Hollandaise sauce; wild mushroom tarts with cream and sherry; deep-fried figs with a gorgonzola sauce served on china spoons; not to mention the caviar display with fresh little blinis and accompaniments set on ice with little shots of vodka. And for afters, drool, drool: china spoons with caramelized crème brulée; apple fritters dusted with cinnamon sugar; fresh fruit tartlets with vanilla and passionfruit mascarpone; and banana won tons with a hot chocolate dip. Need I say more?

> **Blue Strawberry, OPB House, 26/28 Sidney Road, London SW9 OTS**
T · 020 7733 3151 W · bluestrawberry.co.uk

TOO GOOD TO KEEP TO YOURSELF

> From cooking in a field for over a thousand guests, to calming a panicky customer at 11.00 p.m., to organising a three-day overseas Bar Mitzvah celebration including all the flights, accommodation, cars, flowers and food, it would seem that the talents of By Word of Mouth are endless.

> However Sarah Williams, (one of the founders) says it comes down to just three things: well-researched, delicious modern food; never forgetting the personal touch; and complete professionalism (which is why they won't tell us the names of the many celebrities who have graced their books!).

> They have catered at premières and charity

events as well as for private parties, and will do as much or as little as you need. I liked the sound of the marquee they put into Battersea power station and the marionette band suspended over the heads of thrilled guests.

> I say glam, glam, glam, and yum, yum, yum! Minimum quote: drinks and canapés for 50 at £60.00 per head.

> **By Word of Mouth, 22 Glenville Mews, Kimber Road, London SW18 4NJ**
> **T · 020 8871 9566**
> **W · bywordofmouth.co.uk**

SEASON'S HIGHLIGHTS SURE TO PLEASE

> Great food and party design – I first saw 'create' at a show and was stopped in my tracks by the wonderful presentation of their canapés, which I found tasted even better than they looked. Each season create launch a new range of dishes and presentation ideas to wow all you party-goers. They also scour the world to make their tabletop designs exclusive and stylish, always introducing new glasses, china and stunning decorations. At a recent event they presented the canapés on trays made with food-safe wax embedded with glass beads in turquoise, dusty pink and cobalt blue, with the tables swathed in glistening cheesecloth and satins edged with mirrored jewels.

> I really love their mini-meals in porcelain pots – the alternative (more filling) finger food.

> **create food ltd, Unit 4, The Kimber Centre, 54 Kimber Road, London SW18 4PP**
> **T · 020 8870 1717   W · createfood.co.uk**

YOUR WISH IS THEIR COMMAND

> Imagine coming down to breakfast on your birthday and finding the table laid, including gorgeous flowers, breakfast being cooked, a waiter on hand, and all your best mates sitting there. It sounds too good to be true, but all you need to do is drop a few hints

about Delectable Feasts to your loving partner and these guys will bend over backwards to help out.

> I've included them because not only do they do parties and events, through Delectable Events they can also organise your picnic, afternoon tea, breakfast or an intimate dinner party. They recently organised and catered a picnic for 200 where every person got a little picnic box filled with lovely organic and home-made food like griddled honey, lime and ginger chicken salad and char-grilled Mediterranean vegetables. I would love to be invited to a wedding reception where you could lie on rugs and enjoy a picnic – very cosy. Clients include well-known designers and companies.

> **Delectable Feasts & Delectable Events, 23 Crimscott Street, London SE1 5TE**
> **T · 020 7232 3063**
> **W · delectablefeasts.com**

PICNIC OR PARTY – PICK YOUR PLEASURE

> Whether you're planning a private dinner à deux or a wedding for 400 of your closest friends, for a truly bespoke service call Sophie and her team. Sophie has been offering her services as a freelance cook for over 15 years. Her team will travel worldwide and cook anything. They have provided hospitality and catering for TV shows including The Parkinson Show, The Ruby Wax Show and BAFTA's tribute to Dame Judi Dench.

> On a smaller scale, they have provided a sumptuous picnic for two which was enjoyed on the lovely lawns at Glyndebourne. At a country wedding, they transformed the swimming pool into an elaborate centrepiece of a Brazilian nightclub by adding flaming torches, floating lily pads and a massive water fountain. And not to leave out the children, they have styled a Monsters Inc party for 30 eight-year-olds.

> For a dinner party for eight, expect to pay from £30.00 per head, with a supplement for staff. They can also provide china, cutlery, linen, glasses and wine.

> **Sophie Douglas-Bate, Edible Food Design, Unit 22, Southbank Business Centre, Ponton Road, Nine Elms Lane, London SW8 5BL**
> **T · 020 7622 5444**
> **W · ediblefooddesign.co.uk**

"RHUBARB" ARE NO FOOLS

> Nine years ago, Lucy Gemmell combined her passions for food and design to create "rhubarb" food design, now considered one of the top caterers/party-planners in the UK working on over 400 parties a year. They will play as large or small a part in your event as you desire, from catering for intimate dinners to large sit-down affairs, buffets, or delightful selections of canapés. Once you see what they can do though, you'll probably want them to plan the entire party for you.

> Their past successes include numerous blockbuster premières, society wedding receptions and celebrity birthday parties; they also have a very impressive corporate client list.

> They have a stunning range of glassware, china and cutlery (many made exclusively for "rhubarb") and offer food with a modern twist. They are renowned for their fabulous presentation — and it's not just their food: staff appearance is a high priority and they can even go the extra mile and dress in amazing outfits. How about their rubber party with food served on rubber trays by rubber-clad staff? Kinky!

> Pieter-Bas Jacobse, the MD, believes 'the impossible only takes a few seconds more'. They once flew in a sommelier all the way from the Netherlands to open bottles of wine costing £10,000 and, on another occasion, pulled an entire event together in two hours after it had accidentally been booked for the Wednesday rather than the Tuesday night. Now that's the kind of people I want around in a crisis!

> **"rhubarb" food design, Rhubarb House, 5–25 Burr Road, London SW18 4SQ**
> **T · 020 8812 3200 W · rhubarb.net**

If you're worried the big boys of catering might find your event somewhat on the small side to make it worth their while, read on for some little gems.

PUTTING ON A SHOW

> With a background in theatre design and years of experience working with top event and production companies, Emma Baker has now set up on her own. What I love about her is that you can go to her for the smaller things, like your invitation design, place-card settings or table plan, or use her vast experience, sharp eye and talent for perfection to put together your whole event. She designs the most amazing canapé trays and you can commission a bespoke one, or hire them from her fascinating collection. For example, she recently did a Halloween Party making the canapé trays from witches' hats and gravestones — they looked stunning. Such unique creativity means she is in great demand for private parties, weddings, fashion shows, launch events and premières, but you can be assured that whatever your party dreams, making them come true will be Emma's top priority.

> **EB Event Design**
> **T · 07786 657 760 W · ebeventdesign.co.uk**

HEAR YOUR GUESTS GASP

> Idyllic Days offers a fabulous vintage china hire and styling service. Imagine walking out into a garden where the tables are covered with antique lace tablecloths, fresh flowers and pastel-coloured vintage cake stands overflowing with the latest must-try cup-cakes. Tea is served in the most delicate

rose-patterned china and tealights are flickering softly in vintage candle holders. This is just one of the scenes Samantha Freeman can create if she styles your wedding reception or elegant garden party. And you don't have to wait till summer, Samantha is just as at home transforming your indoor venue into a breathtaking winter wonderland, with all that vintage pressed glass flickering in the soft candle light. The perfect opportunity to wear that impulse-buy fake fur capelet!

> If you would prefer to style the party yourself, you can simply hire her fabulous vintage china, glassware and silverware. Having worked with some of the top caterers and florists, she can obviously point you in the right direction in those areas, too.

> Her styling service is available at £300.00 per day. Hired goods are extra, approximately £5.00 per head for place settings, sugar tongs, sugar bowls, milk jugs and cake stands.

> **Idyllic Days, The Haven, 2 Underwood Road, Haslemere, Surrey GU27 1JQ T·01428 656267 / 07887 510 556 W·idyllicdays.com**

A DECADE OF DELICIOUSNESS

> Iona always gets her work through word of mouth and has been cooking up wonderful treats for over 10 years. She can come and cook for an intimate dinner party for eight, a big bash or even breakfast in bed (*see page* 251), and is happy to organise any other part of your event, from decorations to flowers, to full silver-service staffing.

> Iona offers great personal service and loves mixing food cultures, with Moroccan and Scottish food her own favourites to cook. She mainly works in London, but will travel and can use all your kitchen paraphernalia or bring her own — it's your call.

> **Iona Grant T·07720 443 132 E·iona@macunlimited.net**

INDULGE IN A LITTLE KIWI COOKING

> Having been at three parties where Suze Catering had been serving the most sumptuous canapés and meals, we booked them to cater at our own wedding reception. I'm delighted to tell you that the food was absolutely divine, a perfect New Zealand meal, and the service was second to none. They can supply all staff, linen, food and drink. They have a great selection of menus and canapés, including New Zealand mussels wrapped in bacon with pesto, fried quail eggs on chorizo sausage, and Grand Marnier and chocolate filo triangles. Delish! Tom and Sue are a truly gracious, unflappable couple who will go out of their way to cater for your every need. Among their many clients, they have cooked for the All Blacks and the Black Caps (the NZ cricket team). Howzat!

> **Suze Catering T·020 7491 3237 W·suzewinebar.com**

WONKIE'S GOT HER PLANNING HEAD ON STRAIGHT

> Wonkie from Zest Events is always keen to help, no matter what your budget. She says it's all about 'being clever with the money available'. She recently organised an incredible proposal with an audience for a client and his unsuspecting bride-to-be. It began as the couple waited for the film to start at the cinema. Instead of the normal string of trailers, up on the screen came a declaration of his love, followed by the big question... Meanwhile Wonkie (with a spy carefully placed at the cinema updating her) was back in the couple's house preparing a wonderful romantic dinner for two, complete with chefs, a waiter and stunning floral arrangements. After the lucky girl accepted, her fiancé then had to get her out of the cinema and back home, not actually allowing her to watch the movie. When they walked out of the cinema all the local press were waiting to take their photo — it was the real red-carpet treatment!

> They're a small company offering an intimate service and happy to face any logistical challenge head on in the most serene and professional manner.
> Zest Events, 2 Swan Mews, London SW6 4QT **T·020 7384 9336 W·zestevents.co.uk**

RED CARPET TREATMENT

Film parties are all the rage, darlings, so it's time to host your own private film screening. Show your favourite film, or invite a bunch of friends to watch an old classic on 'movie nights'. Some of these cinemas are located within gorgeous hotels, so why not make it even more enjoyable and stay the night as well as they often offer a discount for a package deal.

BOOK OUT THE WHOLE SHOW

> Firmdale Hotels have several state-of-the-art screening rooms. Charlotte Street Hotel and Covent Garden Hotel offer a 'Be a Movie Mogul For The Night' package, where you can entertain 10 or more of your friends with a movie of your choice, preceded or followed by either a three-course meal or a champagne and canapé reception. All this for just £50.00 per person.
> Or take a bunch of friends to one of their Weekend Film Clubs. You can dine in the hotel's restaurant, enjoying a two-course meal, glass of wine and the movie for only £35.00 per person. Covent Garden Hotel offers a Saturday Film Club and Charlotte Street offers a Sunday Film Club.
> Log on to see the month's selections of either classics or new releases.
> **Be a Movie Mogul T·Bookings 020 7287 4434**

> Saturday Film Club, Covent Garden Hotel, 10 Monmouth Street, London WC2H 9HB **T·020 7806 1000**
> Sunday Film Club, Charlotte Street Hotel, 15-17 Charlotte Street, London W1T 1RJ **T·020 7806 2000**
> All the Firmdale hotels can be viewed online at **W·firmdale.com**

SHOW ME THE MOVIE!

> One Aldwych has a 'Private Give Me Movies' programme where you can relax in luxurious, Italian-made, blue-leather cinema seats and enjoy a glass of champers and popcorn as you watch a film of your choice (which you bring on DVD or video). This is followed by an amazing three-course dinner in a private room at £48.50 per person (including service charges and VAT). You need to invite a minimum of 20 guests (maximum 30).
> Or you could just hire the screening room for £95.00 an hour (weekend rate) or £125.00 per hour (week-night rate), for a minimum of two hours. They have hosted hen parties, had people watch their own wedding video, and hosted a movie-themed birthday party. The room has even been hired for two, for a wedding proposal – a complete surprise for the lucky lady who accepted, then snuggled down to champers and the movie *When Harry Met Sally* – yes, yes, yes!
> **One Aldwych, London WC2B 4RH T·Nick 020 7300 1080 or Kyla 020 7300 0700 W·onealdwych.co.uk**

CULTURE ON THE COAST

> The delightful Hotel Tresanton (see full listing on page 133) will let you hire a movie room from £250.00. They have a huge selection of videos and films, and the room can seat up to 40 theatre-style. They can also provide little nibbles for you (at extra cost) to enjoy while you're watching the movie.
> **Hotel Tresanton, St Mawes, Cornwall T·01326 270 055 W·tresanton.com**

THE ULTIMATE HOME CINEMA

> This is probably my fave idea – host your own movie night at home. CVS will come round and set up the projector, DVD (if you don't have one), sound system and big screen – all you do is pop the popcorn, chill the champers, invite your best mates over and press play. Or, if you can't agree on a movie, you could plug in your computer game or playstation for the kids' party, or plug in a tuner (also for hire) to watch a sporting final or MTV music. Worth a thought… a friend hosted a Eurovision Song Contest party – with every new contestant everybody at the party drank that country's beer or wine. The costumes were a thing of wonder on the big screen, and they also ran a sweepstake on outcome.

> You can hire screens sized from 6 ft to 12 ft, and Colin, from CVS, gives the tip that you need to check the height of your ceiling (most are 8 feet high) before ordering the largest screen. The average cost, including equipment hire, delivery and collection, and set-up of a projector, sound system and 6-foot screen, is £184.00. Extras costs would be hire of a DVD or tuner (if you wanted to watch TV or cable), a larger screen, plus VAT. Cost includes delivery within the M25. They will deliver nationwide, but deliveries outside the M25 will incur an extra delivery charge.

> **CVS International T· 0800 018 6564 W· cvsinternational.co.uk**

TOP OF THE POPS

> Oh, my goodness! I tried this gorgeous popcorn at the Homes & Gardens Fair and nearly ate the whole display – it was so delicious. We're not just talking ordinary popcorn here – this is American-style gourmet popcorn, available in flavours such as Bombay-style Masala, pink Himalayan crystal salted, salt & vinegar, sour cream and chive, traditional salted, white cheddar, caramel drizzled with chocolate and – my absolute favourite – caramel.

> Ear-to-Ear won a prize at Top Drawer for the best Gift Food range and were snapped up by Selfridges & Co to supply their store (view a list of other stockists online). You can buy the popcorn in tins or bags with many options. If you're salivating over the choice of flavours, opt for the sampler range – a bag of six different flavours – from £13.49. Or you could try six medium tins from £31.97; individual tins are available from £10.00.

> It's not the cheapest, but it's by far the scrummiest I've ever tried. The perfect accompaniment if you're throwing a film party.

> **Ear-to-Ear, Alpha Business Centre, 7-11 Minerva Road, Park Royal, London NW10 6HJ T· 020 7681 7941 W· ear-to-ear.com**

DRESS HIRE & FANCY DRESS

FANCY DRESS

DIVE INTO THE BIGGEST DRESSING UP BOX IN THE WORLD

> I bet you didn't know that over 160 years ago Angel Morris was one of the first people in the world to hire out costumes. In 1840, actors flocked to his cart to hire costumes prior to an audition, as in those days they literally had to dress for the part. All these years later, Angels now have over five miles of rails packed with beautiful clothing.

> Angels The Costumiers (sister company to Angels Fancy Dress) is the leading supplier of costumes to the UK and international film industry. They have over one million costumes, many of which have earned Oscars for Best Achievement in Costume Design. The great news for us is that each year a percentage of these are released into

the fancy dress side of the business, so the majority of the 5,000 costumes available to hire have previously featured in movies. So yes, you too can hire a costume that has been worn in *Braveheart* or *Shakespeare in Love*.

> Their buyers travel the world to search for that must-have costume to add to their selection – what a great job! You can buy the more commercial costumes from as little as £3.00 and their wig, mask and accessories section is fantastic. Trained assistants are on hand to help you achieve the perfect look – just ask Elton John or Mick Jagger, who have both been known to hire a costume or two. Prices: Hire costumes from £50.00 (last fitting 4.30 p.m.).

> **Angels Fancy Dress, 119 Shaftesbury Avenue, London WC2H 8AE T·020 7836 5678 W·fancydress.com**

GUESS WHO'S COME TO DINNER

> I've always wanted to throw a masked ball and I'm already planning one for my husband's fiftieth, which is still a few years away! One Sunday at Spitalfields Market we came across Wood 'N' Things, a great shop with a fantastic selection of Venetian masks, among the other collectables, toys and fancy dress. The masks are all created by Venetian artisans in the traditional way using the finest materials. They had over 80 in the shop – gorgeous colours, glitter, feathers, painting and decorations. Think how much fun you could have choosing them for all your friends.

> You can order online (delivery 1-3 working days) where they have a selection of around 45 designs, or mail order via the shop. Prices from £35.00.

> **Wood n Things, 57 Brushfield Street, Old Spitalfields Market, London E1 6AA T·020 7247 6275 W·woodnthings.uk.com**

DRESS HIRE

CHOOSE TO HIRE AND YOU'LL NEVER TIRE

> The lovely Pauline and Lisa will help you find that all-important dress which is going to make every head turn. Newly opened in Edinburgh, they offer over 250 dresses, including Amanda Wakeley, Donna Karan and a vintage selection. They stock sizes 6-22, with a three-day hire period (available for longer if needed) at very reasonable prices.

> You can also choose from their large range of accessories including shoes, handbags, jewellery, pashminas and gloves, from as little as £5.00. The good news is you don't even have to hire a dress to hire their accessories. They stay open late and can accommodate small parties, but what I love the best is that after a telephone consultation they will visit you in your hotel room with a selection of their finest.

> **The Dress Hire Co, 58 St Stephen Street, Edinburgh EH3 5AL T·0131 226 5894 W·thedresshirecompany.com**

FIVE HUNDRED WAYS TO BE FABULOUS

> No, they don't start at size 0, but a 4 is good enough for most people (and they go up to size 28). Froxy Lady has a reputation for hiring out amazing dresses – and what's more they have around 500 different designs for hire or sale. In fact, their dresses have been worn to all the glitzy charity balls and even by Miss England. They also offer accessories and shoes and bags.

> Froxy Lady dress hire is run on an appointment-only basis (six days per week), to ensure that you can shop when it's convenient for you, with no time constraints and no next customer waiting. If you can't get to Hertfordshire, don't fret, they also offer a nationwide ordering and shipping service. Prices: from £80.00

> **Froxy Lady, 29 The Copse, Hemel Hempstead, Herts HP1 2TA T·01442 217 276 W·froxylady.com**

WHY BE SEEN IN THE SAME DRESS TWICE?

> With hire prices from as little as £45.00 and a choice of over 200 dresses available (including Jenny Packham and Vera Wang) in sizes 8-26, you're bound to be the belle of the ball after a visit to Jo McLaren's.

> The gowns are arranged in categories, including elegance, ball gown and prom, velvet, cocktail, beaded and curvaceous. They also hire costume jewellery and accessories – the beautiful extras are sourced from designers in the UK and the USA, and are all included in the price of the garment hire. They also offer a good selection of men's formal wear, including dinner suits, morning suits, top hats and Highland dress.

> They offer very flexible hire terms, over the weekend or on a weekly hire, but you can also hire for longer occasions. So if you're off on a little cruise perhaps and want to look the part at the captain's table, you don't have to blow your entire clothing budget on evening wear. And all the dresses and menswear are available to hire or to purchase, so if you can't bear to give up the dress you were wearing when you met your future husband on that romantic cruise, you don't have to!

> **Jo McLaren Dress Hire 156 Waldegrave Road, Teddington, Middlesex TW11 8NA T· 020 8977 3207 W· jomclarendresshire.com**

BE PROUD OF YOUR ONE NIGHT STAND

> An invitation to a posh event doesn't have to mean that your credit card bill turns the same colour as that glamorous red carpet! Book an appointment in advance to choose from over 500 dresses for hire (sizes 6-18), and the staff at One Night Stand can take one look at you and know immediately what will look stunning. This will save you the hassle of trying on loads of dresses and help you avoid those less than flattering mirror moments! Their collection includes some designer

dresses from the likes of Jenny Packham and Ben di Lisi, with all stock being purchased from new collections, and minor alterations can be undertaken if necessary.

> Then choose that finishing touch from their large range of accessories – it couldn't be less stressful.
Prices: Dress hire from £80.00; jewellery from £10.00

> **One Night Stand, 8 Chelsea Manor Studios, Flood Street, London SW3 5SR T· 020 7352 4848 W· onenightstand.co.uk**

For Men's Dress Hire see page 59

See also Dress Agencies page 146

ENTERTAINMENT

ROLL UP, ROLL UP

> We always used Crowd Pullers when we produced big conference events, as they provide skilful, imaginative, intelligent and very funny street performers. From bands to solo acts, the choice is fantastic and you're bound to find the perfect entertainer, meet-and-greet or party performer.

> **Crowd Pullers, 14 Somerset Gardens, London SE13 7SY T· 020 8469 3900 W· crowdpullers.co.uk**

MAY THE FUNK BE WITH YOU

> Whenever I go out dancing these days I feel the need to hold up a placard demanding the return of disco dancing. Call me old school, but I just don't get all this techno, rave and rap at all. So if you, like me, want to let your flares flap and your lapels let off steam, live a little on Planet Funk. They're the most fantastic 70s-themed, soul, funk and disco eight-piece function band I've ever danced to. They've been entertaining at parties, balls and weddings for over 13 years and my sister,

Liz, hired them for her fortieth. We literally wore down our platform shoes with dancing, not to mention our poor throats as we sang at the top of our voices to the likes of Sister Sledge, Village People, Bee Gees and The Jacksons. Don't be shy, blame it on the Boogie! Prices from £1,200.00.

> **T·Charlie 01844 261 579 / 0770 200 6218**
> **W·planet-funk.co.uk**

HAVE THE STARS OF THE FUTURE PLAY AT YOUR PARTY

> For a wonderful surprise my sister-in-law, Victoria, organised a string quartet at our wedding reception. It was over 10 years ago, but I still remember the beautiful music they played. I didn't realise that musicians from the Royal College of Music can be hired for external engagements. Mary Cosgrave runs the department that books out students and can help you find exactly the right kind of entertainment to set the atmosphere and please your guests. They not only offer string quartets, but harpists, flautists, guitar soloists/ensembles and jazz ensembles – in fact, any combination of musicians playing any manner of music, be it Celtic, Greek, percussion, Latin American or easy listening. They recently supplied a quartet for a James Bond party and they played all the theme tunes from the Bond movies. Bet you can't name them all!
> Prices: Usually £100.00 per musician, plus a small booking fee to the College.

> **Royal College of Music**
> **T·020 7591 4367 E·mcosgrove@rcm.ac.uk**

A-Z Party List see pages 37-41

FLORISTS

Whether you buy flowers once every 12 months on Mother's Day (the biggest flower-buying day of the year), or keep your home stocked with fresh blooms on a weekly basis, you are contributing to a market worth over £1.5 billion. From the fragrant stall at the station, to exquisite custom-made arrangements, there are way too many established and new florists with great talent to list them all here, so I've stuck to the ones I know who offer that little bit extra.

CUT FLOWERS WITH A SHARPER EDGE

> I was completely stopped in my tracks by Jamie's wonderful arrangements at the Designer Wedding Show (*see page* 61). As a rising young star of the world of floristry, who already has an international reputation for his amazing displays, from London to New York and Tokyo, he draws his inspiration from the cutting edge of fashion. Using more flowers and less foliage, his prices are very reasonable, with bouquets starting from £35.00. The final presentation is gorgeous: go online to see his beautiful creations – I love the hand-tied bouquet he made for a wedding and the vintage cake stands covered in roses and tiered like a cake.

> Word gets out quickly and he already has a following from the film and fashion worlds. What's great for you and me is that he also shares his creativity and knowledge with fab courses, from one day to two weeks, at his new floristry school (details online).

> **Jamie Aston, 226 Great Portland Street, London W1W 5AA**
> **T·020 7387 0999 W·jamieaston.com**

THINKING OUTSIDE THE VASE

> Oh, my goodness! I nearly purchased one of everything in this shop. I was oohing and aahing, not only at their amazing bouquets

(from £30.00), but also at the flowers and architectural plants planted in a-m-a-z-i-n-g holders and planters – unusual orchids and helibores, twisted bromeliads and spring bulbs...

> Matthew and Gary trained in Holland and Germany and are very influenced by European floral design. Their creativity knows no bounds and last year they decorated more than 80 weddings. At one winter wedding they decorated an upside-down Christmas tree chandelier consisting of a natural blue spruce tree wound with flickering fairy lights and wired with mirrored squares and long silver, mirrored baubles suspended over the top table. They also did a garden wedding where the garden had no plants so they had to work for three days creating and decorating foliage trees.

> But they don't only do weddings – they will decorate any affair and can even deliver a lovely arrangement, perhaps as a 'thank-you', in one of their fab containers. Same-day delivery can be arranged within a 10-mile area of either of their shops, and they can arrange delivery further afield on request. They have recently been awarded the prestigious accolade of Master Florists.

> **Fabulous Flowers, 63 Banbury Road, Oxford OX2 7PG T·01865 511 811**
> **or 9a Bride Street, Abingdon, Oxfordshire OX14 3HN T·01235 520 346**
> **www.fabulousflowers.biz**

THE COMPLETE FLORAL FANTASY

> Orlando goes the extra mile for his clients and that's why they keep coming back for more. He's credited with being one of London's top florists and was once asked to sneak into a famous actresses's house at 4.00 a.m. to fill the downstairs full of rose petals and arrangements of roses and tulips as a surprise. Lucky lady!

> He is known for adding other gorgeous pressies to the flowers, and has at various times been asked to pop into Tiffany for a piece of jewellery, and pick up the best champagne to accompany flowers.

> From special dinners to weddings, he has had to fly in ostrich feathers from South Africa, source black orchids for a designer and send an extra-special gift to a movie star!

> He offers nationwide delivery and you can order a hand-tied, vase arrangement or an arrangement in any bespoke container. Prices: from £35.00.

> **Orlando Hamilton, 59 Saint Helen's Gardens, London W10 6LN T·020 8962 8944**

SWEET-LIPPED SURPRISES – SAY IT WITH FLOWERS

> Most little boys spend their time out in the garden kicking around a football or soaking each other with huge water pistols. Robbie spent his time smelling the roses and tending to his cabbage patch. Flowers have been a passion for him since he was a little boy and the infatuation is still growing.

> Often referred to as the 'Jamie Oliver of the flower world', Robbie loves doing wild and wonderful designs, especially large installation work. Recent spectacular pieces include a huge pair of lips made entirely out of flowers, giant liquorice allsorts made from rubber and flowers, and a large bar wall with hundreds of flame-coloured dahlias in Perspex screens. Robbie uses familiar flowers in ways people don't expect and, as he says himself, 'to say I am obsessed with flowers is a bit of an understatement'.

> Any event, be it large or small, is approached with equal verve. At a recent wedding ceremony he created an aisle with four arches of white roses with a central blossom tree, made from painted white birch and white orchids. He then had just one hour to change the room around for the party, for which the flowers were hundreds of red roses!

> Besides decorating events worldwide, Robbie has filmed his own TV show for Channel 5 and offers a couture bouquet service for delivery within the London area from £50.00. These glorious creations are made from flowers purchased that morning specifically for each bouquet, and they arrive nestled luxuriously in handmade, be-ribboned boxes. For same-day delivery the order must be in by 10.00 a.m. and, unusually, the bouquets contain no foliage, just beautiful flowers.

> **Robbie Honey, The Studio, Arch 69, New Covent Garden Market, Nine Elms Lane, London SW8 5PP**
> **T·020 7720 3777 W·robbiehoney.com**

FLOWERS ON FILM

> From the Cannes Film Festival to Posh and Beck's wedding, there is no stopping this man, and there's no one style or design to which he adheres. Unsurpassed in his commitment to his clients, you will often find Simon and his team rummaging amongst country antique fairs to find the perfect containers and props to decorate events.

> Arranging the flowers for the hit film *Four Weddings and a Funeral* sparked offers to design and create flowers for numerous TV shows and films, and also inspired Simon to write five books about his work. He has decorated locations throughout the world and has a regular slot as resident floral expert and style guru on TV.

> Honoured to have been commissioned by Her Majesty to decorate Windsor Castle for the reception to celebrate the marriage of Prince Charles to Camilla Parker-Bowles, he also shares his design secrets with eager students at the Great Flower Academy, where he offers courses from dinner party decoration and wedding flowers to Christmas designs.

> **Simon J. Lycett, Arches 270-272 Bethwin Road, London SE5 0YW**
> **T·020 7277 3322 W·simonlycett.co.uk**

RAW STYLE ON THE RED CARPET

> Founded by Kally Ellis and Ercole Moroni, McQueens' philosophy is 'use the finest raw materials, the latest skills, but keep it simple'.

> They create floral art for some of the world's most glamorous parties and are well known for their styling for the *Vanity Fair* post-Academy Awards party. Their private-client list consisting of top celebs remains a closely guarded secret.

> Their small selections of traditional and modern hand-tied bouquets (from £35.00) are only available for delivery within the London area, but they will deliver their scented candles and McQ toiletries nationwide.

> The McQueens floristry school attracts students from all over the world with its wide array of courses, from one-day workshops on vase arrangements, wedding flowers, hand-tied bouquets, table centres and buttonholes (£210.00), to a five-week career course (£4,200.00). A one-day private course is also available on application (from £410.00).

> **McQueens, 70-72 Old Street, London EC1V 9AN**
> **T·020 7251 5505 W·mcqueens.co.uk**

FUSS FREE AND FANTASTIC

> Jane Packer's signature is 'floral designs that inspire without being fussy' — and they certainly inspire me whenever I pass one of her shops, now found in London, New York and Tokyo. It would seem I'm not alone, as her clients include designers and celebs.

> As well as offering wonderful flower courses, she has produced more than ten books, a range of home products and a new DVD guide, Jane Packer — Flowers for the Home.

> I went on one of her fabulous courses and made a handbag completely from flowers and leaves. I went on to use a pair of fishnets, glitter, photo mount, 14 beautiful roses, a white china vase and willow to

create a stunning arrangement which looked exactly like a handbag (can you spot a theme here?). I thoroughly enjoyed the day and can highly recommend it.

> Jane delivers flowers and other lovely goodies nationwide from as little as £22.00 through janepackerdelivered.com, and they can usually arrange same-day delivery (within a five-mile radius) from the stores listed below.

> **Jane Packer Flowers: 32-34 New Cavendish Street, London W1G 8UE T·020 7935 2673 and 5th Floor, Harvey Nichols, 109-125 Knightsbridge, London SW1X 7RJ W·janepacker.com W·janepackerdelivered.com T·0845 074 6000**

FAR-FLUNG FLORAL FAME

> Having previously purchased two of Paula's floristry books I was already a fan, but I only discovered her original shop in N1 when the stunning floral decorations in the window caught my eye and I nearly crashed the car!

> She's been described as 'the most brilliant florist in London', has demonstrated and lectured around the world and written ten best-selling books. As one of the most famous and well-respected florists in the world, her devotees include the A-list, along with various royalty, presidents and Heads of State.

> Paula offers a fabulous flower school, including a one-day bridal workshop, and has concessions in Liberty, Selfridges and the Conran forecourt at Brompton Cross.

> Wonderful arrangements can be delivered from £50.00, or hand tied from £30.00.

> **Paula Pryke Flowers, The Flower House, Cynthia Street, London N1 9JF T·020 7837 7336**

> **Liberty Flowers by Paula Pryke, Liberty plc, Gt Marlborough Street, London W1R 6AH T·020 7573 9563**

> **Paula Pryke Flowers at Brompton Cross, Michelin House, 81 Fulham Road, London SW3 6RD T·020 7589 4986**

> **Paula Pryke Flowers at Selfridges London, 400 Oxford Street, London W1A 2LR T·0207 318 3894**

> **Paula Pryke Flowers at Selfridges Birmingham, Upper Mall East, Bullring, Birmingham B5 4BP T·0121 600 6716**

FLOWERS FIT FOR A KING

> Famous for his work on prestigious events, celebrity weddings – even a Royal Wedding – Rob is in demand around the globe for his fantastic floral designs. He is a perfectionist and whether it's for your party, Bar or Bat Mitzvah, wedding or dinner table, he wants his natural-looking designs to have that 'wow' factor.

> Luckily for us he delivers nationwide with prices starting at £40.00 (plus delivery and VAT). Ring him to order a stunning bouquet that can be hand tied or delivered in a vase (from £50.00).

> I also love Rob's fantastic prop-hire service, used by stylists, magazines, caterers, party planners and Mrs Jones from next door. You can hire containers made of pewter, steel, terracotta, silver, glass or Perspex, wonderful candelabras, night-lights and lanterns. Very popular at the moment are his decorative urns, which he'll paint any colour to suit your occasion. You're welcome to hire the props on their own and not fill them with his wonderful flowers – but where's the fun in that?

> **Rob Van Helden Floral Design Ltd, 8 Tun Yard, Peardon Street, London SW8 3HT T·020 7720 6774 W·rvhfloraldesign.com**

FOLLOW YOUR NOSE IN WILD WEST LONDON

> Undoubtedly you will probably have heard about Nikki Tibbles and Wild at Heart for their fresh and inspirational approach to

flowers. Renowned for supplying spectacular displays to the fashion industry, boutique hotels and the media, Nikki says, 'We like to take the traditional flowers, like peonies and roses and arrange them in a modern way, luxurious but simple.'

> With tied bunches and dinner-party decorations, arrangements for weddings and hip parties, Wild at Heart can cater for an intimate dinner for two or a party for 2,000. They do more than put the flowers in the centre of the table, though. They can help you out with the styling of your party as well. They will send couture bunches of flowers anywhere in London, with prices from £35.00

> Wild at Heart, The Turquoise Island, 222 Westbourne Grove, London W11 2RJ T·020 7727 3095 W·wildatheart.com
> Wild at Heart at Great Eastern Hotel, Liverpool Street, London EC2M 7QN T·020 7618 5350

LOOK FOR THE LITTLE BLACK BOX

> Woodhams are best known for their striking, contemporary, hand-tied arrangements, which arrive in their signature black box, but you can also order one of their lovely containers. They focus on compact styles, usually keeping to one colour palette.
> In 1994 Stephen Woodham, the company's founder, was one of the youngest designers to win a Gold Medal at the Chelsea Flower Show. He has since spent 11 years building a great business and an elite team.
> Woodhams Landscapes is also regarded as being at the forefront of contemporary garden design and floral events, offering designs from urban gardens to country estates.
> They have an extensive client list and if you saw the Brit Awards when an award-winning singer (no names, please) fell into the display of cacti (ouch!), that was one of their designs too! Prices from £40.00 – unfortunately, delivery is only available in London.

> Woodhams, One Aldwych, London WC2 4BZ T·020 7300 0777
> For garden design or flowers: 45 Elizabeth Street, Belgravia, London SW1W 9PP T·020 7730 3353 W·woodhams.co.uk

NEED TO KNOW

> W·florists-uk.org is a comprehensive online guide to UK florists businesses. When I wanted a florist to deliver to Stratton Audley, a small village in Oxfordshire, I found that I had missed the deadline for next-day delivery with my favourite florists, but I found a local florist through this site who were able to deliver a divine arrangement the same day, and I even saved some money!

> W·flowers.org.uk is the site for The Flowers & Plants Association, offering an unbiased, non-commercial source of expert advice. You can find all manner of flower facts, trends, care tips, flowers by month, flowers by colour, botanical and common names, and information about scented flowers. Great for planning a wedding or for those moments when you just have to know whether *convallaria* is actually a lily of the valley or that *zantedeschia* is an arum.
> It also has a handy section recommending retailers and floral deliveries.

> W·masterfloristsdirect.com is definitely one for your favourites list as it's a fabulous resource for putting you in touch with the finest florists in the UK. Caroline Marshall has opened her little black book and listed her approved florists after 'realising that too many consumers ended up with rubbish designs that didn't represent good value'. They also have a very useful Gift Ideas section to inspire you before you chat to the florist.

SERVICE WITH A SMILE

BESPOKE LINEN

WHEN OFF-THE-SHELF DOESN'T MEASURE UP

> We have a table that is 275 cm long, and when we were house-hunting it always revolved around the question 'will the table fit'? Being an awkward size, we always used table mats as we couldn't find a tablecloth the right length. That is, until we found Purple and Fine Linen. Not only do they sell pure linen, plain tablecloths and napkins in standard sizes and contemporary or antique designs, they can also make up linen to fit unusual or awkwardly-sized tables. They receive orders to grace the huge dining rooms of castles and stately homes as well as the tiny tables on ships. Their clients range from me and you to celebrities and barons. If you're using their made-to-order service, allow three weeks.

> The largest tablecloth they've been asked to make was for an oval table measuring 260 cm x 760 cm — glad I'm not ironing that! They've also been asked to make a 5.5-m chocolate-brown linen runner and monogrammed linen napkins for every guest at a wedding reception. My favourite order, though, was from a city banker who ordered linen napkins with buttonholes so they could be attached to shirts — he'd seen this in an old Audrey Hepburn movie!

> Oh yes, they also make custom fitted-linen sheets for larger-than-king-sized beds.

> **Purple and Fine Linen, Faber House, Ibstone, Buckinghamshire HP14 3XT**
> **T · 01491 638 184**
> **W · purpleandfinelinen.com**

See page 2, The Dining Room Shop
Also see page 67, The Linen Merchant

DON'T DRINK AND DRIVE

YOUR FOLD-AWAY DESIGNATED DRIVER

> I love this service — if you've had one too many, Scooterman rides his scooter to where you are, then folds it away into a sealed bag, puts it in the back of your car, fastens you in the passenger seat and drives you home. (That is if you can remember where you live!)

> The only thing he can't help you with is your hangover. The office is only open after 5.00 p.m., so don't bother phoning before, and they're insured to drive any car up to £50,000.00 in value.

> They operate in greater London, Manchester, Bristol, Cardiff and Cheltenham but will go further if given 24 hours' notice.

> **Scooterman T · 0870 242 6999**
> **W · scooterman.co.uk**

HELPING HANDS

If you enjoy the challenge of organising it all yourself and just need to hire in staff and/or equipment, here's a good selection to get you started.

SERVICE WITH A STYLE

> Always in the press covering the hottest functions with their bar and waiting staff (*see page 5*), At Your Service can send you champagne bartenders, table and wine waitresses/waiters, cloakroom attendants, hostesses, canapé waiters, and tray staff.

> The team are happy to meet 'n greet, take coats, pour drinks and serve nibbles, all with a professional, highly-trained and well-mannered approach. It's for good reason that they've been hired to work at prestigious product launches, film premières, weddings and private parties.

> Not worried about convention, they can provide staff in all manner of uniforms, from

male waiters dressed in only a white tie, pink tutu (covered in fairy lights) and ballet shoes, to waitresses dressed in cheongsams. They can even provide tray staff dressed as geisha girls with full make-up – nice for an afternoon tea party.

> At Your Service can provide transport if you're hiring quite a few staff, and they can also offer kitchen porters to support caterers through their 'Sherpa' section. Try to book at least five days in advance.

Prices range from £14.00 per hour (plus VAT) for waiting staff, to £19.00 per hour for a co-ordinator; price on application for costumed staff. You need to factor in travel costs (especially if staff are required before 7 a.m. or after 11 p.m.) and their meals.

> **At Your Service**
T · London 020 7610 8610; Oxford 01865 304 078; Bristol 0117 905 5131; Birmingham 08704 130 430; Manchester 0161 2777 830
W · ays.co.uk/atyourservice

LURE A BARISTA

For those who may not know, Barista is Italian for coffee-house bartender (not a lawyer with a funny wig), and they will come to your house and serve your guests the perfect cappuccino, latté, espresso or even liqueur coffee.

I had heard that a well-known coffee house offered this service, but after trying for over a month to find the details and leaving loads of messages with marketing and customer services I had given up! Very unlike me. However, after all my searching I have found Kurt, who is the bee's knees and in huge demand.

An alternative is to hire the coffee machines separately and then poach your favourite member of staff from your local coffee house. They'll probably be happy to earn a bit of extra dosh on their night off.

CAFFEINE HITS A NEW HIGH

> The lovely Kurt Stewart will drive his mobile café to you and serve up all manner of coffees, cappuccinos, lattés, teas and hot chocolates. Cakes and pastries are also available, I tried them at a vintage fair and they were fresh and delicious, not to mention that it is all Fair Trade and organic.

> Outside London, don't fret, he can put his mobile espresso unit onto a trailer and travel nationwide (p.o.a.).

> If you're having a very swish do and don't want the mobile unit (which is all self-powered), he can set up inside as long as there is mains power. Kurt offers high-quality organic coffee and charming service at reasonable prices (weddings/parties from £250.00).

> **Kurt Stewart T · 0794 675 8295**
W · fullsteamespresso.com

THE GREAT HIRE OF LONDON

> Forget wooden trestles and linen tablecloths! I saw this fabulous furniture for hire at the Designer Wedding Show (*see page* 61), but don't be put off if you're not in the market for a wedding, they can set you up for any event where you have more guests than you own chairs and you want to make a style statement.

> Their great selection includes Perspex tables, stunning glass candelabra, Philippe Starck Louis Ghost chairs, black or white leather sofas, gilt mirrors and bean bag chairs, to mention just a few of their range. They try to cater to everyone's budget, with no minimum hire.

> **CIPI Ltd, 37 Maida Vale, Studio A, London W9 1TP**
T · 020 7121 0333 W · greathire.co.uk

CLICK ON A CATERER

> While spending hours surfing the net for a traditional fish-and-chip van to hire, I found this invaluable association. You can choose

from their extensive drop-down menu to search for mobile caterers who will come to your party or event to serve you an array of delicious delights. The choice of over 160 mobile units was quite unbelievable, including those specialising in vegetarian/ vegan food, Victorian food, organic, tandoori, spit roasts, waffles, strawberries & cream, potato wedges and dips, American milk-shakes and even licensed bars. Search their members list online, or they also offer a very useful printed directory for £20.00.

> **Mobile & Outside Caterers Association, NCASS, Centre Court, 1301 Stratford, Road Hall Green, Birmingham B28 9HH**
T · 0871 504 1780
W · ncass.org.uk

CATERING FOR EVERY TASTE

> If you're less than confident about your cooking, these would be the perfect waiters for you to hire. You could serve rats tails on toast and your guests wouldn't even notice as they would not be able to stop looking at your lovely staff, who all just happen to be working models. Unfortunately, you cannot just hire the model staff — you must also use their catering services, but as this starts from as little as £10.00 per guest and is excellent, I don't think you'll find that a problem. They can also provide chefs, hire equipment, lighting or transport. They can cater for dinner parties, buffets or a canapé reception, and are very flexible.

> Ex-model Sophie Gray set up Model Catering and she'd love to organise your whole event, especially if you're thinking of having a themed one. She has recently organised a party with waitresses dressed as geisha girls with wonderful painted faces and costumes, exotic orchid decorations and Japanese food. Sophie's biggest challenge to date was serving 1,500 guests in half-an-hour in a very confined space. Good job she's not claustrophobic!

> I love her Deli Delivery service, where they deliver seven days' worth of frozen meals — all you need to do is thaw and cook them; the perfect present for a new mum. (For further information, *see page* 284.)

> **Model Catering, 697 Harrow Road, London NW10 5NY**
T · 020 8964 1712 W · modelcatering.com

See also Busy People (page 52) and Caterers (pages 11-16)

ICE SCULPTURES

PUTTING THE 'OH!' IN H2O

> You've probably seen Duncan's work without even knowing it as his ice masterpieces appear regularly in film, television and advertising. He's been hand sculpting ice for over 30 years with Japanese samurai chisels, and his mould-free creations have garnered him an international reputation.

> His website contains inspirational pictures of his previous works of art — I loved the Christmas crackers, life-sized saxophone player and fridge, not to mention the beautifully sculpted hand draped in jewellery. His largest indoor sculpture to date has been a 40-foot-wide fantasy castle for a glam wedding. Duncan delivers across Europe, with miniature sculptures starting from £80.00.

> **Duncan Hamilton Ice Sculptor, 33 Wimbledon Stadium, Riverside Road, London SW17 0BA**
T · 020 8944 9787 W · icesculpture.co.uk

THINK OUTSIDE THE BOX

> When you think ice, you might think G&T. Think bigger, these guys have talent, with a capital T.

> They can deliver tubed, cubed, crushed, flaked or dry ice for your bash, but what they're highly sought after for is their themed ice masterpieces.

> At their massive tenth anniversary party they showcased their work by creating all manner of ice sculptures, including a gorgeous chess board, a funky bar with bottles suspended in ice, a chandelier and fountain, poser tables, sunflowers stacked in ice, stunning vases, and even the chairs you sat on – bet it wasn't for long! Truly art in ice.

> What's also great for a party is their fruit and flowers in ice, and I can't *not* mention the ever popular luges, which they introduced into the UK market over 12 years ago. Sadly I'm not into Vodka luges, where you wrap your mouth around an ice willy and receive a shot of Vodka to the back of the throat, at least not if you're twenty-fifth in the queue. However, some are… Those who agree with me can perhaps order a classic vase or delicate swan to display your flowers.

> Go online and check out their ice Volkswagen car – it took eight tonnes of ice and 350 sculpting hours. Then they parked it in the street – absolutely fantastic!

> When I win the lottery, I'm going to throw a big party and order one of their ice living rooms – simply stunning, and the cold should discourage the 4.00 a.m. laggers!

> The ice bars and ice rooms will generally last around six to eight hours, unless you're in a marquee in the height of summer with temperatures over 32 degrees – then your guests might start to lick them!

> They have great customer service and will pull out all the stops to achieve your desired result, including nationwide and European delivery, and free 24-hour delivery within London, with a minimum order of just £11.00.

> **The Ice Box, Unit A35–36 New Covent Garden Market, London SW8 5EE T·020 7498 0800**

> **Also Ice Box Scotland, Unit 23, Fisherrow Industrial Estate, Newhailes Road, Musselburgh, Edinburgh EH21 6RU T·0131 665 6315 W·theicebox.com**

A PARTY IDEA
HAVE YOU EVER THOUGHT ABOUT…

See also the A-Z Party Guide page 37

DARE TO GO DOWN TO THE CELLAR!

> I wish I'd known about this venue for my fortieth birthday bash; it would've been great fun and unique. Your guests can be collected in vintage limos (and, if you ask nicely, they'll even throw in a vampire or two!) and blindfolded for the journey to the undisclosed location in Central London. This is where Simon Drake, magician extraordinaire, entertains you in his House of Magic.

> On arrival you'll be greeted with champagne and then offered a tour of The Haunted Cellar, home to subterranean spooks. You will also be invited to sit in the 'Whispering Chair' to have your fortune told. Next you sit down for a silver-service dinner, or (if you want something less formal) chow down on canapés, before being entertained by Simon and his mind-blowing magic extravaganza.

> Simon has made special appearances for the Royal family, as well as Elton John and Tina Turner. He has made numerous TV appearances and has become internationally renowned as one of the most original, creative and shocking illusionists in the world.

> I love his answering message where you are greeted by Rafe the Butler – very amusing! Exclusive hire – price on application.

> **Simon Drake House of Magic, London T·020 7735 4777 W·houseofmagic.co.uk**

PUT ON YOUR PARTY FACE

> I used to love Madge in the Dame Edna show shoving the badges on the guests and decided to use the idea for a party. The novelty of it went down a treat and I'd definitely do it again. Russell Turner at

Digital Expression can make up 55-mm button badges with text or pictures (or both). Simply email him the names or photos of your guests and he will send you the badges within two days. It costs from £15.00 for ten; however, enquire about a discount if you want large numbers. The only guests they're not suitable for are the under-threes, due to the non-safety-pin type.

> To make it even more genuine, hire a look-alike Dame Edna and Madge from Jez at Fake Faces, who have over 600 look-alikes on their books.

> **Digital Expression, 21 Jasmine Avenue, Chapel Park, Newcastle Upon Tyne NE5 1TL**
> **T · 0191 264 3207 W · poshbadges.co.uk**

> **Fake Faces T · 0800 652 2842**
> **W · fakefaces.co.uk**

STATIONERY

EXQUISITE STATIONERY

These days we couldn't live without e-mail for business, convenience and keeping up with far-flung friends. However, a printed-out e-mail invitation looks pretty shoddy on the mantelpiece and a virtual thank-you note is virtually an insult! When it comes to the personal touch, remember, E is for etiquette not e-mail, so fish out that fountain pen and, most importantly, make sure you have the right stationery.

OFF-THE-STREET SERVICE

> A lovely family-run business – one of the few, if not the only one, where you can come off the street and sit down with a designer and design your stationery. Their customers return again and again for their wonderful bespoke range and they offer every kind of printing.

> **Alistair Lockhart Limited, 97 Walton Street, London SW3 2HP**
> **T · 020 7589 0000 W · alastairlockhart.com**

IT'S ALL IN THE DETAILS

> Ellen McGrath paints the most exquisite gouache (favoured by Persian and Indian miniature artists) illustrations. You may have seen her fashionable stationery with painted images of bags, dresses, flowers and glamour images. She also offers a bespoke service for social and wedding stationery.

> Inspired by the Orient, catwalk fashion and style icons from the past, her company Anzu also offers journals, note cards and invitations. Her Details of the Day cards for weddings are divine.

> She also offers a design service for businesses – fabulous letterhead, business cards or images for your website.

> You can't buy her stationery online, but if you key in your postcode it will direct you to the nearest stockist for her greeting cards, journals and stationery range. If you want bespoke, give her a call.

> **Ellen Mcgrath, Anzu T · 020 7193 0189**
> **W · anzu.co.uk**

SAN FRANCISCO STYLE

> Stephannie wowed the press with her couture tri-fold wedding invitations; she wowed me with her absolutely stunning range of stationery that she has been designing since she was a young girl. I would give anything in the world to be able to illustrate and scribe the way Stephannie does. Having worked for many years as a fashion illustrator and calligrapher in New York, she has now moved to San Francisco with her French dog Didier. In fact, Stephannie is inspired by all things French and says they 'have a wonderful elegant, sometimes whimsical style that I incorporate into my work'.

> The tri-fold wedding stationery folds out to include the invite, reply card and map

(or other related wedding information), tied in with gossamer ribbon and subtly illustrated with a little personalised drawing. Naturally she does other wedding designs as well – I loved that her envelopes were lined in colourful Japanese papers and her illustrated maps had very personalised, exquisite tiny drawings (see her other website **W·couturemaps.com**).

> She also offers gorgeous birth announcement cards, business cards, printed paper napkins, personalised name cards and general calligraphy.
Prices: tri-fold invitations from $30.00 each for a minimum order of 100.

> **Stephannie Barba, Couture Calligraphy and Stationery, 625 Scott Street, 403 San Francisco, CA 94117 T·+1 415 437 6001 W·stephanniebarba.com**

INVITATIONS TO PLAY

> After completing her degree at Goldsmiths, Lucy started designing Christmas cards. They proved so popular that people were soon asking her for other designs. Inspired by 1930-1950s haberdashery packaging, Lucy makes quirky and interactive cards and products with her unique style of illustration and design. I love her novel 'Come to Dinner' postcards which can be cut and folded into a table shape. She also makes a height chart which you can send in the mail, advent calendars, and wonderful interactive cards where the receiver can make a poodle out of a balloon, make up a tooth-fairy box, stitch a message, or play old-fashioned parlour games.

> For bespoke Christmas, wedding, christening or other stationery, allow two months from the initial meeting to print. You can order from her website or look at her list of stockists.
Prices: Bespoke designs from £300.00 plus printing; individual occasion cards from £4.00

> **Lucy Jane Batchelor T·07941 006 513 W·lucyjanebatchelor.co.uk**

PUTTING EMAILS TO SHAME

> If, like me, you're frequently jotting 'thank you' or 'thinking of you' notes to friends on gorgeous stationery, then you need some of the lovely Billet Doux correspondence cards with accompanying gold-tissue-lined envelopes. Ornate gold borders with delicate flourishes are offered on plain, At Home or Thank You cards. Colours include white, mixed (soft pastels or bright blue, pink, yellow, green and purple). The Taj Bindi range is decorated with a jewelled bindi which adds that extra touch of glamour. Cards are sent either boxed or in a wallet.
Prices: from £12.50.

> **Billet Doux, The Old Dinosaur Museum, Kingston Road, Worth Matravers, Dorset BH19 3JP**
T·01929 439 003 W·billetdoux.co.uk

PERFECTION IS ON THE CARDS

> Elena was formerly an embroidery designer for leading fashion designers, but now she creates the most luxurious, exclusive range of embroidered stationery and textiles. She designs wonderful wedding stationery and party invitations, and hand-makes them, adding exquisite special touches.

> You can use one of her existing designs and personalise yourself (prices are from £4.25 per card) for a fab invite.

> I have been buying her general correspondence cards for years and love it when her new designs come out so I can stock up my card box.

> **Elena Deshmukh T·020 8647 6905 E·elena.cards@virgin.net**

A CENTURY OF SKILL

> Did you know that hand-engravers work back to front and upside down? No wonder it took Barry Turner seven years to learn the skill from his father. Barry's now one of the few remaining old-school hand-engravers (many printers have moved to machine

engraving). For a truly stunning invitation I would choose hand-engraving every time.

> Now over 100 years old, Downey & Co established its reputation as a specialist in fine hand-engraving, but by the 1970s the company expanded into print. They now offer engraving, blind embossing, foil blocking, lithography, thermography and letterpress. They can create family crests, monograms, company logos, decorative initials and a great range of symbols. They can also hand make any shape or size of envelope in a huge variety of materials.

> All three Turner brothers, Barry, Grahame and Christopher, offer superb customer service and exceptional printing. They really do sweat the small stuff to bring you perfection and will try every which way to achieve your desired result. Clients have included Cartier, Burberry, De Beers, Mont Blanc and Theo Fennell, to name a few. Having looked at over 30 invitations that they have produced over the last year or two, I can honestly say I would be extremely proud to send out any one of them.

> **Downey & Company, Peterley Business Centre, Unit 1, 472 Hackney Road, London E2 9EQ**
T· 020 7739 8696 W· downey.co.uk

HEARD IT ON THE GRAPEVINE

> Karen Bartolomei and her company Grapevine produce absolutely stunning, exclusive engraved and letterpress invitations and accessories. I saw her work at a wedding show in New York and was blown away. Her unique invitations are presented in beautiful boxes (with optional added trinkets), as a booklet, or on stunning paddle fans – the choice is endless. Their designs have included a boxed booklet invitation on a bed of live moss for a wedding in a botanical garden, and an elegant invitation booklet announcing a wedding in Rome, honeymoon in Paris and reception in Boston.

You can enjoy many of their lovely designs on their website.

> Beautiful calligraphy, fonts, coloured papers and creative design all combine to showcase exquisite stationery that will make your guests give your invitation pride of place on the mantelpiece. Prices are top end, but boy are they worth it!

> **Grapevine, 105 N Street, Boston, Massachusetts 02127**
> **T· From USA 800 994 3799 / from outside the USA +1 617 268 9409**
W· grapevineweddings.com

HANDMADE HEIRLOOMS

> If you are looking for the crème de la crème in invitations, you are certain to find it at Hannah Handmade. Andrea Liss and her very talented team use the world's finest materials, including fancy jacquard and dupione silk ribbons, cloisonné enamels, semi-precious gemstones, fresh orchids, exotic and handmade papers, and luxurious fabrics, coupled with the finest printing and exquisite detailing. They possess master-level skills in the techniques of hand calligraphy, origami, sewing, beading and embroidery to ensure that your custom invitations, handmade cards or paper accessories meet Hannah's award-winning standards of excellence. They believe 'your invitation will be like no other ever seen, an unforgettable heirloom to delight your guests and create an aura of anticipation'. Pricing begins at $3,500 for a custom project, and is based on the complexity of the design, materials used and printing process.

> **Hannah Handmade**
T· (toll free) 1 800 670 6703 / from outside the USA +1 847 864 8292
W· hannahhandmade.com
E· info@hannahhandmade.com

STATIONERY'S MOVING UP IN THE WORLD

> Hazlitz opened their doors in 2004 to much acclaim. Their stationery is produced using traditional techniques, and they have top illustrators design distinct motifs and illustrations.

> Naturally they can create gorgeous bespoke invitations, birth announcements, christening cards, party invites and correspondence cards. They also offer a ready-to-write selection of notelets with embossed emblems such as a chandelier, bathing beauties, powder-puff girls and cupcakes. Just pop in to the shop to buy their ready-to-write notelets; if you require your own bespoke range, motif or emblem, please phone for an appointment. Prices: for the ready-to-write, from £20.00 for a box of 12 cards and envelopes.

> **Hazlitz Bespoke Stationery, 18 Coulson Street, London SW3 3NB**
T·020 7225 7590 W·hazlitz.com

Jody Hyde-Thomson, see page 44

DRAWN IN BY TALULA

> When I first saw Andrea's cards in Liberty, I bought one of every design as they were so glamorous. Think men in tights and painted ladies with names like Talula Bumble, Siousie Choux and Miss Lipgloss — one customer even rang her and asked to speak to Lottie Loveday! Her cards are all hand-painted watercolours with added glitz and sparkle. As long as she has at least six weeks' notice, Andrea will create one-off party or wedding invitations or Christmas cards. Although she doesn't have her own website yet, you can purchase a good selection of her work through **W·art-is-a-tart.com**.

> **Andrea Kett T·07790 568 295**

A DYING ARTFORM REVIVED

> For a striking invitation, I don't think that you can beat letterpress. The image or type is debossed onto the card, giving a lovely soft, hand-wrought appearance — it looks especially effective if you include an image, or even print the text over an image. It was becoming a lost art but now, thankfully, is becoming much more popular again.

> The family-run business, Letter Press of Cirencester, have a wonderful reputation with well-known stationery designers and the public alike as a traditional printer offering personal and wedding stationery at very reasonable rates. They can work with you on a bespoke basis for the design of your invite or stationery. Beside letterpress, they also offer litho and thermo-raised printing and die-stamping, and they offer a wide range of print finishes such as plate sinking, gilding or blind embossing. Ribbon and envelope linings are available in colours to match your ink, and the envelopes can be lined in tissue, or the currently very popular paper with a metallic sheen.

> They have over 150 agents in the UK and Ireland, so phone them for your nearest stockist. Allow three weeks for printing, although they do offer an express five-working-days service for £32.00 extra.

> **The Letter Press of Cirencester, 3-9 Cripps Road, Cirencester, Gloucestershire GL7 1HN
T·01285 659797 W·letterpress.co.uk**

THE CHOICE IS NOT ALWAYS BLACK AND WHITE

> If you're looking for a charming, helpful designer who will give you the very best of service with exceptional quality, look no further. Susan O'Hanlon will spend as long as it takes to find the perfect photograph from her collection of top photographers' work to make your wedding invitation. She was chosen as *Elle* and *You and Your Wedding* magazines' favourite stationer, has been featured on GMTV, has designed many a celebrity wedding invitation, and has just produced 4,000 invites for the wedding of

one of the richest men in the world. She also offers a calligraphy and monogram service. Prices: from £2.40 per invitation
> **Susan O'Hanlon, 14 East Common, Gerrards Cross, Buckinghamshire SL9 7AF T·01753 887 659 W·susanohanlon.com**

FUNNY FANTASTIC, NOT FUNNY PECULIAR
> Mary Beth Fiorentino is the hair twister and Amy Elizabeth Hayson is the hypochondriac, and along with their other peculiar foibles they thought Peculiar Pair Press a rather apt company name. They produce wonderful letterpress invitations, stationery and occasion cards with great attention paid to detail and quality. I love their printed, addressed envelopes in the package for brides, with addresses in wonderful fonts printed slightly off centre — they look really striking. Lovely designs, flourishes, fonts and images — good enough to frame! Custom designs start at $30.00 a set based on 100 sets. If ordering from overseas allow at least four months.
> **Peculiar Pair Press T·Mary Beth +1 415 812 7247; Amy Elizabeth +1 415 407 7247 W·peculiarpairpress.com**

CHILDHOOD INSPIRATION
> All R. Nichols' designs are initially created as little paper collages, which he attributes to his sixth-grade skills of cutting and pasting. He introduces new designs twice a year and they're all limited editions, so keep checking and buy them quickly as they sell out fast.
> They're printed on the finest quality, cream-coloured stock in two formats: small folded cards and flat postcard style.
> His card ranges are categorised: Beauty, Baby, Party, Pets, Shopping, Holiday, Garden, Paris and so on — I find it hard to choose as there are so many I want. Sending a couple of boxes to someone would make a lovely housewarming present.

> You may well have seen his illustrations in the book *French Women Don't Get Fat* (Mireille Guiliano, Knopf) — I'm a huge admirer of such talent. The great news is he now ships worldwide.
> **R. Nichols Stationery T·+1 407 628 4899 W·r-nichols.com**

DESIGNED TO PLEASE
> When I saw Louise's stationery I was in awe and spent a long time looking at the beautiful examples — your dilemma will be what design to choose. Don't baulk at the prices, you are not only paying for quality but a for package which, depending on the design, includes the invitation, evening invitation, order of service, place names, thank-you letterheads, accommodation list and envelopes. She also offers other specialist stationery and you can order individual items. Her current designs can be reproduced in any colour, adapted, or you can have a completely new design. Beautiful hand-finishing, lovely touches and great designs.
> **Louise Richardson T·0771 267 3456 W·louiserichardson.co.uk**

DO YOUR GUESTS AN EXQUISITE FAVOUR
> I wish, I wish, I wish that my mantelpiece could boast a wedding invitation created by Sherri Weese. Her company name says it all, they are Simply Unique. All her invitations are custom made and are inspired by designer wedding dress collections and luxury style icons from around the world.
> The 'Monique' invitation has a rhinestone buckle and Midori ribbon sitting gracefully on the letterpress invitation, which is presented in a co-ordinating silk box. The 'Paris' pays tribute to Chanel's sense of style — a stunning rhinestone buckle graces the top of a custom silk box and inside is a luxurious letterpress invitation embossed with perhaps your monogram or themed motif and mounted onto a padded layer of

matching or coordinating silk. Invitations start from $46.00 depending on materials used.

> **Sherri Weese, Simply Unique Invitations**
  T · +1 703 216 3192
  W · simplyuniqueinvitations.com

FILE UNDER 'MUST HAVE'

> Sorry. I can't resist putting in *theweddingfile* because we publish it as well, and, after all, we've had loads of lovely comments from brides-to-be who said they couldn't have managed without this unique planner. The luxury A5 personal organiser has over 200 pages in 17 sections for the bride to record everything. It's a great keepsake for the event, with useful pockets for receipts and cuttings, and stacks of room for all your notes, sketches, lists and to-do's. You can order it online or over the phone.

> *theweddingfile* T · 0870 443 0035
  W · theweddingfile.com

GOOD ENOUGH FOR THE ROYAL GARDEN PARTY!

> Established over 25 years ago, this is another great family-run business. The Wren Press owns its own factory and uses a unique combination of traditional skills and modern technology. The team can offer a fantastic range of party invitations, from shaped to shiny, along with bespoke wedding, birth, correspondence and Christmas stationery. I love their range of brightly coloured sets of correspondence cards with envelopes. The Wren Press has been awarded two Royal Warrants, and I hear that another well-known Elizabeth always orders her Christmas cards from them and them alone.

> With offices in London, Dublin, New York, South Africa and Hong Kong, they can offer a worldwide service (see the website for details of their international offices)

> **The Wren Press, 1 Chelsea Wharf, 15 Lots Road, London SW10 0QJ**
  T · 020 7351 5887 W · wrenpress.com

ONLINE STATIONERY

SEND SOMEONE YOU LOVE A SMILE

> I haven't laughed so much in ages – log on and choose personalised cards for all your friends. The Spoof and Humour sections are absolutely brilliant; you can add names, photos, funny headlines and stories to mock magazine covers and newspapers, personalise well-known humorous cards, or go for a more dignified look. Cards can be sent directly from Moonpig, or why not order your year's supply and have them ready to send out when the occasion arises. There were so many I wanted. I spent hours giggling my way round their website. Prices: from £2.99 plus postage and packaging.

> **Moonpig T · 0845 4500 100**
  W · moonpig.com

> I've fallen in love with **W · namemaker.com** where you can order personalised wrapping paper and ribbon in stunning colours. Makes a wonderful and unique way to present your gift. I ordered wrapping paper with a printed Christmas greeting from my family and it came from the USA within two weeks. Allow longer near the holiday season.

'MUST VISIT' STATIONERY SHOPS

CORRESPOND WITH CARE

> Nemeta (formerly Bureau) in Covent Garden is a great shop that caters for all your stationery needs, desires and just because …, and as they source their stock from the best French, Swiss, German, British and Italian manufacturers, you'll certainly find something unique here. New in is their personal organiser range with luggage to match, and fine precision Swiss pencils with diamonds!

They have a fantastic selection of greeting cards and coloured card with envelopes, and they're also expanding their gift range, so they're well worth a visit. Printing is also available.

> **Nemeta, 10 Great Newport Street, Covent Garden, London WC2H 7JL**
> **T·020 7379 7898 W·nemeta.com**

CAN'T SAY NO TO THAT SCANDINAVIAN STYLE

> Designed and made in Sweden, with over 800 different types of papers and related products and over 200 cards and envelopes – think colour and minimalist, pure and simple stationery. This divine stuff made me want to buy eight empty journals in different colours – I just hope my life gets interesting enough to fill them! Their A4 cloth ring-binders are some of the smartest around and would sit proudly on any desk, as would their sleek chrome office accessories. I'm addicted to their spring pen-holders, which you can attach to any book to hold your pen – and since last Christmas all my friends are too!

> With two stores in London and over 50 stores in 15 countries (see online) there's no excuse not to visit!

> **Ordning&Reda, 186A Kings Road, London SW3 5XP**
> **T·020 7351 1003 W·ordning-reda.com**
> **Also in Selfridges, 400 Oxford Street, London W1A 2LR T·020 7318 3654**
> **and 21 Swan Lane, Guildford GU1 4EQ**
> **T·0148 388 8440**

BIGGER IS BETTER WHEN IT COMES TO CHOICE

> Not only is Paperchase one of the best contemporary stationers around, but it has one of the largest selections of greeting cards and, top of my list, hardly any of them have teddy bears on them. Do you know, I still receive 'cutsey' teddy-bear cards and I'm in my *early* forties!

> It's fantastic for crafty types and budding artists, and along with all the usual stationery things, they stock a great selection of handmade papers from around the world. At Christmas they offer up some unique decorations, and I'm a huge fan of their lovely notebooks. Monthly – no make that weekly – visits are a must. If you go into their flagship London store, prepare to spend a long time as you will shop on all three floors.

> If you can't get to a branch, you can also browse through their enormous range online and buy by mail-order.

> **Paperchase, 213-215 Tottenham Court Road, London W1T 7PS**
> **T·020 7580 8496 W·paperchase.co.uk**
> **82 branches nationwide: ring 020 7467 6200 for your nearest**

ALWAYS GO TO THE SOURCE

> Based in the USA but happy to ship to the UK, this has to be one of the best stationery shops I've visited. I recently went to the Chicago store and spent over two hours browsing – OK, shopping! What I love about them is that you can buy different sized cards with lovely edges in a range of stunning colours and then add letterpress, monograms, messages, decorative overlays – all manner of do-it-yourself bits, only limited by your imagination. They also offer gorgeous linen stationery folios filled with beautifully decorated cards and envelopes, wonderful boxed do-it-yourself invitation kits, every size and colour of envelope, as well as envelope labels and seals, ribbon, decorative punches and every other accessory you could ever need. They live by the motto 'Do something creative every day', and with materials this great you just try and stop me.

> **Paper Source**
> **T·in the USA 1-888-PAPER-11 / from outside the USA +1 312 906 9678**
> **W·paper-source.com**

NOTE TO SELF: BUY THE BEST

> Smythson is the shop for haute couture stationery. Established in 1887, it is renowned for its range of leather books, stationery, journals and accessories. I'm completely addicted to their gorgeous notebooks, which look even more gorgeous if you have them gold- or silver-stamped with your own message, title or initials (£4.95 per letter – allow seven days). I've bought the Born to Shop, I Love You and Domestic Goddess note books (among other things), and every year I order the pink Bijou Portobello Day Book and enjoy the lovely compliments I receive whenever I bring it out of my bag.

> On my wish list are their Fashionista and Style Notes notebooks and their soft, pale blue correspondence card box, filled with tiny, silver heart die-stamped cards – just divine. Their bespoke invitations and stationery are sheer perfection, with one customer even ordering visiting cards for his dog! Along with the stores listed below, there are also concessions in Selfridges and Harvey Nichols in London, and Heathrow Airport Terminals 3 & 4.

> **Smythson of Bond Street, 40 New Bond Street, London W1S 2DE**
  T · 020 7629 8558; for Mail Order 08705 211 311 W · www.smythson.com

> **Also 135 Sloane Street, London SW1X 9AX**
  T · 020 7730 5520

> **and 4 West 57th Street, New York, NY 10019 T · +1 212 265 4573**

> *To make your stationery look ultra luxurious, line the envelope with tissue paper to match your ink – it looks absolutely gorgeous.*

CALLIGRAPHERS

*If your handwriting says six-year-old rather than sophistication, you have two options: sign yourself up for one of the excellent calligraphy classes on offer – I went to one at City Lit (**T · 0207 831 7831 W · citylit.ac.uk**) – or call in the experts. Forget fancy fonts on your laptop, a professional calligrapher will design gorgeous invitations, place cards, scrolls and menus to give your special event unforgettable elegance.*

CARVED-IN-STONE EXCELLENCE

> Highly recommended by London Scribes, I phoned Mark who then sent me a selection of the breathtaking work he has produced over the last 25 years. With a background in stone carving, he was recently asked to carve 250 slate place settings for a fiftieth birthday dinner and hand deliver them to Cyprus! He is now working on another party for which he is engraving in Perspex an individual named menu for each guest – what a lovely thing to take away with you after the party.

> His penned seating cards and envelopes cost from £2.00 (per piece); menus (printed on heavy card) with individual names at the top cost approximately £350.00 for up to 200. Mark does all the printing for you and can also pen little illustrations with the lettering. Your only problem will be choosing food to live up to the menus!

> **Mark Brooks**
  E · calligraphy@markbrooks.net

ORIGINAL STYLE

> Two words sum up Sally Mangum's work – absolutely beautiful. Sally offers a wide range of calligraphy, including place cards, hand-designed invitations and menus, monograms, diplomas, maps, and stunning pen and ink

illustrations. She can provide small quantities of originals or one master copy for you to have printed.

Prices: from £1.00 each for simple place cards; minimum charge £30.00

> **Sally Mangum** T · 07764 195 754
  W · sallymangum.com

MASTER STROKES

> A Master Calligrapher and member of the highly-prestigious Guild of Master Craftsmen, Annie has taught and written calligraphy for over 25 years and is trained in the arts of illumination, heraldry and calligraphy. She scribes for the most illustrious clients and had the honour of being chosen to scribe the Queen Mum's 100th birthday scroll. I met her many years ago at the City Lit when I did a beginners' calligraphy class, and she still teaches there one day a week.

> She has just been commissioned to produce a gorgeous one-off poetry book using illumination on vellum, and her work over the years has included certificates, book inscriptions, society wedding invitations, party invites, scrolls for visiting Heads of State, anniversaries and jubilees. What I love about Annie is that even though she works for royalty, she still believes your order is special and will produce her most beautiful work.

Prices: from £1.00 for a place card or £3.00 for an invitation and envelope; minimum charge £30.00

> **Annie Moring** T · 01708 476 691
  E · anniemoring@ntlworld.com

A-Z PARTY GUIDE

ADD A LITTLE *PIZZAZZ* TO YOUR PARTY

Do you sometimes know you need a little expert help, but you don't know where to turn? Worry no longer, I've ransacked my Rolodex and emailed all my contacts for the most unusual, entertaining or simply fab suggestions. Here's my 'hot' party A-Z.

> *An Astronaut Jukebox* – Forget the DJ, go for a 6-foot, life-size, touch-screen, digital astronaut jukebox. From £400.00.
  T · 01604 473 101 W · jukebox45s.com

> *Butlers* – Freelance butlers are a rare breed and Adrian Olinsky is a real find. He can lay the table, select china and glasses, choose the wines, plan the seating arrangements, flowers and décor, greet your guests and serve, as well as offering personal aide services. Adrian will travel nationwide and says his secret is in 'knowing what people need without them asking'.
  Adrian Olinsky T · 01494 670 107

> *Candles* – Non-drip candles (dinner-party, nightlights, church, floating, pillar, beeswax, bistro and gold and silver) with great prices offered for bulk buying.
  Gifts on the Green T · 020 7736 0740
  W · candlesontheweb.co.uk

> *Cleaners* – Surely the worst part of throwing a party is the cleaning-up. Call in these guys and they will leave your venue spick and span. What bliss!
**Absolutely Spotless T·020 8932 7360
W·absolutelyspotless.co.uk**

> *Coloured Linen* – You can hire over 30 colours/designs of tablecloths and napkins from Coloured Linen Hire. They can provide linen for square, round and oblong tables, also white, ivory or black chair covers and accessories.
**T·0194 886 0597
W·colouredlinenhire.co.uk**

> *Chitty Chitty Bang Bang car* – Yes, the actual original from the movie is available for hire. Make a fine, four-fendered impression!
T·01789 204 300 W·chittygen11.com

> *Dance floor* – Think *Saturday Night Fever* with flashing multi-coloured squares – it even shows you the dance moves. From £800.00 including delivery and installation.
Funky Floors T·0785 484 3838

> *Digital Paparazzi* – Dressed as 1950s reporters, or any theme to suit, 'performing' photo-graphers snap away, then you and guests can go online to relive the night's highlights! Guests can download their favourite or incriminating photos at no extra charge.
T·01623 811 467 W·digitalpaparazzi.co.uk

Entertainment – Whether you want them to sing their hearts out or make you laugh until you cry, here are a couple of great entertainment agencies:

> *Sternberg Clarke* – Can provide the whole A-Z of entertainers, including great bands, dancers, speciality acts and novelty acts, such as an origami artist and a numerologist. They say, 'if an act exists, they know about it; if it doesn't, they can create it'.
T·020 8877 1102 W·sternbergclarke.co.uk

> *Search Party* – Fantastic and innovative activities and entertainment. I loved the Basil Fawlty and Manuel look-alikes whom you can invite to attend your party, and the inflatable pub. Perhaps best not to combine the two!
T·01423 711 806 W·searchparty.co.uk

> *Fish & Chip Van* – The lovely Geoff will come and cook you fish and chips from his traditional fish-and-chip van. Hugely popular for weddings. Travels nationwide.
**Geoff Allen Catering T·01668 283 276 /
07876 506 837**

> *Grape Debate* – A fantastic wine-tasting game with a quiz and a blind taste-off. I loved their champagne and imposter challenge. Bet you can't guess it – hic!
T·01784 442 593 W·grapedebate.co.uk

> *Hire, Hire, Hire* – Make your guests feel at home with squishy beanbags to lounge around on (five colours; £30.00 for up to five days' hire). For the less flexible among us they also provide leather sofas!
**Spaceworks T·0800 854 486
W·spaceworks.co.uk**

> *Hire Your Head Attire* – Hectic have gorgeous colours, styles and embellishments and they're happy to customise their hats to complement your outfit. From £30.00.
**Hectic Hat Hire T·020 7381 5127 / 07971
968 099 W·hectichathire.co.uk**

> *Ice-cream Van* – Hire Lola's 1970s refurbished ice-cream van. Ice-cream and sorbets are made daily, contain no GM and are mostly organic. Scrummy flavours include melon & ginger sorbet, lavender ice-cream, and valhrona chocolate sorbet with a brandy snap. £200.00 for two hours (London) plus £3.00 per ice-cream; £300.00 within 40-mile radius of London.

Lola's on Ice T· 07871 797 260 W· lolasonice.com

> *Inflatables* – If your party needs a little pumping up, you can hire fantastic inflatable sculptures, props, people, decor or even a castle.

Airtechs T· 0777 624 1700 W· airtechs.co.uk

> *Jumicar* – This is a fantastic idea for your child's party (for ages 6+). The children drive real (junior-sized) cars, and learn all about road safety. You'll have them driving in no time, sitting their test and even earning their driver's licence. Branches in Bristol, Dorset, and Nottinghamshire.

W· ukjumicar.co.uk

> *Karaoke* – At Lucky Voice Private Karaoke you can hire private rooms (nine available). Sing whatever songs your heart desires from a playlist of over 5,000, and tuck in to Yakitori Grilled Skewers, Yasai Karaoke, Tsingtao Rolls or other delectables from their Japanese-inspired menu.

T· 0871 223 2507 W· luckyvoice.co.uk

> *Kimono Girls* – wearing traditional Japanese outfits can serve your food and drinks at your next sophisticated soirée.

JAC Recruitment T· 020 7623 9900

> *Luxury Toilets* – So luxurious you won't believe you're not in a five-star hotel. Years of experience offering travelling trailers through to bespoke systems.

Igloos T· 01438 861 418 W· igloos.co.uk

> *Luxury Toilets* – Andyloos can be installed inside almost any structure – great black and white colour scheme, large mirrors and spot lighting (ALVAC range). Can travel nationwide and overseas.

Andyloos Ltd T· 01905 345 821; for South West 01726 861 656 W· andyloos.com

> *Mobile Coffee Van* – Let Kurt from Full Steam Espresso serve your guests lovely cappuccinos, lattés, teas or hot chocolate, and let them munch on a cake or pastry or two. From £250.00.

Kurt Stewart T· 0794 675 8295

> *Mobile Catering* – NCASS is the association for all mobile catering operators – their list is phenomenal (*also see page* 26).

W· ncass.org.uk

> *Marquee Décor* – To hire bespoke and stunningly stylish linings and decorative overlays, call the expert stylists Justine and Simon from Crescent Moon. But why stop with a marvellous marquee? They also offer complete event design and production.

Crescent Moon T· 0800 083 84 80 W· crescent-moon.co.uk

> *Napkins* – Make your event stand out with a black-and-white photo printed onto your disposable napkins. NPK will even add any terms of endearment you wish. Great prices and good choice of colours.

NPK Napkins T· 0845 644 7017

> *Organic Wines* – Vintage Roots have a fantastic selection of organic wines, beers and spirits. They also offer selections for vegetarians and vegans, and biodynamic products.
T·0800 980 4992 W·vintageroots.co.uk

> *Photo Booth* – Entertainment and souvenirs for your guests rolled into one. From £2,200.00 for a week's hire.
Photo-Me-International T·01372 453 399 W·photo-me.co.uk

> *Pickpockets, Liars and Cheats* – Great laugh, great entertainment, no harm done
T·0121 743 1600 W·pickingpockets.com

> *Props* – One of the best selections to be found, with over 50,000 props and 10,000 costumes. They also offer a full range of special event services working around the globe and have designed parties for many a celebrity.
Theme Traders T·020 8452 8518 W·themetraders.com

> *Quick Help* – Cheated a bit here under Q, although I could have mentioned the Queen look-alike (great to have seated at one of your party tables) or a Queen Tribute Band. The County Fetes website will help you find what you're looking for. A great list for any event organiser who needs to hire anything for a party.
W·countyfetes.co.uk

> *Rickshaws* – Click on the hire section and get yourself a traditional Indian rickshaw, either self-drive or with a driver if you can't bear the exercise!
The London Bicycle Tour Company T·020 7928 6838 W·londonbicycle.com

> *Salsa Stilt Dancers* – This company have the most amazing collection of entertainers and unique acts, so you're guaranteed to find exactly what you need. Besides the salsa stilt dancers, I love Bridie the Irish Tea-Lady, who will serve you tea and cakes from her seven-foot musical trolley.
Missing Link Productions T·020 7739 7713 W·circusperformers.com

> *Star Car Hire* – Famous fleets of replica cars from the movies or television: *Starsky & Hutch* Gran Torinos, *Back to the Future* DeLoreans, a Batmobile, Del Boy's Reliant Robin...
T·0845 017 5017 W·starcarhire.co.uk

> *Teepee* – Party in traditional teepees, Yurts or Kåtas with dreamcatchers, flokati rugs, faux ocelot rugs and faux wolfskin throws. You can cook up a treat in the central fire-places, and the children can have their own little teepee where they can be entertained with music and stories, an original feather war bonnet and talking sticks.
The Stunning Tents Company T·0118 988 2355 W·stunningtents.co.uk

> *Table Plan* – Set in ice... simply fabulous.
The Ice Box T·020 7498 0800 W·theicebox.com

> *Vodka Luge* – Not only can Ice Box build fantastic ice sculptures (*page 27*) including ice aquariums, chandeliers, martini glasses

and sushi bars, but their Vodka Luges are unlike any you've ever wrapped your mouth around! A dragon's head, perhaps?

**The Ice Box T·020 7498 0800
Scotland 0131 665 6315 W·theicebox.com**

> *I Thee Web* – Great all-round website with luxurious offerings
W·luxuriouswedding.com

> *Zzzzzzz* – You'll need plenty of these after a party with all the pizzazz I've listed here!

CHRISTMAS

Although I wouldn't quite go as far as that modern yuletide anthem and wish it could be Christmas everyday, every year I do absolutely love it and start preparing in about October. However, from a little research among friends, I know I'm probably in the minority on this one. There's a lot of 'bah humbugging', fatigue, stress and anxiety out there in the run up to Christmas day, so I hope that this section will help you relax and survive – even enjoy – the festive season.

The first step in the successful run-up to Christmas is grabbing a little ME-TIME...

BELLE-OF-THE-BALL STATUS GUARANTEED
> If you want to indulge in a spot of five-star festive hair treatment, pop along to Daniel Galvin's luxurious salon for his bespoke Christmas Party Package (available throughout December). Arrive after a hectic day at work with your glad rags in hand and unwind with a complimentary glass of bubbly to get you in the festive mood. Your hair will be washed, conditioned and styled for a show-stopping party entrance. You can even have a luxury manicure or pedicure to top it off (at an additional cost). Then slip into your party dress using the salon's celebrity private dressing room and your daywear will be returned to you, free of charge, by courier the following day. At the bargain price of £55.00, it certainly beats fighting for cubicle and mirror space at your work loos!
> **Daniel Galvin, 58–60 George Street, London W1U 7ET
> T·020 7486 9661 W·danielgalvin.com**

LET'S HEAR IT FOR HARI
> Hari's, on the Brompton Road, is a fantastic salon to visit for all sorts of self-esteem boosting treats. Not only do they have great

stylists, colourists and beauticians (*see page 234*), but they also offer an array of treatments to transform you for your big night out.

> For your last-minute hot date, all you need is about 30 minutes for a blow-dry and mini manicure as they will all work on you at once for extra speed. If your hair is in need of a good conditioning, they have several wonderful options. For the ultimate in luxury, go for the caviar hair mask while sipping champers, enjoying caviar canapés (can't get enough of that stuff!) and relaxing with a head and shoulder massage. All topped off, of course, with a manicure.
Prices: from £30.00.

> **Hari's, 305 Brompton Road, Knightsbridge, London SW3 2DY**
T · 020 7581 5211 W · harissalon.com

SOMETHING TO POUT ABOUT

> Whether you need a quick fix or a major overhaul before your big night out, don't stress, head to Pout. The team of top make-up artists in this relaxing boudoir setting have worked on fashion shows and music videos with some top celebrities.

> A Mecca for many women in search of a certain gloss, Pout offer bridal make-up services, brow plucking, cosmetic bag makeovers, even fashionista sessions where you can get your favourite celebrity look. Try their hugely popular, semi-permanent eyelash extensions: called Luscious Lashes, they use different-sized and individual lashes to create a volumising effect that really opens up your eyes — you won't be able to stop fluttering them!

> They also offer great 'girls' nights in' (by appointment) where you can have your own private shopping evening with music, drinks and nibbles and lots of one-on-one help to find your new look. £60.00 per person.

> **Pout, 32 Shelton Street, Covent Garden, London WC2H 9JE**
T · 020 7379 0379 W · pout.co.uk

Then it's back home and time to find the perfect CHRISTMAS TREE...

SORTING YOUR TREE FROM A TO ZEE

> If the thought of dragging a 6-foot Christmas tree home on public transport (I've seen it done!) or vacuuming pine needles out of your car till late March doesn't appeal, opt for home delivery from BuyaTree. You can order up to an 8-foot tree online; however, if you need a bigger tree phone them as they can supply trees up to 25 feet tall. Just for comparison, Trafalgar Square's tree is 65 feet high! You can be assured of quality as they are members of the BCTGA — I didn't have a clue either: the British Christmas Tree Growers Association.

> And if you don't have a Von Trapp-sized family to help you out, they also offer the service of decorating your tree, tree stands, wreaths, extra holly and mistletoe, and removal of the tree after Twelfth Night! I also love their service of buying the decorations for you — just give them a colour or theme and they will research and buy the most spectacular decorations from the most exclusive fashion houses in London.

> If you order a tree before December, they offer reduced prices. Prices rise the nearer you get to Christmas from £46.95 for a four-foot tree or £56.95 for a six-foot Nordman non-drop, including free delivery within central London (£5.50 for other parts of London and with last delivery date being 23 December — my order is already in!

> **BuyaTree.com T · 0845 458 2425 W · buyatree.com**

Now it's time for the DECORATIONS ...

Whether it's getting teary-eyed over a loo-roll, crepe paper and cotton wool Santa brought home from nursery, or proudly hanging last year's must-have tree delight from Harvey Nicks, unpacking the decorations box each year has to be the best part of Christmas for me. However, I know some of you love it all being done for you, or perhaps you just don't have the time, so here are some great people who can act as your festive fairy godmother.

SAY HELLO TO KITTY

> Not only is Kitty Arden an artist and designer with her own range of beautifully made bespoke gifts, she is also responsible for the gorgeous re-branding of Prestat's packaging. Who better to decorate your tree at Christmas, or provide you with beautiful wreaths and table decorations, or even a themed table for that special dinner party?

> She has decorated for some of the most exclusive parties, and you'll need to book well in advance as she is very popular. Prices on request.

> **Kitty Arden T·020 7351 3331 W·kittyarden.com**

LIGHTING UP YOUR NEIGHBOURHOOD

> Once you've let John and his team work their wonders on your Christmas tree, the rest of the house will look down-right shabby in comparison, so it's a good job he makes fantastic wreaths, garlands and table decorations as well, not to mention his stunning floral arrangements. With top names on his client list, be prepared for an admiring crowd to gather outside your windows on those dark December nights! The service starts from £500.00 and includes delivering and dressing the tree, lights, decorations, and the dismantling and removal of the tree after Christmas.

> **John Carter Flowers, 2–5 The Engineering Works, 2 Michael Road, London SW6 2AD T·020 7731 5146 W·johncarterflowers.com**

See page 24 for Woodhams

A BERRY GOOD DEAL

> Holly has been used for nearly 2,000 years to bring festive cheer into our homes in the darkest part of winter. Holly by Post is a family-run business that delivers freshly-picked holly from their orchard in Somerset. They guarantee that you will not find fresher holly anywhere.
Prices: from £14.99 a box; last orders 18 December

> **Holly by Post, Keirles Farm, Thurloxton, Taunton, Somerset TA2 8RH T·01823 412 318 (p.m. only) / 07970 858 536 W·hollybypost.co.uk**

MAKE ROOM AT THE INN FOR QUALITY

> Now that Finn, our young son, has requested some nativity figures for Christmas, I have begun my search for either vintage or lovely plain wooden pieces. I was lucky enough to find some at a car boot sale, but there were only three shepherds. Now I have found Once A Tree, who supply carved wooden nativity scenes, and they will sell you individual pieces so you could build up your nativity scene over the years. I love their Holy Family, a three-piece set carved in Alder from Germany (£24.00) and the three Hallelujah Angels, also from the Thuringian Forest in Germany (£26.50). They can ship worldwide.

> **Once A Tree, 255 Old High Street, Perth PH1 5QN T·01738 636 213 W·onceatree.co.uk**

GIVE YOUR HOME A LITTLE VA-VA-VOOM!

> You probably all know VV Rouleaux, which I believe is one of the best trimmings and passementerie shops in the UK, if not the

world (*see page* 211). What you probably don't know is that Annabel Lewis can actually come to your home at Christmas and decorate your tree and house with bespoke jewelled wreaths, birds, crystals, shiny beads and baubles. She'll send you a brochure so you can see the range of her wonderful products, which grows by the day. Buyers beware – you'll want all of them! Price is on application, so phone the Trade Vaults if, like me, you can't resist this fantastic service.

> **VV Rouleaux Trade Vaults** T · 020 7627 4455 W · vvrouleaux.com
> **102 Marylebone Lane, London W1U 2QD** T · 020 7224 5179
> **54 Sloane Square, Cliveden Place, London SW1W 8AX** T · 020 7730 3125
> **94 Miller Street, Merchant City, Glasgow G1 1DT** T · 0141 221 2277
> **38 Brentwood Avenue, Jesmond, Newcastle upon Tyne** T · 0191 281 3003

And don't you dare forget anyone on your CHRISTMAS CARD list...

We send 2.4 billion greeting cards each year, around 70 per cent of which are Christmas cards. At least 80 of these are sent by my family, and I know that's quite restrained! I love receiving unique Christmas cards, especially if they have been handmade or are bespoke. If you fancy sending a more personalised card, why not have one of these fabulous designers create your next festive greeting. Sometimes it can even be cheaper than buying boxes of printed cards. Also, save the cards you receive to use as Christmas labels next year: cut up all your favourites, punch a hole through them and thread them with ribbon – it will save you a fortune on labels.

ART IMITATING LIFE
> You may well have seen Jody's witty, stylish illustrations in *Tatler*. She has also illustrated little booklets for Harrods magazine

The best way I have seen Christmas cards displayed was at my friend's house: She had bought old wooden pegs (some had even been turned into little fairies by painting the top as a face and using vintage materials for the outfit), and hung the cards from vintage ribbon using the pegs to hold them. It looked great.

supplements. As long as you book a long time in advance, Jody can design a unique, personalised Christmas card for you that will take pride of place on all your friends' mantelpieces. You will receive the original art work (which you can later frame), from which you then need to have your invitations printed. Her detail is phenomenal – if she has to draw a certain car she will look at hundreds of car magazines; when she draws people, she studies them from the way they slouch to how they hold their handbag and tie their hair; and she illustrates pets just as well.

> And if you're blown away by her Christmas cards, she can also do wedding invitations, menu cards, place-cards and initials.
> The artwork typically starts at £500.00; if you have a very small drawing in mind, Jody will negotiate a price with you.
> **Jody Hyde-Thomson T · 020 7589 0537**

For other fab designers who offer Christmas card design, check out those featured under Stationery pages 29-37.

Andrea Kett offers fabulous bespoke cards (see page 32), as does Ellen McGrath from Anzu (see page 29)

Pulling the Other One – CRACKERS

GUARANTEED TO CRACK A SMILE

> Clare will make you the most wonderful handmade, genuinely luxury Christmas crackers that will be the talking point of your table. The crackers can be made from just about anything: beautiful textiles to match your tablecloth, gorgeous Japanese art papers, well-known newspapers or delicate Italian papers. The decorations on the crackers are fabulous, including feathers, organza ribbon, pearls, natural hydrangeas and lavender (for the gardening range crackers), beads and baubles.

> Gifts inside are upmarket and unique – from a mother-of-pearl caviar spoon, to a small radio pen, to fashion jewellery. The crackers all go off with a bang, and include the obligatory laugh – I nearly started – joke. Thankfully though, there are no hats – wouldn't want to mess up the hair would we?

> Clare can also provide you with a couture level of crackers. They are amazing – tell her about the intended recipient and she will make you the perfect cracker. You can order bespoke crackers year-round for birthdays, weddings, anniversaries or dinner parties. She can deliver anywhere within the UK, but unfortunately not overseas because of the regulations about the bangers!
Prices range from £10.00 to £25.00 per cracker, depending on the level of luxury, and you need to allow around six weeks for ordering and delivery (so order in October for Christmas).

> **Clare Hutchison, Froufrou & Thomas, 5 Bower Hinton, Martock, Somerset TA12 6JY
T·01935 825 124
W·froufrouandthomas.co.uk**

CRACK A SMILE WITH A UNIQUE SURPRISE

> Totally Crackers specialise in making handmade crackers for Christmas, weddings, parties (including kids') and corporate events. You can choose your paper, decoration and the contents, so they're exclusive to you. I loved the idea they had for a wedding cracker – they printed the name of every guest at the wedding onto the cracker wrapping and each guest received one as a favour. And with no minimum order, except the Design Your Own (minimum of 100 crackers), you can order a single cracker or several hundred.

> They have a selection of gifts for you to choose from, or you can send them your own special gift, which they can pop into the cracker. They have a good selection of papers, ribbons and accessories, but if you don't see something to match your colour scheme, let them know and they'll do their best to source it.

> They also run a monthly competition to win a luxury cracker filled with goodies – just send them a child-friendly joke that they can use in their crackers.
Prices: Mini (£1.35), Fill Your Own (£1.40), Classic (£1.70), Slide Apart (£2.55).

> Allow four to six weeks when ordering between one and fifty crackers.

> **Totally Crackers, 4 Matthews Lane, East Boldre, Brockenhurst, Hampshire SO42 7WJ
T·01590 611 041 W·totallycrackers.co.uk**

COUTURE CRACKERS

> I have written about the very creative Jeannine from Lost for Words in the Shopping and Presents section (*see page* 200). One of her very unique bespoke gifts is her most amazing party and Christmas crackers. Each cracker is filled with a teeny personalised booklet made for each recipient. The little booklets are created by Jeannine after she has gleaned from you all the low-down on

your friends and loved ones – you can also provide her with favourite photos.

> And once you surprise your friends with your unique present they will quite simply be 'Lost for Words'
> The crackers cost £175.00 (for four) – I simply must order some.
> **Lost for Words, Lancaster House, 237 Sussex Gardens, London W2 3UD**
  T · 020 7262 2292 / 07802 815 336
  W · lostforwordsonline.com

TOO GOODE TO BE TRUE?

> Opened in 1827, this house of luxury offers a pledge of quality to its discriminating customers. Thomas Goode is recognised by many as the best fine bone china, crystal and silverware shop in the world and has three warrants to supply the Royal family. But what's that got to do with Christmas I hear you ask. Well, they also offer wonderful Christmas crackers and you can choose anything from the shop (within reason) to go inside. Just to give you an idea: previous customers have ordered crackers containing porcelain figures, napkin rings, table-setting place-name holders, candle holders and little china boxes. They take a couple of weeks to make up and, obviously, prices depend on the gifts enclosed. You could also choose their bespoke crackers, which they make up in boxes of six for £350.00 or £750.00.
I couldn't finish here without telling you to read about their gorgeous bespoke china range (*see page* 74) that would just complete your festive table setting.
> **Thomas Goode & Co, 19 South Audley Street, Mayfair, London W1K 2BN**
  T · 020 7499 2823 W · thomasgoode.co.uk

Then you have to FEED everyone…

DINNER IS SERVED (BUT NOT BY YOU)

> If you want the full Monty for Christmas Day but can't cook or won't cook, then The Christmas Dinner Company is the answer. Come 23 December, they will deliver everything you need for the perfect Christmas dinner, all prepared and ready to go. The ingredients are carefully selected from quality producers, including Kelly Turkeys and Duchy Originals.
> You receive an instruction booklet, digital kitchen timer, linen apron, cooking guidelines and a time planner, along with great recipe ideas for leftovers. All your veggies are peeled and ready to cook, and all your gravies and sauces are made. Each pack contains your turkey, organic honey and rosemary cocktail sausages, organic chestnut and apple stuffing, and organic Christmas fruits and cognac stuffing, honey-roast parsnips, Brussels sprouts with chestnuts and pancetta, citrus-glazed carrots, potatoes, gravy, bread sauce, cranberry sauce, Christmas pud, brandy butter, mince pies, olive oil, goose fat, vodka and a roasting tin. Prices: £450.00 for six to eight people, or £650.00 for 10-12; expensive, I know, but what a great present to give someone who is hosting Christmas Day. Sorry, but it is only available to mainland UK.
> **The Christmas Dinner Company**
  T · 0845 607 2512
  W · thechristmasdinnercompany.co.uk

Preparing the PANTRY

Don't know about you, but I can taste the difference between frozen and fresh, organic or battery, and although I only eat poultry and fish (not red meat), I like to know the animals have been well looked after before I tuck in. Many of us like to support local, small-scale producers who invariably hand-make yummy goodies that taste like nothing else. So here are my recommendations for where to buy all your Christmas fare.

Cheese

CHEESE LOVERS UNITE

> Not everyone is like my father, who couldn't go to bed without his nightly glass of port and piece of Stilton, but many of us like to indulge at Christmas. Order your cheese board this Christmas from The Fine Cheese Company and they can recommend their favourites from a selection of over 60 varieties. You can order right up till 14 December, and their minimum order is just £25.00 plus delivery.

> And if you're a cheese-aholic, then relief is on hand. They also offer a Monthly Cheeseboard that you can order any month, or *every* month, for £29.50 (delivered) – very popular as a Christmas present. They have even designed wonderful crackers to scoff with particular cheeses. I love the walnut oat digestive with goat's cheese, or Red Hot Chilli Crackers with Cheddar. I also regularly stock up on their chutney, relish, oils, honey, wine, delicious savoury nibbles, chocolates and biscuits. For something truly different, check out their fabulous Artisan Cheese Wedding Cake.

> **The Fine Cheese Company, 29 & 31 Walcot Street, Bath BA1 5BN**
> **T · 01225 448 748 W · finecheese.co.uk**

YOU CAN'T SAY CHEESE WITHOUT SMILING

> Whenever we have a dinner party I pop into Selfridges (any excuse!) to stock up on Neal's Yard cheeses and other delectable morsels. If, however, you're not quite as devoted to wandering round food halls, you can order over 72 cheeses through Neal's Yard's website. You don't even have to plan far in advance as they offer a two-day delivery service within mainland UK (excluding some parts of Scotland).

> Apart from tasting fantastic, Neal's Yard's cheeses also have fabulous names. It's always amusing to tuck into a Stinking Bishop at the end of a meal, or to ask your guest to 'Please pass the Verulamium' after you've had a few! For the full cheese experience, head for one of their branches in Covent Garden or at the Borough food market, one of the finest destinations for food shopping in London.

> **Neal's Yard Dairy, 17 Shorts Gardens, Covent Garden, London WC2H 9UP**

> **or 6 Park Street, Borough Market, London SE1 9AB**
> **T · 020 7240 5700 (Covent Garden) / 020 7645 3554 (Borough Market) / Mail Order 020 7500 7653**
> **W · nealsyarddairy.co.uk**

Chocolates

(See also Divine Bespoke Chocolates page 255)

A TASTE OF THE COUNTRY

> From the Dorset countryside, Chococo is a husband and wife-led team (their six-year-old daughter being their chief chocolate taster!) making wonderful handmade chocolates, flavoured and filled with delicious ingredients, for example, fresh Dorset cream (no preservatives), lemon curd, or Moroccan mint and honey. They use fair-trade products where possible or products sourced from ethical producers, and all their chocolates are suitable for vegetarians, are GM-free, and contain only natural ingredients.

> For Christmas they make solid chocolate Christmas cards with 'Merry Christmas' in 10 different languages, but what I especially love is their Advent box with 25 numbered chocolates — yum, yum! I also couldn't get enough of their scrumptious hand-dipped dried fruits.

> Their fantastic packaging has won design awards and ensures that their chocolates make a lovely gift, not only for Christmas, but throughout the year. They won Gold at the Great Taste Awards (the Choccie Oscars) for Wild Thing — a marbled dome of plain & white chocolate with a centre studded with a whole griottine cherry soaked in kirsch surrounded by a plain chocolate ganache — wow!

> They're happy to produce bespoke chocolate gifts, from creating new chocolates to person-alising with labels and matching colours for an event, and their Wedding Queen, Lynne, will sort out all your favours.

> They can host children's parties or, if you can pop along to their shop any Monday to Saturday (10.00 a.m. - 5.00 p.m.), you can watch them making the chocolates.

> Last orders for Christmas should be placed two weeks before the big day, but check their website for the most up-to-date information.

> **Chococo, The Purbeck Chocolate Co, "Cocoa Central", Commercial Road, Swanage, Dorset BH19 1DF T · 01929 421 777 W · chococo.co.uk**

CHOCOLATE, CHOCOLATE AND NOTHING BUT THE CHOCOLATE

> I bought some James Chocolate in a deli in Sherbourne — lovingly handmade, with no additives or preservatives, using a secret blend of the world's finest chocolate couver-ture, it was absolutely delicious. The chocolate range includes colourful chocolate fish, cute pigs, big yummie slabs, and — a very classy gift idea — a nifty box (made from chocolate) topped with fruit and nuts and filled with delicious pralines.

> Specifically for Christmas there are hand-decorated chocolate Christmas trees and Christmas pudding-shaped truffles, while the Mosaic Bar, an impressive one kilo of indulgent chocolate in nine separate tiles, decorated with fruits, nuts, marshmallows and drizzled chocolate, would be a choco-holic's dream Christmas present. It's on my Christmas list and I'm afraid no, you can't have any, not even a little!

> Drop into one of his retail Bar Chocolat shops and you can not only stock up for Christmas, but also sit down and enjoy an ultimate hot chocolate with a triple nut brownie.

> **James Chocolate T · 01749 831 330 W · jameschocolates.co.uk**

> **Bar Chocolat stores:**

> **19 The Mall, Clifton Village, Bristol BS8 4JG T · 0117 974 7000**

> **3 Argyle Street, Bath BA2 4BA T · 01225 446060**

A LITTLE PIECE OF HANDMADE HEAVEN

> Montezuma's (or Monty's to friends) offer a fantastic selection of chocolate bars, truffles, dollops, big bits, fudge, drinking chocolate and more. All their chocolate products are made from organic cocoa from the Dominican Republic or Peru, and for the other ingredients they source the best products from around the world. Better still, most of their chocolates are certified organic. The times they aren't are when it's been impossible to get organic ingredients, for example Cointreau!

> Their whole range is made by hand with great care and passion and with a complete love of chocolate. I love their Create A Kilo — choose from a list of ingredients to have your very own big slab of flavoured chocolate. They also offer hampers, wedding chocolates, and even a chocolate club — mmm, yummy chocolates delivered every month. They've won many awards, including the Organic Food Award for chocolate, and with amazing

ingredients like geranium, bergamot and four peppers, you'll be spoilt for choice. Try Montezuma's Revenge, a truffle filled with chilli, tequila and lime, or if you like a traditional Christmas, stock up on snowmen, Christmas trees and candied oranges.

> There are Montezuma's stores in Brighton, London, Winchester and Chichester, and a store in Windsor where you're invited to pop in if you happen to be visiting the Queen! (See online for store details)

> Last orders for Christmas by 17 December.

> **Montezuma's T·01243 537 385 W·montezumas.co.uk**

Ham

EXPERIENCE SELLS

> Established in 1828 and still in the hands of the same family eight generations later, Richard Woodall Ltd is probably one of the oldest family-run businesses in Britain today. They rear their own pig herd and use no chemical additives, preservatives or added water. Having perfected their prepared hams over the course of nearly two centuries, they have also been awarded the Royal Warrant for their Cumberland sausages, Cumberland hams and bacon. For an uncooked ham that will feed 20 people, expect to pay £55.00 plus £7.00 delivery. You should order by 1 December.

> **Richard Woodall Ltd, Waberthwaite, Cumbria LA19 5YJ T·01229 717 237 W·richardwoodall.co.uk**

Turkeys

FIRST COME, FIRST SERVED

> Graigs have won many organic food awards for the quality of their produce (*see page* 51) and an award for Best Home Delivery Service. They offer what they call the Rolls Royce of organic turkeys – top-of-the-range,

from a chicken-size up to 10-kg – and a less expensive, free-range turkey which is additive free. Orders are taken up to the first week in December, but they have a limited stock and sell out quickly, so it pays to get organised in November.

> **Graig Farm Organics, Dolau, Llandrindod Wells, Powys LD1 5TL T·01597 851 655 W·graigfarm.co.uk**

A BIRD ON THE FARM'S WORTH TWO IN THE FREEZER

> Paul Kelly knows everything there is to know about turkeys, which is why his award-winning Kelly Bronze are beautifully moist and full of flavour. The turkeys roam freely in pastures, fields and woodland and are completely drug-free. They are grown to a mature age, hand-plucked and hung for 10 days to let them develop their full flavour.

> From £51.38 for a 4-kg bird, order by 18 December for nationwide delivery. Or you can save yourself a tenner by collecting from the farm, right up till Christmas. Paul says he has never turned anyone away empty-handed!

> **Kelly Turkey Farms, Springate Farm, Bicknacre Road, Danbury, Essex CM3 4EP T·01245 223 581 W·kellyturkeys.com**

FREE-RANGE FLAVOUR

> Fresh, oven-ready Woodlands Farm Organic Bronze Turkeys can be collected from the farm or home delivered. Raised in small groups free to wander the fields and woods, they are healthy, contented birds with a fine gamey flavour. Prices start at £9.00 per kg, plus £8.00 delivery. They recommend ordering by the end of November.

> **Woodlands Farm, Kirton House, Kirton, Boston, Lincolnshire PE20 1JD T·01205 724 778 W·woodlandsfarm.co.uk**

Salmon

FISHING FOR COMPLIMENTS

> A fine-food mail-order company, Forman & Field specialises in traditional British produce from small, independent producers. A one-stop shop for a wonderful gourmet Christmas, it could be the answer to all your culinary prayers.

> They offer a range of wild, organic and smoked salmon by Britain's oldest salmon smokers, H. Forman & Son, who are particularly famous for their smoked Scottish wild salmon. A whole side of Scottish wild salmon costs around £100.00 for 1.4 kg, which is enough to feed 15. Last orders December 10.

> **Forman & Field, Stour Road, Fish Island, London E3 2NT**
T·020 8221 3939 W·formanandfield.com

WHERE THERE'S SMOKE THERE'S FLAVOUR

> Ummera has a reputation for offering one of the best smoked salmon in the world. They can deliver their GOLD award winning smoked organic salmon and smoked silver eel to most countries worldwide, often overnight.

> **Ummera Smoked Products Limited, Inchybridge, Timoleague, Co. Cork, Ireland**
T·+353 23 46644 W·ummera.com

Vegetables

WILLING AND ABEL

> I love Abel & Cole not only for their superb organic food and drink, but also for their organic vegetables Christmas box. They also have a great section on their website where you can look up recipes, storage tips and nutrition information for all the veggies they offer.

> The Christmas box is priced from £22.50 and contains enough veg for up to six people. You

should order by the first week in December. Unfortunately, they do not deliver nationwide just yet but can deliver to most of London, the home counties and large areas of the south west and east of England.

> **Abel & Cole Limited, 16 Waterside Way, Plough Lane, Wimbledon, London SW17 0HB**
T·0845 262 6262 W·abel-cole.co.uk

THESE GUYS REALLY KNOW THEIR VEG...

> If being recommended by Rick Stein and winning numerous organic awards isn't proof enough that these guys produce top quality goods, I can also tell you that they have received the Great Taste Gold Award. Rod and Ben pride themselves on the variety, freshness and good quality of their box scheme. They grow 70 different organic crops and insist that the produce arrives at your door within 18 hours of leaving the farm. They believe 'the best tasting food is food picked in season and eaten in season'. They can also supply honey (non-organic), wonderful fresh soups and pesto (which I loved), and organic eggs from their own hens. Their website has some fantastic recipes; I made the Artichoke Rosti — yum yum.

> The bumper Christmas box is full of healthy favourites and costs £40-50.00 plus delivery (standard range £10-14.00). Last orders 16 December, with delivery available within mainland UK.

> **Rod and Ben's, Bickham Farm, Kenn, Exeter, Devon EX6 7XL**
T·01392 833 833 W·rodandbens.com

All manner of goods

KEEPING IT REAL

> Shelves heaving with their own divine produce and best foods from Britain and around the world — The Real Eating Company's many awards are well deserved. Treat yourself or a friend to one of their

three hampers (each come in two sizes) — The Best of British, Spanish Gourmet or Italian Gourmet — or sample some of their jams, chutneys, mince pies, choccie brownies, cheeses and Christmas puds. Their ginger-bread houses are particularly show-stopping and are so popular they need to be ordered two weeks in advance. Order a small one at £45.00, or if you're feeding the 5,000, opt for a 2-foot tall one at £75.00.

> Making use of the next-day delivery service, last orders can be placed up until the eve of the last working day before Christmas.

> **The Real Eating Company, 86/87 Western Road, Hove, East Sussex BN3 1JB T·01273 221 444 shop / 01273 221 441 for queries about online shopping W·real-eating.co.uk**

Christmas Hampers

> We all know and love the hampers you can have delivered from Fortnum & Mason, Harrods, Selfridges and Harvey Nichols (not to mention their divine packaging):

> **Fortnum & Mason: W·fortnumandmason.com T·020 7734 8040**

> **Harrods: W·harrods.com T·020 7730 1234**

> **Harvey Nichols: W·harveynichols.com/hampers T·020 8957 5030 Shopping Team**

> **Selfridges & Co: W·selfridges.com T·0800 123 400; for overseas customers +44 113 369 8040**

For picnic hampers see page 261

I also wanted to let you drool over a few other options…

THE ULTIMATE FOODIE FANTASY

> I still can't quite believe this hamper. You must order it two to three weeks before Christmas and, at £1,000.00 each, it's no

wonder they are delivered by Securicor! It includes an entire Pata Negra Ham on the bone (air-dried in Southern Spain using only the pure-bred black Iberico pig and prized by many as one of the greatest culinary ingredients in the world), a whole side of smoked wild salmon, half a kilo of caviar, and either a fresh foie gras en torchon with truffles or a wonderful selection of handmade chocolates.

> For those with a slightly smaller budget this year (start saving for next year), I also love their children's hamper at just £29.99. This is a big box painted like a London bus and filled with a kilo of Christmas sweets — chocolate sardines, candy canes, chocolate coins, multi-coloured sugar-coated puffed rice, chocolate cars, fruit and caramel lollipops, and jellybeans — aren't you full yet! They can actually deliver this hamper year round, so it would also make a nice birthday gift. Order before 16 December for Christmas delivery.

> **Cornucopia Foods Ltd, 3 Albion Close, Newtown Business Park, Poole BH12 3LL T·08450 633 699 W·cornucopiafoods.co.uk**

THE TRUTH IS IN THE TASTING

> Graigs are loved by their customers and by the good people who give organic food awards. They work with over 200 farmers and taste everything they sell to make sure you are only buying the best. Their huge range of produce includes meats to baby food to gluten-free products to alcoholic drinks.

> They offer two Christmas hampers: the Gourmet (£76.50), a hamper for four; and the excellent-value Luxury Hamper for up to eight people (£168.50). The contents of your hamper may vary, but it will include things like smoked salmon, Christmas pudding and Christmas cake, mince pies, brandy butter, chutney, cheese, Italian biscuits, Brazilian coffee, paté, Green & Black's organic

chocolate, and a bottle each of red and white wine (all organic). Orders are taken up to the first week in December.

> **Graig Farm Organics, Dolau, Llandrindod Wells, Powys LD1 5TL**
> **T·01597 851 655 W·graigfarm.co.uk**

It's not only Santa who needs little helpers...
I know we all aspire to being Superwoman,
but never be afraid to admit you need help.
Here are some great services that will relieve
some of the pressure.

IF YOU WANT SOMETHING DONE, ASK A BUSY PERSON

> Put these Busy People on your speed dial immediately – the lovely Lyn can send you help for all sorts of things (*see main entry, page 85*). Invaluable in the midst of Christmas chaos, Lyn has helped clients with shopping, cooking, baby-sitting and even wrapping presents. Either provide the materials yourself or pay a little extra and Busy People will bring themed wrapping materials, tree decorations, or supply serving staff to hand out your drinks and nibbles. Prices vary depending on the job, but to give you an idea, you would pay £13.00 per hour for waiting staff and £15.00 an hour for present wrapping. What price can you put on staying sane?

> **Busy People**
> **T·020 8981 8972 / 07974 308 668**
> **W·busy-people.co.uk**

TEAR UP YOUR TO-DO LIST

> It's not only top executives and celebrities who can benefit from a personal assistant. We all need an extra pair of hands once in a while and never more so than at Christmas time. With clients as far flung as Cambodia and Salt Lake City, the jobs carried out by this innovative team are not easily categorized. One client's wife in Salt Lake City was pregnant and had a complete craving for Greek yoghurt, which she couldn't find anywhere. Andrea tracked down a wholesaler in New York and begged and pleaded with them to send a pallet of yoghurt to her – she was delighted! Another client phoned at 4.00 p.m. the day before moving home to tell them that the street he was moving to was closed all that next day for the May Day demonstrations and asked how could he get the removal truck in? Andrea sorted everything out for a smooth move, and needless to say this client is still a client three years later!

> The service costs £30.00 per hour for up to four hours, or book a block of 10 hours for £25.00 per hour. If you buy a block of hours, you have up to 12 months to use those hours on jobs – a great Christmas gift that keeps on giving. Their motto is 'If it is legal, moral and feasible, we'll be happy to help.'

> **Cushion the Impact, 68 St Peter's Street, London N1 8JS**
> **T·020 7704 6922**
> **W·cushiontheimpact.co.uk**

NOTHING PLAIN ABOUT THIS JANE

> Jane is known as the 'Gift Wrap Guru', and I was joined by clients from around the world when I went to her one-day gift-wrapping course. Having travelled the globe in search of presentation at its best, Jane has always been inspired by the high standards of gift wrapping in the USA, the Far East and Japan. I too love beautiful packaging and have a whole room filled with things that I use to wrap my presents, but I have always struggled with the bows and hated all the sticky tape showing and the uneven corners. I was definitely in need of help from an expert, as I really believe that it doesn't matter how much you spend on the present inside, an artistically-wrapped gift is a thing of beauty and will delight whoever receives it.

> The course covers wrapping basics, and we learnt how to wrap a box, a bottle and a

cylindrical shape perfectly, as well as how to do the very sophisticated Japanese pleating. We took a break for a scrummy two-course, home-cooked meal before we got back to ribbon-tying, bow-making and handmade envelopes and gift bags.

> The most fun part was learning how to use all sorts of things from around the home in the presentation process – even a kitchen scourer, wallpaper and a daily newspaper.

> Jane offers five wonderful courses, either in Lincolnshire or London: Gift Wrapping; Card Making For All Occasions (Jane has made over 70,000, supplying Harvey Nichols and other well-known stores); Handmade Christmas Cards; Table Dressing; and Wedding Preparation and Ideas. In Lincolnshire the one-day courses cost £75.00 per person; in London £95.00 per person. She will also run private courses in your home or workplace, which at £230.00 for a half-day or £300.00 for a whole day are good value if you have up to five friends join you (includes all handouts and materials, but not lunch or travel expenses). She also runs a mail-order service selling ribbons and other wrapping supplies and ready-made decorations.

> **Jane Means, 64 High Street, Coningsby, Lincolnshire LN4 4RF**
> **T·07986 830 866 W·janemeans.co.uk**

GIVE YOUR GIFT A LIFT

> Carmen and Marie (two sisters) set up The Wrapping Company in 2003. I love their bespoke giftwrapping service – either send them your presents and they'll wrap and return them, or have them over to your house to wrap all your presents. Diaries permitting, they can come over right up to Christmas Eve – bookings open in October and they do get very booked up, so try to book well in advance.

> Prices start from £160.00 for half a day in the London area. The cost obviously depends on what you want to have wrapped, and they will give you an all-inclusive quote after a consultation.

> They also provide a mail-order/online service for classic and contemporary giftwrapping products and accessories from the UK and abroad. If you're ordering their paper, ribbons, tissue or accessories, last day for orders is usually around 18 December (check online).

> Their services aren't only for Christmas, although this is the most popular. They will also wrap presents for parties, weddings, corporate, anniversaries or baby gifts. I asked Carmen what was the hardest thing they have been asked to wrap – can you believe it was an aeroplane? We're talking thousands of metres of wrapping paper here!

> **The Wrapping Company, 7 Broomhall Road, Woking, Surrey GU21 4AP**
> **T·01483 823 023 W·thewrappingco.com**

Because I shop so much, I often pick up the perfect Christmas gifts for friends or family throughout the year. I sometimes even buy in the January sales, which saves me a fortune. Unfortunately, when I plan so far ahead I often find that the nicest gifts creep out from the bottom drawer to sit on my dressing table or appear in my kitchen! However, if you're like my friend who has 88 presents to buy for her extended family, if you can't face the crush in the stores, or if you're stressed by online mailing deadlines, see page 70, Rachel Meddowes, for some Christmas-shopping help.

Survival Guides for Christmas-time –
Fantastic books that will help you through the
Christmas period

IT'S A WRAP

> A lovely little book that will inspire and instruct you on how to wrap absolutely anything – even the rather unimaginative book or CD voucher for that hard-to-buy-for person.
> I loved the way they show you how to tidily wrap a cylinder and bottle, and the alternative and more interesting method of wrapping a book, along with how to make envelope bags and handmade envelopes. I enjoy wrapping my loved-ones' gifts, using all sorts of vintage trimmings and flea market finds, so much so that it's often more fun than unwrapping my own gifts. Unless of course it's that Hermes bag I couldn't even afford to join the waiting list for.
> *Gift Wrapping*, **Lucy Berridge and Charlotte Packer (Ryland, Peters & Small)**

GET SILLY WITH JILLY

> Jilly's book made me laugh so much last December that I almost forgot the frantic stressfulness of the approach to Christmas. Being a complete games addict, I loved the section where, along with old favourites such as Charades, she suggested a game for only two people which has me weeping with laughter. Here it is: 'Mr and Ms Stressed each sit down with a bottle of whisky and a glass. Both finish drinking their own bottle; then one of them goes out of the room and knocks on the door, and the other has to guess who it is.'
> *How to Survive Christmas*, **Jilly Cooper (Bantam Press)**

FLOSSED TURKEY AND FROZEN CANDLES

> Based on the popular BBC programme, *Trade Secrets – Christmas*, an invaluable book bringing you every possible tip, scam and downright cheat to help you achieve the perfect celebrations. As they say, 'May your baubles sparkle, your turkey be plump and your tree hold all its needles.' Here are some of their useful tips:

> Use dental floss (not the mint-flavoured kind!) to tie up and stitch your turkey
> For extra-tasty roast potatoes, make a hole through the potato with an apple corer and push a piece of rolled-up bacon inside, then roast as usual
> Tart up old decorations and baubles with a can of metallic spray paint
> Save up egg boxes to store delicate bauble decorations
> You can prolong the burning time of a candle by putting it in the fridge for a day before lighting.

> How did we get ever get through Christmas past without knowing those?

> *Trade Secrets – Christmas*, **Annie Ashworth and Meg Sanders (Orion, A Division of the Orion Publishing Group)**

WEDDINGS

THE COMPLETE
A-Z WEDDING GUIDE

I'm completely obsessed with everything to do with weddings and you'll often find me sobbing by the side of the pavement when I see a bridal car go past! I find it all extremely emotional. Also, I have kept my finger on the pulse of what's hip and happening every year for the last ten years in the wedding business, for publishing theweddingfile *(see page 34) and writing for wedding magazines. This section could be huge – I did contemplate having a separate little book just for weddings (watch this space!) – so what I've done, for this edition, is just list products, sources and services without too much waffle. That way I can tell you about twice as many fab things in half the space. So, for a complete change of pace, read on!*

> BEAUTIFUL BOOKS – Fabulous bespoke wedding books
Lightmonkey T·020 8299 2552
W·lightmonkey.co.uk

> ADD A LITTLE FANCY TO YOUR FLORALS – Swarovski crystal or rhinestones – flowers, monograms, hearts or single stones
Bouquet Jewels T·+1 480 361 7335
W·bouquetjewels.com

> ALL BOXED UP – For favours or keepsakes – a very good selection of plain and coloured boxes, including wrappings, bags and accessories.
All Boxed Up T·01202 672 200
W·all-boxed-up.co.uk

> ARTIST-IN-RESIDENCE – Charles Burns creates fantastic silhouettes within 90 seconds using a pair of scissors and black

---

JUST ASK ANNABEL

If you want your venue, reception table and wedding cake to look unique, but design is not your strong point, don't worry. The very talented Annabel Lewis of VV Rouleaux fame offers a wedding decoration consultancy for brides-to-be. I bought some of her stunning table numbers decorated with ribbon, flowers and diamanté, and was thrilled with the effect. Prices on application.

Annabel Lewis: for enquiries call
VV Rouleaux Trade Vaults
T·020 7627 4455

paper. Give one to your guests for a memento and keep the other for your album.
Charles Burns T·0118 947 6637
W·roving-artist.com

> BOXING CLEVER – Not only do they have great storage boxes for your wedding dress, shoes and accessories, they also have lovely favour boxes.
The Empty Box Co T·01306 740 193
W·emptybox.co.uk

> STRESS-FREE CO-ORDINATION – Unflappable, professional and stress-free wedding co-ordinator.
Christine Dewar T·01372 477 199
W·weddingsolutions.org

> LET THEM EAT CAKE – Extraordinary cakes that will wow your guests *(see page* 251*)*.
Savoir Design T·020 8877 9770
W·savoirdesign.com

> 'ART-BREAKINGLY BEAUTIFUL – Hand-painted, modern wedding cakes. I love the Golden Tree – a stunning three-tiered, heart-shaped wedding cake with extravagant gold leaf,

painted with colourful butterflies, flowers and birds.
T·020 8290 4981 W·amandastreeter.com

> DIVINE WITH A CAPITAL D – Funky, inspiring cakes, cookies and favours (*see page 252*).
**Peggy Porschen T·020 7738 1339
W·peggyporschen.com**

> CHOCOLATE CREATIONS – Beautifully decorated chocolate creations.
**Purita Hyam T·01403 891 518
W·chocolateweddingcakes.co.uk**

> CLOSE UP ON THE CAKE – All the stars book Mich Turner.
Little Venice Cake Company T·020 7486 5252 W·lvcc.co.uk

> A TASTE FOR CELEBRITY – Bespoke cutting edge designs.
**Linda Fripp Designs T·01722 718 518
W·lindafrippcakes.co.uk**

> CROWN IT – Spectacular jewelled flowers, monograms and crowns to top your cake.
**Debra Moreland, Paris
T·+1 513 542 8345 W·paristiaras.com**

> A BAG TO BITE INTO – Divine chocolate handbags, great favours.
W·chocochocohouse.com

> CONFETTI TO REMEMBER – Personalised photo confetti.
**Confetti T·08870 840 6060
W·confetti.co.uk**

You can buy Vera Wang, Reem Acra and other designer wedding or bridesmaids' dresses on Ebay. Some of the dresses have not been worn and are offered at an absolute steal. When I looked there were 50 Vera Wang dresses – one that was worth $5,300.00 sold for $850.00 – and 31 dresses by Reem Acra, with a grand total of 15,583 wedding dresses up for sale!

THE TALENTED MS TAYLOR

You may have read about Julia in the fashion section (*see page* 172), but I want to let you know about all the other lovely things she does for weddings. She can make beaded flowers or butterflies for your hair adornment, add a little beading to your wedding dress or veil and even create a small pair of earrings. She can also make your shoes match your dress either by adding beading, appliquéing lace, adding feathers or dyeing them. She's very talented and I'm so jealous!

Julia Taylor T·020 7289 3966 by appointment only

> MAKE A CLASSY IMPRESSION – *Very* classy. Engrave a message or monogram on a champagne bottle.
**T·0870 190 0072
W·engravedchampers.com**

> STAND ATOP YOUR CAKE – Exquisite, bespoke silk and mixed-media miniatures of you and hubbie-to-be.
**Kathy Scott T·01379 643 995
W·kathyscott.co.uk**

> BROWNS IS THE NEW WHITE – This store has scoured the world for the best in bridal fashion: Reem Acra, Christian Dior, Azzedine Alaia, Colette Dinnigan, Monique Lhuillier.
**Browns Bride T·020 7514 0056
W·brownsfashion.com**

> TAKE THE LEAD WITH BEADS – Exquisite beaded wedding dresses.
**Jenny Packham T·020 7730 2264
W·jennypackhambride.com**

TOP OF THE LIST TO ASK FOR A FAVOUR

Karen makes the most exquisite, luxury favour boxes I've ever seen, handcrafting her hand-painted or material-covered boxes with divine embellishments – a gold shoe, a ceramic wedding cake, a silver heart or a ring with diamonds. She works with silk, satin, crystals, gold, fresh-water pearls, silver and diamonds.

Karen spent over two years researching the perfect components and only uses the best available. She makes them for weddings, Christmas or individual one-off gifts – for example, one man ordered a silk box mounted with a gold shoe with three diamonds which can then also be worn as a necklace. The favours come complete with a wrapped chocolate or a filling of your choice. Prices: £2.75–£225.00.

Karen Lowe Designs **T·01865 715 669 / 07814 930 592**
W·karenlowedesigns.com

> BE A ONE-OFF – Unique and fabulous creations (*see also page* 61).
Basia Zarzycka **T·020 7730 1660**
W·basia-zarzycka.com

> WED IN A WANG! – Vera Wang wedding dresses.
The Wedding Shop **T·020 7838 0171**
W·weddingshop.com

> MINIATURE MEMORIES – Sell your dress, keep the couture-quality miniature replica by Heather Menzies.
Miss Periwinkle **T·+1 877 867 8977 / +1 516 375 3807** **W·missperiwinkle.com**

> DYEING TO GET IT RIGHT – Shoes, veils, lace and bags can all be dyed to match or complement your dress. They offer other wonderful services, such as bespoke shoes, accessories and a fantastic fabric selection, with over 6,000 fabrics.
The Wedding People **T·01254 382 029**
W·theweddingpeople.co.uk

> YOU'VE GOT TO HAND IT TO THEM – Go nowhere else for exquisite bespoke embroidery.
Hand & Lock **T·020 7580 7488**
W·handembroidery.com

> IT'S WHAT'S ON THE OUTSIDE THAT COUNTS – Unique & colourful boxes for gifts and favours.
Big Tomato Company **T·020 8968 1815**
W·bigtomatocompany.com

> A FINE AFFAIR – Favours, labels, sweets and ribbon.
Edgbaston Fine Detail **T·0121 246 7550**
W·edgbastonfinedetail.co.uk

> FOR YOUR FAVOURITE PEOPLE – To make gorgeous pressies, buy little monogram stickers, CD tins, favour boxes or favour cards.
T·(USA toll free) +1 877 79 FAVOR (32867) / +1 714 259 9800
W·weddingfavorites.com

> LITTLE GEMS – Mini favours, beautifully boxed and would look great with your monogram.
Little Cakes **T·01932 872 115**
W·littlecakes.co.uk

> PUTTING THE FAB IN FABRIC – Great selection, including wonderful couture fabrics.
Joel & Sons **T·020 7724 6895**
W·joelandsonfabrics.co.uk

> 'YOU WILL IMPRESS YOUR GUESTS' – Personalised fortune cookies.
> **T·01279 793 090 W·fortune-cookies.co.uk**

> FILE UNDER LUXURY – Had to put it in, seeing as we publish it! Not to blow one's own trumpet, we have been told it's 'one of the best around'.
> *theweddingfile* **T·0870 443 0035**
> **W·theweddingfile.com**

> MANLY MAKEOVER – Gorgeous men's grooming products and services.
> **Geo F Trumper T·020 7272 1765**
> **W·trumpers.com**

> SPACE-AGE STYLE – Great treatments and fantastic selection of grooming products.
> **Space.NK.Men T·020 8740 2085**
> **W·spacenk.com**

> GROOM THAT GROOM! – For the finishing touches take him to Heidi Klein.
> **T·020 7243 5665 W·heidiklein.co.uk**

> MAKE IT YOUR OWN – Swarovski initial handbags (Mrs PW).
> **Scrumptious Design T·0870 240 6672**
> **W·scrumptiousdesign.co.uk**

> STOCKING UP – Bridal hosiery.
> **W·tightsplease.co.uk**

> MAKE A BREAK FOR IT – Three years' research produced this fab collection of honeymoon destinations.
> **Ultimate Honeymoons T·0870 350 0464**
> **W·ultimatehoneymoons.co.uk**

> NO BOYS ALLOWED – Hen pampering in style, Girls Night In at The Berkeley. Divine treats await.
> **T·020 7950 5490**
> **W·theberkeleyhotellondon.com**

> HANDS UP FOR PAMPERING – Pedi and mani hen treatments.
> **The Nail Lounge T·020 7287 1847**

> ROOST YOUR HENS – 26 rooms in a stunning hotel and you've got a great hen night!
> **Fifty Four Boutique Hotel T·020 7761 4000**
> **W·54boutique.co.uk**

> HEAD-TURNING HATS – Heavenly!
> **Philip Treacy T·020 7730 3992**
> **W·philiptreacy.co.uk**

> ROOM FOR TWO – Great little site for hiring self-catering properties that sleep two – perfect for your honeymoon.
> **T·01326 240 028 W·thelittledomain.com**

> YOU SCREAM, ICE-CREAM – Hire a '30s-style ice-cream tricycle from Wedding Trikes and keep your guests cool. (They can also offer pop-corn, Pimms or cocktails.)
> **T·020 8851 7398 / 07958 722 251**
> **W·weddingtrikes.com**

ESPECIALLY FOR CHOO

> If there's one thing that could make you feel even more special than slipping on a pair of Jimmy Choo's on your big day, it would have to be slipping on a custom-made pair in the same fabric as your wedding dress. I'm still upset that no one told me before I got married, but yes, this magical service does exist. You can have beautiful beading added for a slipper truly fit for Cinderella (no extra charge for wearing them after midnight!). Prices start at £500.00 and you should allow three to four weeks for your order.

Jimmy Choo Couture, 18 Connaught Street, London W2 2AF T·020 7262 6888

> KOSHER CREATIVITY – One of the best kosher caterers.
Tony Page T· 020 8830 4000

> FLATTER YOURSELF – Innovative lighting.
Fisher Productions T· 020 8871 1978
W· fisherproductions.co.uk

> EVERLASTING GLAMOUR – Nail gel manicure lasts three weeks. It's fantastic! 35 nail bars UK-wide.
Nails Inc T· 020 7529 2340
W· nailsinc.com

> DON'T MAKE IT UP AS YOU GO ALONG – Make-up lessons to make you look gorg, or let him glam you up for your special day.
Mathew Alexander
T· 020 7495 1122

> INITIAL IT – Your very own beautifully designed monogram (*see page* 70).
Caroline Brackenridge T· +1 212 288 8864
W· monograminc.com

> MEN IN BLACK – Men's dress hire at Lipman & Sons
T· 020 7240 2310 W· lipmanandsons.co.uk

> MORE MENSWEAR – Formal wear hire, tailoring and alterations.
Buckleigh of London T· 020 7730 0770
W· buckleighoflondon.com

> MAGICAL MARQUEES – Designers 'par excellence'.
Crescent Moon T· 0800 083 84 80
W· crescent-moon.co.uk

MONOGRAMS

When you are a single woman, you would use the first letter of your given, middle and family names to create a monogram. A woman might make her surname initial oversized and use it in the middle, flanked by her given and middle name initials. For instance, Anne Thurston Smith would be AST. When a woman marries, she drops her middle name and adds her husband's surname. So, if Anne were to marry George Perot, her initials would change to APS.

A man is lucky; he keeps his same three initials throughout his life – unless he and his wife share a monogram on certain wedding gifts. For example, as a married monogram on engraved silver, etched crystal, or embroidered linens. In this case the monogram would be APG.

Printed with kind permission from Monogram Inc see page 70)

> ORGANIC PLEASURES! – Divine catering using the finest, freshest and seasonal organic ingredients.
Passion Organic T· 020 7277 6147
W· passionorganic.com

> THROW-AWAY THRILLS – Bespoke and disposable paper wedding dresses.
Rachael Sleight T· 07795 528 274
W· rachaelsleight.com

YOU DON'T BRING ME FLOWERS ANY MORE

I've already mentioned the unique paper wedding dresses by Rachael Sleight (*see page* 59), but I have to tell you that she also makes divine paper bouquets. Made from a continuous array of perforated, pleated petals, Rachael can make them in any size. As they're all handmade to order, allow four weeks for delivery. Don't forget that paper symbolises the first year of marriage too.

**T·07795 528 274 W·rachaelsleight.com
E·rachael@rachaelsleight.com**

> I CAN'T BELIEVE IT'S NOT SILK – Magical paper wedding dresses and accessories – totally breathtaking by Mireille Etienne Brunel.
**T·(Paris) +33 1 4548 2613
W·etienne-brunel.com**

> TRAVELLING LENSMAN – Beautiful photography; specialises in overseas work.
**Contrejour T·020 8670 1234
W·contre-jour.co.uk**

> RELIVE IT WITH REPORTAGE – Award-winning, stunning photography.
**Stephen Swain T·020 8371 8726
W·stephenswain.com**

> SNAP THEM UP – Highly sought after.
**Lovegrove Photography T·01275 853 204
W·lovegroveweddings.com**

> AND LEFT ONE, TWO, THREE – Make your opening dance spectacular by learning the quick step, foxtrot, samba, waltz or tango without bruising your new husband's feet!

And who better to learn from than the four-times undefeated World and European Tango Supreme Champion and World Cup winner and All England professional ballroom championship grand finalist, Paul Bottomer. Lead on!
Paul Bottomer T·020 8372 8150 / 07960 736 925 W·dancematrix.com

> ROLLS ROYCE OF RIBBONS – The Rolls Royce of printed ribbons, used by many designers.
**Mistral Management T·020 8231 8911
W·mistralmagic.co.uk**

> ALL TIED UP – Customised hand-woven ribbon and labels – great service.
**GB Labels T·01646 600 664
W·gblabels.co.uk**

> YOU CAN'T HAVE TOO MANY ROSES – Make your own arrangements with wonderful old-fashioned organic scented roses. Sold in bulk (minimum 100 roses), May-October.
**Country Roses T·01206 273 565
W·countryroses.co.uk**

> DO-IT-YOURSELF DELIGHT – Make your own wedding rings.
**Wedding Ring Workshop T·020 7831 2909
W·weddingringworkshop.co.uk**

> SHORTCUT TO LOVE – Shortbread hearts iced with monograms from Konditor & Cook.
**T·020 7261 0456
W·konditorandcook.com**

> THE PERFECT FIT – Must-have shoes – can be made up in any fabric.
Gina Shoes T·020 7235 2932 W·gina.com

> TONE IT UP – Dye your shoes or their own brands. Worldwide.
T·01392 207 040 W·rainbow-club.co.uk

A WONDERFUL BESPOKE SERVICE FOR YOUR ENGAGEMENT RING

1 Boyfriend goes to Wint & Kidd and chooses a diamond in any size, carat and shade

2 Wint & Kidd beautifully wrap the raw stone in a brivka – for the uninitiated, a paper wrap – inside a beautifully hand-made lacquered box with a temporary clip ring

3 Boyfriend pops the question and girlfriend says 'Yes'

4 Girlfriend goes to the boutique (with boyfriend) and chooses own setting. Ring fits perfectly and boyfriend – now fiancé – gets a million brownie points!

Wint & Kidd, 237 Westbourne Grove, London W11 2SE T·020 7908 9990 W·wintandkidd.com

> STAND-OUT STYLE – Unique, beautifully embellished wedding stationery.
Clementine Invitations T·+1 203 314 3011 W·clementineinvitations.com

> STEP OUT OF THIS WORLD – Stunning shoes.
Basia Zarzycka T·020 7730 1660 W·basia-zarzycka.com

> ENGRAVED ON YOUR SOLE – Personalise your shoes with words or memorable dates printed on the soles.
Beatrix Ong T·020 7449 0480 W·beatrixong.com

> SWEET ENOUGH – For gorgeous heart-shaped and decorated sugar cubes head to Fortnum & Mason.
T·020 7734 8040 W·fortnumandmason.com

> SAY IT WITH SILK – For simply divine couture invitations (see page 33).
Simply Unique Invitations T·+1 703 216 3192 W·simplyuniqueinvitations.com

> BEST IN SHOWS – The only wedding show you need to visit. Stall-holders are heavily vetted, so only the best are represented. Held twice a year in February and October.
T·0870 190 9098 (box office) W·designerweddingshow.co.uk

> TIARA TO TOP THEM ALL – Over 600 hand-crafted headdresses and tiaras. Also antique tiaras dating from Napoleonic times available to hire.
Basia Zarzycka T·020 7730 1660 W·basia-zarzycka.com

> RECEPTION RAJ STYLE – Raj tents, exotic furniture, lighting and accessories for hire.
Raj Tent Club T·020 7820 0010 W·rajtentclub.com

> TALK OF THE TEEPEE – Wow your guests with an unusual marquee. Great fun.
The Stunning Tent Company T·0118 988 2355 W·stunningtents.co.uk

> TOP IT OFF WITH TRADITION – Top hats to keep from James Lock & Co.
T·020 7930 8874 W·jameslock.co.uk

> ALL THE TRIMMINGS – Exciting trimmings, printed ribbon, flowers and braids.
Barnett Lawson Trimmings T·020 7636 8591 W·bltrimmings.com

> FIT FOR THE TOP TABLE – Fantastic selection of tableware for hire.
Toptable Hire T·01327 260 575 W·toptablehire.com

> INITIAL IMPRESSIONS LAST FOREVER – Surprise your new hubbie with silk nightwear proclaiming your married name.
Monogrammed Linen Shop T·020 7589 4033
W·monogrammedlinenshop.com

For the perfect bridal lingerie or strapless bra, see Fashion – Lingerie page 161

> DON'T MISS A MOMENT – Top video production.
T·020 7924 6978
W·thefilmingbusiness.com

> VINTAGE GLAMOUR – For vintage dresses and accessories you can't beat Virginia.
T·020 7727 9908

> JUST ASK ANNIE – Fabulously gorgeous!
Annie's Vintage Clothes T·020 7359 0796

> HIGHLY RECOMMENDED – Victorian, 20s, 30s, to early 70s wedding dresses.
T·020 7328 1398 / 07951 866 896
W·thevintageweddingdresscompany.com

(See pages 176-178 for further details on vintage dresses)

> 21ST-CENTURY CELEBRATIONS – Your own wedding website.
W·mydigisite.com

> SPOT THE BOGUS WAITER – Hugely entertaining – your guests will be in stitches.
Spanner in the Works T·01905 353 551
W·spanner.co.uk

> WORLDWIDE WONDERS – Upmarket wedding website for links to the best on offer in the world of weddings.
W·luxuriouswedding.com

> IT COULDN'T YURT TO TRY ONE! – A beautiful alternative to a marquee. LPM have one of the largest yurts in the world which can accommodate up to 500 people for dining. Can also provide teepees and vintage tents.
LPM Bohemia T·0870 770 7185
W·lpmbohemia.com

> ZOO – Perhaps a zoo if you needed a venue! For a comprehensive list of zoos (and aquaria, etc.) worldwide, go to **W·zoos-worldwide.de**

A PAINTING'S WORTH A THOUSAND PHOTOS

Anne's work is so lovely and unique that I had to include her, even though she's based in New York – she'll travel world-wide so you need to know about her. Anne sets up her small easel and brushes and a stack of textured hand-pressed paper and gets to work painting wonderful water-colours of the wedding day – so different to having a wedding photographer. Anne works quickly and discreetly to produce graceful, flowing lines and a hint of detail. She does not paint any facial features, yet everyone recognises themselves immediately. Anne finishes her paintings at home – just a slight touch-up before packaging the 11 x 15 paintings into a silk-covered presentation box or a hand-tooled leather portfolio. You'll receive 8-12 paintings. Fees vary depending on location and time required.

Anne Watkins T·+1 212 866 0057
W·annewatkins.com

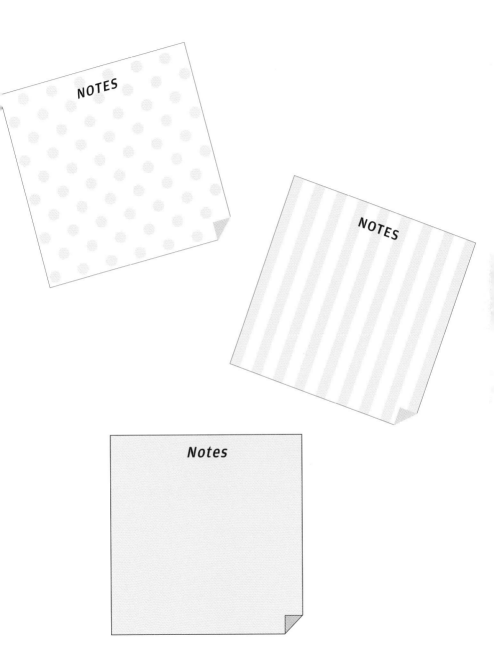

HOME

CLEANING DOMESTICGODDESS

STYLECONSULTANTS BEDDING

MONOGRAMS WALLPAPER LINEN

DIYSAVIOURS STORAGEBOXES

CLUTTERTHERAPISTS PHOTOS

HOUSEPROUD

ANTIQUECUTLERY

HOUSESITTING ITSOLUTIONS

HOUSESWAP RESTORATION

HOME INTERIORS

BEDS & BEDDING

EVERY DUVET DESERVES ITS DAY

> This family-run business has been renovating duvets and pillows for over 20 years. Now in its second generation, the lovely Isolde Lawlor told me that it's the only business in the UK that offers to renovate your down-filled duvets and pillows. They cut open your old duvet and clean all the down in their cleaning machine (no dry-cleaning allowed), which removes all the old disintegrated down and dust. After a thorough drying, they pack it into a new cotton cover and they can also add more down if it's gone a bit flat. If you have an unusual-sized bed, they can even make a duvet to suit your requirements. The renovation process usually takes four to five working days; however, if you can't be without your duvet, they can offer a same-day service by appointment at no extra cost. Prices: For a double duvet expect to pay £111.00 (£29.00 for the cleaning and £82.00 for the new cover); single £75.00.

> **Austrian Bedding Co, 205 Belsize Road, West Hampstead, London NW6 4AA**
  T · 020 7372 3121

QUILT WHILE YOU'RE AHEAD

> Way back in the last century, Joan used to watch her great aunt collect wool shearing in the Welsh fields, wash it, spin it and put it in a quilt. She's had a passion for the art form ever since. Joan lectures around the UK on the subject of quilts and Victorian and Edwardian textiles, and has been sourcing and skilfully repairing vintage textiles for years. She has a vast collection of top-quality Welsh quilts, Welsh wool and checked blankets, Victorian and Edwardian textiles, including bed linen, nightwear, children's garments, period clothes, and shawls. You can purchase directly from Joan (strictly appointment only).

> **Joan Howells, 120 Charles Street, Milford Haven, Pembrokeshire SA73 2HW**
  T · 01646 692 170
  E · davidbwlchgwyn@hotmail.com

ARE YOU DOWN WITH EIDER?

> Do you remember snuggling under a satin eiderdown on a rainy day while staying at your Gran's? If you want to recreate that sense of luxury and warmth on your own bed, there are a few select companies that make 100 per cent British eiderdowns. Robert Dare and his family are one that has been keeping the craft alive since 1946. Robert says many orders are from interior designers who want a luxury bed-covering, and each eiderdown is a handmade, one-off piece.

> The eiderdown can be covered in satin, crêpe de Chine or taffeta-look, or polycotton, in a large range of colours. One customer simply sent a piece of wallpaper to them saying she wanted them to match the green — and they did! They can also make the eiderdown up in your choice of fabric to match curtains or other bedding. There are six different stitching designs to choose from, along with frilled or piped edging — I'd love a pillar-box red, art deco design, and I'm told rose and gold are the most popular colours.

> They also offer hard-to-get bed linen, and an eiderdown and duvet re-covering service for that vintage piece you can't bear to throw away. They've just re-covered an eiderdown given to a couple as a wedding present in 1932! Contact them for an informative booklet on the eiderdown, along with some samples of the colour range. Robert, Fran and Chris are also very happy to talk you through the whole process on the phone. Price: feather and down-filled, double eiderdown £305.00; polyester hollofibre-filled eiderdowns from £200.00.

> Keys of Clacton, Gorse Lane Industrial
Estate, Unit 9, Stephenson Road, Clacton
on Sea, Essex CO15 4XA
T · 01255 432 518
W · englisheiderdown.co.uk

FIT FOR A KING-SIZE

> If you opted for the super-king-sized bed
for yourself and put a large circular one in
the guest room, buying new sheets may be
proving a bit of a challenge. Fret not (excuse
the pun), The Linen Merchant can make
sheets in any size and can even add some
lovely embroidery if the fancy takes you.
Depending on choice of sheet, they can
offer up to 44 colours, and they also offer
silk sheets. The largest they have made to
date has been for a 10-foot wide bed –
'There were ten in a bed…'

> **The Linen Merchant, 11 Montpelier Street,
London SW7 1EX**
T · 020 7584 3654
W · thelinenmerchant.com

REASSURING BEDSIDE MANNER

> As a young girl I remember being somewhat
worried when I was tucked in and told not
to 'let the bed bugs bite'. I wish I'd known
about the mattress doctors and their free,
no-obligation, two-minute test clean. I don't
think you want me to go into details about
the decaying skin, fungi and dust mites'
do-does, because if I do, you'll never want to
lay your head again. Suffice to say this is an
excellent service if you suffer from allergies,
asthma, eczema or hay fever. The Mattress
Doctor is now a franchise working under the
Mattress Doctor brand, and they'll clean your
mattress hygienically without the use of
chemicals. Prices vary, depending on where
you live; phone for details.

> **The Mattress Doctor, World Head Office,
8 Mountbatten Drive, Ringstead,
Northants NN14 4TX**
T · 0845 330 6607 W · mattressdoctor.co.uk

GET A PARK LIFE

> Megan Park designs gorgeous clothes,
evening bags and scarves so exquisite that I
just can't get enough of them. Her prints are
created using hand-carved wooden blocks,
her dyes are produced by one man from
memory, the glass beads are stitched one
by one and the embroidery applied by hand,
so it's not surprising that quality and work-
manship are now Megan's trademark.
In 2002 Megan launched her home collection
(following her ready-to-wear collection),
which includes pillows, cushions, throws
and quilts. Her hand-embroidered, lavish
silk quilts are available in single to king sizes,
from £400.00. See online for stockists and
her ready-to-wear collection.

> **Megan Park T · 020 7739 5828**
W · meganpark.co.uk

*The Monogrammed Linen Shop can make
sheets any size – see page 70*

*Jane Sacchi has a wonderful selection of
antique linen, bedspreads, sheets and
pillowcases – see page 74*

Also see Purple and Fine Linen page 25

CURTAINS

For curtain cleaning, see page 78

HANG ON TO BARBARA

> Barbara came round to our new home and
rehung our old curtains so cleverly that they
looked like they were made for the new
windows. She also shortened some curtains
I'd bought at an antique fair – even finding a
dry-cleaner who cleaned them for just £5.00.
She can make pelmets, curtains, tie-backs
and roman blinds at very reasonable prices,
and is fantastic at making suggestions that
don't cost the earth. Always obliging, friendly
and fast.

> **Barbara Pearce T · 020 8524 3779**

CUTLERY

GOLD PRIZE FOR SILVER HUNTING

> A friend of mine cannot say enough good things about Sanda Lipton. She recently had help in clearing up after a massive dinner party, but unfortunately one of her pieces of antique silver cutlery went missing. She thinks it was thrown out with the scraps – bring back any memories? Maybe not with the antique silver – but one particularly hectic Christmas morning I famously threw out our Alessi tin-opener and neatly put the tin lid in the drawer!

> Happily, my friend is no longer one knife short of a cutlery set. Take your incomplete cutlery set to Sanda and she will source a similar or identical piece for you. And if you can't visit her, then simply photocopy the back and front of the piece and send it to her and she will try to source more than one example so you have a choice. She says sometimes it can be done very quickly and others, depending on the piece, can take up to six months to find, but she never gives up. She also offers advice on silver collecting, renovation and repair and can buy pieces for you at auction.

> **Sanda Lipton Antique Silver, Third Floor, Elliott House, 28a Devonshire Street, London W1G 6PS**
> **T · 020 7431 0866 / 0783 666 0008**
> **W · antique-silver.com**

ONE IS SILVER, THE OTHER IS GOLD

> If they require a little bit of TLC, Elisabeth Bailey will take care of all your antique cutlery, picture frames, candlesticks and tea sets. Offering a silver and gold restoration service, she can replate and repair anything from carving sets, cutlery and candlesticks to your tea set. Knives can be rebladed and mother-of-pearl handles replaced. Spruce up your dressing table by having your silver hairbrush and mirror restored and your silver picture frames revelveted. (A piece of cutlery costs £6.00 to replate.)

> Elisabeth also offers a fabulous made-to-measure cutlery drawer holder made from velvet or moleskin in an array of different colours (from £500.00). Allow six weeks for delivery. She can collect and return items in central London and offers a nationwide service.

> **Elisabeth Bailey, Kensington Silver**
> **T · 020 8740 0451 / 07939 532 036**

FABRICS & TEXTILE ART

MAKE THAT CURTAIN CALL

> I was drawn to Victoria's previous work of beautiful bespoke embroidery and tiny embroidered buttons. Now she's focusing on machine-embellished trims, creating a wonderful collection for you to use on upholstery, curtains and soft furnishings – all of which can be uniquely tailored for you. The Appliqué collection is made in velvet, wool felt, linen and suede. The handcrafted, designed pieces have been researched from some of England's historic residences and the Russian dynasties of the 18th century.

> If you require something tailored, you provide the fabric and Victoria will embroider something on it based on her extensive range of designs. Victoria is very happy to come and visit you, or you can phone for an appointment if you wish to visit her studio. Prices: from £170.00 a metre (minimum 12m); allow 6-10 weeks for delivery.

> **Victoria Bain T · 020 7498 9262 / 07971 280 795 W · victoriabain.co.uk**

CLASSIC CONVENIENCE

> Vintage French textiles are so sought after now that it's becoming really hard to find any pieces that are larger than half a metre, barely enough for a small cushion. Kate

loves French influences, so has launched a range of cotton and linen fabrics inspired by original vintage French designs, including wonderful roses on cream linen, cameos and ribbons, small rosebuds on duck-egg blue, as well as lovely plain and dark linen, from £24.00 per metre. But don't just stop at buying her fabric – she also has a wonderful range of accessories, including lavender-filled boots, cushions, covered baskets, corsages, doorstops and covered matchboxes.

> **Kate Forman Designs Ltd, Long Barn North, Sutton Manor Farm, Bishops Sutton, Alresford, Hants SO24 OAA**
T · 01962 732 244 W · kateforman.co.uk

YOUR HOME'S IN SAFE HANDS

> Read page 162 first to learn a little about Hand & Lock, then get on the phone to order bespoke soft furnishing fabrics, including curtains, tablecloths, bedspreads and cushions. They've worked with private clients and interior designers from around the world, and will help you develop your own fabric and embroidery ideas or inspire you with their existing design book.

> **Hand & Lock, 86 Margaret Street, London W1W 8TE**
T · 020 7580 7488
W · hand-embroidery.co.uk

REGAL RELAXATION

> Don't let the art of embroidery, goldwork, stump work, decorative tassels or silk shading be a thing of the past. Head to Hampton Court Palace and the Royal School of Needlework to immerse yourself in these different techniques, in a taster day or a longer class or course. I've already done two fabulous courses, Beadwork and Goldwork, and believe me you don't need any previous experience – I could barely thread a needle when I first went. Established in 1872 to teach the art of hand-embroidery, the sense

of history is incredible as you sit and sew enjoying the fine views overlooking the Palace gardens.

> **Royal School of Needlework, Apartment 12A, Hampton Court Palace, Surrey KT8 9AU**
T · 020 8943 1432
W · royal-needlework.co.uk

For textile restoration, see page 91

INTERIOR STYLE CONSULTANTS

If flicking through interior magazines leaves you dissatisfied with your own humdrum home, but you don't have the time or the know-how to initiate the much-needed makeover yourself, help is at hand. You need a style consultant (they're not interior designers), who will visit you, spend lots of time finding out what you love, what you dream of and, more importantly, what you wouldn't touch with a 10-foot curtain pole, before sourcing the most divine items to transform your home.

Collectively, the ladies listed here have worked for years styling rooms for magazines and ad campaigns, editing and writing interior features and even the occasional book, so you're in more-than-capable hands. Forget spending your weekends traipsing round town in search of 'you'll know it when you see it', they know exactly where to go, what to pay, what's in and what's not, the best stores and dealers and, most of all, how to make your friends green with envy.

ENJOY YOUR HOME MORE, FOR LESS

> Belinda's worked on some fabulous projects. She's styled for celebrities, written books, worked on *Livingetc, Elle Decoration* and *Homes & Gardens*. Check out her website, you'll be desperate to be her next client. Belinda has spent many years editing and

writing fantastic features on trends, interiors, shopping and room makeovers. If you're overwhelmed with home style options, she's happy to pay you a visit and share her vast amount of knowledge and her 'less is more' attitude.

Prices: from £150.00.

> **Belinda Buckley T· 07958 477 494 W· belinda buckley.com**

SHOP TILL SHE DROPS!

> Rachel has worked on *Harper's Bazaar* (formerly *Harpers & Queen*) for over nine years and, by hiring her services as a Lifestyle Shopper/Stylist, you can get your hands on her amazing little book of contacts and insider knowledge of shops, auction houses, fairs, markets, artisans, salvage yards and warehouses. If you're like me, shopping with a retail guru is your idea of heaven, then you'll be with Rachel every step of the way, but if the mere idea of it fills you with dread, she's happy to go it alone and seek out and buy the selected items for you. She can help you achieve that perfect-looking interior, sort out that awkward space in the living room, and even buy and wrap unique, often handmade or vintage, gifts for the toughest people on your Christmas list. Expect to pay around £200.00 for half a day.

> **Rachel Meddowes T· 07770 511 969**

MONOGRAMS

LET CAROLINE MAKE YOUR MARK

> I've always wanted my initials on sheets and, having scoured antique markets, shops and stalls, I find that my own initials aren't that easy to come by. So I was delighted to find Caroline who has set up her company designing custom monograms.

> Once you have chosen your unique monogram, she can arrange to have them embroidered onto sheets, napkins, towels and bathrobes, or even transferred to stationery or engraved onto crystal, sliver and other metals. You can choose from Victorian, Gothic, Deco or Modern styles, and they can be left plain or embellished with squiggles, loops, flowers or curls (*see page* 59 for Caroline's monogram etiquette).

> The design fee is $450.00, which entitles you to eight designs including revisions. If you choose machine embroidery, as opposed to hand embroidery, then there is an additional set-up fee. They are exquisite and the embroidered items will become beautiful family heirlooms. You will need an appointment to visit Caroline's workshop, but you can also order via email.

> **Caroline Brackenridge, Monogram Inc, 225 East 73rd Street, New York, NY 10021 T· +1 212 288 8864 W· monograminc.com**

A PILLOW TALKING PIECE

> The Monogrammed Linen Shop offers all manner of wonderful goodies and present ideas. Their in-house service can add embroidery to practically anything, and you have a choice of scripts, coloured threads and designs. They offer both hand- and machine embroidery – their exquisite hand-initialling uses 17th- and 18th-century stitching patterns, which looks gorgeous on Egyptian cotton bed-sheets (which can be made any size) or brightly coloured napkins. They can even embroider napkins with an initial to match your monogrammed china! Baby gifts can be embroidered with the child's name and date of birth, or how about a gift for your host such as an initialled cosmetic bag, pillowcase or bath towel? I love that you can take in a child's drawing and have it embroidered onto a pillowcase, an extremely popular gift for grandparents.

> Allow one week for any in-house embroidery, four to six weeks for something more intricate, and eight weeks for hand-stitching. They will ship overseas.

Prices: embroidered initials from £10.50;
£12.00 for a name.
> **Monogrammed Linen Shop 168-170 Walton
Street, London SW3 2JL
T·020 7589 4033
W·monogrammedlinenshop.com**

*For monogrammed dinner services see
pages 73-74*

PHOTOGRAPHIC
CUSTOMISATION
FABRICS / BAGS / CANVAS /
WALLPAPER

*How would you like your favourite photo blown
up life-size on a canvas or transferred to fabric
or wallpaper? Wouldn't any granny just love a
photo of beloved grandchild made into a
jigsaw, tile or handbag?*

BEST GIFT AWARD'S IN THE BAG
> Be-A-Bag was born in 2001 as an innovative
charity promotion. The idea was such a
success that, thankfully, Anya has decided
to carry it on and now offers 12 styles of
customised bag, from a mini wash bag to
the Trolley. For me, it's a toss up between
the Trolley and the Shopper.
> It has been much imitated, but for me, I feel
never equalled. Send in your own photo to be
lovingly transferred to your choice of wash
bag, tote bag, evening bag, nappy bag,
weekend, shopper, tote, trolley or despatch
bag (great for men).
> Prices: from £75.00; allow six to eight weeks
for delivery
> Concessions and stores are worldwide – see
website for further information.
> **Anya Hindmarch, 15-17 Pont Street,
London SW1X 9EH
T·020 7838 9177 W·anyahindmarch.com**
> **or 63 Ledbury Road, Notting Hill, London
W11 2AD T·020 7792 4427**

CAT'S EYE FOR DETAIL
> The Centre for Advanced Textiles can
digitally print any natural woven fabric
(cotton, silk, linen, wool, etc) or customise
striped furnishing fabric in your own colour
combinations. Digital printing costs from
£25.00 per metre depending on quantity,
plus the fabric. *See page* 151 *for further
information.*
> **CAT, Centre for Advanced Textiles,
The Glasgow School of Art, 158 Renfrew
Street, Glasgow G3 6RF
T·0141 353 4742 W·catdigital.co.uk**

GET A HANDLE ON LOVE
> Contrado's photo books and notebooks
make fantastic presents, but don't stop there!
Every time I go online they seem to amaze
me with a new idea they've created on how
they can put your loved ones image onto an
item. Among the other things Contrado can
personalise with a photo, including the great
keepsake tin, jigsaw puzzles, banners, wallpaper and folding screens are their great
range of bags and holdalls in leather or
canvas. Their Pop Art bag is fun and with
prices from £29.95, with quick delivery of
seven to 14 days, you can be sure to tick off
a few people on your present list.
> Contrado state that the image will not
scratch, flake or fade.
> **Contrado, Unit 10, Shaftesbury Centre, 85
Barlby Road, London W10 6BN
T·020 8960 4567 W·bagsoflove.co.uk**

PERFECTING THE ART OF LIVING
> Easy, peasy – send them a photo, either a
print or digital image, and Learn to Dream
will send you a wonderful creation of PhotoArt.
They offer a great choice of materials,
including art paper, canvas, clear acrylic,
and silver finish. They also offer image blocks
and Paralax, which is their own multi-layered
technique that enables the colours of your
image to change depending on the position

of the observer and the time of day, creating an interactive art piece.

> You can order bespoke wallpaper which is fantastic, and they can also work with an original drawing.

> **Learn to Dream, Coate House, Ground Floor East, 1–3 Coate Street, London E2 9AG T·0845 456 4033 W·learntodream.co.uk**

GET ON BOARD

> The amazing selection of photos from 55max's archives, including famous Getty images, make for funky travel and wash bags. Of course, you can also send in your own photographs to create lovely keepsake gifts. I love the montage of photos that they can artfully create into a magnetic display board: send 20 of your photos, notes or even poems and for £85.00 (plus delivery) they'll scan all the material and three weeks later you'll receive a snazzy magnetic display board.

> **55Max Bespoke Service, 6 Lonsdale Road, London NW6 6RD T·020 7625 3774 W·55max.com**

SIT ON YOUR FAVOURITE PHOTO

> Mybiggerpicture offers some novel personal-ised photo gifts. Apart from the usual canvas bags and mugs, they offer unique items like the slim-line DAB radio, glasses' case, tea cosy, oven glove, dog bowl, photo tiles and deckchairs. You can send them a photo, child's drawing or even a handwritten poem. Allow approximately 21 days for delivery with prices from as little as £10.00

> **Mybiggerpicture, PO Box 466, Macclesfield SK11 7WL T·01625 421 226 W·mybiggerpicture.com**

FAMOUS IN YOUR OWN LIVING ROOM

> Well-known for their Andy Warhol-style portraits, it's also worth checking out the other 10 styles Youareart offer, from oil portraits to simple graphic style. Send them your photo, and their top artists and graphic

designers will get to work designing just the right look and colours. They'll show you ideas you may not have thought of and you approve everything before it is applied to the canvas. Allow four to eight weeks for the whole process. Obviously prices vary depending on canvas size, style, original photo and the finish, but to give you an idea, a 40×40 cm, Warhol-style picture on stretched canvas and wooden frame would be £277.00; a 15×10 cm (postcard-sized) stretched canvas on a wooden frame, for the pet oil paintings, would be £99.00.

> **Youareart T·020 7384 1113 W·youareart.co.uk**

For personalised chocolates with image see pages 255 and 293 or cakes page 254

TABLEWARE

LONELY TEACUP SEEKS PERFECT SAUCER

> Chinasearch, established in 1988, is considered Europe's largest china matching and replacement service, with more than 4,000 patterns from over 40 manufacturers. Not only can it supply discontinued china and tableware worldwide, it can supply pottery, stoneware, porcelain, earthenware, glassware and cutlery, and can post you anything from a saucer to a complete dinner service. And it's not just a service for the clumsy or unlucky; plenty of customers use Chinasearch to add to their service, for example, making an eight-place setting up to a 12. Requests are filed on their search register and they contact you once the piece is found. They had a French film company phone them as they needed a very old Wedgwood black basalt teapot for their film and they had only 10 days to find it – Chinasearch came up trumps!

> **Chinasearch Ltd, 4 Princes Drive, Kenilworth, Warwickshire CV8 2FD T·01926 512 402 W·chinasearch.co.uk**

HEAD WEST FOR CHINA

> All the kitchen, gourmet and harder-to-find cooking products on offer at Kitchenshop have been used and recommended by their experts. We love their monogrammed china made from the finest porcelain and hand-decorated in the USA. The fine white china is trimmed in gold or platinum, with a modern block or elegant script monogram. They also offer a custom service where they can hand-decorate almost any design onto the china. A family-owned company, they will ship worldwide with a minimum export order of eight place settings (that includes dinner plate, side plate, soup bowl, cup and saucer).

> Kitchenshop.com, 7419 Metcalf, Suite 385, Overland Park, KS 66204
T·+1 913 438 2511 or within the USA 888 834 2511
W·kitchenshop.com

DINNER SET AND MATCHED

> This family-run business not only covers the classics but also modern pieces. Matching China supplies replacement china for discontinued patterns by Royal Doulton, Wedgwood, Royal Albert, Denby and others. They also sell items from a number of current china patterns at discounted prices. Really useful if you've broken a piece or want to build up your collection – at last you won't have two of your eight guests eating off your Beatrix Potter plates! Superb service with orders usually sent out within a day.

> Matching China, 65 Scott Street, Dundee DD2 2BA
T· 01382 666 260 W·matchingchina.com

FORGIVE AND FORGET, COMPLETE THAT SET

> If you only have seven plates in your dinner set and no one will own up to breaking one, let it go. Log on to W·replacements.com and get some closure. They have over 10 million pieces in their inventory and can probably replace any old or new china, crystal, silver or collectible. With over 200,000 patterns going back over 100 years, and with an astonishing seven million customers world-wide, satisfaction is practically guaranteed. Their website offers many useful sections, including an image library, in-depth dinnerware knowledgebase, and pattern identification.

> Replacements Ltd, 1089 Knox Road, PO Box 26029, Greensboro, NC 27420
T·+1 336 697 3000 or within the USA +1 800 737 5223
W·replacements.com

INITIAL YOUR OWN PIECE OF HISTORY

> Josiah Spode the First invented the formulae for fine bone china in the 18th century and became famous around the world. And with fame came orders from some of the most distinguished individuals, including royalty, eager to get their name all over it.

> If you dream of joining the élite and owning a quality dinner service with your own monogram, crest or even your own design, Spode's commissioned service is the perfect place for you.

> You'll choose from seven tableware patterns and, as part of the standard service, the motif can be applied in 22-carat gold or single colour, in a choice of four elegant lettering styles. For an additional cost, you can choose multi-colour, raised colours or even raised gold. If you wanted a full banqueting service, they can produce one to your very own design or you can design it with their studio art director (poa).

> Minimum order 100 pieces and allow 10 weeks for delivery from your order confirmation.

> If you fancy visiting, they have a great visitor centre, factory tour and museum, as well as several shops where you can purchase their best china, a factory shop (60 per cent off

high street prices), a clearance shop, crystal shop, cook shop, gift emporium and a Christmas shop.

> **Spode, Church Street, Stoke-on-Trent ST4 1BX**
> **T · 01782 744 011 W · spode.co.uk**

KNOW WHERE TO GO

> If you find it hard to match a pattern to a picture on the internet, this is the company for you. You can visit their warehouse to search for your piece, but you might be overwhelmed, as they have over one million pieces – 4,000 patterns from 70 manufacturers, from the 1900s onwards. The company started as a ceramic collectibles business but was soon overtaken with the demand for discontinued tableware.

> Their state-of-the-art technology took five years to develop, then it took an incredible two years to load all the stock onto the database.

> They're also a major retailer and will buy your old china, pieces of which may now prove very elusive to track down, so you can purchase one of their new services (discounts offered).

> I asked Kim if I could come in and search for 60 odd floral china teacups and saucers for a vintage tea party, she said she would be able to give me 600 if I wanted! With their extremely knowledgeable, friendly and efficient sales team, I probably wouldn't look anywhere else.

> **Tablewhere? 4 Queens Parade Close, London N11 3FY**
> **T · 020 8361 6111 W · tablewhere.co.uk**

TOO GOODE FOR WEEKDAYS

> Thomas Goode opened for business in 1827 and originally produced china for international royalty. Almost two centuries later, they still have three warrants to supply Royal families. It is recognised as the best fine bone china, crystal and silverware shop in the world, a true house of luxury.

For discerning customers they will create bespoke pieces and sets. Their hand-painters can match a vintage design from china or will work from a photo, watercolour, piece of fabric, wallpaper, or any other source that is copyright free. If you need inspiration, their museum and design archive has fired the imagination of many customers who wished to create their own service.

> **Thomas Goode & Co, 19 South Audley Street, Mayfair, London W1K 2BN**
> **T · 020 7499 2823 W · thomasgoode.co.uk**

MOVE AWAY FROM THE SUPERGLUE ...

> If you're actually there when a piece of your wedding china or part of your dinner service gets broken, stay calm, pick up the pieces and Zelli Porcelain will lovingly restore it for you. Well-known for their passion for porcelain and their desire to bring you the finest of today's traditional and contemporary designs. Their gallery displays wonderful porcelain art, and work from all six major porcelain manufacturers, especially Meissen. Every piece is handmade out of purest porcelain, many from over a hundred different moulds.

> They offer a bespoke service for tableware and can paint anything from a family crest or bird to lines of poetry.

> **Zelli, 55–57 Chiltern Street, London W1U 6ND**
> **T · 020 7224 2114 W · zelli.co.uk**

TABLECLOTHS

ACCESSING ANTIQUE BEAUTY

> Well-known for dealing in antique linen (made of flax), sheets and pillowcases, Jane also manufactures new linens to the same standard as the old, which are now becoming increasingly harder to find. Working with a master weaver in Scotland, she can provide

you not only with wonderful bespoke bed linens, but also elegant bespoke table linen, especially useful for an oversized table.

> Her clients have included exclusive restaurants and small hotels, and she's currently making some divine linen with a logo and monogram woven into the damask for a yacht owner. Depending on the complexity of your order and cloth availability, allow four to 12 weeks for delivery.

> **Jane Sacchi T·020 7351 3160**
  W·janesacchi.com

Also see The Dining Room Shop page 2, and Purple and Fine Linen page 25

WALLPAPER

The choice of wall decoration these days is unbelievable and I'm sure that in years to come some of today's new wallpapers will be collectors' items in their own right. Even if you can't afford the whole room, just doing one wall will make an impressive style statement and if you fancy yourself as a bit of a modern-day William Morris, with some of the companies below you can even have a go at designing your own.

PAPER PARADISE

> Deborah has been designing and hand-printing her papers with *trompe l'œil* photographs for over seven years. You can commission unique wallpaper – as have Soho House, Selfridges and Paul Smith – or buy one of her designs. There are at least 40-50 designs to choose from, with some silk-screened by hand, some digitally printed and some hand painted. The designs are fabulous and I'd love the filing wallpaper for my office, the standard lamp for my small bathroom and the Cho Cho couch for anywhere.

> Bespoke wallpaper panels start from £500.00, her readymade wallpaper is £150.00 for a

56x330 cm drop, and individual cut-outs such as frames, shoes & bags, paper plates or ducks range from £35.00 to £45.00.

> **Deborah Bowness T·07817 807 504**
  W·deborahbowness.com
  E·wallpaper@deborahbowness.com

BRICKS ARE SO 2006

> This is the bee's knees if you have an ugly outside wall or shed, or if you just want something unique for your garden. Susan Bradley has come up with a laser-cut trellis, which you can order to fit the space you have, using it singularly or commissioned as a huge wall-art piece. The fixing allows plants to grow up and through the 'wallpaper', which looks incredible when lit up.

> The Outdoor Wallpaper is made to order in your choice of material and finish. You can choose from satin-brushed stainless steel, mirror-polished stainless steel, rusted mild steel (for an aged look), powder-coated steel in many colours, and Perspex in various colours and translucencies. Susan's designs have won international acclaim and she has many awards under her belt, not to mention being featured in all the top interior and design magazines worldwide. You can commission a bespoke design for outdoor (or indoor) spaces, and international orders are very welcome. My favourite is the Perspex flowers, which a customer ordered in black and hung inside on a white wall – it looked fab! Prices: from £150.00; for bespoke orders, allow up to six weeks.

> **Susan Bradley, Studio 11, Pennybank Chambers, 33–35 St Johns Square, London EC1M 4DS (Strictly by appointment only) T·07905 484 542 W·susanbradley.co.uk**

GET IN THE FRAME

> Graham & Brown have some fab products, including the Frames wallpaper, which I think is great for a kid's room, bathroom or one wall in your kitchen. It consists of differently

sized empty frames that you can fill with your own paintings, photographs, scribbles and lists. Designed by Artists Taylor and Wood, the wallpaper costs £20.00 a roll. I also liked their products that transform surfaces – look at some great ideas online.
> Do check you are on the UK website as products may differ to other countries.
> **Graham & Brown T·UK 0800 328 8452 / USA +1 800 554 0887**
  W·grahambrown.com

CARRIE ON UP THE WALL!
> You may well have seen Rachel's New Shoes wallpaper, as it was originally commissioned for Sex & The City. Among other awards, Rachel was named Crabtree & Evelyn Young Designer of the Year at the *Homes & Gardens* Classic Design Awards 2005. She manufactures bespoke wallpaper and ready-made products, and you can currently order her New Shoes wallpaper and her lace-cut stickers which stick on walls and windows. The designs can be ordered in a great variety of colour ways and patterns. Her long flower panel wallpaper kits (which come with a whole pack of stick-on motifs) and transfer sets are available to order online. International shipping is available.
> **Rachel Kelly, Interactive Wallpaper**
  W·interactivewallpaper.co.uk

INTERIOR TIME TRAVEL
> Based in the USA, Secondhand Rose has been selling vintage wallpapers for over a quarter of a century and has one of the largest collections in the world. Their categories include: rare and unusual papers, floral, kitchen, bathroom, novelty, chinoiserie and mylar, and date from the 1860s to the 1970s. The choice is superb, with some absolutely stunning geometric prints that would really make a statement. Prices range from $70.00

per roll to $1,200.00 for a triple-roll of an original Frank Lloyd Wright design. They also offer vintage lino. Worldwide shipping is available.
> **Secondhand Rose, 138 Duane Street, New York, NY 10013**
  T·+1 212 393 9002
  W·secondhandrose.com

STAY INSIDE THE LINES
> I remember getting into big trouble for colouring on the walls when I was a little girl, but these days it's positively the done thing. After you've hung up your Wallpaper-By-Numbers (that's the hard bit), all you need is your paints, felt tips or pencils, and away you go. Designs include dogs, palm trees, gerberas, pineapples, butterflies and lots of other colourful or calming imagery. The wallpaper is just £40.00 per 10 metre roll, or £60.00 with the DIY paint kits. Jenny also offers kids' wallpaper borders for painting (£18.00 per 4.5 m x 15 cm roll).
> **Jenny Wilkinson T·07939 401 631**
  W·jennywilkinson.com

PASTING THE PAST
> This very useful US website offers many links to suppliers of reproduction wallpaper, books about wallpaper, wallpaper museums, and professionals in the historic wallpaper industry.
> Not to mention the fabulous Jim Yates, a masterpaperhanger with a passion for the historic home.
> **W·historicwallpapering.com**

If you like to be the first to know about the most fabulous companies and ideas in far flung places, log on to W · springwise.com and let their 8,000 spotters of smart business ideas do the sleuthing work for you. It makes for some fascinating reading; here are a few of the places that impressed me:

FAST AND FABULOUS

> blik make fantastic self-adhesive wall decals that will transform your walls in minutes. There are Mod graphics, birds, flowers and designs by Keith Haring and Charles & Ray Eames which all look like paint once they've been applied. If you get bored, the decals are removable, so just choose another design and update your walls, windows, ceilings, tables or even floors. I just had to order the Glass Stiks for my next party, they look fabulous, oh yes and the chandelier for the wall, and the ...

> **blik, LLC, PO Box 1663, Venice, CA 90294**
> **T · +1 866 262 blik (2545)**
> **W · whatisblik.com**

GET STUCK IN PARIS

> A great collection of wall coverings from young British and European designers (including Deborah Bowness, *see page* 75). You can order wallpaper by the metre, hand screen-printed, *trompe l'œil,* wallpaper kits, embroidered wallpaper, illustrations, stickers and hand-finished adhesive friezes. Images include stacks of books, fake bookshelves, green chair, flowers, birds and cutlery. You can order online or visit the store in Paris, which is open noon till 7.00 p.m Monday-Saturday.

> **The Collection, 33, rue de Poitou,**
> **75003 Paris**
> **T · +33 1 34 80 07 23**
> **W · thecollection.fr**

BY NAME AND BY NATURE

> These Wonderful! vinyl graffiti letters are such a great find that I'm ordering some immediately. Use them to cover part of a wall in your office, laundry room, kitchen or hall, and it will look like you've painted them on. You can turn a favourite quote, poem, nursery rhyme, sentiment or recipe, in fact anything at all, into wall graffiti, choosing your own colour, type style and size, or just choose one of their designs. The design arrives as one piece (no individual letters which you have to position), and you just press on and peel off. It's also easy to remove, won't damage your walls and will stay put until you remove it. On their website they have a fantastic photo album showing loads of ideas that people have ordered and put up in their homes – I love the one a lady ordered for her kitchen: 'I cooked once and decided it was a bad idea'. There's a wide selection for children's rooms and wedding presents, as well as monograms. I'm ordering my son's name to put above framed black and white photos of him growing up.

> **Wonderful! 2807 Delmar Drive, Suite B,**
> **Columbus, OH 43209**
> **T · +1 877 557 5675**
> **W · wonderfulgraffiti.com**

HOUSE-PROUD

HOUSE-KEEPING

CARPETS / CURTAINS / FURNISHINGS

COLOUR ME COMFY

> If your sofa is in dire need of a makeover, what about dying it Treacle Brown, Moss Green, another of the 17 colours on offer from professional dyers Harry Berger, or even your own choice of shade? As well as having an unbeatable reputation for their extensive textile knowledge, the Berger brothers are rated by their peers as one of the five very best dry-cleaners and dyers out of around 4,700 in the UK. Not only can they dye loose covers, they can also dye miscellaneous soft furnishings and garments. So while changing your sofa, why not change the curtains, cushions and your not-so-favourite outfit too, for the perfect couch-potato camouflage! They can usually complete orders in two or three weeks, but will consider urgent orders. Go on, be brave — white is so last-season!

> **Harry Berger, Specialist Cleaners and Dyers, 25 Station Road, Cheadle Hulme, Cheadle, Cheshire SK8 5AF
T·0161 485 3421 / 0161 485 7733
W·harryberger.com**

BANISH THOSE BLOTCHES

> You're lying on the wine-stained sofa looking at the dried baby-food stain on the curtains, when you notice that old dog-sick on the carpet! It's time to call Cadogan. Not only will they come to your home and take away any loose covers, cushions and curtains that need to be specially cleaned, but they'll also repair any lining and clean your carpets and rugs, too.

> **Cadogan Company, 3 Enterprise Way, Triangle Business Centre, London NW10 6UG
T·020 8960 8020**

DO YOU DREAM OF CLEAN LIVING?

> For all carpet, furnishing and curtain cleaning (take-down and rehang service offered), at home or off-site, you can trust the well-established company that the big-name stores use. James Turtle On-Site Services can clean anything from antique rugs to sofas, and any material or floor covering, including leather. They can come round to give you a free estimate or offer advice by telephone or email.

> They recently drove all the way to Devon to rescue a newly laid carpet — it had already been cleaned by two cleaners who hadn't managed to get the gravy stains out and in fact had made it a lot worse. James Turtle On-site were able to restore it to good-as-new condition. They cleaned all our rugs when we moved but I have to admit their curtain-cleaning quote was a little out of our price range.

> **James Turtle On-Site Services, Unit 5, 4a Manorgate Road, Kingston upon Thames KT2 7EL
T·020 8546 4222 W·on-siteservices.co.uk**

GENERAL CLEANING

MEN IN SHORTS CLEAN DOWN UNDER

> You've probably heard about how spotless these Aussies will leave your house after they come round for the big clean. Or was it the fact that quite a few of them are men in short shorts? If you've had major renovations and your house looks like a bomb has hit it, then they'll clean it from top to toe. They'll give you a detailed quote for each item to be cleaned, but to give you an idea of cost: to spring-clean a one-bedroom flat £110.00-£130.00, a five-bedroomed house £200.00-£250.00.

> They offer a seven-day, 24-hour service, even at short notice, and they also offer carpet, upholstery and window cleaning, with a

minimum call-out charge of £80.00. Used to dealing with end-of-tenancy, moving-in and after-builders cleans, they can also deal with fire or flood damage, and can dry-clean your curtains on site. They even cleaned the Big Brother house!

> **Absolutely Spotless, Head Office, 106 Wellesly Road, London W4 3AP T·020 8932 7360 / 020 7839 8222 W·absolutelyspotless.co.uk**

A CLEAN HOUSE FOR THE COST OF A MEAL

> I wouldn't normally put in any cleaning agencies, as a good service usually boils down to the individual cleaner in the end. However, this one is so reasonable – they will find you a weekly cleaner for a monthly fee of £19.97 plus £6.00 an hour (3 hours per week minimum). And they have other great services I love their One-off Spring Clean @ £10.00 an hour, After-Party Clean @ £11.00 an hour and, the most useful as anyone who has had builders in will attest to, the After-Builders Clean @ £12.00 per hour. (All with a minimum of four hours per visit.) It's also great that you can pay by credit card, if you don't have the ready cash (charges apply). You provide all the cleaning equipment or they can provide it for an extra cost.

> They also offer a very handy carpet, upholstery and steam-clean service, and can do your ironing. They cover all London postcodes.

> **Perfect Clean, Unit G41, Waterfront Studios, 1 Dock Road, London E16 1AG T·0800 195 7848 W·perfectclean.co.uk**

OVEN CLEANING

What busy person wouldn't want someone to come and clean their oven! There are many franchises and small companies operating throughout the UK. I think you'll be very pleased with these:

ANGEL IN MARIGOLDS

> What a find! The lovely Fiona will come and clean your oven so well that it will look like a showroom model. One of the first to set up in the south-east London and Kent area over eight years ago, Fiona enjoys offering a personal service to many new and long-term customers, so chooses not to franchise out her jobs. Fiona is a woman with many strings to her bow – she is a qualified nurse and a trained massage therapist, and can offer ayurvedic or aromatherapy massage. So why not have a relaxing massage and then have your oven cleaned using eco-friendly products? Actually, she'll happily clean your whole kitchen if you wish. Her motto is 'Love to do the jobs you hate', which is just fine by me.
Prices: Oven cleaning from £45.00, Aga from £75.00; Massage £50.00 per hour.

> **Fiona George, Oven Angels T·01892 514 552**

RIGHT UP YOUR STREET

> I love this group because when I entered our postcode, E11, into their map locator (under Booking Enquiry on their website) I got several representatives that we could phone, whereas on other sites I had tried the postcodes E8, E11, E17 and even N1, and kept getting 'not available'. Oven Clean have cleaned over 500,000 ovens with their non-caustic, fume-free, eco-friendly process. It takes them approximately two hours to remove all the grease, fat and burnt-on carbon deposits, and they can also clean your hob, microwave, range, Aga, extractor fan or BBQ. What are you waiting for?

Prices: from approximately £40.00 for a single oven; available UK, Eire and Australia!

> **Oven Clean T·0800 731 7913
> W·ovenclean.com**

LET SOMEONE ELSE 'TO DO' IT FOR YOU

> You know it's on your list of household chores, but somehow it always seems to fall to the bottom of the list, to be done when you have time. Well now you don't need the time, you just need a minimum of £26.00 (single-oven price) and The Oven Cleaning Company will leave your oven looking spic and span in an hour. They will also clean hobs, extractors, microwaves, ranges, Agas and Rayburns.

> One of the first companies to offer a domestic oven-cleaning service, they've been operating for over eight years and have over 50,000 regular customers with 10 vehicles on the road, covering the UK and Ireland. They only use non-toxic, biodegradable products. Your oven can be used as soon as they finish, with no lingering smells. They also offer an electrical repair service, will replace bulbs and filters, and can organise replacement seals and parts.

> **The Oven Cleaning Company, Jacobson House, Crossways, Churt, Farnham, Surrey GU10 2JD
> T·01428 717 174 / 01428 717 176
> W·theovencleaningco.com**

WHEELIE BINS

I want to puke/hurl/throw up/vomit when I see the bottom of our outside rubbish bin and you must be joking if you think I'm going to clean it! Now help is at hand if you want to stop your stomach churning on Tuesday nights! I love these wheelie-bin hygiene companies who are popping up all over the country, either as small concerns or big franchises.

HYGIENE GETS THE GREEN LIGHT

> Green Cleen have just celebrated their tenth anniversary of cleaning domestic and commercial bins. Covering most parts of the UK, they also operate in Ireland, France, the USA, Canada and Australia.

> Phone their head office and they'll put you in contact with your local franchisee. They will clean any bin on a one-off basis (£7.00) or offer a four-weekly clean at £3.50 per clean (incl. VAT), with discounts if you pay in advance.

> **Green Cleen, UK Booking Office, 18 Ladfordfields Industrial Park, Seighford, Staffordshire ST18 9QE
> T·0800 0150 880 / 01785 281301
> W·greencleen.co.uk**

SAY GOODBYE TO DUSTY BIN

> The Wheelie Bin Cleaning Company is a nationwide franchise from the Omni-Kleen group. From their main office in South Wales they can put you in touch with your local operator. Some do offer a one-off clean; others require you to take up the service on a regular basis. They all offer a bin washing, deodorising and lining service for your wheelie bin(s), and some will wash the non-wheeled black bins too.

> Although the website leans more towards becoming a franchisee, you can book a wash online or contact many of their operators under the link to The Network.

> Ian and Janet Bundle run the regional office for South East England. If you live in this area,

give them a call and they'll send someone round to make your bin the sweetest smelling in the street. Prices range from £2.50 to £3.50 per clean.

> **The Wheelie Bin Cleaning Company, Head Office, Omni-Kleen Ltd, Mwyndy Cross, Mwyndy, Pontyclun, Mid-Glamorgan CF72 8PN**
> **T · 01443 237 800 W · wheeliebin.co.uk**
> **Ian and Janet Bundle, South-East Regional Office T · 020 8404 7672**

DOMESTIC GODDESS
STATUS

Great little products, services and webbies to help us in our bid for domestic goddess status:

SOFT OPTION
> We all know you can't chuck your favourite cashmere cardie in the washing machine, and the only options for it are dry-cleaning or hand-washing. In fact, rather than dry-cleaning, cashmere will respond better to being hand-washed in luke-warm water. To help us out, Brora make a special cashmere shampoo (£5.00) and de-fuzzing comb (£2.00), which I've used to great effect.
> **W · brora.co.uk T · 020 7736 9944**

CHECK IN THE CASHMERE CLINIC
> If your favourite cashmere cardigan or sweater has been attacked by those pesky moths, or you've spilled Chicken Jalfrezi down the front, call on the Cashmere Clinic who will lovingly restore it. They offer a mending and cleaning service for knitted cashmere, and have great success with fixing holes. They offer a Europe-wide mail-order service or you can visit the Clinic personally (by appointment only).
> Prices: mending from £15.00 per hole; cleaning from £20.00
> **Cashmere Clinic Limited T · 020 7584 9806**

PUT A SMILE ON YOUR FACE

I think the Extreme Ironing World Championships, where contestants must find the most extreme place to iron a garment is highly amusing. There are people furiously competing for the world record and are prepared to iron nude on top of a very high mountain, iron in the jungle of Guatemala, in a Mayan temple, squatting between two high rocks in South Africa, and even underwater in Madagascar! Go on, you know you want the DVD!

W · extremeironing.com

E.R. TIPS FOR THOSE OOPS MOMENTS
> DrClean is a great website for fabric-cleaning tips, including carpet cleaning, with a comprehensive stain-removal chart, loads of advice, and special products and services, such as their emergency spillage kit or the best fuzz-remover.
> **W · drclean.co.uk T · 020 8421 8866**

FIGHTING STAINS WITH FIZZ
> I can't believe how much I've learnt from some sites on the internet, and this fantastic site is no exception (so think the other 20 million visitors they've had visit their site).
> It started with a group of cleaning professionals getting together to exchange tips and techniques. There are now over 1,300 free cleaning tips and product reviews, along with very useful home remedies, available to read at your leisure – for example, articles on how to remove the smell of skunk, how to clean your keyboard and even a link to W · urine-off.co.uk, a very useful product!
> **W · howtocleananything.com**
> **E · howtocleananything@home.com**

THE FINE ART OF LAUNDRY

> The Laundress has the most fabulous range of luxury fabric care and speciality detergents that are just so gorgeous you'll probably just want to sit them on your laundry shelf. However, if you can bear to open any of them you'll love the unique fragrances, with essential oils – Cedar, Baby, Lady or Classic.

> I love their Travel Pacquettes which you can slip into your luggage or handbag. They come in a pack of eight little black-and-white striped sachets of either Stain Solution, Delicate Wash or Wool & Cashmere. Their Travel Pack is a must for any globetrotter, or you could also buy their Starter Kit which has six of their best-selling products in a striped zip pouch with their Laundress Recipe Card.

> Their products tick all the right boxes: they're plant-based and made with organic materials; they're dye, sulfate, phosphate and chlorine free; there's no bleach; and they're 100 per cent biodegradable – simply fantastic.

> A full list of stockists can be found online and I'm delighted to find that Fortnum & Mason (020 7734 8040) are stockists.

> **W·thelaundress.com**

NOTHING TOUCHES TOCCA

> I would have gone to the ends of the earth to get a bottle of the Tocca Laundry Delicate, the wonderful smelling wash for fine fabrics – great for lingerie, hosiery, silks and cashmere.

> Indeed, I went to quite a few big stores in London to try to track it down, phoned all sorts of leads I'd been given, then accidentally came across a bottle at a shop called **Prey** in Bath (*see page* 189).

> There are four fragrances – Cleopatra, Florence, Touch, and the only one I've tried so far and love, Stella. Even the packaging is gorgeous, you open up the box and it says 'love yourself'.

> Tocca also offer a fantastic gift set of the four mini-laundry travel sizes with a lingerie wash-bag, all packed in a gift canister.

> I've checked their online shop and they ship internationally but the shipping costs currently seem to be a flat rate, so rather expensive if you're just ordering one bottle. However, now I've done some more sleuthing, I'm delighted to say you can buy it at a little girlie boutique in Darlington – OCD. Jenny Davis, the owner, is very happy to mail it to you. She sells the 230ml bottles for £13.00 and the travel kit for £40.00 (plus postage). She has a customer who buys six bottles at a time – every six weeks – so I'm not the only fan!

> **Tocca Laundry Delicate W·tocca.com**

> **OCD, 28 Coniscliffe Road, Darlington, Durham County DL3 7RJ T·01325 469 880**

HOME SERVICES

CLUTTER THERAPISTS
OR ORGANISERS

AMATEURS NEED NOT APPLY

> The Association of Professional Declutterers and Organisers (ADPO) was founded in 2004 to help you find a professional organiser nationwide. Their website includes a very useful directory including people who can help you in all manner of ways.

> W · apdo-uk.co.uk

DISCOVER YOUR INNER DESK

> You may have read her book or, more likely, seen her on TV, as Sue Kay really is the decluttering expert. The lovely Sue will come over and set up or sort out your home office, helping you plan your space more effectively. Your filing systems will be neat and efficient, your desk will be clear and those towering piles of paper will be a thing of the past. Sue says 'a clutter-free, organised desk with all your notes and material properly filed will save you time, reduce your stress and ultimately free up your energy for your work'.

> Sue's decluttering doesn't stop at the office. She can help you in the rest of your home and even with moving home. Sue only works in London, but she's the founding member of the Association of Professional Declutterers and Organisers and has set up a great website to help you find a declutterer or organiser nationwide (see above). Her website has lots of other great links, including storage solutions, how to sell your stuff, home services, and hints for moving, and she also offers a useful monthly newsletter.

Prices: Minimum £150.00 for three hours.

> Sue Kay, No More Clutter T · 020 8444 5149 07974 076 675 W · nomoreclutter.co.uk

LIVE AS THE OTHER HALF (PER CENT!) DO

Created by Cosima Somerset, Concierge London was set up to deal with all those 'I simply can't cope' lifestyle management issues. Cosima and her expert staff will calm you down, offer practical assistance and find the solution to all those niggling everyday problems.

For their (very grateful) clients, they've found the ideal home, hired staff, organised fabulous parties, sorted moving from another country, arranged wardrobes into seasonal choices, got tickets for sold-out events, rented a chateau over the New Year, and found someone to explain to the non-English speaking cleaner that one didn't dust the priceless Georgian sideboard using fly spray!

They set themselves apart from the other concierge services by having not one, but two dedicated members of staff who will look after you. If you want to eat at a top London restaurant, they don't just book the restaurant, they choose the table, pre-pay the bill and pre-order the wine. If they're booking your summer villa, they'll fly there and check that everything is as you like it ... favourite foods are stocked in the fridge, staff are briefed on your pet hates, fabulous excursions are set up and top restaurants are booked and visited to make sure they're up to scratch. Naturally, membership is very select and is by proposal only, with fees starting from £5,000.00 a year, plus monthly invoices for any additional time used.

Concierge London Limited, Studio D3, The Depot, 2 Michael Road, London SW6 2AD T · 020 7736 2244 W · conciergelondon.co.uk

CLUTTER EXPERT COMES OUT OF THE CLOSET

> Annya set up the first declutter/personal organisation consultancy in the UK six years ago, but still remains one of the best kept secrets in London. Why? Because no-one wants their friends to know they've had a declutterer or personal organiser round! She's had to work under cover, even pretending to be someone else when a partner has unexpectedly come home. Well, now with all the TV programmes, articles and books around about time management, organisation and decluttering, it is perfectly acceptable to hire any number of professionals to help run your home, your office and your life in general.

> Annya really knows how to clear your room, your house, even your head! She particularly remembers one client who had paperwork going back to 1930! And that's not all she offers: She can work with you on time management, running your home, helping with staff issues, and even show your children how to keep things tidy. She's worked with clients with low budgets and those where the sky's the limit. Annya works nationwide and offers a very personal, friendly and efficient service.

> **Annya Ladakh, Clear Space**
> **T·020 7233 3138 W·clear-space.co.uk**

SOPHIE'S ITCHING TO RESTORE YOUR SANITY

> This company was recommended by Rachel Meddowes (*see page* 70). Sophie can come and clear your life, home or office of clutter, leaving you feeling calm, organised and in control. Just call her Mrs Practical – she loves to come in and restore order. She has run 10 holiday cottages in Devon while the owner was away, including sorting all the inventories; helped a family with a 35-room house move home; sorted out an estate in Gloucestershire by filing and categorising

their family history from 1700 to 2004, even found restorers for some of their dilapidated antiques and sold off antiques they no longer wanted; and has created a great bedroom for a boy and girl who were begrudgingly sharing (and arguing), making a girl zone, a boy zone and a fun zone which the kids adore – in fact, you can't get them out of the room!

> The Order Restorers will work anywhere in the country, and even have a client in Paris. They work within budgets and deliver great results.
> Prices: £40.00-£60.00 per hour or £300.00 per day (7.5 hours).

> **Sophie March & Co, The Order Restorers, 17 Worple Street, London SW14 8HE**
> **T·020 8878 2402 / 07792 545 328**
> **W·sophiemarch.com**

FREE YOUR MEMORIES FROM THE BOX IN THE LOFT

> My friend has spent the last two years trying to organise her 10-years' worth of photos into some sort of order, and she still has five years to get through! This is just the sort of challenge Jeanetta loves. She'll come and sort through your photos (with you) or you can sort through them and then just hand them over to Jeanetta who will create 'works of art' by arranging them beautifully into collages and albums. She can also add any relevant ephemera, which is always a nice touch. She has a client from the USA who has sent her all her photos to create wonderful memory books.

> Jeanetta charges £45.00 per hour, but will negotiate if you require her to sort the material with you as well as complete the albums. I'm sure you're thinking I'll get round to doing it myself – believe me, you won't, most of us don't, and I include myself here – I have four years of photos of our son to sort through! So don't feel you're being lazy, just find time to call Jeanetta.

> **Jeanetta Rowan Hamilton T·020 7584 3030**

And after you have cleared all your clutter, you may need to:

REGIFT YOUR JUNK

> Any Junk will pick up quite literally anything from your garden, office or home, and have even been known to do the odd palace, embassy and houseboat, too. They'll take away anything from single items to truck loads, which they aim to recycle and reuse through local charities, auction houses and recycling depots. Prices start from £47.00, but also factor in any congestion and parking charges and surcharges for some items. Currently they only serve the central London area, but they will consider going further afield, subject to the size of the clearance. If they can't reach you at the moment, watch this space, as their expansion plans mean that within the next two years they will cover a much wider area.

> **Any Junk T·0800 043 1007 W·anyjunk.co.uk**

DIY SAVIOURS

ALL YOU NEED IS LYN

> Lyn has sent me office help, an electrician, gardener and someone to fix the TV. She was motivated to set up Busy People by the sheer frustration of being a busy working woman and not being able to get the help she needed herself. She provides all the usual services, like gardening and odd-jobs, as well as meeting unusual requests such as cooking Mexican food, mural painting, antique furniture restoring, finding a house presentation specialist when you decide to sell, French tuition or a driver. There's not much she can't help you with. *See page* 52 for her special services at Christmas, *or page* 99 for her PA Confidential part-time secretarial service.

> **Busy People T·020 8981 8972 / 07974 308 668 W·busy-people.co.uk**

DIAL FOR YOUR OWN HANDY ANDY

> OK, so you could try your hand at replacing that broken cord for the sash window or mending that broken door-handle but, let's face it, you really don't want to ruin your nails! 0800Handyman will put up, pull down, mend, fix, stick and assemble whatever your heart desires. Even a small-scale plumbing or electrical job won't faze them as they've worked on over 41,000 jobs since 2001. They cover 11 areas (see online), and in most areas charge £20.00 + VAT per half-hour plus a small call-out fee.

> **0800HandyMan Ltd, 8c Commodore House, Juniper Drive, Battersea Reach, London SW18 1TW T·0800 426 396 W·0800handyman.co.uk**

SCORE A GREAT TRADESPERSON

> HomePro.com is one of the UK's largest quality-ranked directories of home improvement professionals and is free to people looking for a vetted trade professional. Performance scores are provided by previous customers, and references are available. There's an extensive drop-down menu with a choice of over 40 tradespeople, including architects, landscape gardeners, painters and decorators, re-upholsterers, plumbers and electricians. I was impressed, as usually east London postcodes don't return many results – not so on this website. I found vetted professionals in nearly every section – much better than just searching the classified ads in the local paper. They also have an extremely useful homebuilding works contract, which you can use with your builder.

> This seems to be a great site. It is funded by charging the trade professionals small fees to cover vetting and reference gathering, and for Insurance-Backed Guarantee policies and other advertising on the website.

> **HomePro Insurance Services,**
> **Quadrant House, The Quadrant, Hoylake,**
> **Wirral CH47 2EE**
> **T · 0870 7344 344 (option 5 to find a**
> **professional) W · Homepro.com**

DON'T TRY THIS AT HOME
> You've bought some 'self-assembly' furniture and now you're faced with instructions that are just drawings, or written in strangely translated English, and the floor is covered with 32 nails, 46 screws and three odd-looking plastic bits. What you need is Screwdriver – the company, not the cocktail! – who after eight years is now the UK's largest flat-packed-furniture assembly service.
> Just phone them with the item number/ description and if it's on their database they'll give you a quote for assembling it; otherwise, they charge a £42.00 minimum call-out fee plus £9.00 per quarter-hour. They won't carry out other odd jobs or carpentry, plumbing or electrical work, however they will dismantle furniture in preparation for moving it to another room or house.
> **Screwdriver T · 0800 454 828**
> **W · screwdriver-flatpack.co.uk**

IN THE COMFORT
OF YOUR HOME

DRY-CLEANING & LAUNDRY
HOME-DELIVERY

WARNING: IT MAY SHOW UP YOUR SUIT
> Established in 1983, the customers – who have included diplomats, TV personalities, lawyers and top business executives – will attest to this company's wonderful service. They don't just do beautifully-laundered (starched or unstarched) shirts; they also offer a comprehensive dry-cleaning service with free collection and delivery from/to your workplace or home. Your shirts will receive tip-top treatment, with any missing buttons replaced, and collars and cuffs treated. They use state-of-the-art equipment and offer a hand-finished service. One customer regularly sends in fifty shirts for cleaning! Shirts can be folded, boxed or hung on hangers. Mainly covering central London, they also cover some areas outside London, so check the postcodes list on their website. Prices: from £2.10 per shirt.
> **Just Shirts of London, Unit 5c, Heron**
> **Industrial Estate, Alliance Road,**
> **London W3 ORA**
> **T · 020 8992 2777 9.00 a.m.–4.00 p.m.**
> **W · justshirtsoflondon.co.uk**

TAKEN TO THE CLEANERS
> I used this fab service all the time when I lived in SE16, but now I live too far east – boo hoo! It couldn't be more convenient: The Laundry Box pick up your dry-cleaning, laundry and alterations, and deliver them back promptly, all nicely cleaned or repaired. Their service is available to around 27 London postcodes (see online, or phone to see if they cover your area), with a minimum order of £25.00 per collection.
> Prices: e.g. two-piece suit from £11.50; trousers £5.40; duvet cover £7.90
> **The Laundry Box, 1 Shad Thames, off**
> **Tooley Street, London SE1 2PB**
> **or New Crane Wharf, New Crane Place,**
> **London E1W 3TS**
> **T · 020 7403 0808 W · thelaundrybox.co.uk**

WHITER-THAN-WHITE RESULTS
> Servicing some top London firms, White Rose Laundries and Dry Cleaning Direct is a family-owned business established back in 1972 when flares were wide and collars were huge!
> Their seven-day-a-week collection and delivery service, usually between 8.30 a.m. and 6.30 p.m., with a three-day turnaround and very reasonable prices, make White Rose

a useful number to store in your phone directory. They offer laundry and dry-cleaning, repairs and alterations, leather and suede care, shoe repair, curtain, carpet and upholstery cleaning, and specialist cleaning/storing of bridal-wear and ball-gowns. Their delivery service covers the London area from W12 to E1.

> **White Rose Laundries Ltd, Head Office, 9 Gayford Road, London W12 9BY
T · 0800 783 7457
W · whiteroselaundries.co.uk**

FOR THE MAN WHO HAS EVERYTHING

If your husband has ever longed for his own Gentleman's Gentleman, but can't quite spring for a permanent Jeeves, put him in touch with Stephen Haughton from Burfords.

Stephen offers a wonderful service for men or women who have the kind of couture clothes that demand a high level of care. Stephen is a modern-day valet who will keep your wardrobe in mint condition. He offers a weekly or fort-nightly service, and comes and collects your shoes for polishing and your suits for a full service, which usually entails a sponge clean and press, replacing any lost buttons (often having to source unusual ones), and repairing and pressing linings. He has had some private clients for over 10 years and also offers 'surgeries' at some of the smaller banks in the city. Stephen is also very willing to travel in his passion for caring for good clothes.

Prices: Full service for a suit, from £14.00

**Burford Valet Service T · 020 8355 3481
M · 07774 476 327**

Other home-delivery dry-cleaning/laundry services:

> **W · cleancleartidy.co.uk** T · 07999 048 953 (south-west London)

> **W · 123Cleaners.com** T · 020 7289 9123

HOME SWAP

Our friends swear by house swapping – they've swapped their London home for a house in Aspen for a fantastic skiing holiday, an apartment in Italy for a beach holiday and a three-bedroomed home in Vancouver for touring western Canada. With two young children, they say it cuts the cost of their holiday in half.

Most agencies charge an annual membership fee for which you get access to their database of members from around the world, who are often also happy to exchange cars as well. However, the agencies do not vet their members and they don't take any responsi-bility for their actions, so please ensure you carry out all necessary checks beforehand, including that insurance on your car and/or home.

I've chosen three of the most popular home-swapping agencies and listed others that may be of interest:

HOTEL-FREE HOLIDAYS

> Homebase Holidays is a UK agency established back in 1985. I found a gorgeous house in the East Hamptons where we could do some major celebrity spotting, a trendy New York loft apartment, not to mention a wonderful apartment by the beach in the south of France. There are some lovely holiday homes to exchange on this site, which is super-easy to use and offers a very low subscription rate of £29.00 for one year or £39.00 for two years.

> I loved that there is a great selection of pictures for each property; the trouble was I couldn't stop clicking every property on offer!

> **Homebase Holidays T · 020 8886 8752**
W · homebase-hols.com
E · info@homebase-hols.com

HOME FROM HOME (ONLY MORE GLAM)

> Want to stay in a three-bedroom house on the beach in Western Cape, South Africa, looking out at whales, incredible birds and spectacular views? Or how about a six-bedroomed house in Tokyo with Japanese pond and garden? Or perhaps an apartment in downtown New York that sleeps six? Without paying anything for accommodation? All you need is a house you think visitors would like to stay in and an annual membership in Home Link (£115.00).

> You'll have access to 13,070 members in over 69 countries. Home Link, who are rated as one of the best home-exchange organisation in the world, print an annual directory, display all their homes online (you can view them before joining), and also offer help and information regarding home swapping, including their 'Ten International Principles'.

> **Home Link, 7 St Nicholas Rise, Headbourne Worthy, Winchester SO23 7SY**
T · 01962 886 882 W · homelink.org.uk

PLAN YOUR ESCAPE TODAY

> Started in 1953, Intervac is now an international organisation with over 10,000 listings in 50 countries. It has individual agencies in many of the countries represented, so you usually have a national organiser as a direct point of contact.

> I liked that it listed new entries in the last seven days. When I entered my holiday wish list, it returned 610 possible holiday swaps. Of course, I could narrow it down by refining my search, but I was just looking and dreaming! Intervac also publishes two colour catalogues a year, and you can receive one

with your membership (£74.99 per annum with discounts and promotions available).

> Brian Hayes is responsible for the UK operation, and Intervac have a woman, now in her eighties, who has completed over 300 swaps and has had the most incredible adventures. Other possibilities are available via the website: you can rent a property (some members have two homes), do a non-simultaneous exchange, a long exchange or even a B&B swap. (Other countries have their own contact – please check online)

> **Intervac UK T · 0845 260 5776**
W · intervac.co.uk

Some other agencies:

> **W · exchangehomes.com** – US site; one-year subscription $50.00.

> **W · homeexchange.com** – 17,000+ listings; useful ABCs of exchanging home, including sample letters and agreement forms; annual membership $99.95

> **W · ihen.com** – International Home Exchange' US site; also offers large selection of privately-owned rentals if you don't want to exchange homes; annual membership $39.95

HOUSE-SITTING

Did you realise that your home insurance often becomes very limited if the house is left unoccupied for more than 30 days? Even if you're not going away for that long and just need the peace of mind that someone is looking after your home, pet and/or garden, then perhaps you should consider a house-sitter.

Some house-sitters are employed by an agency after rigorous vetting, others are self-employed, so do check references and insurance. Most agencies charge a registration fee plus a daily fee for the sitter, usually with food and travelling expenses as extras. Pet care, if offered, is also an extra charge, and other services are often available. We have a friend whose house-sitter takes them to the airport, stocks their fridge for when they return, does some PA work and looks after their dogs, not to mention watering their garden.

See also Pet-sitting Services pages 303-305.

HAND OVER YOUR HOME

> In 1995 Susie Johnston came home from a family holiday to find that their house had been ransacked. Besides being traumatised and angry, most upsetting was the fact that irreplaceable heirlooms and family keepsakes had gone. In 1997 she set up The Home Service – their sitters want you to 'know they care when you're not there', so you can look forward to coming home to a clean house, happy pets, healthy house-plants and a tidy garden. Sitters are interviewed in their own home prior to being employed and your house guardian can be supported by a regional manager.
Prices: £25.00 registration fee; £30.50 daily fee (animals extra), £6.00 per day food allowance, plus travel expenses.
> **The Home Service, Unit 4 Potkins Lane, Front Street, Orford, Suffolk IP12 2SS**
T · 0845 130 3100   W · housesitters.co.uk

HOME ADVANTAGE ASSURED

> With over 51,000 bookings since they opened in 1980, Homesitters have nearly 1,000 meticulously vetted employees nationwide. All house-sitters are personally interviewed and abide by a strict set of rules whilst looking after your home, garden and pets. As one of the first home-sitting companies, Homesitters have built up a strong relationship with insurance companies who recognise the benefits of using this kind of service, and they are highly recommended for probate work. You'll always meet your house-sitter prior to heading off on holiday, and Homesitters make an enormous effort to ensure a perfect match. That said, if you find yourself suddenly called away from home, they can cover a short-notice booking.
Prices: £30.00 registration fee; £35.00 per day (with small additional increments for the care of pets) plus a daily food allowance (currently £6.00) and travel expenses.
> **Homesitters Limited, Buckland Wharf, Aylesbury, Buckinghamshire HP22 5LQ**
T · 01296 630 730   W · homesitters.co.uk

KEYS AND LOCKS

SECURITY IS KEY

> This is a keyholding service for domestic and commercial properties. They provide a Key Guard (all licensed by SIA), who can attend your premises following requests or alarm activation. They can also make pre-arranged visits at timed intervals. All keys are security coded and when not is use are sealed in their secure control room.
> **CMS Keyholding, 10 Pascal Street, London SW8 4SH**
T · 020 7627 0344   W · cmskeyholding.com

HASSLE-FREE HELP AT HAND

> One in four of us have locked ourselves out at some point and we've also wasted millions

of working days waiting for workmen and deliveries to turn up. Well, if you pay The Keyholding Company a one-off registration fee (£24.00), followed by a monthly fee (£12.50/£17.95), they'll not only let you back in when you lose or forget your keys, but will also send someone to wait at your home for a service person or delivery. You can also have your parcel delivered to them, then have them bring it over at your convenience.

> They're on call 24 hours a day, seven days a week, for alarm responses, lost keys or other circumstances. And best of all, they offer a reliable, vetted contractor desk to provide tradesmen to take care of any property maintenance or emergency.

> The Keyholding Company is accredited by the National Security Inspectorate to Gold standard, and all the key wardens are full-time employees who have been thoroughly screened. They also offer a house-check service if you're away, whereby they can clear post, turn lights on and off, and keep a watchful eye on your property. They operate in all 32 London boroughs — check online for postcodes covered.

> **The Keyholding Company, 2 Cotswold Mews, 30 Battersea Square, London SW11 3RA**
T·0870 770 6880
W·keyholding.com

IDEAL FOR SECRET GARDENS

> This unusual company can supply old-fashioned keys to fit most antique locks. They also restore old locks, including removing paint and dirt, repairing broken springs and replacing any missing parts. They provide a worldwide mail-order service — you can send them your lock and they'll provide a key to fit. It's a great service if you have an old jewellery box, or if you want to be able to lock some rooms in your period house.

> **Richard Doughty, Lock Restoration Company**
T·0775 412 9793 / 01294 829 229

RESTORATION

CONSERVE YOUR ENERGY, STOP YOUR SEARCH

> What a great site! You'll find professional conservators and restorers for all manner of antique items among the Conservation Register. If you've got a leather book that's fraying round the edges, an antique clock that won't chime, a dingy oil painting, a tapestry that's looking a little threadbare, or even an historic building in need of some tender loving care, you'll find the expert you need here.

> They also offer guidance on caring for your art, antiques and decorative features of buildings.

> **W·conservationregister.com**

TOO GOOD TO BE NEW

> If you've chipped the edge of your vintage champagne glass, Facets can grind and polish it to look like new. If you've lost the stopper for a crystal decanter they can match it, or even remove it if it's got stuck.

> Facets specialise in the restoration of objects made of glass and silver. They can repair broken glass and then using grinding and polishing techniques can eliminate the evidence of damage. They can supply glass liners for salt cellars in blue, clear, frosted, green, ruby or cranberry glass, and make a new silver top for scent bottles. They can clean cloudy bottles or decanters, and replate or repolish cutlery. Oh, and I mustn't forget to mention that they can supply chandelier drops, from stock or made to order.

> I saw a fantastic vintage vanity case at an antique fair; everything was intact except the silver-mounted tortoiseshell comb, which was all broken. I phoned Facets who said they could replace the comb, with hand-cut imitation tortoiseshell of course, and re-bristle the hair and clothes brush in the case as well.

> Service is by appointment only, except on their open day, which is usually a Tuesday from 11.00 a.m. till 4.00 p.m. — please phone to confirm before you go. They also offer a UK and international postal service.
> Facets, 107 Boundary Road, Leyton E17 8NQ
> T · 020 8520 3392 W · facetsglass.co.uk

STITCHES IN TIME

> The Textile Restoration Studio will clean, repair, support, mount or provide storage for all types of antique textiles, including samplers, lace, embroideries, tapestries, costumes and costume accessories. They will provide a free examination and condition report, although there is a charge for a home visit. Customers have included private individuals, churches and stately homes.
> The Textile Restoration Studio Postal Address only: 2 Talbot Road, Bowdon, Altrincham, Cheshire WA14 3JD T · 0161 928 0020 W · textilerestoration.co.uk

RESTORING BEAUTY

> As HJ Hatfield and Sons have been restoring for nearly 200 years, their reputation as leaders in restoration of furniture, art works and fabrics is well earned. Restorers and conservators of English and French 17th- to 20th-century furniture (including lacquer work), they have metal workers, wood turners, gilders, porcelain restorers and upholsterers on site, not to mention their skilled specialists in cabinet-making, polishing, carving and upholstery. They can undertake restoration of ormolu mounts, marquetry, works of art and paintings, — in fact they are able to restore virtually anything (glass excepted).
> Customers usually send them the item for restoration, but they can travel to collect or restore in situ depending on the project, and they also take international commissions.

> HJ Hatfield and Sons, 49 Clapham High Street, London SW4 7TN T · 020 7622 8169

For lock restoration, see page 90

STORAGE BOXES

CHAMPION BOXERS

> All Boxed Up is a great online store for boxes, bags and packaging. There's a minimum order of £10.00 and you have the handy option of next-day delivery.
> W · all-boxed-up.co.uk

STORAGE TO SHOUT ABOUT

> Conservation By Design offer an unbelievable choice of storage boxes, cans and envelopes for dedicated, high-quality conservation storage. They can provide acid-free boxes for storing antique fabrics, letters, cards, baby keepsakes, photos and negatives, or even your vintage handbags. They can hand- or machine-make any box to your own requirements and supply European, Japanese and Indian papers. They also offer all sorts of drawers, display and showcases. Personal visits by appointment only.
> Conservation By Design, Timecare Works, 5 Singer Way, Woburn Road Industrial Estate, Kempston, Bedford MK42 7AW T · 01234 853 555 W · conservation-by-design.co.uk

CONQUER YOUR CLUTTER

> The Empty Box Company's homepage is all about their handmade wedding-dress boxes, but click on Products and you'll see a great selection of storage boxes for office and study, sitting room, baby keepsakes, hats, toys and under-bed storage. You'll be spoilt for choice with over 40 different sorts of boxes in over 70 designs including floral,

stripes, plain and children's patterns that will smarten up any room of the house.

> What I love is their bespoke service. Send them a piece of material or that left over piece of wallpaper and they will cover any sized box for you.

> **The Empty Box Company, The Old Dairy, Coomb Farm Buildings, Balchins Lane, Westcott, Nr Dorking, Surrey RH4 3LW T·01306 740 193 W·emptybox.co.uk**

FILE UNDER STYLE

> russell+hazel is a fab company in the USA who have made stationery and storage look funky, sensational and smart. I love their new Audrey collection for 'refined filing and stationery effects for the impeccable office.' Colourful binders, folders and storage boxes, expandable tote filing bags (very stylish) and assorted labels will make your storage and filing look so inviting you'll be able to knock 'sort out desk' off your 'to do' list forever!

> If their website isn't enough to inspire you and should you ever find yourself Minneapolis-bound, head straight for their incredible flagship store. You can stock up on storage and attend one of their great after-hours events to help you with all your personal organising. For the rest of us, they do ship internationally – yipee! They also tell me that their products will soon be winging their way over the pond to be stocked in some of our top stores, so stay tuned!

> **russell+hazel, 901 3rd Street North, Suite 115, Minneapolis, MN 55401 T·+1 612 313 2714 W·russellandhazel.com**

> **Shop: 4388 France Ave South, Minneapolis, MN 55410 T·+1 952 929 9000**

SCANDINAVIAN STACKING

> If your shoe collection is verging on out-of-control, treat yourself to a stack of these fantastic Danish 'Hotel' boxes. You can pile them up in up-to-10-foot towers, or just use

them individually. Log on to purenomade (design section) to see them displayed fabulously around the home and to give you some ideas on how you might use them. There are 16 snazzy designs and every six months new designs will be introduced. I simply must have some. They have stockists worldwide (see list online).

> **Pure Nomad W·purenomade.dk**

> **UK stockist: T·08708 921 903 W·designmyworld.net**

MOVING HOME

With the help of my mum, we've worked out that I have moved house 32 times in 46 years, including 13 moves before I was 11! Call me peculiar, but I actually really like the admin involved in moving home – I have my moving-home folder and meticulously tick though all the lists. Every time I pack up for another move I uncover things in the loft that I'd forgotten about, take a trip down memory lane and chuck out a load of stuff that doesn't need to move with us. Well, actually only a little bit of stuff, because I'm such a hoarder!

The average homeowner moves every seven years, although I know one couple who have lived in the same house for 52 years, talk about putting down roots! For most people, the mere thought of moving is worse than pulling teeth, so picture walking into your new home to find your utilities connected, your linen and furnishings all beautifully laundered, change-of-address cards printed, and the house spic and span ready for the bulk of your unpacking. These are the firms or individuals that can help:

100 PER CENT MORTGAGE GOLD

> Two of the most stressful parts of house buying are arranging the mortgage and the exchange. Gavin Davis can smooth the whole process for you by offering unbiased advice

on mortgages and mortgage-related insurance. Whether you need help with a first-time buy, moving home or a remortgage, I can't recommend him enough. He'll go through all the options in as much detail as you want – he told us things no other broker had bothered to tell us and very importantly, saved us money. He's always there to help, weekends and out of hours, even chasing real-estate agents and banks on your behalf, and he does it all with a great sense of humour – which believe me, you will need!

> **Bespoke Mortgages Ltd, Dephna House, 24-26 Arcadia Avenue, Finchley, London N3 2JU**
T · 0870 754 2688 / 07931 550 627
W · bmortgages.co.uk

MAKE A CLEAN START

> In the fashion section I've mentioned Blossom and Browne's Sycamore for their luxury laundry service, not to mention their useful travel-packing service (*see page* 148). They also have a very useful service where they'll come and take away all your soft furnishings, linens, towels or dry-cleaning, then deliver them to your new home, beautifully laundered. They can rehang the most elaborate curtains and pelmets and re-cover your sadder-looking pillows.

> **Blossom and Browne's Sycamore T · 020 8552 1231 W · blossomandbrowne.com**

S.O.S. SARAH OR STRESS?

> Sarah is so efficient that she'll arrange and supervise your entire move from start to finish, whether it's domestic or international. It's not just the logistics of packing, unpacking and moving, she'll see to all the endless admin – utilities, redirection of mail, new-address cards, and so on – even filling the fridge at the new place and throwing a house-warming party! She said her biggest challenge so far was either moving two houses over nine floors to fit into a four-floor, double-fronted

house, or the one large-house downsizing where the contents were going in 14 different directions! In one job she filed 750 compact discs into alphabetical order and put over 7,000 books onto new shelves in a library in exactly the same order as in the previous home...
Prices: from £3,000.00

> **Sarah Kampe, Moving Solutions**
T · 07976 296 838
W · moving-solutions.com

SEARCH SMART FROM THE START

> The time spent looking for the right property can be a stressful, time-consuming, even depressing period. London Property Match is a home-finding service that Suzanne and Sarah set up to help busy buyers find the perfect property.

> They offer a personal property-search service in the Central, South and West areas of London, and they'll sort out the 'must see' from the 'will never be'. No more trudging round totally unsuitable properties wasting your precious weekends and evenings. They can find you a studio, flat or house from £400,000 to £4,000,000+, They often have first dibs on looking at the new properties coming onto the market as estate agents know that their clients mean business.

> Not only will they find your ideal property, they can hold your hand all the way, negotiating the best price and oversee the entire buying process which we all know can take months. It's great for first-time buyers as they take you through the minefield of house buying. They can introduce you to surveyors, solicitors and architects, advise on refurbishments and offer project management services.

> They work on an initial retainer fee, plus a final fee of one per cent of purchase price.

> **London Property Match, Suzanne Emson**
T · 020 7223 0952 / 07802 737 268

> **or Sarah Snow T · 020 7881 5235 / 07977 069 235 W · londonpropertymatch.com**

IF IN DOUBT, LET SOMEONE ELSE DO IT!

> These efficient bods work for private and corporate customers, and guarantee to save you time, money and energy. They offer two services – standard and premium – from recommending removal firms, organising the change of address, etc, to finding schools in your new area, arranging temporary storage, making a list of the best of the local amenities, hanging all your pictures, even interior design. They have experience with international moves, especially to France and America.
Prices: from £195.00

> **The Moving Consultancy T·020 7942 0571
W·themovingconsultancy.com**

BOXES AND PACKAGING

BOXING CLEVER

> If you're not using your removal firm's packing services or boxes, or you're moving home with a little help from your friends, then this is a fantastic website. You can order all your professional moving boxes and packing supplies such as bubble-wrap, tape and furniture protectors. If you're not sure how many boxes you'll need or what size, PacknMove offer handy kits including a variety of boxes and supplies. We're not just talking normal boxes here; they have special divided boxes for glasses and mugs, plate boxes, CD and DVD storage boxes, archive boxes, wine storage boxes, even made-to-measure boxes.

> And if it doesn't fit in a box, they offer loads of suitable coverings for sofas, curtains, or chairs. We loved the floor protector – roll it out and the self-adhesive, non-slip, protective covering will guard your floors and carpets from wet, muddy feet and constant footfall whilst everyone traipses through. (£24.99 for a 20-metre roll). You can also download an excellent moving checklist.

> They'll deliver anywhere in the UK, with free delivery on all orders over £75.00.

> **PacknMove, 9-13 Marsh Green Road, Exeter EX2 8NY
T·0800 698 5101 W·packnmove.co.uk**

HELPFUL WEBSITES

> **W·estateangels.co.uk** – This handy website doesn't list actual properties, but fill in just one form with all your particulars and it will be sent to all the relevant estate agents within your chosen area. You can also enter a postcode and look at the average house prices within that area and/or download lists of local surveyors, builders, electricians and cleaners, etc.

> **W·findaproperty.com** – A leading property website to help all you house-hunters looking to buy or rent your dream home. I loved their independent editorials, including a property market review, a section where you can ogle the real luxury stuff, the report on estate agency fees for sellers, and useful local information such as council tax rates, school performance ratings and crime statistics, along with a guidebook to each area.

> **W·rightmove.co.uk** – Another website connecting home-hunters with properties to buy or rent. It includes a useful house price index and a handy holiday-homes-to-rent section.

> **W·fish4Homes.co.uk** – My last search on this website produced 318,647 homes for sale with all the usual handy sections you'd expect to find on a property portal.

> **W·primelocation.co.uk** – Quality properties will be found on this extremely popular website. Over 3,000 leading UK estate agents list all their properties on here. They offer a

very valuable email property alert for users and also offer a great selection of over 50,000 properties from estate agents in over 40 other countries.

> **W·propertyfinder.com** – This website lists over 340,000 properties for sale or rent, so you're sure to find a few that interest you. Good resources and information and they not only list UK properties, but ones from Australia and New Zealand as well. Perfect if you're thinking of moving down under.

USEFUL 'HELP ME' WEBSITES

KNOW THE RISKS
> This website gives great free advice (as a guide only) on the environment surrounding your prospective home. You've seen in the news the devastation that can be caused by natural disasters, so if you're worried about flooding, subsidence, toxic waste contamination, or landslip, log on and key in the postcode. Homecheck will give you information by postcode area only on over six risk categories, including any planning permission in the area. This sort of information is rarely covered in property surveys and has been collected from public sources such as the Land Registry and Health and Safety Executive. You can also get helpful facts on the Home Information Pack (HIP).
> I checked out our new home and found, to our relief, that it was low in most categories. For a more specific environment report on your particular house, you can order a Homecheck Professional Report (£32.00 plus VAT).
> **T·0844 844 9966 W·homecheck.co.uk**

SUSS OUT YOUR STREET
> I couldn't believe this site! I entered our new street address and it listed all the houses in the street and the most recent price that had

been paid for each house. You can then purchase an online valuation report (you can look at a sample), which lists information such as neighbourhood price trends, value range, selected comparable houses in the street, historic house prices, sales-to-asking price ranges, time to sell (on average) and approved agents. They say it's the same report that is used by mortgage lenders.
> **W·hometrack.co.uk**

DON'T MAKE A MOVE WITHOUT IT
> Voted Website Of The Day by listeners on BBC Radio 2, helpiammoving.com is packed with free, independent advice on moving home, including where to get free moving quotes, storage companies, handy checklists to tick off and keep you serene and organised, fun for the kids when moving, and even printable change of address cards.
> **W·helpiammoving.com**

LESS TIME FOR A CHANGE
> This handy website offers a free change-of-address service and a great moving guide. Follow three easy steps and, voilà, you've told all companies and organisations that you've moved home. You can also send a free e-card to all your friends, which will save you a lot of time and money on stamps.
> **W·iammoving.com**

STEP IN THE RIGHT DIRECTION
> Type in your street address or postcode and you'll get a handy map that you can print out. It's just the thing to attach to the invitations for your big house-warming party.
> **W·streetmap.co.uk**

CHECK OUT YOUR NEW 'HOOD
> This 'real-life guide to your neighbourhood' tells you loads of things you may want to know about your new area. I really liked the section that helps you find your nearest chemist, doctor, swimming pool or gym,

and the News & Views section, where you can ask the locals things like where to find a really good handyman.

> Even if you're only contemplating moving to an area, you can use it to find out about house prices, property types and renting.
> **W · upmystreet.com**

Here are a few useful sites if you're thinking of moving overseas:

SEND YOURSELF A CARE PARCEL

> If you've ever paid a 200 per cent mark-up in a speciality deli just to stock up on your beloved Marmite, PG Tips, Heinz Baked Beans, HP Sauce or a can of Guinness, you'll realise just how wonderful this company is. Run by the lovely Celine and Laura as a family business, they'll send any British grocery item, including Marks & Spencer products, anywhere in the world. They personally go and shop for you and check all sell-by dates and quality.
> They send baby foods and goods to a customer in Japan, Green & Black's chocolate to a well-known celebrity who has a second home in America, and even loo paper and pickled onions to a customer in Boston.
> Delivery to EU countries usually takes 3-5 days, and allow 5-20 days to the rest of the world. Reasonable shipping costs are included, but you will be responsible for any extra taxes or duty imposed on receipt of your parcel.
> **T · 01227 365 070**
> **W · britishsupermarketworldwide.com**

SUPER SERVICE FROM HOME

> Run as a hobby, Mike Rushforth has done the huge community of Brits abroad a great service by providing this 'expat yellow pages'. It contains a wealth of useful information and links, including BBC News, articles, recruitment and travel, all with a great sense of humour. It's perfect for those living in irony-free zones.
> **W · expats.org.uk**

REMOVAL
FIRMS

NO JOB TOO LARGE

> Over 80 per cent of Cadogan Tate's business comes to them by word-of-mouth. Although their prices are not the lowest, in this case you really do get what you pay for. With quality staff, vehicles, warehouses and, most importantly, endless know-how (they run the London training centre for their industry), they'll tailor their removals service to exactly suit your needs, however demanding.
> We know of one customer who called at Thursday lunchtime to arrange the transfer of all the fine art and antiques from his two London properties to one of his two stately homes. He wanted it to be rearranged to look its best for a visit by 'two very important people'. The problem was that they were arriving at 10.00 a.m. the following Monday!
> It took 72 hours' frantic work, using eight trucks and 20 men – and a picture restorer requested on Saturday morning, located by Cadogan Tate before lunchtime and collected by the customer's helicopter an hour later – and the customer declared himself completely delighted and quite happy to pay the five-figure bill. Sadly the royal guests were unable to make it after all!
> Cadogan Tate have depots in London, the Home Counties, Paris and New York, and can handle business, residential, fine art and worldwide moving, shipping and storage.
> **Cadogan Tate, Cadogan House, 239 Acton Lane, Park Royal, London NW10 7NP**
> **T · 020 8963 4000 W · cadogantate.com**

INTERNATIONALLY APPRECIATED

> This is a family business highly recommended by friends who used them for their massive house removal. I invited them round for a quote and Matthew's mum, the charming Ann, went through everything with me. She also showed me an excellent portfolio

complete with thank-you letters and references. They offer free packing materials and wardrobe cartons, and can even transport your car or piano.

> They have offices in the UK and Spain, with a weekly service to/from France. They can relocate a single item if you want, so when you spot that amazing armoire in the French market and Easyjet won't let you bring it home with you, you know whom to call.

> **Matthew James Removals and Storage Limited, 'The Firs', 6 Poyntell Crescent, Chislehurst, Kent BR7 6PJ**
> **T · UK 0800 040 7907; Spain +34 800 2435 2435 W · matthewjamesremovals.com**

HISTORICALLY HELPFUL

> I can personally recommend Scott's as they helped us with our recent house move. When we sold our home, the house we were moving to wasn't ready, so after packing all our belongings (into two trucks) they stored everything for two months, then moved us in. Naturally, we used their packing service as well. It would have taken me a month of Sundays to pack up all my collections. My office filled 70 boxes before they even started on the rest of the house! They were very helpful, went out of their way to accommodate all our requests and were super-patient while I directed the furniture to one room, then changed my mind and got them to move it again... and then one more time... and they were still smiling!

> A great family-run business established in 1918, their prices are very reasonable and we've recommended them to others who've also been delighted with them.

> **Scott's Removal Service, Head Office, Thornton House, Nobel Road, Edmonton, London N18 3BH**
> **T · 020 8807 8007 W · scottsremovals.co.uk**

MOVING-HOME SURVIVAL KIT

This does not go with the removal men but travels securely in your own car so you have all of the essentials to help you through the first few nights:

address book; batteries; bed linen; biscuits (the removal guys will love you); books, toys and videos/DVDs for the children; bottle opener; *breakfast provisions*; can opener; candles and matches; cash for tipping the removal guys; CHAMPAGNE and glasses to toast your new home; cleaning equipment – lots of kitchen roll, bin liners, vacuum cleaner and spare bags; cleaning products; cooler bag if fridge not readily available; extension lead; kettle (with cord!) with accompanying tea, coffee, milk, sugar and cups (include enough for the removal men); first-aid kit; kitchen knife; *light bulbs*; mobile charger; pet food; scissors; soap and towels; toilet paper; *tool kit* or basic tools, especially screwdriver, penknife, screws, nails and hammer (you may need to whack up a few pictures); torch; valuable documents like passports, driving licence, etc; a *smile* and a *stiff upper lip*!

HOME OFFICE

SERVICES & PRODUCTS

HELP YOURSELF

> Bizhelp24 is a useful website for UK-based small businesses. It offers business and financial information on start up, employment entitlements, contracts, home-working, company names, debt collection, accounting and IT. There's also interesting news, articles (over 400) and services. Well worth a look.
> **W · bizhelp24.com**

SOS – SAVE OUR STRESS LEVELS

> Your printer has just run out of ink and your document is half printed. Dial Cartridge SOS who will jump on their scooter and deliver very reasonably priced ink cartridges or laser toners to you within 90 minutes, including Saturday within West and South-West London, or within three hours within central London.
> If you live outside these areas, next day delivery is available to anyone in the UK. Mine certainly arrived the next morning and delivery was free (on orders over £20.00). They can also deliver paper, CDs, and a good selection of stationery. Lovely friendly service.
> **Cartridge SOS T · 0207 731 1144 / 0845 9007 999**
> **W · cartridgesos.co.uk**

JOIN THE FEDS TODAY

> Set up with the aim of protecting and promoting the interests of the self-employed and all those who run their own small businesses, the Federation of Small Businesses has over 195,000 members. You can join if you have your own business and employ fewer than 200 people.

> The Federation campaigns on many issues for small businesses, and offers great benefits, including: free legal advice covering employment and commercial law; insurance; free tax advice and support with any inspection by the Inland Revenue or Customs and Excise; loans; a platinum credit card; preferential rates on factoring, telecoms, medical insurance; independent financial planning; and discounts on various internet services. You'll more than cover your annual subscription fee with their excellent banking package, which offers free business banking, interest on credit balances, a free overdraft facility, business loans, no charge for transactions, including unlimited cheques paid in or out, and no monthly service charge. I pay a fortune in business banking charges and the lower your turnover the more most banks seem to want to charge. When I can get out of my current e-commerce contract, I'm certainly considering moving over to this fantastic package, as it would save me thousands.
> Unbelievably, you get all this for a £30.00 registration fee plus an annual subscription rate starting at £100.00 (tiered by number of employees).
> **Federation of Small Businesses, Sir Frank Whittle Way, Blackpool Business Park, Blackpool, Lancashire FY4 2FE**
> **T · 01253 336 000 W · fsb.org.uk**

MAKING HOME WORKING WORK

> Besides offering the usual desks, chairs and storage solutions, Home Working Solutions offer some great ergonomic accessories. The copyholder that sits in front of your keyboard (Q-doc or Docuglide) is fab and the USB massage ball is an absolute must – no more RSI, stiff neck, sore back and squinting eyes.
> **Home Working Solutions Limited, 500 Chiswick High Road, London W4 5RG**
> **T · 020 8956 2880**
> **W · homeworkingsolutions.co.uk**

SAVE THE SQUID!

> Inksaver is a PC-based programme that allows you to control the amount of ink you use from your cartridge without affecting your print quality. It lowers your ink consumption; you get a lot more life out of your ink cartridges, thereby saving you money. Current UK stockists include Staples, Amazon and PC World. A full list of distributors and retailers worldwide is available online.

> **Inksaver T· +1 800 663 6222 / from outside the USA +1 604 296 3600 W·inksaver.com**

BUDGET-COMPATIBLE CARTRIDGES

> Ink Worldwide, a family-run business, offers inkjet and toner cartridges and cartridge refills at prices that no small business can afford to miss. I print pages and pages for all the research I do and the original ink cartridges cost a fortune – when I have to change both my black and colour cartridges I'm looking at just under £50.00. Here you can buy alternative ink cartridges for a fraction of that price – I was able to buy compatible black and colour cartridges for £21.98 and, wait for it, in a pack of FIVE, so I got 10 cartridges for less than the price of one black ink original. The compatible inkjet cartridges are manufactured to internationally recognised standards, come with a 24-month warranty and have even received awards. All UK mainland deliveries are free (and mine arrived the next day).

> **Ink Worldwide T· 0161 969 3200 W·inkworldwide.co.uk**

BOSS FOR A DAY

> The lovely 'I can do anything for you' Lyn from Busy People (*see page* 85) has set up PA Confidential, which offers secretarial support to small businesses and private individuals at their office, the client's office or the client's home. This support can include setting up new business templates, forms, payroll, invoicing and VAT, research, PowerPoint presentations, word processing, database creation and management, book-keeping, and IT set-up and support.

> The inspired part about it, I think, is that you can hire a PA for as few as four hours, from £15.00 per hour. No job is too small, but if your office is, they can offer a 'virtual PA' service that means you don't have to provide any equipment or desk space.

> **PA Confidential T· 020 8980 9091 / 07980 334 038 W· paconfidential.org.uk**

GARDEN OFFICES

The humble garden shed used to be a place you sneaked off to for a quick puff or to read the paper and escape your in-laws. Not any more. In many homes, this valuable space has now been occupied by a designer home-office. Forget the rush hour, leave home at 8.59 a.m. and make it to your desk before the clock strikes nine.

Depending on your budget, you can now order the most fabulous huts, log cabins, sheds, offices and studios. They can come fully insulated, with electricity, phone lines, burglar alarms, security lights, gorgeous wooden floors or carpet, balconies and decking. One thing you do need to check is your planning permission – most garden offices won't require planning permission, but different councils have different rules and you may even find your title deeds don't allow an erection!

Budget-wise, you should expect to pay between £5,000.00 and £20,000.00. Be sure to check if any quoted price includes the groundwork, which could be a substantial extra. You can find loads and loads of companies offering these home offices, so I've done some of the legwork for you. If you work from home, I guarantee you'll want one.

AS SEEN ON TV

> You may well have seen this company on Channel 4's Property Ladder. I would love to have the 'CS Classic 35' log cabin installed in our garden (look at the pics online), but sadly we don't have the room. A small log cabin starts from £2,845.00 for a self-build or £6,995.00 fully assembled, which includes the building base, electrics, double-glazing, insulation, heat, light and power, with a fine timber interior.

> **CreateSpace UK Ltd, 1 Victoria Square, Birmingham B1 1BD**
> **T·0121 616 0310 W·create-space.com**

THE GREAT ESCAPE

> You can alter the designs of any of these buildings to meet your needs, but they all have gorgeous lines with an open, spacious feel and lots of glass. Prices start at £16,000.00, for which you receive a very substantial construction with double-glazing, plastered, painted walls, recessed lights, electrics, phone line and heating. Also included are a patio or terrace and down lights on the overhang. The Garden Escape claim that the insulation in their designs are 30-40 per cent better than in most homes.

> **The Garden Escape Ltd, Up Beyond, Wye View Lane, Symonds Yat West, Herefordshire HR9 6B**
> **or 9 Belgrave Place, Brighton BN2 1EL**
> **T·0870 242 7024**
> **W·thegardenescape.co.uk**

COMPACT SOLUTION

> To become the proud owner of your own Henley home-office, all you need is a 2.8 m x 3.8 m space in your garden. They say their Compact Office range remains the best selling personal office in the UK, and everything comes as standard, including lighting, electrics (six sockets plus a fuse box), double-glazing, security features and fully-insulated walls, floors and ceilings.

A Henley Compact Office Vista will cost you £5,775.00 including delivery and same-day installation. It doesn't require footings in most locations and if you're moving home it can even be dismantled in just five hours.

> **Henley Garden Buildings Ltd, Rowen House, 28 Queens Road, Hethersett, Norwich NR9 3DB**
> **T·0870 240 7490 W·henleyoffices.com**

GIVE YOUR GARDEN FURNITURE A HOME

> I can so easily imagine myself working in the Moderno or Cubano from this great collection of outdoor rooms. I think I'd also be cosy and productive in the little Solo (perfect for the smaller garden). These garden rooms start from £7,323.00 and Rooms Outdoor is very happy to come and complete a free garden survey so you can get the optimum design to suit your requirements.

> **Rooms Outdoor Limited, Studio 3B, Clapham North Art Centre, 26–32 Voltaire Road, London SW4 6DH**
> **T·020 8332 3022 W·roomsoutdoor.co.uk**

If you want something a little more unusual, what about a gypsy caravan?

FANCY A LITTLE OFFICE ROMANCE?

> You can buy an original gypsy caravan to convert into your home office. The lovely Hugh, who is very passionate about his work, can undertake services and repairs, and even help with sourcing the right one for you if you don't fall in love with one on his website. He says they're cosy, warm and waterproof.

> **Hugh Chapman T·01736 811 090 / 0777 563 1317 W·gypsy-caravans.co.uk**

MY OFFICE FOR A HORSE!

> The Gypsy Caravan Company will actually build you a caravan, to meet your own specifications, complete with furniture. The standard model does include a bed, which you may not want if you're thinking of using

it as an office, but they can provide them without furniture, too. The Reading Caravan is built from solid timber, with hardwood used for the axles, steps and wheels (it can be moved around the garden with a couple of strong bodies), fully-opening windows on all four sides, and working sliding shutters. Inside the fully-furnished caravan there is a single bed which can extend to a double (with a huge storage space underneath), extending table, built-in seating with storage lockers, traditional fireplace and mantelpiece, wardrobes with hanging rail, bookshelves, galleried shelving and a side table with cupboards underneath. It will be painted inside and out; you can choose your own colour scheme and fabrics. (Note: the maximum headroom is only 6 ft 1 in.) They also offer second-hand gypsy caravans. Prices: Reading Caravan, fully painted, complete with furniture £9,845.00, without furniture £9,100.00 (+ VAT and delivery).

> **The Gypsy Caravan Company (Norfolk)**
T· 01953 681 995 / 07717 402 845
W· gypsycaravancompany.co.uk

IT SOLUTIONS

You're two hours from a vital deadline, your computer crashes, you work from home and there's no helpful person at the end of a free phone line because the warranty has just run out. Don't panic and don't call in that favour from your computer-savvy mate just yet. Here are a few shortcuts from those in the know that will hopefully get you out of trouble.

OPEN ALL HOURS
> We've all been there: it's 2.00 a.m., your work was due in eight hours ago and your computer has just shut down on you. Who can you call at this ungodly hour, when you need your machine fixed right NOW? Thankfully Stephen Cullen, Director and

Founder of OOH IT (Out Of Hours IT) saw a need in the market for a 24-hour emergency IT maintenance and support service for small companies and those of us working from home.
> You can opt for their annual maintenance/ support contract (from £400.00 per annum), or you can pay their call-out charge for each visit (from £100.00 per hour). They work mainly with PCs but can also attend to Macs if necessary. They're based in Wimbledon but, unlike some agencies, are happy to travel to your home anywhere in London.
> If computers scare you and something always goes wrong at the most inconvenient times, you'd be the perfect customer for PoziMon, their PC safe-guard system. This programme allows them to remotely monitor your computer and notifies them if it looks like your disk space, hard drive, back-up system or the like is developing a problem. They'll usually be able to rectify it before it gets too serious. Talk about peace of mind! If you feel this is a service for you, give them a call and they'll chat to you about your requirements and sign you up for the 24-hour service if needed.
> Daytime visits can of course be scheduled anytime to help you with IT issues from set-up to maintenance.

> **OOH IT T· 020 8543 6364 W· oohit.com**

BETTER THE BEVIL YOU KNOW
> Nothing I've ever thrown at Bevil has fazed him. He's round in a jiffy if the problem needs on-site attendance, or if he can he'll sort it out for you over the phone. He has a wealth of knowledge about Macs and software programmes, and is also very PC literate. Bevil was marvellous when I was just out of hospital after a caesarean with a nine-day-old baby and we were burgled. He sent over a loan Mac so I could continue my business — it arrived quicker than the police did! His company, Templeton Smith, is a

Mac-authorised reseller and you can often get a really good deal on new kit. He offers a free initial consultancy visit to assess your present IT set-up and needs, and thereafter charges an hourly rate of £75.00. That sounds a lot, but he's very quick so you'll get your money's worth, especially when being offline for just one day could cost your business a lot more.

> **Templeton Smith Ltd T· 0845 123 3807 / 020 8947 7832 / 0777 552 4065 W· templeton-smith.com**

MEETING ROOMS & SERVICED OFFICES TO HIRE

If you live on the 14th floor, a garden office is not going to work for you. What about a flexible lease or licence for furnished office space, meeting rooms or a virtual office? You can often take the space with as little as one month's notice, without the large capital expenditure and running costs of a conventional lease. All manner of services are offered, including secretarial support, courier services, fax and photocopying, staffed reception, personalised telephone answering, utilities and maintenance. You usually only have to pay extra for meeting room hire, photocopying and telephone call charges. Many companies offer virtual business services, where if you're not ready to hire an office you can use their services for calls, faxes, mail and meeting rooms.

VIRTUALLY STRESS-FREE
> Lenta provide serviced offices, meeting rooms and virtual offices in London, Watford, Swindon, Swanley and Norwich. You can hire their meeting rooms by the hour or the day, and make full use of their high-tech telecom systems. If you don't need office space, you

can also sign up for their Virtual Business Service. It's great that you only need to commit for one calendar month, so don't have a long lease to pay.
> Phone the extremely helpful Vanessa who will take you through the possibilities and costs.
> **Lenta T· 0800 515 622 W· lentabusinesscentres.co.uk**

If you're setting up a new business, here are two books that will help you on the path from panic to profit:

The White Ladder Diaries, Ros Jay (White Ladder Press)

As soon as I finished this book I started reading it again and making detailed notes. It's a fascinating week-by-week diary of setting up a new business – in this case a publishing company with a difference. Of course a lot of the information will be applicable to many other types of businesses. See their website for a list of their other innovative books.

T· 01803 813 343 W· whiteladderpress.com

Anyone Can Do It, Sahar and Bobby Hashemi (Capstone Publishing Ltd)

You'll read this really quickly as you won't want to put it down. Written by brother and sister, Sahar and Bobby Hashemi and their personal journey in starting Coffee Republic. I loved this book and found it very inspiring with great tips and contacts.

NO-FUSS NETWORKING

> Probably one of the largest serviced-office providers in the world, with 750 prime office locations across 60 countries, they can offer fully-furnished, single-person office space, executive, open-plan, team rooms and hot desking. Prices are by negotiation, as it all depends on the location, office size and duration of stay.

> Another fabulous service is their Network Access programme, which allows you worldwide access to their lounges, offices and meeting rooms for £199.00 a year for individual members, lower for multiple members.

> **Regus Head Office 3000 Hillswood Drive, Hillswood Business Park, Chertsey, Surrey KT16 0RS**
  T · 0870 880 8484 W · regus.co.uk

Also look at:

> **First Base** – Offer space in London and Southampton T · 020 8600 2500
  W · fbase.com

> **Acacia Offices** – T · 020 7483 3434
  W · acaciagroup.co.uk

> **Workspace** – Offer offices, studios, workshops and light industrial units in London.
  T · 020 7369 2389 W · workspacegroup.co.uk

> **W · serviced.co.uk** – A great site to help you find serviced office space. Locations are listed A through Z, and there are several choices offered in most areas.
  T · 0800 980 1938

TRAVEL
HOLIDAYWARDROBE
LUGGAGE   CARHIRE
FUNKYDESIGNERHOTELS
SKIING
BEAUTY/GROOMINGPRODUCTS
BOOKS
TOURS
TRAVELPRODUCTS

AIRPORTS

AIRPORT TRANSPORT

CLICK IT TO RIDE

> If you don't know how to get from the airport to your destination and don't want an expensive taxi ride, then book a-t-s (Airport Transfer Service). It is available from over 120 airports in 20 countries, with over 4,000 routes. They offer comfortable minibuses with English-speaking drivers on a shared transfer, or you can book the slightly more costly transfer by private car delivering you safely to your hotel or villa.

> **T· 0709 209 7392   W· a-t-s.net**

JOIN THE CLUB

> How would you like to be met by a chauffeur at the airport on your departure and return? He will take your car to a secure off-airport car park nearby and bring it back to you when you land. The service is available at Heathrow, Gatwick, Stansted, Manchester, Edinburgh, Bristol, Exeter, Newcastle and Birmingham airports from £24.95 plus the daily parking charge.

> When we were laden down with luggage, this was a great service to use. Naturally, they also offer just the airport parking without the meet-and-greet service. Other services include city parking, airport lounges and Chauffeur Drive Express.

> **BCP Club   T· 0870 013 4535**
> **W· parkbcp.co.uk**

KEY TO A SMOOTH DEPARTURE

> This valet parking service is offered at 11 UK airports, including Glasgow, Bristol and Manchester. Drive to the terminal doors, let Purple Parking park your car while you get on with checking-in and jetting off. When you get back, they'll have your car waiting for you outside the terminal, they'll even load all those shopping-laden suitcases into the boot for you. Alternatively, you could just use their Park-and-Ride service. Prices depend on duration and period of stay.

> **Purple Parking   T· 0845 450 0808/**
> **+44 (0) 20 8813 8130**
> **W· purpleparking.com**

HANDLING HEATHROW

If you're always sure you're missing something special as you rush through to the departure gate – plan ahead. British Airport Authority (BAA) produce great little guides to each of Heathrow's terminals. These booklets list check-in zones, all the shops and facilities, restaurants and cafes, walking times to gates, locations of cash machines and a lot more useful information. If you phone up, they'll send you one, but the information is also on their website W· baa.com. They also offer a couple of other great services you might like to know about – completely free:

SHOPPING COLLECTION SERVICE

> Did you know that if you're travelling within the EU you can shop at any of the stores at Heathrow and collect your purchases from the collection desk in Arrivals when you return? This is great for bulky or fragile items that won't benefit from a romantic city break! This service is also available at Stansted, Gatwick, Glasgow, Aberdeen, Edinburgh and Southampton airports.

SHOPPING INFORMATION CONSULTANTS

> Shopping Information Consultants will, at no charge, point you in the right direction for all your shopping needs or offer help and advice – never again will you miss out on those sale-price Chanel sunglasses. Just look for staff dressed in a green uniform in the departure lounge. Even more impressively, if you know that the brand you want is at one

of the terminals that you are not passing through – like that Smythson notebook with gorgeous pink lining – the personal shopper will bring the items to you or, if you have time, she can whisk you to the other terminal using her magic pass. The service is available on the day, but we suggest you pre-book this via W·baa.com/shopping.

SOME USEFUL NUMBERS
> **BAA Advance T·0870 000 1000**
Use their one-stop shop to pre-book parking, pre-order your foreign currency for collection at the airport or book your travel insurance.
> **Bus & Coach Information**
T·0870 580 8080
> **Heathrow Airport T·0870 000 0123**
For all flight times etc.
> **Heathrow Express T·0845 600 1515**
A speedy 15-minute trip from London Paddington to Heathrow – avoid fighting with your luggage down the tube stairs and escalators! The first train leaves Paddington at 5.10 a.m., then they go every 15 mins thereafter up to 1.30 a.m. Prices: open return, valid for 30 days £28.00; single £14.50.
> **London Transport Information**
T·0207 222 1234
Great for finding out how to get from A to Z via bus and/or tube.
> **National Rail Enquiries T·0845 748 4950**
> **Skycaps T·020 8745 6011**
W·skycaps.com
The airport porter service to help you with all that heavy holiday shopping! Did you know that if you are travelling solo with children the service is free, as it is if you are a senior citizen, disabled or require special assistance? For others, the service is £8.00 for up to five bags. Book the service at least two days before travelling.

After waiting patiently for my next international trip to make a tax-free Gucci purchase, I was somewhat annoyed to find that the Gucci store was at Terminal 3, whereas I was at Terminal 4. Grrrrr! I wish I'd known about those personal shoppers! To save you this frustration, here is a list of all the airside shops (after security). All the shops are listed on the BAA website with phone numbers and shop hours, so do check as sometimes they change. Warning: This list could be totally boring to some readers – it's here for the shopaholics who will love it!

HAVE SOME FUN – TERMINAL ONE
> Austin Reed, Bally, The Beauty Centre,* Books.Co, Boots (pharmacist available 6.00 a.m. - 9.30 p.m.), Burberry, Caviar House, Chocolate Box, Clarks, Collection,† Dixons, Gassan Diamonds, Fat Face, fcuk, Glorious Britain, Goldsmiths, Hamleys, Harrods, HMV, Hugo Boss, Hugo Woman, LK Bennett, Links of London, Manicure Express, Mulberry, Omega, The Pen Shop, Perfume Gallery, Rolling Luggage, Sunglass Hut, Swarovski, Tie Rack, Timberland, Thomas Pink, Tumi Luggage, Vodafone and WH Smith.
> Plus, of course, your tax- and duty-free – World Duty-Free, World of Whiskies and The Cigar House.

The Beauty Centre offers a hand-picked selection of the world's top beauty brands, along with some cult products. I love their Exclusive Travel Kits for nails, hair, or skin from the likes of Christian Dior, Estée Lauder, Clinique, Lancôme and Clarins. They also have the exclusive UK rights (also at Gatwick) to sell Victoria's Secret make-up, gift sets, body range and perfume. Best bargain: the selected perfumes, which are updated regularly, with some up to 40 per cent off high street prices.
***T·020 8745 1679**.*

*†Collection is a glam new accessories outlet, stocking jewellery, sunglasses and luxury handbag brands including Marc Jacobs, Chloé, Dior, Moschino and D&G **T·020 8745 7694**.*

SO MUCH TO DO — TERMINAL TWO

> Austin Reed, Bally, Barbour, Books Etc, Boots, (pharmacist available 6.00 a.m. - 9.30 p.m.), Burberry, Case, Caviar House, Dixons, Fortnum & Mason, Gassan Diamonds, Glorious Britain, Hamleys, Harrods, HMV, Naturally Cashmere, The Pen Shop, Perfume Gallery, Rolling Luggage, Sunglass Hut, Swarovski, Tie Rack, Timberland, Thomas Pink, WH Smith and World Shopping.
> Tax- and duty-free: World Duty Free and World of Whiskies

THE PLACE TO BE — TERMINAL THREE

My personal favourite, you can shop till you drop in this terminal and with its recent £100 million revamp, it now includes a Mulberry shop, so check in nice and early. Shops include:

> Armani, Bally, Boots (pharmacist available 6.00 a.m. - 9.30 p.m.), Borders, Bulgari, Burberry, Cartier, Caviar House, Chanel, Chocolate Box, Christian Dior, David Clulow, Dixons, Dunhill, Emporio Armani, Ermenegildo Zegna, Glorious Britain, Gucci, Hamleys, Harrods Way In, Hermès, HMV, Jo Malone, Kurt Geiger, Mac, Mappin & Webb, Mont Blanc, Nike, Paul Smith, Reiss, Salvatore Ferragamo, Smythson of Bond Street, Sunglass Hut, Swatch, Tie Rack, Thomas Pink, Tods, Versace, World News, Zegna.
> Tax- and duty-free: World Duty Free, World of Whiskies and The Cigar House

I WANT MORE! — TERMINAL FOUR

> Accessorize, Agent Provocateur, Asprey, Austin Reed, Bally, Boots (pharmacist available 6.00 a.m. - 9.30 p.m.), The Beauty Studio,* Borders, The British Museum Company, Burberry, Bulgari, Cartier, Caviar House, Chanel, Chocolate Box, Church & Co, Cigar House, Dior Studio (make-up/ fragrances/skin-care) Dixons, Escada, Glorious Britain, Gucci, Hackett, Hamleys, Hargreaves Sports, Harrods, Hermès, HMV,

Links of London, Mappin & Webb, Mulberry, Naturally Cashmere, Nike, The Pen Shop, Salvatore Ferragamo, Smythson of Bond Street, Sunglass Hut, Swarovski, Ted Baker, Thomas Pink, Tie Rack, Tumi and WH Smith
> Tax- and duty-free: World Duty Free, World of Whiskies and The Cigar House

*The Beauty Studio offers travel kits you won't find elsewhere and cult ranges. The Terminal Four store offers Mac, Molton Brown, Origins and Clarins among others. There's also a men's bar offering skin-care ranges from Molton Brown, Clarins, Clinique, Biotherm, Shiseido and Lab Series. **T·020 8757 1418**.

STOP-OVER SAVIOURS

> I've just returned from New Zealand after a tiring 36 hours' travelling. At Sydney I had an eight-hour wait at the airport and I can tell you I was bored, tired and longing for a bath. So I'm thrilled to hear about Yotel (from the founder of all things Yo!). Opening summer '07 at Heathrow Terminal 4 (opened in Gatwick's South Terminal in June), and one of the first UK hotels to be actually situated at the airport, you can book one of their 10.5 sq metre hotel cabins from £40.00 (standard room) for a night, or just £25.00 for four hours. If you're delayed in transit, or have a really early morning flight and want to stay the night before, then I suggest you book immediately. Amenities include *en suite* bathroom, free internet access, on-demand movies (on a flat screen) along with 62 TV stations (careful you don't get so ensconced you miss your flight), eat-in 'grazing' menu and automated check-in/out.
> You can book online or through the customer services number during office hours (there is a £5.00 charge to book over the phone). I was very impressed that you could change the font size on the website, if like me, you're lacking in the visual department.
> **W·yotel.com   T·0207 100 1100 Customer Services**

LUGGAGE
LUGGAGE SERVICES

HOW MUCH IS PEACE OF MIND WORTH TO YOU?

> I seem to remember when I was young, free and single, that I could set off for a week's trip with a small and stylish carry-on case. Now our family holidays require planning of military precision, involving huge amounts of stress with excess-luggage fees, lengthy waits at the carousel – one unfortunate pram even ended up on the wrong continent!

> Next time I'm going to treat myself to a stress-free trip by sending all our bulky items (including my husband's golf clubs) with First Luggage. In association with FedEx, this company collects everything but your hand luggage from your home or office the day before departure, and delivers it straight to your hotel or accommodation in the majority of European, and all USA destinations prior to your arrival.

> Prices vary according to which country your luggage is collected from and dropped off at, so check out the charts on their website, but for me checking in last minute and strolling off the plane straight into a cab at our destination will be priceless.

> First Luggage   T · 0845 270 0670
  W · firstluggage.com

LET YOUR LUGGAGE LEAD THE WAY

> Arriving in France on our most recent holiday, we found to our horror that our luggage had not accompanied us on the flight. For once I'd been super efficient and packed my husband's, my baby's and my luggage all in the one suitcase, instead of the four or five that I usually travel with. But it hadn't paid off – we had absolutely nothing for any of us. So I can only thank companies like Flymycase that will forward your suitcase and baggage, including golf clubs and skis, to your destination. Flymycase is a courier delivery service operated in association with FedEx, currently covering all EU countries, the USA, Caribbean Islands and Hong Kong. Delivering a suitcase to France would cost you £59.00, your skis £35.00, and a suitcase to Hong Kong would cost £159.00. You need to book seven days in advance for any destination. Flymycase tell us that 20 million bags are lost or misdirected by airlines worldwide each year – next year I'd rather none of them were mine.

> W · flymycase.com   T · 08452 700 680

ONE PRICE SUITS ALL

> Luggage Free promise to pick up, plastic wrap and tag your luggage, including pushchairs and golf clubs, and deliver it at your destination in perfect condition. They charge from $1.50 per pound, internationally from $5.50 per pound (plus a pick-up fee), with set rates for golf clubs, skis and bikes. Instead of waiting in long queues for security checks and risking the unpleasantness of having a customs agent go through your bags, all you have to do is arrive relaxed at your hotel where you will find your luggage waiting for you – sounds ideal to me.

> Luggage Free, 153 West 27th Street, Suite 903, New York, NY 10001
> T · +1 212 453 1579 or within USA 800 361 6871   W · luggagefree.com

PACKING

GETTING A GOOD FLIGHTS SLEEP

> Cris Notti has probably the best selection of silk sleep masks I've seen. Each one has a lace-like strap and they come in a fantastic selection of designs and colours – I simply couldn't choose just one. Get one to wow

your fellow flyers on your next long-haul trip. You'll probably also be tempted by their jewellery rolls and fabulous travel cases. Prices: from US$20.00 with international delivery.

> **Cris Notti, 11320 Chandler Blvd. #G, North Hollywood, CA 91601**
> **W·crisnotti.com**

TAKE THE 'NO CHECK-IN' CHALLENGE

> I just adore this website – and 10/10 to Doug Dyment, who gifts this vast supply of unbiased and extremely useful information to all of us. Doug believes 'over-packing heads the list of the biggest travel mistakes' and believes there are two kinds of luggage – 'carry-on and lost'! After notching up countless trips, reading hundreds of articles on the subject and, yes, even attending seminars on packing techniques, he is the 'go-light guru'. The challenges are what to take and how to pack it, both of which Doug will amusingly answer for you, also providing great checklists and resource sections along the way.

> Check-out the link to The Universal Packing List which generates a customised packing list for your journey after you have answered a few questions such as what accommodation you're using, gender, length of trip, max/min temps, activities, personal info such as 'I do/don't wash my own clothes', method of transportation, etc. You receive a very extensive list back, and if you find that just too much and just want a more convenient checklist then download Doug's. He loves the travel adage: 'Take half as many clothes and twice as much money.'

> **W·onebag.com**

Holiday laundry – Finding the return to reality hard work? At least let someone else sort the suitcase. Have your laundry picked up, washed, folded and delivered back to you (see page 148).

And for a simply fantastic little suitcase for children which they can pull, sit on and ride look at Trunki (see page 297)

HOLIDAY WARDROBE

CUSTOMISE YOUR CURVES

> Oh, my goodness, what a simply fantastic idea! The lovely Jenny and Kathryn offer a wonderful bespoke swimwear service. Fancy a silver bikini with mother-of-pearl ring accessories? Or perhaps you've seen a picture of a 1950s Hollywood starlet lounging by a pool in your perfect suit. The world is your oyster.

> Biondi offer made-to-measure bikinis and one-pieces in a fabulous selection of Italian fabrics. With the first consultation they will take you through the design and shape, and offer very useful advice on what would best suit your figure shape, while at your first fitting you can change any part of the design. They also offer a large selection of accessories – diamanté, mother-of-pearl and wooden ring trims or charms, along with embroidery and other embellishments.

> And the best bit is if you can't get to them, they'll come and visit you at home (within the M25) to measure all those bits you want to show off to the world and all those bits you'd rather hide! They take approximately two to three weeks to make, although allow up to six weeks over the busy summer period. Prices: £195.00 to £350.00 for their top of the range swimwear.

> In their luxury, holiday boutique, they of course offer a lovely selection of clothing, swimwear and travel accessories, and now they also have an online shop with some gorgeous things. I simply have to have the cashmere slippers – divine!

> **Biondi, 55b Old Church Street, London SW3 5BS T·020 7349 1111**
> **W·biondicouture.com**

BUZZ OFF, BUGS!

> A friend of mine planning a trip to South America was determined she would finally win the battle of the bugs on this trip. She did a little research online and came across Ex Officio's range of clothing (for the whole family) that has been treated with insect repellent, creating an invisible and odourless protective barrier around the clothes and body. A spokesman for the company, Tom Smithburg, explained: 'The idea was originally driven by the US Armed Forces' need to protect field troops, and after seven years' research it was proved highly effective in repelling mosquitoes and ticks, along with ants, flies, chiggers and no-see-ums.'

> My friend reckoned if they were good enough for the American army, they were good enough for her. And apparently, her trip was transformed by the 30+ UPF sun protection, quick drying, convertible, high warmth but lightweight, odour-, stain- and water-resistant and wind-proofing qualities of her new clothing. The shirts, hats, socks, shorts, fleeces, sweatshirts and pants (including the Men's Buzz Off No-Brainer Pant!) may not all be catwalk material, but nor is an intrepid traveller covered in infected bites.

> Ex Officio clothing is currently only available online in the USA, but they have international distributors, and the clothes are available through speciality outdoor, travel and luggage stores across the USA and throughout the world. We all love a little international shopping challenge!

> **Ex Officio T· USA only 0800 644 7303; from outside the USA +1 206 644 7303 W· exofficio.com**

STOP HIDING UNDER THAT SARONG

> After many years of dreading that first-day-by-the-pool, pale and not so interesting look, this year I discovered the preholiday secret that the supermodels have known about for years. Instead of a last-minute scramble up

and down the High Street, you can pick up a flattering bikini, the perfect sun hat, wrap and sunglasses and get a one-minute Mist-On Tan, all at the one-stop Heidi Klein shop. You may also be tempted by the Body Polish Treatment and a whole list of other beauty treatments, but there's always the next trip. If you don't want to be let down on the beaches by the state of your partner or children, head for the newly opened Chelsea store – great for the whole family.

> **Heidi Klein, 174 Westbourne Grove, London W11 2RW T· 020 7243 5665 or 257 Pavilion Road, Chelsea, London SW1X 0BP T· 020 7259 9418 W· heidiklein.co.uk**

THE SUMMER OF MY CONTENT

> What a great find for those off in search of winter sun – a shop that sells spring and summer clothes throughout the year. And another bonus for London, there's free private parking right outside.

> Open every day of the week except Sunday, this tempting boutique offers a continually-changing selection of beachwear, kaftans, dresses, skirts, trousers, tops, jackets and great accessories from hats to flip-flops.

> **Laura Tom's Summer House (The Gasworks), Redloh House, 2 Michael Road, London SW6 2AD T· 020 7736 3393 W· lauratom.com**

TRAVEL PRODUCTS
YOU CAN'T BE WITHOUT

BE CLEVER: BE CLEAN

> If you've ever tried to wash 15 pairs of knickers with your last drop of travel shampoo in a sink with no plug, you'll know how little fun it is. For the more organised traveller, Changes in Latitude's store and website offers a great selection of travel

accessories (currently they do not ship outside the USA). You can print out a very handy free packing checklist, with over 120 reminders which will lower the stress levels before you set off.

> Their travel laundry products include inflatable hangers, laundry lines, travel washing powders and flat sink stoppers. Start packing...

> **Changes in Latitude W·cil.com**

> **Travel Store, 2525 Arapahoe, Boulder, CO 80302 T·USA toll free 1 866 786 8406/ 303 786 8406**

SPLASH OUT ON A SURVIVAL KIT

> I like to window-shop on this website and absolutely love its graphics, sleekness and stylish products. While browsing the shopping sections, enjoying names like Jet Comfort and Just In Case I've been tempted by many things (unfortunately they only ship within the USA).

> There are great gifts for travellers, from make-up bags to chic dog-carriers. The Mobile Foodie Survival Kit is very novel — they reckon you can 'doctor up even the most repulsive meal on the go' using this handy kit stocked with all the essential herbs and spices, plus indispensable extras like tabasco sauce and wasabi'!

> **W·flight001.com**

FEELING A BIT DEFLATED?

> I'm not the best of sleepers when it comes to aeroplanes, but my new JetRest made a world of difference. You unroll it, rather than inflate it, so it is a little bulky to pack, but it's more than worthwhile. Made in a range of fabrics, including cashmere, it's so cosy I also used to pop it behind my son's head when he fell asleep in his buggy. It's also great for a quick nap in the car — but not when you're driving! From £19.95.

> **Jet Rest T·0870 739 1591 W·thejetrest.com**

PERFECT PRESSIE

> We have this wonderful old leather suitcase which I bid for at an auction — paid too much for it in the end as I'm a bit like a dog with a bone that just won't let go when I really want something! Anyway, it does have wonderful old travel stickers on from the times when hotels and airlines would brand guests' luggage. Laughing Elephant (great name) has produced a selection of boxed sets of 20 vintage replica luggage labels for $8.95 — the perfect stocking stuffer for a travelling friend or relative and a good way for them to recognise their bag on the carousel.

> **Laughing Elephant T·+1 206 447 9229/ within the USA 800 354 0400 W·laughingelephant.com**

EASY TRAVELLING

> I love, love, loved Magellans for showing me so many fabulous bits and pieces that I'd never have known I needed! Appliances, footwear, clothing, health, in-flight comforts, luggage, maps and books, packing aids, and toiletries and kits — you'll spend ages browsing. Look at the portable luggage scale — a handy, lightweight scale to weigh your luggage (up to 75 lb), so you'll never be caught paying excess baggage fees again. Their Dry Case Set is a must too, a 100 per cent leak-proof pouch to keep your toiletries from leaking over your luggage or to keep small valuables dry (even when submersed in water).

> The website also has very useful travel tips, including what exactly you are allowed to carry on board.

> **Magellan's T·+1 805 568 5400 or within the USA 800 962 4943 T·UK 0870 600 1601 W·magellans.com**

HOPE FOR THE BEST: PREPARE FOR THE WORST

> Few things put more of a dampener on one's holiday spirit than an unexpected bout of

diarrhoea, vomiting, back pain, allergies or a urine infection. You can't prevent any of these occurring, neither can you predict the unfortunate fall or infected bite or cut, but you can be prepared for them.

> If you travel with Medipac, chances are you'll be covered for most travel-related medical situations, because theirs is one of the best-stocked medical kits I've seen. It offers a number of prescription medications, dressings, sutures, sterile needles and syringes (£79.99). The company, e-med, also offer worldwide consultations with your own London based online doctor by e-mail, or for a personal consultation in London. These doctors can give you medical advice, a diagnosis, a referral (UK only), or even a prescription. There is a membership fee of £20.00, with a £15.00 consultation fee.

> **Medipac T·020 7806 4028 W·e-med.co.uk**

A LITTLE BIT OF WHAT YOU FANCY

> This is a must-visit website for anyone who travels frequently, especially now the airlines have set a maximum 30ml product size for carry-on. Their products are also great for camping, in the car and handbag essentials. The website was set up by the Shrater family who wanted a one-stop shop for travel-size condiments, travel accessories and various other travel-size items. They now stock hundreds of products, including many items that are not available for retail sale anywhere else. They also offer handy kits such as baby care on the go, laundry, dorm care, and cold and flu care packages.

> If your order value is over $20.00 shipping is free within the USA; they also offer international shipping. Among all the usual personal care items, I also found some other very useful mini goods, including hand warmers, contact lens solutions and stain removers – just excellent. Some calorie-conscious customers take the mini 'light'

dressings into restaurants, and other products have even been taken on board the space shuttle!

> **W·minimus.biz**

IF IN DOUBT, CHEAT

> Despite hours spent in the classroom struggling to get to grips with 'to be' and 'to have' in various European languages, few of us can say anything truly useful once we're in a French, Italian or Spanish boutique, hotel or bistro. With these discreet, postcard-size, laminated Pigeon Cards, full of useful words and phrases, you can stop speaking loudly and slowly in English and charm your waiter into keeping those cocktails coming. You can buy them from Amazon.co.uk, bookshops or from Gazelle Book Services.

> **Pigeon Cards T·01524 68765 (Gazelle Book Services) W·pigeoncards.co.uk**

TOYS FOR TRAVELLERS

> If you're planning to travel far from luxury hotels and multilingual staff, you could probably do with a 16-language electronic translator and quick-drying clothes. For a full range of wonderful and useful items for the traveller or mobile lifestyle that you never knew existed, visit travelproducts.com. I think the Pack-Mate compression bags are fab – they allow you to pack twice as much and they are really useful for dirty laundry.

> With over 60 product categories, you will find exactly what you need and all products are fully guaranteed for one year, wherever you decide to take them!

> **W·travelproducts.com**

Calendula cream is a First Aid essential – no holiday bag or medical kit should be without it. It's excellent for soothing prickly heat, sunburn, bee-stings, cuts and grazes, bruises, nappy rash and dry skin.

BEAUTY & GROOMING
PRODUCTS

My trusty wash bag seems positively roomy now there's a fantastic range of one-use, one-dose, individually packed skincare and little mini travel products. It's so much easier these days than when we had to do the decanting into little bottles ourselves. Now if the makers of contact lens solutions could just learn that less is more…

YOU'LL BE THE BEES KNEES

> If you like to try before you buy, The Head-to-Toe Starter Kit containing miniatures of Burt's Bees best-sellers, from Beeswax Lip Balm to Avocado Butter Hair Treatment, is the place to start. Stockists include Harvey Nichols, Fenwicks and Fresh & Wild, or you could buy it online at W·bathandunwind.com (£15.99).

> My friend Ruth swears it cured her cracked and dry feet. Great site with some great brands — you may well find yourself buying a lot more than the starter kit!

> **Burt's Bees T·For stockists
01628 898 410**

JUST WHAT THE DOCTOR ORDERED

> Long recognised as the essential beauty travel companions, Dr. Hauschka's organic products come in chic travel-size metallic cases and are made with pure botanical ingredients. The fabulous Daily Face Care Kit consists of Cleansing Cream, Cleansing Milk, Facial Toner, Moisturising Day Cream, Rose Day Cream and Quince Day Cream, while The Daily Body Care Kit contains Quince Body Moisturiser, Rose Body Moisturiser, Hand Cream, Blackthorn Body Oil, Rose Body Oil, Lemon Bath, Body Wash Floral and Body Wash Fresh. And now there's a new Daily Bath Care Kit with five travel-sized bath oils, each with different healing and reviving properties — Lavender Bath, Lemon Bath, Rosemary Bath, Sage Bath and Spruce Bath. I have used all the kits and love them all, especially the dainty sizes which take up no space at all.

> **Dr. Hauschka T·For stockists
01386 791 022 W·drhauschka.co.uk**

FABULOUS SOLUTIONS FOR THE FREQUENT FLYER

> If anyone should know about looking great at 30,000 feet, it's an international flight attendant. Kati Kasza founded Evolu Botanical Skincare of New Zealand because she couldn't find any products to resolve the problems with her skin while working on long-distance flights. All the products are made with botanical ingredients and 100 per cent Kiwi spring water.

> One of her most innovative travel products is the Evolu 6-in-1, a fantastic mini kit with six products in one twist-together stack which slips into your handbag or travel bag. It contains a purifying mask, soothing eye gel, night cream, day cream, cleanser and hand & cuticle cream (£19.00).

> Internationally you can purchase via the New Zealand website and although prices are listed in US dollars you can pay online in Australian dollars, UK sterling, US dollars, euros or Japanese yen. All products are shipped from New Zealand.

> In the UK you can purchase online from W·evolu.co.uk.

> **Evolu Botanical Skincare
T·NZ +64 9 376 7255 W·evolu.com**

NO FRILLS: MINI THRILLS

> With a policy of no advertising and simple, no-frills packaging, Kiehl's are able to offer you small quantities of the most efficient ingredients available. Well-known for their reputation for generous free samples, with a 'try-before-you-buy' philosophy, you can go in-store for a consultation and come away with all your holiday products without parting

with a lot of your holiday fund! They know you'll be back to buy them after you've sampled. I simply love their products and always have a tub of Simply Mahvelous Legs Shave Cream (no, that's not a typo) which gives me the best shave ever. And to get my hair as silky smooth as my legs, I trust in Creme with Silk Groom.

> If you can't get to the main store, they offer a mail-order service and (in the UK) the products are also available at Space NK, Harvey Nichols, Selfridges Oxford Street and Selfridges Birmingham. Visit Kiehl's website for international stockists.

> **Kiehl's London Store, 29 Monmouth Street, London WC2H 9DD**
T · Mail order 020 7240 2411 W · kiehls.com
(online ordering with delivery to USA only)

BAG YOURSELF A BEAUTIFUL LANDING

> We all love and know Jo Malone products, and it's always such a treat to receive any of her products as they're so beautifully packaged. I always take her travel candles away with me, as they help me to relax straight into a new hotel room, but now I won't leave home without her In-Flight Travel Bag. It's a dinky, smaller version of the Essential Travel Bag, and is available in very classy black or cream. Filled with ginseng day-moisturising cream, green tea & honey eye cream, protein skin serum, juniper skin tonic, avocado cleansing milk, lime, basil & mandarin body lotion and a refreshing grapefruit cologne, you'll step off that plane looking and feeling like you've just spent a day in a spa. Price: £72.00. See online for further stores worldwide.

> **Jo Malone, 150 Sloane Street, London SW1X 9BX T · 020 7730 2100**
T · 020 7720 0202 Mail Order
W · jomalone.co.uk

DABBLE IN A LITTLE M&S

> For some great mini products Marks & Spencer is the place to go. Don't wait to go on holiday; they're perfect even if you just plan to crash at a friend's house. They offer a cute Short-Haul Kit that neatly stores a mini shower gel, hand cream, lip balm, travel toothbrush and toothpaste and a mirror which comes in a soft pink bag (£5.00). I particularly love the fragrance free, dinky facial wipes for cleansing, toning and make-up removal that are smaller than a pack of handbag-size tissues (£2.50). These products are available in stores nationwide (or online) but it might be worth phoning ahead before schlepping in to your nearest branch.

> **Marks & Spencer T · Stockists 0845 302 1234**
W · marksandspencer.com

THE ULTIMATE MULTI-TASKER

> When it comes to dinky little products, I especially like Nivea lip-gloss-sized deodorant. The DRY Compact pump spray not only fits into your handbag but it also lasts around 80 days — if only my husband would stop stealing mine! You should also stock up on Nivea Creme as it is a little-known fact that it prevents ingrown hairs, soothes your lips, is ideal to prevent that ugly red nose when you have a cold, prevents your nails drying out when you rub it into your nail bed and cuticles, and it will help to cool and hydrate your skin if — ouch! — you've been silly enough to get sunburnt — all from their 25 ml motif tin. Lastly, you mustn't go away without Nivea Visage Cleansing wipes in a handy re-sealable small pack. They're soap- and alcohol-free, and even remove waterproof mascara. Available in most pharmacists and supermarkets.

> **Nivea Careline T · 08456 448 556**
W · nivea.co.uk

LET TINY TREATS TRANSFORM YOUR TRIP

> On a recent hen-weekend, the bride gave us all take-anywhere travel kits with fantastic travel-sized products in a sleek black neoprene zip-up bag. What we all liked best about these REN kits was that all their products are free from petrochemicals, sulfates, synthetic fragrance, animal products, synthetic colours, parabens and all that nasty stuff. Even better, each travel bag is suited to all skin types and contains six great products: facial wash, moisturiser, repair cream, facial serum, body wash and body cream (£18.00).

> Available at SpaceNK, Selfridges and selected stores, or via their website.

> **REN T·Stockist details 0845 225 5600 W·renskincare.com**

SPACE SAVERS AT SUPERDRUG

> Pop into the travel section at Superdrug for a great selection of mini toothpaste, shampoos and conditioners, antiperspirants, body sprays, sun-care, cute talcs and other really useful bits. With over 900 stores nationwide, you're bound to find one near you – their website has a handy store locator.

> **Superdrug Stores T·0800 096 1055 W·superdrug.com**

HOW TO SURVIVE LONG-HAUL IN STYLE (AND SMELL GOOD, TOO)

> As the former Health and Beauty director of *Vogue* magazine, Kathy Phillips should know what works ... and this does. Working in partnership with Geraldine Howard and Sue Beechey of Aromatherapy Associates, Kathy has created This Works, whose bath and body oils and accessories are formulated using 100 per cent natural plant oils and the highest calibre of raw materials from around the world. All the ingredients are free from mineral oils, synthetic colour or fragrance, petro-chemical or GM ingredients.

> I love TheTravel Kit (£35.00) containing eight essential miniature travel products. It includes Turbo Balm for moisturising and hydrating; Energy Bank Bath and Shower Oil; Deep Calm Bath & Shower Oil; One for All, for whenever you need antiseptic and soothing relief; Breathe In, which I find indispensable when I'm travelling or feeling run down; Quick Spritz to hydrate and refresh your skin; Enjoy Face and Body Lotion which feeds and hydrates any part of your face or body; and Stay Cool Eye Serum for when your eyes need a little TLC.

> **This Works, 18 Cale Street, London SW3 3QU T·020 7584 1887; Mail order UK 0845 230 0499 W·thisworks.com**

If you can't resist an exclusive tax-free temptation, check out the Beauty Centre/ Beauty Studio at Heathrow Terminals. They offer wonderful travel products you won't find anywhere else. Sssh! See page 107-108

*Also see **minimus.biz** page 113 for fabulous mini travel products*

And for the men...

MIKRO MANAGING

> I think this website is fantastic and every man who travels frequently should buy a supply of Mikro products, and every self-respecting partner (I include myself here) should try to nick some of them. The compact, credit-card sized, single-use personal care and grooming products come in disposable five- and seven-piece packs, including shave & toothpaste kits, combination kits, and overnight kits. He can choose from aftershave balm, brushless shaving cream, deodorant wipes, hair gel, shampoo, shower gel, toothpaste, and disposable triple blade razors. They also offer hand wipes, hand gel, shoeshine wipes and overnight kits and bags (from £0.99).

> **Mikro Travel T·020 8346 5169 / 07944 344 363 W·mikrotravel.com**

THE GIFT THAT KEEPS ON GIVING

> What do you give the man who has everything? Something that makes him smell delicious! Space.NK.MAN is a completely indispensable travel kit which comes packaged in a very smart black wash bag and includes eau de toilette, body wash and shave cream (£30.00).

> **Space.NK.MEN, 8 Broadwick Street, Soho, London W1F 8HW T·020 7287 2667 W·spacenk.co.uk**

---

*The most **appreciated gifts** are those with a bit of thought behind them. So why not see a **special friend** off in style with a **personalised travel kit**. If you need a few ideas, I never travel without...*

- **ELIZABETH ARDEN'S EIGHT-HOUR CREAM** – a multi-purpose cream great for dry lips and skin

- **CASHMERE SOCKS** – use on the plane and in bed – cosy, cosy

- **EVIAN SPRAY** – spray your face regularly and step off that flight fresh and glowing

- **TEA TREE OIL** – dab this under your nostrils while flying – I read somewhere that this prevents 'germs' and colds, and it seems to have worked for me

- **PASHMINA OR CASHMERE SHAWL** – for cuddling, and warmth of course

- **A BUNDLE OF MAGAZINES** – to catch up on all the latest fashion and news – then I leave them on the plane to lighten my load. You can't go wrong with *Vogue*, *Harper's Bazaar*, *Travel & Leisure* and *Tatler*

- **LAVENDER OIL** – I rub it on my temples at the slightest sign of a headache or put a few drops in the bath to relax at my hotel

- **HELIOS HOMEOPATHY SPECIFICS FOR THE TRAVELLER** – a fantastic kit containing 36 homeopathic remedies for everything from upset tummies to prickly heat. It's light and compact, and has proved invaluable for all sorts of ailments and conditions. My friends said the kit I lent them was the most useful thing they had packed on their trip to India and Bali. (01892 537 254)

- **JET REST** – a divine little ergonomic pillow (*see page* 112)

- **AEROLATTE** – sad but true, wherever I'm staying I simply must have a frothy cappuccino – yum, yum. This travel version comes with a case and takes up no room at all!

- **MINI HOT WATER BOTTLE** – with a cashmere cover. This Works (*see page* 116) offers one with a little pocket on the front with a muslin cloth that you can dab with a few drops of your favourite essential oil – breathe and relax and stay warm.

- **LA PRAIRIE** – one of the best skin creams I've ever used – I never leave home without the Anti-Aging Complex and the luxurious Skin Caviar Luxe Cream (*see page* 219)

INFORMATION
BOOKS & MAPS

A QUEST FOR ANSWERS

> It's amazing what is on offer through the web – at Mapquest you can find places, airports, hotels and restaurants in Europe and North America. I was able to find a business I'd been looking for in San Francisco in a matter of seconds. You can also print out a map and directions. How did we cope in the olden days?

> W·mapquest.com

MR & MRS SMITH

You simply must have this book on your bookshelf, or at least buy it for someone who loves to stay in stylish places. *Mr & Mrs Smith* is a fantastic guide to must-stay places that have all been checked anonymously. The book's design is fab, and it includes a section of things **Worth Getting Out of Bed For**, along with pages devoted to packing, how to fly a kite and how to throw a Frisbee, and a diary of events. The **At a Glance** section puts each hotel into categories: price, great for kids, spas, village life, coastal etc. When you buy the book, you also receive a Smith card which gives you exclusive offers at participating hotels such as a free bottle of champagne, picnic hamper, free room upgrade or late check-out. The first edition featured the UK and Ireland and they have now brought out a European Cities and European Coast & Country collection.

Mr & Mrs Smith, **Spy Publishing**
W·mrandmrssmith.com

BOOK THE HOLIDAY – BUY THE BOOK

> This very old, famous travel bookshop is amazing – I went in for a couple of things and came out with seven, including a fantastic travel guide and city map. Stanfords offer a huge range of travel literature, stationery, atlases and other travel bits, so even if your next holiday seems a long way off, it's the perfect place to go and dream...

> **Stanfords, 12-14 Long Acre, Covent Garden, London WC2E 9LP**
> **T·London 020 7836 2260**
> **Bristol 0161 831 0250 W·stanfords.co.uk**

Also see page 184 for fantastic shopping guides

NEED TO KNOW BASIS

ACCESSING YOUR EMAIL OVERSEAS

> We all know that prices charged for accessing the internet when you are overseas can often be exorbitant, especially in hotels. If you are footing the bill, not your company, then take a look at these other options. First though, check that your current ISP doesn't offer a global roaming plan. If not, I suggest **W·ipass.co.uk.** Another site worth looking into is **W·i2roam.com** which offers one of the lowest-cost roaming solutions with secure access to email and the web while on the move; while **W·freedomlist.com** provides you with an ISP directory. And for a list of internet cafes around the world, try **W·cybercaptive.com**

SORRY YOU'RE CALLING ME FROM WHERE EXACTLY?

> You'll love this idea if you, like me, have ever been hit with a £200.00 mobile phone bill on returning from a trip. When I was in New Zealand, even if I only spoke for two seconds I was charged £1.50 – simply outrageous. Now all you do is buy a foreign SIM before

going abroad, insert it into your phone and let your favourite friends and family know the new number that they need to call to get you overseas.

> You'll see major savings whether you talk via mobile phone, a landline or online throughout the world.

> This company is the leading supplier of NZ SIM cards – receive incoming calls for free, make calls from just 18p and have your new local number before you leave the UK – just top up with vouchers on a pay-as-you-go system locally.

> **0044 Ltd   T·0870 950 0044 W·0044.co.uk**

DON'T SWEAT THE SMALL STUFF

> Will your mobile work in Los Angeles? Will you need a travel plug for your hairdryer in Australia? What is the international dialling code for Venezuela? Steve Kropla's comprehensive lists offer worldwide phone, plug, electrical and telephone information. He also offers a list of handy resources and places to buy the accessories that allow you to remain connected. You may have never thought that the day would come when you would be so thankful for a clearly-set-out table of worldwide phone plugs, but when you're stuck in Brazil and your boss is screaming blue murder for a lost report in Birmingham, you need to get online – now!

> **W·kropla.com**

DREAM BEYOND YOUR MEANS

> Everyone waxes lyrical about this site and it's often voted one of the best for travel. Offering luxury travel properties, special offers, exclusives and auctions for the sophisticated traveller, Luxury Link is a good place to find hotels, resorts, spas, yacht charters, villas and some of the most desirable cruise packages in the world.

> **W·luxurylink.com**

TIME TO CONVERT

> I use this every time I travel. This site gives you foreign exchange rates and their FXCheatSheet is great – print it out, cut it out and end up with a useful little purse/wallet-sized sheet to tell you exactly what you are spending. I feel absolutely lost without it.

> **W·oanda.com/convert/cheatsheet**

OKAY, IT'S RAINING OUTSIDE!

> **W·rainorshine.com**

ARE YOU SITTING COMFORTABLY?

> If you can't wait till you're on board to find out if you have a seat with extra legroom, or a seat that doesn't recline, or all about your in-flight entertainment and meals, then I suggest you take a look at the highly informative seatGuru.com.

> Offered with 40 different airlines, from Virgin Atlantic, BA and Singapore to United, SAS and American Airlines.

> **W·seatguru.com**

GET THE INSIDER INFORMATION

> The website of my favourite US-published travel magazine, *Travel and Leisure*, has great archived articles from previous back issues. I was delighted to find all the best vintage shops in the USA by entering 'best shops vintage' into the search facility. It also offers hotel, restaurant and destination guides among other very useful information.

> **W·travelandleisure.com**

SAY GOODBYE TO MAP READING MAYHEM

> If you've ever wondered whether it's cheaper to fly, train, hire a car or drive when you visit Europe, put this website into your Favourites – it is fantastic.

> Type in any two addresses, anywhere in Europe, and it will give you precise instructions on how to get there with information on road tolls, estimated journey times, tourist attractions, hotels and

restaurants en route. And, best of all, it will even show you the location of radar speed checks (in France) and road disruptions. With directions this clear, you just can't go wrong – and you can't argue either!

> **W·viamichelin.com**

LET THEM DO THE QUEUE

> One of the few companies to deal with passports and visas that do not answer their phone with an automated 'Press 48 buttons before you can speak to anyone' routine, this passport and visa service is still busy despite the new changes and laws easing modern-day travelling. Currently they can help you with your British Passport Application (new, lost – not overseas – and replacement), and also offer a visa service. As they are visiting the main embassies on a daily basis, they're always fully conversant with current requirements. Fees vary depending on country charges, but expect a handling fee from £40.00.

> **Visa and Passport Service**
> **T·020 7229 4784**
> **E·visa-passport@btclick.com**

WOW THE LOCALS

> It's always worth trying to speak some of the language of the country you're in – your hosts will love you for it, even if they can't understand you... With 6,800 known languages, the trick is to be selective. This website offers a great range of language dictionaries from Abenaki to Zulu. It's never been so easy to book a room in Maori, or charm a Prussian with a little love poetry.

> **W·yourdictionary.com/languages**

WHAT'S THE TIME MR WOLF?

> With world clocks and time-zone convertors, this is a very handy site. I also like the world-clock meeting planner – great if you're teleconferencing with people in different countries and you want to find a time that

will be convenient for everyone. And for a little bit of fun, it will tell you when you are 10,000 days old, count you down to the New Year or tell you what date it is in 5,000 days' time – oh yes, and when it's a leap year in case you had any ideas about proposing!

> **W·timeanddate.com**

GOING UNDERGROUND

> A really useful site if you're planning to use the underground/subway on your travels. This site gives you access to the world's underground systems, including maps, a route finder, which also includes approximate travel time, and links to interesting places.

> **W·subwaynavigator.com**

SERVICES
CAR HIRE

SERVICE WITH A SMILE

> A company with one of the best reputations in holiday car hire and lovely customer service. You can book a car rental in the UK from £17.00, France from £20.00, Spain from £11.00 and the USA from £13.00 – these are all daily rates and intended as a guide to show you just how reasonable their pricing is. (Holiday Autos is part of lastminute.com.)

> **Holiday Autos T·0870 400 0011**
> **W·holidayautos.co.uk**

INSURE AGAINST NASTY SURPRISES

> Did you know that if you damage your rental car it could cost you over £500.00, even if it's not your fault? Just a tail-light? – they could also charge you for the time the car is off the road – suddenly it's looking very costly. I'm sure you've been asked if you want excess

insurance when you've picked up your rental car and this is normally offered on a per-day basis. Insurance4carhire offers low-premium annual cover with unlimited use including an excess waiver covering damage to the vehicle, theft, window and tyre damage, and covering all additional drivers on the rental agreement, from as little as £49.00 per annum.

> **Insurance4carhire T · 020 7012 6300 W · insurance4carhire.co.uk**

Luxury car hire

ARRIVE IN STYLE

> Drive through the English countryside in a Ferrari F430 Spider F1, arrive in style in a Bentley Continental GTC at your showy friend's next birthday party, or cruise to a halt outside this month's hottest restaurant in a Lamborghini Murcielago. All these and more can be yours when you join the supercar club, Ecurie25.

> Membership costs £9,200.00 (per annum) plus a £750.00 one-off joining fee, which buys you points that you then exchange for use of the cars. During the course of your annual membership, you'll typically experience 35 days' driving these gorgeous cars. Enjoy the car whilst not having the worry of ownership, depreciation, insurance and servicing – how fab is that?

> Membership is open to those with UK or non-UK driving licences; you do have to be at least 25 years old and they only enrol a restricted number of members, so sign up quick. Mmm, which dream-car shall I drive next?

> **Ecurie25 T · 020 7159 2543 W · ecurie25.co.uk**

CHAUFFEURS

YES, M'LADY

> Twenty-one years in business and over 4,500 members speaks for itself. Members of the British Chauffeurs Guild are available to drive your car on a daily, weekly or long-term basis. Phone Lesley who will sort you out with a self-employed, permanent or temporary chauffeur. As they drive your vehicle, you will need to ring your insurance broker and make sure they are covered. The suited chauffeurs have all been on an intensive training course and are available 24 hours, 365 days of the year. Minimum charge is five hours @ £8.00 per hour, however you also have to pay a £23.50 agency fee per day, £5.00 travel costs, and any congestion charges and parking costs, so it could soon mount up – but what a treat!

> **British Chauffeurs Guild, 13 Stonecot Hill, Sutton, Surrey SM3 9HB T · 020 8641 1740 W · britishchauffeursguild.co.uk**

BOOK NOW FOR THE BAFTAS

> First choice for celebs, or so I've heard – Browns Chauffeur Hire offer an extensive list of cars from £42.00 per hour, or a Bentley or Rolls Royce for £75.00 an hour. They pride themselves on outstanding customer service, are very discreet and offer friendly, professionally trained, uniformed chauffeurs. They offer a nationwide service.

> **Browns Chauffeur Hire, 3 Victory Way, Heston, Middlesex TW5 9NS T · 0870 050 0605   W · bchlondon.com**

ALWAYS MAKE AN ENTRANCE

> I first booked one of the fabulous Karma Kabs for my husband's fortieth birthday and it arrived in true Bollywood-style. All the cars have different arty interiors – mosaic, chandeliers, zebra print … and they drive you s-l-o-w-l-y to your venue. There's no rush as

top speed is, as Sacha the owner states, "As fast as you can push" ... and we drank a bottle of champers in the back. Drivers have great knowledge and can give you advice on shopping or restaurants. Famous for delivering celebs to opening nights and fashion functions, this is the perfect gift for the 'star' in your house. Sacha and Tobias (owners) believe the journey is more important than the destination – all trips considered.

> **Karma Kabs T·020 8964 0700 W·karmakabs.com**

BIKER CHIC

> Celebrities are using it, business people are using it, so why aren't you? What with all the speed bumps, wrongly phased traffic lights, road works and sheer amount of cars in London, this truly is the quickest way to get from A to Z. Prices are on a zone system and, in some instances, slightly more than a black cab fare.

> **Virgin Limo Bike, 5th Floor, Communications Building, 48 Leicester Square, London WC2H 7LT T·020 7930 0814 W·virginlimobike.com**

HOLIDAY NANNY HIRE

MARY POPPINS IN CYBERSPACE

> A useful site to have in your Favourites, nannyjob.co.uk lists childcare positions, sought and offered. You could advertise that you want a nanny for three weeks for your trip to Antigua – you'll have no shortage of responses. Or if you don't want to wade through all the CVs, you can view all the UK childcare recruitment agencies and ask them to send you a shortlist of candidates – they would have already checked the CV, employment history and completed a CRB check. It also offers other great services, such as babysitters, nursery schools,

employment advice, special needs, overseas agencies, Au Pairs abroad, and helpful questions to ask at the interview. When I logged on, there were 3,221 jobs available and 3,162 nannies or child-carers looking for work.

> **W·nannyjob.co.uk**

TRUST IN TINIES

> With 22 branches in the UK, Tinies Childcare offer temporary and permanent childcare. All carers have a minimum of two years' experience, have been personally interviewed, and reference and CRB checked. Tinies offer holiday nannies for both the UK and abroad. The weekly fee to the agency is £90.00, plus you pay the nanny's entire expenses and then £7.00 per hour for childcare. Tinies can also offer maternity nurses.

> **Tinies Childcare T·020 7384 0322 W·tinies.com**

NORLAND NANNIES TAKE TO THE AIR

When we travelled to NZ on the 27-hour flight, I said to my husband, 'What they need is a little area for children to play, crawl and be entertained.' Well hats off to Gulf Air for providing, not the space, but a Norland-trained Nanny on all wide-bodied aircraft flying long-haul routes. How wonderful to have a nanny who is skilled in entertaining the children on the long flight and calming crying babies. She'll even feed your baby while you have a nap. Available to passengers in all classes, these seats are selling fast and not just to people with children – it's great for all the other passengers as well!

W·gulfairco.com

*Also look at **W·gumtree.com** which lists all sorts of offers from nanny and babysitting to selling your buggy. Our friend Louise, who now has four children under five, has found wonderful au pairs and mother's help through this site.*

SIGHTSEEING & TOURS

NEVER MISS THE MAIN EVENT

> This is a brilliant site – one you should log on to each and every time you go travelling. It allows you to plan your leisure time according to your interests and never miss an exciting event. Key in where you are going and choose from a drop-down menu of themes, from adventure to visual arts. I was intrigued by the 'bizarre' and wondered what it would offer my family on our trip to New York the following week. I loved the nine suggestions: one at the Empire State Building where on 1 February every year a selection of incredibly fit and fearless competitors gather to race up the 1,575 stairs from the lobby to the 86th floor. It is an invitation-only race (see online for an application form)
> The site is simple to use, up-to-date and speedy, with great cross-references for phone numbers, addresses and websites.
> **W·whatsonwhen.com**

LIVE FOR THE MOMENT

> This fabulous site is about 'the things you do when you get there'. There are over 4,000 tours and sightseeing products on offer, just waiting for you to key in your destination or choose from a selection of activities. Naturally I picked shopping and was delighted to discover that for £30.00 I could attend a New York Fashion Show; £14.00 would buy me a seven-hour tour of the Gucci and Prada outlets in Florence with up to 50 per cent discounts; and £28.00 was the small price to pay for an eight-hour shopping spree in Melbourne ... Mmm, hard to decide which one!
> Okay, for those of you who want to be a bit more adventurous, you could try a Seven-Day Tornado Chasing Tour (remember the film *Twister*?), take a Grand Canyon Jeep Tour, try a Seadog Speedboat ride on Lake Michigan, or ride your own four-wheeler through the Valley of Fire. My choice would be to participate in Top Dog Air Combat, where in San Diego you fly with active duty marine corps and navy pilots.
> If you know someone who is off on a holiday, why not surprise them with a ticket for a once-in-a-lifetime activity once they get there – I bet it will be one of the best presents they ever receive.
> **W·viator.com**

For shopping tours see page 194

A PLACE TO STAY

HOTELS WORTH A NIGHT OR TWO

It's time to get personal – massive resort complexes with 1,000 identical rooms are so 20th century. Now it's all about unique boutique hotels and personalised style. I thought being offered a selection of 11 pillows (including anti-snore, buckwheat and magnetic therapy) and nine honeys for my tea when I was in New York, and four firewoods for my hearth in Boston, was about as customer-centred as it got. I've since found out from jet-setting friends that I ain't seen nothin' yet ...

One particularly large acquaintance of mine swears by hotels that cater for the taller client and once stayed in a hotel where if you tried

out the bed and bought it, your accom-
modation was free. Another friend was told in
one establishment that she could borrow a
goldfish for her room if she was missing a pet,
and at other times has enjoyed a butler-drawn
bath with fresh rose petals, a choice of
30 soaps, foams, salts and oils chosen from a
leather-bound catalogue and, her children's
favourite, the glow-in-the-dark dinosaur soap.
And it's not only in America: I've heard that
Europe leads the way in letting you choose
your own furniture and even your bedcover
from a sleeping menu. It's a long way from
getting excited about an electric kettle and an
en-suite toilet!

FUNKY | DESIGNER

A DIGNIFIED RETREAT

> Chic Retreats has been founded with a lot of
hard work and determination by Lulu
Townsend. She represents private and
personal boutique hotels and villas with no
more than 30 rooms. Many are owner
operated, offering a fantastic personal
service and a passion for ensuring you have
the holiday of a lifetime. As Lulu says, "You
are a guest rather than a room number."

> You can book any one of the hotels online,
but even better, if you become a member,
(£20.00), you receive many benefits which
can include reduced rates, upgrades,
complimentary dinners and a massage, not
to mention the inspiring directory listing with
over 120 villas and hotels worldwide.

> Lulu has just included the fabulous Riad Noir
d'Ivoire in Marrakesh which she says is
"absolutely divine" (from €180). Peanuts, the
donkey, will take your luggage on arrival,
they issue you a mobile phone when you go
shopping and you only need push a button if
you get lost in the Medina! There is luxury
accommodation with a choice of six

bedrooms – one master suite, three junior
suites and two double bedrooms. A Jazz Bar,
traditional steam room, 24-hour massage
room, and a fabulous shop where they can
make anything in 24 hours are all on hand.

> The Riad also offers a heated courtyard pool,
jacuzzi and a chillout zone on the roof
terrace. And a lovely touch, if you're sitting in
the courtyard and it becomes too hot, a very
fine spray mist will cool and refresh... What,
you haven't booked yet?.

> **Chic Retreats T · 020 7978 7164 /**
07879 812224   W · chicretreats.com

COOLER BY DESIGN

> If you're overwhelmed by the choice of where
to stay – go to the experts. The world's most
state-of-the-art hotels have been brought
together in a collection called Design Hotels
and new members are joining every year.
Their website will tell you everything you
need to know about each hotel and show you
photos, along with special rates. To focus
your options yet further, these are my top
'design' choices:

> The Gray is one of Milan's most jealously-
guarded secrets, with 21 guestrooms – two
offering private steam rooms and two with
separate private gyms – you'll need to book
quickly to beat the fashionistas.

> If business or pleasure should take you to
Nottingham, the only place to stay is the Lace
Market Hotel. Modern bespoke furniture,
brushed steel finishes and natural colours
add to the overall feeling of 21st-century
style. We suggest you book one of the three
funky studios.

> The Outpost, in Kruger National Park, would
be worth it simply for its outside bath with
views to die for. There's plenty more, in fact,
but I don't want to spoil the surprises!

> And of course we can't leave out New York
and the wonderfully inspiring Chambers
Hotel that is an inner-city retreat famous for
its apartment-like touches and superior

amenities. Book a suite with a terrace with panoramic views where you can sit back with a glass of champers and enjoy the buzz of the Big Apple.

> Book any of their hotels online or through the toll-free international reservation numbers (see online for each country's number). And if finding the best hotel is a hobby of yours, buy and drool over their fab bi-annual magazine (€10).

> **Design Hotels T·00 800 3746 8357**
  W·designhotels.com

WHAT A FOXY NUMBER

> If you're heading to Copenhagen, be sure to stay a night or two at Hotel Fox. Originally the hotel came together as an event – Project Fox – linked to the launch of a new car from Volkswagen – The Fox. Volkswagen invited 21 young designers from the fields of graphic design, art and illustration to create the interior of Hotel Fox. Sixty-one rooms and 21 artists produced some unique and amazing ideas, with each room an individual piece of art. The rooms cater to a variety of moods – you can choose mystical rooms with magicians, jesters and fortune-tellers, rooms filled with text and typography, foxy women, friendly monster creatures, mock surveillance cameras or punch bags, and one with a tent in the middle of the room.

> They offer all the usual services – great breakfasts, high-speed internet, flat screens and a roof terrace – and I especially love their minibar bags which you customise from the Hangoverbag, Moviebag or Loversbag. They also offer a fab 'Ask Me' service, where their panel of experts can point you in the right direction for hip shopping, including the best second-hand shops, music, clubs, restaurants, sport or art.

> Try their Tour de Fox, a three-night stay in three different rooms (from 605DKK per person per night) which should give you an overall flavour of this groovy hotel. Individual

room rates range from €125 for the small to €215 for the extra large rooms (all rates include breakfast and VAT).

> **Hotel Fox, Jarmers Plads 3, DK-1551**
  Copenhaagen V, Denmark
  T·+45 33 95 77 55
  bookings +45 33 13 30 00 W·hotelfox.dk

NIGHT NIGHT, SLEEP TIGHT

> I have never, ever seen such an unusual and interesting hotel as the Propeller Island City Lodge. Each guest receives a different experience, as everything is custom-made for each room. Styles range from the tame Room 44 with futuristic computer paintings, to the rather extreme Room 31 where you can choose to sleep in a coffin or in the labyrinth below!

> Everything at the Lodge was created by the German artist Lars Stroschen who wants you to feel like you're 'living in a work of art'. Their website is very comprehensive and shows you a picture of each of the 30 rooms. In Room 3 you can sleep in a castle which has its own miniature golf course; the bed in Room 12 is suspended from the beams with ship's rope; Room 23 is the upside-down room – all furnishings hang from the ceiling and you sleep and sit in boxes beneath the floorboards; you access the bathroom of Room 27 through the wardrobe; and in Room 42 you can sleep in a cage or the double bed and soak in the beautiful wooden bath with balcony. I know I wouldn't even be able to go into the diamond-shaped Room 15, which is completely decorated with mirrors – I'd spend my whole time wondering 'does my bum look big in this room?'!

> What's more, I love the fact that if you fancy checking out another room, flip the sign on your door to 'I'll show you mine if you show me yours' and go and have a good snoop.

> They're even under legal obligation to write 'Instructions for Use' for every room, which you are given when you check in! Prices:

rooms €69–€190 for one person and an additional €15 for each further person in the room (some rooms sleep four); breakfast €7 per person.

> **Propeller Island City Lodge, Albrecht Achilles Str. 58, 10709 Berlin, Germany T · +49 30 891 9016 until noon / +49 163 256 5909 W · propeller-island.com**

EVER THOUGHT OF SLEEPING UNDERWATER?

> Probably one of the most unusual places for a hotel I have ever seen, the Utter Inn is the place to stay as long as you don't suffer from claustrophobia. Built by Mikael Genberg, a local artist and sculptor who has built one tree-house hotel, one underwater hotel, one café – where you drink coffee in chairs that are five metres high – and one toilet! He believes we all need to experience fear and risk-taking from time to time.

> Utter Inn (or, in English, Otter Inn) is situated on Lake Mälaren near Västerå, approximately 100 km west of Stockholm (Ryanair flies daily from Stansted to Västerå).

> It looks like a small Swedish red house with white gables, except that it floats. As a guest, you're taken 1 km out onto the lake by an inflatable boat, receive your instructions and then you're on your own, except if you have opted for the Deluxe option, in which case you'll be visited later that evening with supper. Three metres down, you'll be staying the night in twin beds with little else other than a bedside table. Oh, did I mention the panoramic windows in all directions? Anyway, it is tiny and you'll feel like you're in an aquarium. This unique experience costs from £50.00 per person, including dinner and breakfast delivered by boat.

> **Utter Inn, Lake Mälaren – Sweden T +46 (0) 2139 0100 (Tourist information Västerås) E · malarstaden@vasteras.se**

PURE HEAVEN

ARE YOU READY FOR A SECOND HONEY MOO?

> If you are organised enough to book far in advance, Babington House in Somerset is the perfect place to take the one you love. There are 28 bedrooms in this Georgian, country-house hotel and usually all of them are full. They are spread over four buildings and all have big beds, flat screens, DVD players, satellite, stereos and wireless internet.

> Highlights are their glorious baths, either stand-alone or sunken, and showers with enormous showerheads. If you make it outside, the grounds are extensive, with chapel, lake, tennis courts, cricket pitch and croquet lawn. Bicycles are available, and if the British weather isn't your friend there are indoor and outdoor pools, a gym and a sauna. As if that wasn't enough, The Shop, owned by Lulu Anderson, stocks great clothes, accessories and jewellery.

> Service is superb and they have added lovely touches – every guest is truly treated as an individual. They can put together walks for you or have a nanny baby-sit while you relax in the Cowshed Spa, which offers fantastic treatments – perhaps try the Honey Moo Massage for two. They even offer a private cinema so you can catch up on recent releases without leaving the hotel and, for late risers, the fantastic breakfast is served till noon.

> Other treats, such as games nights, retreats, parties or brainstorming sessions, can be arranged. From £225.00 per night (I have seen last minute offers on their site for £185.00).

> **Babington House, Babington near Frome, Somerset BA11 3RW T · 01373 812 266 W · babingtonhouse.co.uk**

A MONTH'S SALARY CAN LAST A LIFETIME

> When I next get an unexpected windfall I'm going to treat us and our friends to a weekend in Spring Cottage – the memories would last a lifetime.

> This three-bedroom cottage is set in the beautiful grounds of Cliveden House. It sleeps six, has two living rooms, a tearoom (who could live without one?) and a luxury kitchen, complete with your own private butler who will serve you all a sumptuous breakfast. This is included in the price, along with a fully sized fridge, filled with luxury provisions like champagne and wild salmon. The chauffeur is on hand to take you up to the main house for a fabulous dinner, or you could simply call for the chef to come and cook for you in the cottage. Your butler is there to ensure every whim is catered to – fire lit, the beds turned down, drinks in the garden – or he can leave you completely alone if you wish.

> In the secluded garden, where Queen Victoria has taken tea, you could host a fantastic dinner party in the most tranquil setting.

> Use of the spa, sauna, steam rooms, indoor and outdoor pool, and hot tubs are also included in the rate (from £1,695.00 per night), and for a little extra you could book spa treatments or, if you're a nautical bunch, you could hire any of the three luxury vintage boats – *The Belmont*, a 33 foot Slipper launch; *The Liddesdale*, a silent electric canoe or the prize winning *Suzy Ann* – I'll be the one sunning myself on deck with a glass of champagne!

> **Spring Cottage, Cliveden House, Taplow SL6 0JF T·01628 668 561 W·clivedenhouse.co.uk**

CASHMERE SHEETS AND IN-ROOM TREATS

> Cotswold House is a country-house hotel set in an historic town, with beautiful touches that will make it hard for you to leave. You can design your own bedroom with tailor-made options, from choosing the pillow to pre-booking the contents of the minibar to include your favourite tipple. Other in-room surprises include aromatherapy candles and special bath menus, and a collection of classic CDs and DVDs. You will sleep on cashmere under-blankets and Frette linen.

> Each of the 30 rooms is unique, including three suites and several garden cottages. For a truly fairytale break, book Hidcote Cottage with a doorway to your own secret garden and hot tub (from £425.00). Special treats can be pre-arranged, and on one of their designated nights you can hire the entire hotel for up to 60 people at a cost of £11,000 (that's only £183.33 each!) which includes bed and breakfast.

> If there are four of you, it would be good value to pay £181.25 each and book the Old Grammar School Suite which has a fully-fitted kitchen, with the option of a 'chef for the night', a magnificent drawing room, two double bedrooms and two bathrooms (one *en-suite*).

> If you're feeling particularly sociable, they can even cater for a private cocktail party for up to 20 people. And your other family members don't have to miss out on all the fun. Child cots are available and dogs and cats are very welcome. Special packages are available throughout the year so either call them or look on their website. My advice is book now and live life the way it should be. Rooms from £150.00.

> **Cotswold House, The Square, Chipping Campden, Gloucestershire GL55 6AN T·01386 840 330 W·cotswoldhouse.com**

SOMETIMES ONLY THE 'BEST' WILL DO

> This gorgeous 30-bedroom Georgian mansion with its chic interior is set in 55 acres with glorious gardens, a lake and a river. I love the room categories – good, better, great, exceptional and best. The 'best' room really is the best in the house, offering a big modern four-poster bed, a huge bathroom

with a tub for two, superb views over the lake and countryside, and your own private terrace. The other rooms are impressive too. Some are split over two levels, others have a private terrace, others have separate sitting rooms – something for all tastes. Great treatments are on offer in their C-side Spa complete with gym, sauna, indoor and outdoor pools. They also offer an (unsupervised) playroom for children and baby-sitting by prior arrangement. If you are there for the last Sunday of the month, make sure you pop down to Cheltenham racecourse for the weekly boot fair.

> All rates include a full breakfast, VAT and service, starting from £245.00.

> **Cowley Manor, Cowley, Gloucestershire GL53 9NL T · 01242 870 900 W · cowleymanor.com**

VIEW FROM THE TOP

> This magnificent Cornish hotel is set high on a cliff with stunning views over the bay and its own private beach. With just ten rooms, all with elegant, minimalist interiors, my sister-in-law said 'it was the best hotel we have ever stayed in.' A hidden attraction, down a secret pathway in the garden, away from the main hotel and overlooking the beach, is a cabin which you can book from £200.00.

> Driftwood offers a very personal service with unique touches such as picnics and massages. Children are welcome. Prices: from £170.00 including VAT, breakfast, newspapers and morning coffee and biscuits. There is an excellent restaurant and in low season the evening meal is included in the room price.

> **Driftwood, Rosevine, near Portscatho, South Cornwall TR2 5EW T · 01872 580 644 W · driftwoodhotel.co.uk**

A PLACE OF CHARM

> Jeake's House is so charming that after our first night there we simply had to go back for

another stay. The house stands on one of the ancient cobbled streets of Rye and was originally built as a wool store in 1689. Rye is great for shopping, especially antiques and bric-a-brac, and is a bustling market town filled with ancient architecture, cobbled streets, a Norman church, art galleries and friendly pubs.

> Jenny Hadfield and Richard Martin run a relaxed, comfortable, friendly establishment and will go out of their way to accommodate your requests. They can even arrange champagne and flowers in your room for any special occasion. The house is furnished in keeping with its interesting history, with low beams, antique furniture, brass or mahogany bedsteads and a stunning red galleried hall/breakfast room. I loved this colour so much I had to ask Jenny what paint it was so I could buy the same colour for a room in our house.

> If you're planning to stay for a few nights book the Conrad Aiken four-poster suite (£61.00 per person), a lovely, light room with a relaxing window-seat that makes you want to lie and read in the sun. Most of the 11 rooms have *en-suite* facilities and all have been individually restored to create their own special atmosphere – we also love the Radclyffe Hall four-poster suite (£56.00 per person) and the Lowry Suite (£59.00 per person). No evening meals are served, but there's a good selection of restaurants all within walking distance. You can then come back for a night cap and relax in the book-lined honesty bar. If driving, you need to unload your luggage and then park in their private car park which is down the hill. The breakfasts are scrummy, with a choice of traditional or vegetarian. You'll also be very warmly welcomed by their two Tonkinese cats, Yum Yum and Monte.

> **Jeake's House, Mermaid Street, Rye, East Sussex TN31 7ET T · 01797 222 828 W · jeakeshouse.com**

INTERNATIONAL

LOUNGING LAKESIDE

> Writing about Hotel Villagiulia brings back very warm memories. If you take one of the three Villa Giulia (junior suites) with a balcony and glorious lake views (not expensive at €315 and there are deals available for stays of more than four days) you have a fantastic view looking out over Lake Garda. The Hotel has been in the family for over 45 years and the Bombardelli family make you feel so welcome – it is a real home away from home. The hotel grounds and pool (you also have immediate access into the lake for a quick dip if you prefer) are so enticing we didn't want to leave them, although we did drag ourselves off the poolside loungers to hop on a ferry to Limone and Malcesine for the mandatory shopping. I'd like to offer a review of the local restaurants, but the dinners at the hotel were so delicious I don't remember trying anywhere else! Prices from €210 and includes breakfast, the use of the swimming pool and whirlpool, the Turkish bath, sauna and gym, the beach, car park and all local taxes.

> Hotel Villagiulia, 25084 Gargnano sul
  Garda, Brescia, Italy
  T·+39 0365 710 22 / 0365 712 89
  W· villagiulia.it

A GRAND NIGHT INN

> Lake Garda is one of my favourite holiday destinations in Italy, and next time we go back we have promised ourselves we will stay at Villa Feltrinelli. Set in the small town of Gargnano, once described by DH Lawrence as 'one of the most beautiful places on earth', The Grand Hotel a Villa Feltrinelli, originally built in 1892, was painstakingly refurbished in the late 1990s. It now offers 21 individually decorated guestrooms and suites, some with hand-painted fresco ceilings from the 1890s, and all with French porcelain bathtubs. Thirteen of the rooms and the grand library and salon, complete with antique Venetian mirrors, are in the Villa.

> The rest of the rooms are in four guest-houses, the most luxurious of all being The Boat House. This is a charming little one-bedroom house at the water's edge with full kitchen, dining area (opens over the lake), living room, fireplace, outdoor patio, a huge dressing area and a white marble bath. It also has its own sailing boat and dock and valet. From €2800 per night.

> Grand Hotel a Villa Feltrinelli, Via
  Rimembranza 38–40, 25084 Gargnano,
  Italy   T·(+39) 0365 798 000
  W· villafeltrinelli.com

FIVE GOOD REASONS TO STAY ANOTHER NIGHT

> We stayed at Quinta das Sequóias and had originally made a booking for the minimum requirement of two nights – when we arrived we were so-o-o-o taken with this gorgeous house we stayed for five nights (we did have to move rooms though). The views on the drive to the hotel are of the hills, coast and Palace of Le Pena, as Quinta das Sequóias is set amidst the woods surrounding Sintra, just 45 minutes from Lisbon airport. There are only six rooms in the main house, but what rooms, each uniquely decorated. Ours had a great view over the treetops to the Palace and our bathroom was amazing, like showering outside in a rock pool with a waterfall. The interior of the house is filled with antique furniture and interesting collectors' pieces, and you eat breakfast with the other guests in the communal dining room, all seated at the lavishly laid grand table. The grounds are divine – lovely terraced garden with plenty of secluded spots for a quiet read, painting or catching up on lost sleep. It also has a pool and adjoining sauna. Open all year, but sadly they

don't allow children under 12. €145-160 per night, including breakfast, taxes and service.

> **Quinta das Sequóias, Ap. 1004, 2710 Sintra, Portugal T· +351 21 923 0342 W· quintadasequoias.com**

HOME AWAY FROM HOME

HOTEL ALTERNATIVES

If you're fed up with your family running up huge bills on room service, the secret when you visit London is to stay in an all-suites hotel or serviced apartment. They rival hotels for luxury, offer all the usual mod cons of the boutique hotels, and mean you can eat whatever you please and entertain whomever you please, whenever you please. Perfect for the traveller who doesn't like sticking to rules!

THE GOOD, THE BAD AND THE DARN-NEAR PERFECT

> This is probably the one I would choose for an alternative to a hotel when staying in central London. Located just off Regent Street, here one can live, work, eat, relax, sleep and entertain with complete freedom. There are 12 one-, two- or three-bedroom suites, each with all the mod cons and state-of-the-art technology you'd expect, with many of the suites also offering decked balconies and open fireplaces. Bamboo flooring, an organic colour palette and tactile natural materials have been used throughout. With your own private kitchen facilities, you could walk to Selfridges' Food Hall and rustle up a private banquet. Or if you're more of a 'can't cook, won't cook'

guest, then they can organise a private chef to cook for you, or you have the option of 24-hour room service.

> I loved the Big Bar marked 'good' and 'bad' – one of which offers organic *penne* pasta and fruit juices and the other loads of chocolate bars, crisps and lots of alcohol. Everything in moderation is my motto ... and then another serving for luck!

> All suites have a workstation with voicemail, fax and high-speed internet access, while imaginative optional extras include a secretarial service, hire of computer equipment, personal grocery shopping, therapies including Thai and holistic massage, pedicures, Pilates, private fitness training, catered dinner parties and bikes for you to explore the city.

> I also love their website which offers a choice of great tips and guides – really useful stuff. Prices from £260-£640.00 per night.

> **No 5 Maddox Street, Mayfair, London W1S 2QD T· 020 7647 0200 W· 5maddoxstreet.com**

YOUR OWN PRIVATE PLACE

> A five-star town house, all-suites hotel, just three minutes' walk from Buckingham Palace, 51 Buckingham Gate has discreetly welcomed its own fair share of VIP inhabitants, from Prime Ministers to rock stars, sporting legends to film icons, even a reality-TV guru – and I'm pretty sure whoever booked it for him didn't end up fired!

> The three individually-designed buildings contain 82 luxury apartments, including six suites, all of which offer a fully-equipped kitchen, a spacious reception room with suede and leather furnishings, CD and DVD player, fax/printer and dataport, and bedlinen of the finest Egyptian cotton. All apartments also have access to the library, restaurants, fitness and health spa (nominated as one of the world's 100 best spas by *Harpers Bazaar* (formerly *Harper's &*

Queen), nanny service, personal shoppers and chauffeured limousines.

> As if all that wasn't enough, every apartment guest has access to a personal and discreet butler! Your own personal Jeeves just waiting to run your bath, unpack your suitcase, function as a private secretary, or even organise in-room dining for a private dinner party or reception.

> Apartments can be rented for a night or a year, and prices start from £360.00 for a Junior suite. The Deluxe apartments with a personal butler service start from £835.00 a night, but if money is no object, the only way to go is the Prime Minister's Suite: This includes a dining room to seat ten, up to five bedrooms with a spiral staircase linking two suites, personal butler service and superb kitchens stocked with Villeroy & Bosch tableware and finest Wedgewood china. The perfect excuse to invite the Queen round for tea.

> **51 Buckingham Gate, London SW1E 6AF**
T· 020 7769 7766
W· 51-buckinghamgate.com
USA 1 877 528 2503 toll free

BLOSSOM WITH THE BLOOMSBURY SET

> If you, or perhaps an overseas visitor, are looking for a traditional English place to stay, book (them) into The Academy. Set in the heart of Bloomsbury and created by linking five spectacular Georgian town houses together, this hotel offers 49 guest rooms with all the comforts you'd expect from a luxury hotel.

> Restored Georgian décor throughout; some of the bedrooms have split-level bathrooms and free-standing, claw-footed baths, others offer a private patio garden for catching the rays. They also give you personalised business cards on arrival with your room telephone number – lovely touch.

> The Academy features a library, conservatory and two private gardens, so no excuse not to get outside and smell the roses. Prices from £140.00 (not including breakfast).

> **The Academy, 21 Gower Street, Bloomsbury, London WC1E 6HG**
T· 020 7631 4115
W· theetoncollection.com

BECOME TO THE MANOR BORN

> The lovely Lena Proudlock of Denim, Furniture and Photography Fame (*see page 293*) offers her gorgeous-with-a-capital G, five-star, eight-bedroom, Cotswold Georgian town house – Berkeley House. It has been recently refurbished with no expense spared and the stunning décor has been featured in many interior-design magazines from Sydney to Shanghai.

> Situated in Tetbury – a shopping haven for those of us who love antiques – it's also a great place from which to explore the Cotswolds, Bristol or Bath.

> All the mod cons are included, such as luxurious towels, bathrobes, Molton Brown products, PS2 game library and WiFi broadband. The kitchen is a Xera, designed by Italian architects, and is wonderful for all of you who love to cook. However, if cooking is far from your mind, you can have locally prepared, ready-to-eat meals delivered, or a visiting chef, or opt for live-in staff. Therapeutic or rejuvenating treatments can be arranged at the house and Lena, a professional photographer, can also offer her photographic services if you're hosting a party and fancy having the event photographed.

> The main house has seven bedrooms – four doubles and three twins – and three bath or shower rooms, two *en suite*. The kitchen/breakfast room leads into a conservatory dining room (seats 16) overlooking the courtyard garden. There's also the possibility of hiring the new Orangery and attached Coach House as well, providing a large, flexible space for

entertaining (can seat 30 for dinner). And only a minute's walk across the square is the stunning two-bedroomed Bay Tree Court (as well as the new Chipping Apartment). Taking all three properties means you could sleep up to 30 (including four children under the age of eight). The gardens have been designed by Philip Nixon, a two time gold-medal winner at Chelsea Flower Show.

> Berkeley can be rented with or without the Orangery & Coach House; Bay Tree is available with Berkeley or separately. When Berkeley is not let, The Orangery & Coach House are available at £150.00 per night (subject to a minimum three-night stay at weekends). All are available for a three-day weekend, Monday to Friday, a week, a month or longer. Berkeley (ex. Orangery & Coach House) costs from £2,500.00 (including VAT if applicable) for a three-night weekend for up to 14 people, self-catered; £3,350.00 for Monday to Friday and £5,000.00 for a whole week (including Orangery & Coach House).

> **Lena Proudlock, Berkeley House, 4 The Chipping, Tetbury, Gloucestershire GL8 8ET T· 01666 500 051 W· lenaproudlockescapes.com**

GAME, SET AND MATCH TO SLOANE STREET

> Boasting one of London's most fashionable addresses, steps away from Harrods and Harvey Nichols, Durley House is an all-suites hotel with eleven elegantly-furnished suites, each including its own kitchen – so you could create a gourmet extravaganza or host a private cocktail party or a dinner party for eight. You also have full use of the private park and gardens of Cadogan Square, where you can book the tennis courts via reception. They will be happy to organise a tennis coach and loan of rackets and balls. The hotel's butlers will serve you room service 24-hours a day, but there is no restaurant. If you book far enough in advance, you could even have

the whole house. Prices £365-£645.00 per suite.

> **Durley House, 115 Sloane Street, London SW1X 9PJ T· 020 7235 5537 W· durleyhouse.com**

From break-the-bank gorgeous to basic and affordable, there's a large selection of serviced apartments in London.

GREAT SERVICE INCLUDED

> Having done all of the groundwork for you by researching the best serviced apartments in London, this company can offer you a totally independent recommendation, special rates (up to 30 per cent off hotel prices) and great locations. Ring Roy McKenzie, tell him what you want by way of location, price or facilities, and he'll advise you on the best available apartment, anything from a studio to a three-storey town house. Most come equipped with a living room to relax and entertain in, space to work, cooking facilities, washing machines and dryers, use of nearby spas, private parking, dry-cleaning and laundry services, and even a free shopping service. If you want to just book through the website, the apartments are divided into Economy, Mid-Range and Luxury categories, or you can search by area or special offers. Let's say six of you rented a three-bedroom, you'd pay just under £52.00 each for an economy apartment, or for £80.00 each four of you could share a luxury apartment. You can stay from one night to as long as you like (one person has stayed three years!), and if you are relocating to London or staying for extended business, some offer a large board-room. Oh, and you'll get a welcome pack with pre-ordered groceries, very useful if you're arrived from the airport late at night.

> **London Serviced Apartments, Brookscroft House, 26 Second Avenue, London E17 9QH T· 020 8923 0918 W· londonservicedapartments.co.uk**

OH, I DO LIKE TO BE
BESIDE THE SEASIDE

There's nothing like the wind in your hair and the smell of sea air to revive and renew after one-too-many hours stuck in rush-hour traffic. The sound of gulls, the feel of salt spray... hence my quest for seaside hotels, and if you can view the sea while lying in bed drinking a good old cup of British tea, even better!

SNUGGLE UP WITH A SMUGGLER'S VIEW

> For our next wedding anniversary our friends have told us to book into a unique 17th-century inn (reputed to have been the haunt of local smugglers) in the quaint fishing village of Portloe. Specifically, they've told us to book room 201 for one of the best sea views and our own terrace. Following a major renovation programme, the hotel is all pale colours, sea grass, crisp linen, bleached wood and warm welcomes (except if you have children under 12, who unfortunately are not allowed).

> We're especially looking forward to pampering ourselves in The Spa, which offers facials, reiki, reflexology, massage, manicures and pedicures, or an Indian head massage. The 21 bedrooms are divided between three different houses and most of the rooms have either a harbour or sea view (do check on booking).

> The hotel can also organise tickets for you to the popular Eden Project – an experimental biosphere with the largest conservatory in the world. Rooms from £160.00.

> **The Lugger, Portloe, Truro, Cornwall TR2 5RD T·01872 501 322 W·luggerhotel.co.uk**

BOOK A WEEK OF MOTHERING SUNDAYS!

> Probably one of the nicest seaside hotels in the UK, and certainly one of the most family-friendly, Tresanton, a former yachting club, was built from a collection of old houses on different levels. Twenty seven of the 29 bright, light and contemporary rooms, some with a terrace, have views of the sea, and all rooms are furnished with antiques and Cornish art. There are two family suites with terrace, which can accommodate up to three children each. A firm favourite with mums who actually want a break on holiday, the hotel has a spacious children's room, a lovely Wendy House and a cinema to entertain younger guests. Baby-sitting can also be booked in advance and during the summer months a full-time nanny organises activities for the children.

> Tresanton will pack you a picnic, hire you a boat and point you in the direction of local beaches or rivers, or you can hire their 48-ft sailing yacht with crew. Look on their website for the latest events on offer – I'm planning on a great Detoxifying Yoga Package for after Christmas and there are also bridge courses, painting weeks and a Sarah Key Spinal Therapy Programme. Lovely beauty and massage treatments are also offered. Rooms from £175.00.

> **Hotel Tresanton, St Mawes, Cornwall TR2 5DR T·01326 270 055 W·tresanton.com**

IF IT'S GOOD ENOUGH FOR MOVIE STARS...

> Having tried copious times to get a room – I am going to keep trying until I can stay in this lovely 11-roomed hotel on the Holkham Estate. Still owned by the present Earl of Leicester, The Victoria at Holkham is designed around Victorian, Colonial and local themes. Much talked about, as it leads to one of the best beaches in Britain, you may well remember it from its starring role in *Shakespeare in Love*.

> The hotel can organise sailing, horse riding, seal trips and cycling. They offer a weekend package (Friday and Saturday) but you can't book these days on a single-night basis. Ask for the Marsh room for an excellent view and loads of space — but not when I'm trying to book it please! From £120.00, with an extra charge for children of £15.00 (apart from the attic suite).
> **The Victoria, Park Road, Holkham, Norfolk NR23 1RG T· 01328 711 008 W· holkham.co.uk/victoria**

BUDGET CONSCIOUS
LONDON

CHEAPER THAN A CAB FARE HOME!

> You've probably flown easyJet and driven easyCar, so why not go for the hat trick? Look at easyGroup's first foray into accommodation with easyHotel.
> Opened in Kensington, Earl's Court and Victoria, London (and now one in Basel, Switzerland), they offer rooms from £25.00 per night — 'the earlier you book, the less you pay' (but with no restaurant or other services). So if you are staying more than one night, expect to make your own bed unless you pay the extra charges. The rooms do offer a private shower, washbasin and lavatory, and come in three sizes — tiny, small and very small. Some of them won't have any windows, but will of course offer air conditioning. Perhaps not ideal for that special weekend away, but if you can't face a late commute, it's almost certainly cheaper than a taxi fare home — you do however have to book through the website.
> **W· easyhotel.com**

Also See Yotel (page 108)

FOR THE SHOPAHOLIC
LONDON

STYLISH RETREAT FOR A SPOT OF SHOPPING

> Another little gem from the Firmdale Hotels, the Knightsbridge Hotel is a wonderfully comfortable and welcoming place to stay in the heart of the city. You're within a stone's throw of Knightsbridge shopping — Harrods and Harvey Nichols — but you're on a quiet tree-lined street. The 44 bedrooms (and two suites) are each uniquely decorated in modern, fresh, individual designs, from warm neutrals to dramatic bold colours, and best of all there are Miller Harris products in all the bathrooms.
> As well as all the facilities needed by us modern travellers, throughout the honesty bar, the drawing room and the library (which can be hired for functions) there is stunning artwork by Peter Clark, of which I wanted to own at least eight pieces.
> There is a very reasonably priced room service but no restaurant, and do check regarding breakfast as some days the cost of breakfast is not included in your room rate. From £195.00 double; £160.00 for a single. To book any of the seven other Firmdale hotels, visit W· firmdale.com
> **Knightsbridge Hotel, 10 Beaufort Gardens, London SW3 1PT T· 020 7584 6300 W· knightsbridgehotel.com**

ANTIQUE LOVERS' PARADISE

> Only ten minutes from Portobello Antiques Market (can't go wrong there), an unmarked red door leads up into Miller's Residence, a small, luxury, 18th-century-style hotel. There are only seven rooms, five doubles and two suites, with one suite including a kitchen lounge and dining area. Each room is very individual, named after Romantic poets and filled with antiques and other desirables from

a bygone era. I loved the Byron room, but ask for the Tennyson room as it gets the sun all day. In the spacious lounge, decorated with antique furniture, guests sit around the carved oak fireplace helping themselves to wine and spirits at no extra charge. (From £150.00, including breakfast.)

> And if you're no Lovejoy when it comes to antiques they have a Miller's Antique Lovers' Weekend, which is absolutely fab. The offer includes a visit to Portobello Antiques Market, dinner on Saturday night, hosted by Ioana and Martin Miller – the author of *Miller's Antiques Guide* and followed on Sunday with a lovely brunch (maximum of seven couples from £475.00 per couple).

> **Miller's Residence, 111a Westbourne Grove, London W2 4UW T·020 7243 1024 W·millersuk.com**

See also Parkes Hotel (page 166)

HOTELS
BOOKING ONLINE

YOU'D BE MAD TO MISS OUT

> Used by the hotel industry for offering over 500,000 discounted hotel rooms throughout Europe and the UK, you're bound to find the right accommodation for your next trip – after all, they would rather reduce the rate than have an empty bed.

> This site offers reductions of up to 70 per cent on late room bookings on the day you log on for the following week, in four- and five-star hotels, B&Bs, guesthouses and apartments. Each hotel enters its own rate daily to reflect availability. Click on the hotel of your choice and it will give you a unique

reference number to either book online or by phone. Once you have chosen your city, you can then narrow it down by postcode, underground station or district, which is very handy for a big city offering hundreds of rooms. I found a £130.00 reduction in a great hotel in London.

> I can't help but mention that they also have a sister website (W·latelet.com) offering over 50,000 holiday cottages, villas, gîtes and apartments.

> **T·0870 300 6969 W·laterooms.com**

LANDMARK DEALS

> With over 30,000 hotels in 350 major destinations in North America, the Caribbean, Europe and Asia, you can save yourself up to 70 per cent on accommodation in some of the world's most popular and expensive cities. Guaranteed low rates and last-minute deals. And I'm delighted to say they have just added Bed & Breakfast accommodation.

> **T·0871 200 0171 W·hotels.com**

JUST WHAT THE DOCTOR ORDERED

> Tablet Hotels claim they're the cure for boring travel – and I tend to agree. They wade through thousands of hotels to bring you a fine selection that have been through a rigorous review process as well as being visited, anonymously. There is also a handy rating guide from guests who have stayed in the hotels, which I found really helpful when I was making our choice for Singapore (where we stayed at the Scarlet Hotel). There is no fee for a hotel to be included, nor can a hotel pay to be included. They not only list the hotels, but help you through the whole reservation process and can offer some very good rates. They have a top-10 list, where the hotels are categorised (by customer scores) into sections such as Best Hotel Overall, Unusual Hotels, Best of Europe, Beach Hotels, Kid-Friendly Hotels, Seduction Hotels and so on. Well worth a browse. Tablet Hotels have

offices in the USA, Japan, France, Italy and Spain.

> **W · tablethotels.com**

Also look at the fabulous W · unusualhotelsoftheworld.com which offers some very very unique accommodation. Next holiday — sorted!

VILLA RENTALS

If you've ever written 'Wish you were here' on a postcard home and meant it, going on holiday with a group of friends could be for you. However, traveller beware, there's a big difference between sharing an hilarious evening in a restaurant before heading home in separate cabs, and spending a week or two under the same roof in a foreign land. So remember, set some ground rules and make sure there's enough space for the occasional 'time out'.

BOOK NOW FOR A HOLIDAY IN HEAVEN

> Close your eyes and imagine you're on holiday — waking at 10.30 a.m., the children are being looked after by the nanny, so you've been able to have a good lie-in. After breakfast on the terrace (cooked by your own chef), you meet your tennis coach for a lesson, then to cool off you dive into the infinity pool for a quick 20 laps. Lie down on the sun lounger and pick up your novel (such a treat — when did you last read a book?) and catch a few rays before checking on the children, who are having a whale of a time with all the toys and games organised. Then it's off to lunch. The afternoon amounts to one hour of private yoga lessons, a sauna in the spa and a massage which has all been organised for you.

> This may all sound like the hallucination of an exhausted mother, but it can be reality

when you hire a villa from Abercrombie & Kent. You simply have to choose from over 300 spectacular villas, from farmhouses in Tuscany to windmills in Provence and fully staffed resort villas in Cyprus.

> All the villas are personally inspected by the company before being offered to you, and many of them come with swimming pools and maid service. Each villa is graded so you know exactly what kind of property/services to expect.

> As already mentioned, they can offer lovely extras such as chefs, nannies, butlers, tennis lessons, private jets or helicopter transfer. They can even arrange all your flights and car hire.

> **Abercrombie & Kent   T · 0845 0700 618 W · abercrombiekent.co.uk**

PRIVATE PROPERTIES

> Interhome offers private homes and they have exclusive contracts with all the owners. Based in Switzerland, they have over 20,000 quality apartments, houses, rental villas, chalets and cottages on their lists.

> Located in 15 European countries and areas of the USA (Florida and Miami), they also have a good selection of large properties for families. I love that you can choose a 'wish' list of all the properties you'd like to stay at and they can send you a personalised brochure.

> **Interhome   T · 020 8891 1294 W · interhome.co.uk**

SPOILT FOR CHOICE

> I love their mantra: 'He who searches finds …', and you most certainly will find your ideal holiday rental on Latroba's website. You can search by country or by viewing the holiday destination pictures. Trouble is, they have such a lovely selection it's difficult to choose only one. Still there's always next year…

> **W · latroba.co.uk**

WHO SAYS YOU CAN'T GET NO SATISFACTION?

> Want to sleep in Mick Jagger's bed? Of course he won't be in it, but you can rent his very secluded Caribbean, Japanese-style beachfront villa on the tiny island of Mustique. This dream home has six bedrooms (sleeps 10), five bathrooms, a jeep that seats eight, a pool, hot tub, games room, croquet lawn, pond, and a staff of six who can prepare luxurious picnics with the finest crystal and china, champagne and caviar, lobster and succulent fruits. We understand that Mick reviews every application personally, so let's hope you pass the muster (from approx $14,000 to $18,000.00 weekly).

> I don't know about you, but I am saving for the only house on Necker Island in the British Virgin Islands – the private 74-acre island owned by Richard Branson. It has 12 bedrooms (sleeps 28), piano, excellent music system, gym equipment, business facilities, snooker and bridge tables, and a staff of 22. This paradise includes freshwater pools, Jacuzzis, beaches with beach huts, and floodlit tennis courts. You can windsurf, sail, water ski or use the motor launches. You could even use the helicopter landing pad.

> Included in the price are all meals and drinks (yes, we are talking alcohol), all the amenities mentioned above, laundry facilities and a local calypso band for a party evening. It costs $54,000-$75,000.00 per day... I fear my holiday fund is a little short just now!

> For something a little closer to home, you could rent Jane Seymour's very personal country manor house, St Catherine's Court, near Bath, with features dating back to the reign of Henry VIII and Charles I. Recently refurbished, this stunning house now has 17 bedrooms (sleeps maximum of 35), ten bathrooms, 15 acres of gardens and grounds, tennis court, orangery, orchard, croquet lawn, a Victorian plunge pool and medieval church (licensed for British weddings). The romantic dining room is lit only by candlelight, while after dinner the ballroom with grand piano would be perfect for a masked ball (catering extra).

> Some activities they can organise for you include: hot air ballooning, lessons in watercolour painting, ceramic decorating, floral art or tennis, a talk on the history of the house with tour of garden, or a massage. Within a short drive you could be playing golf, fishing, horse-riding, clay-pigeon shooting or having a polo lesson. Included is a full staff, chef and house manager (from $40,000 to $54,000.00 a week).

> All these dream-holiday destinations are available from Overseas Connection, which offers a hand-picked selection of the finest quality properties, so if these don't appeal, or you don't have that kind of spare cash at the moment, then they have a further 4000+ properties to choose from in Europe and the Caribbean. You have to register on the site but it's free and let me tell you, you won't want to miss any of these divine properties.

> You can search by country or geographic region, or even by celebrity villas, and each property shows a pop-up screen calendar indicating rental availability. All services can be provided, from childcare to chefs, fax machines to festivities, and maids to *masseuses*.

> They pride themselves on a very personal service. As Alfredo, one of the owners says: 'Feel free to call us. We will listen to what you are looking for, and our commitment is to assisting you to accomplish your dream. We will work diligently to help you realise it, nearby or abroad, for a week or a lifetime. We never say no and we will accomplish the impossible!' Obviously prices vary hugely – I have picked top-end examples here – but do also check for any additional charges in the way of government taxes and administrative fees prior to renting.

VILLA RENTALS

> **Villas of the World, Overseas Connections, PO Box 1800, Sag Harbor, New York, NY 11963 T· +1 631 324 8455, or from within the USA 888 728 4552
> W· villasoftheworld.com**

AN AMERICAN ABROAD

> Suzanne Pidduck rented her first Italian villa in 1984 and had a hunch that other Americans would appreciate the same. Now her company offers apartments, villas, farmhouses, castles and cottages throughout Europe. The user-review section is a credit to their friendly customer service, and prompt and knowledgeable advice. Whether you want to vacation under the Tuscan sun, lie by your own private pool or escape to an island, Rent Villas is dedicated to being 'the most experienced, the most innovative, and the most customer-obsessed company in the industry.'

> **Rent Villas, 700 E. Main Street, Ventura, CA 93001 T· +1 805 641 1650, or from within the USA 1 800 726 6702
> W· rentvillas.com**

CHECK IN WITH CONFIDENCE ACROSS THE POND

> Whether you're looking to play golf, climb a mountain or lie on a beach, if you're planning to holiday in the USA, Hawaii or Canada and you don't fancy a hotel, then check out the 17,000 condos, villas, cabins, lodges, cottages and vacation homes on this website.

> **W· resortquest.com**

LIVING THE DOLCE VITA

> If you're going to Italy on your next holiday and want to rent a wonderful home, then look no further than this website. Founded by Simon and Barbara Ball with a portfolio of a single house, they now offer around 200 properties, from farmhouses and hamlets to apartments and villas, all on an exclusive basis. Properties are regularly inspected and they work directly with the owners. They encourage you to phone them and tell them your needs and preferences so that they can recommend the perfect place for you, be it a romantic setting with hot tub by the coast, or a castle that sleeps 21. They can also provide maids, chauffeur, cooks and shopping services. Their website has very handy sections, such as Luxury Villas, Villas by the Sea, Large Villas and Honeymoon Villas to streamline your search.

> **Tuscany Now T· 020 7684 8884
> W· tuscanynow.com**

WHITE WALLS, BLUE SKIES, NEW MEMORIES

> This company specialises in villa rentals and distinctive hotels in the Caribbean and Europe. They have some absolutely gorgeous properties on their books. We wanted to go back to Capri as I had lived there over 12 years ago, teaching English as a foreign language. It is such a beautiful island, with the friendliest of people. One of the many properties Wimco could offer us was Villa Mafalda in Anacapri, with views to take your breath away.

> This beautiful home was built by a German aristocrat and dedicated to his wife, a descendent of the Italian Royal Family no less. You can sit in the secluded gardens, surrounded by bronze and marble statues, with a glass of chilled wine, or stay cool inside in the villa which is decorated in typical Caprese style with tiles and white washed walls. A maid service, washing and ironing services, welcome dinner and babysitting are also available. The villa sleeps eight, children are very welcome, and it has a lovely pool.

> **Wimco T· UK 0870 850 1144
> USA 1 800 449 1553 / +1 401 849 8012
> W· wimco.com**

SKIING

*After being lost on a ski slope in severe white-
out conditions and suffering a mild case of
hypothermia, I cannot claim to be enamoured
of the sport, but when a friend asked me if
I knew of a good ski-instructor, I just couldn't
resist putting in this gem of a find.*

OFF-PISTE PROFESSIONAL

> With Martin you'll be getting more than a ski
lesson. With his experience as a fully trained
massage therapist who's worked with
athletes, together with his knowledge of ski
techniques, you'll be offered unique insights
into the benefits you can gain from increased
flexibility. His skiing is at an advanced/expert
level (although he teaches in a non-
professional capacity). What he offers is quite
unique, in that you can book him to join you
and your friends for ski tuition by day and
massage and sports therapy at night. All you
have to do is pick up his expenses – travel,
accommodation and food – plus his fee
(which is negotiable). Go online and look at
his wonderful testimonials (in the Just For
Skiers section), and you'll have him booked
quicker than he can make it down the black
run.

> **Martin Jefferies T·020 7498 5389
W·suppleworx.co.uk**

*Then I thought skipping this section was
probably selfish of me as there will be loads of
you who do find the sport quite exhilarating,
even if we are only talking après ski! So here
are some others you may enjoy.*

TAKE THE LEGWORK OUT OF YOUR
SKI TRIP

> ifyouski.com is a very handy website and part
of the lastminute.com group, so you know
you'll be getting great advice. In fact, you'll
find tons of factual information on over 900

resorts, including lift-pass prices, ski schools,
childcare, piste maps and where you can buy
ski passes online.

> There is a choice of over 2,000
accommodations, in chalets, hotels and
apartments, through more than 40 tour
operators. You can search Worldwide Ski and
Snow Information and Seasonal Prices. I love
the search facility that they've set up for
those of us who are not sure where we want
to go. I had to tick from a number of boxes
including – I want to party all night, want to
shop, want to eats lots, want to swim or
watch a film, then press their search button
which is called 'Fetch Rascal Fetch' (which is
their pet dog). No prizes for guessing which
resort priority I ticked!

> **T·For accommodation in chalets
020 7471 7733/hotels 020 7471 7734/
apartments 0870 739 9399
W·ifyouski.com**

EVERY LITTLE TIP ALPS!

> This website contains resort information for
over 390 resorts, including ski schools,
weather, accommodation, activities and
what's on for children. Handy guides to
number of lifts, snow depth, snowboarding
and how to get there.

> **W·thealps.com**

GET THE VIP TREATMENT

> Whether you're looking for chic designer
style or sheer opulence, with over 11 years in
the business, VIP Chalets have some of the
classiest alpine locations from Val d'Isere to
Méribel. Most of their luxuriously furnished
chalets are either ski in/out or just a few
minutes from the piste by foot or
complimentary shuttle. Your home for the
holiday will include everything you need,
from a Jacuzzi bath, DVD player and balcony
(for that late-afternoon sun), to those special
little extras like lip-salve and toiletries.
Internet access is also now available in an

increasing number of the chalets by modem point for your laptop or communal flat screen for the use of all guests.

> Delicious contemporary menus and wines are included in the price as is a private shuttle service to and from the piste in Méribel.

> If your kids are too young to ski, it won't stop you getting out on the piste, as their excellent childcare provisions will leave you free from worries, safe in the knowledge that the children are having plenty of fun, and being cared for in a safe and happy environment. Their private nanny service has been a runaway success and all their nannies are qualified to NNEB or equivalent standard, hold a First-Aid certificate and have undergone a rigorous screening and training programme.

> Internationally acclaimed as one of the top ski resorts, Val d'Isère offers a unique combination of old world charm and a vibrant international clientele and is one of the liveliest resorts in the world for après ski. If you enjoy shopping, then Val d'Isère has everything from haute couture and technical clothing to art galleries and a few old-style souvenir shops. There is a wide range of body treatments, sauna and steam baths, a swimming pool, gym, outdoor ice rink and a cinema which regularly shows English films. The more active and adventurous can learn to drive a team of huskies, paraglide, rock climb, ride quad bikes and snow-mobiles, or even ride horses. Make sure you remember to leave time to ski!

> **VIP The Chalet Collection T · 0870 1123 119 W · vip-chalets.com**

LIKE TWO SKIS IN A POD

> For a unique break from the rat race, head to the Swiss Alps where you can stay in your own Whitepod. These look so spectacular they may even entice me to hit the Alps! No cars, buses, crowds or hotels, just unspoilt nature. The nine pods, located above Les Cerniers, a small village at the foot of the Dents du Midi, sit on wooden platforms and are modelled on a traditional igloo shape. Each pod has a private front terrace with spectacular views, wood-burning stove, organic bedding and throws, and soft lighting by petrol lamps.

> The Alpine Chalet (located below the camp) houses the lounge, dining room and bathroom facilities. Guests are treated to traditional food prepared by the resident chef, numerous activities with experienced guides, massage in the spa and your own private ski run.

> The Whitepods are reached by snowshoes and accommodate just twenty guests. There are six Expedition pods (from 325CHF), two Pavilion Pods (from 585CHF) and one Group Pod (sleeps 8 from 800CHF). Rates are per pod, per night, and include morning/afternoon tea, with a two-night minimum stay and exclusive of return transfers to the camp.

> **Whitepod, Les Cerniers, Batt. Postale 681, 1871 Les Giettes, Switzerland T · +41 24 471 3838 W · whitepod.com**

HIGHWAY SHOPPING *HEAVEN*

IN THE UK we call them 'boot fairs'. I'm a *huge* fan and I've picked up some absolute **treasures** rummaging amongst many stalls. **In the USA** they are called **Yard Sales**, and they have one particular sale which I am going to visit in August 2008 with my dear friend Barb, who lives in Michigan – very handy for the 127 highway! It's a four-day sale, spanning five states, and always **starts** on the **first Thursday of August**.

It started over 20 years ago as a way of attracting travellers to come off the interstate and on to Highway 127 – hence its nickname, **127 Corridor Sale**. Starting in its birthplace of Jamestown, Tennessee, it now heads north to Defiance, Ohio, and south to Gadsden, Alabama, and stretches for *630 miles*!!

The sale is extremely popular and in 2006 had **over 4,000 sellers** offering every conceivable thing for the collector – **antiques**, kitchen utensils, **jewellery**, furniture, art, decorative sewing, quilts, **vintage toys**, crafts, farm tools, vintage textiles and also **delicious, fresh farm produce** and home-made food. In fact it is now so popular that people book their accommodation up to a year in advance and make this their annual holiday. They come from across America and overseas and often travel the entire 630 miles, shopping to their hearts' content. The **website** devoted to the sale, **W·127sale.com**, offers a link to a list of places to stay along the route, which include an **old school**, **wood cabins** and a **teepee**.

Organisers and County officials have put together a very interesting list of attractions along the route, so there's **something for the entire family**. While mum is bartering for that 1950s first edition cookbook, the children could be off **riding, fishing or hiking**. The area is full of historical culture and you can visit **battlegrounds** and monuments of **the Civil War** and immerse yourself in **Indian History**.

The *scenery* is *beautiful* – rolling hills, waterfalls, botanical gardens, caves and State Parks, including **Big Bone Lick State Park**, where herds of prehistoric mammals once roamed the area, attracted to the warm salt springs.

Festivals and events fill the weekend, not to mention the **Jamestown Jamboree** with *bluegrass* music, *dancing* and *clogging* (the official state dance of Kentucky). The Fentress County Chamber of Commerce are the co-ordinators and can help you with any enquiry. *See you there!*

Fentress County (Jamestown, TN) Chamber of Commerce, P.O. Box 1294, Jamestown, TN 38556 T· +1 800 327 3945 W·127sale.com

FASHION
PERSONALSHOPPING VINTAGE
SALES HANDBAGS SHOES BOOKS
JEWELLERY WEDDINGDRESSES
SUNGLASSES FASHIONGUIDES
DRESSAGENCIES SHIRTMAKER
LINGERIE TAILORS BOOTS WWW
WARDROBESOLUTIONS FABRIC
HOSIERY ALTERATIONS FAIRS

ALTERATIONS & REPAIR

At some point we've all either put on or lost a few pounds and found that our favourite (and guilt-inducingly expensive) designer trousers no longer have that perfect fit. Your local dry-cleaner may be able to do alterations, but often a well-established tailor is a better choice for fantastic results.

BOB'S YOUR (VERY USEFUL) UNCLE!

> If your legs are never quite as long as your trousers', it might work out cheaper to get your trousers hemmed by Bob, than via the shop you bought them in. Having worked in the family business for over 14 years, Bob can alter almost anything, including leather and sheepskin coats, and many famous Bond Street shops send him their work.

> **Bob Tailoring, 124 New Bond Street, London W1S 1DX T· 020 7495 4099**

DON'T DESPAIR, GET A MAGIC REPAIR

> If you've ripped, burnt or torn your favourite outfit (or worse still, someone else's favourite outfit), Thayer Street is the place to go. These mending experts will patch, sew or cleverly disguise the damage. I ripped a gorgeous silk top and after I pulled myself together enough to find out who could save it, they pulled it together with an invisible mend. They also offer a postal service if you can't visit in person.

> **The British Invisible Mending Service, 32 Thayer Street, London W1U 2QT T· 020 7935 2487 W· invisible-mending.co.uk**

TAILOR-MADE FOR FAME

> Sotiris has been a tailor since the age of 12, perfecting his trade on Savile Row. He now runs his own family business offering any kind of alteration, from taking up your cuffs or hems to completely re-sizing an outfit. A favourite with the stars, Sotiris was too discreet to give me many names, but did admit that a well-known movie star takes his clothes to him for mending. He's also famous for his skill with vintage clothes — in fact, he has a customer who can't bear to part with his morning coat which was made in 1919! Quite right, too — they don't make them like they used to.

> **Thimble, 24 Thackeray Street, London W8 5ET T· 020 7938 1161**

WARDROBE MANAGEMENT
IN THE
COMFORT OF YOUR HOME

MAKING DREAMS COME TRUE

> Ten years ago, when I smoked like a chimney and weighed all of seven stone, Julia Dee became my fairy godmother. She altered one of my sister's designer hand-me-downs, till the stunning evening gown 'clung' to me. It turned out to be the dress I was wearing when I met my husband and I have it in my wardrobe still. I can't bear to part with it, even though I can't get it over my arms now.

> Julia can alter or repair anything, including suede and leather, and also offers a wonderful Total Wardrobe Care Service, which men especially love. She'll go through your entire wardrobe and make you justify every item you want to keep. These will be hung nicely, and the rest will be relegated to the bin, re-built (especially good with vintage), stored or given away to charity (no... please not the dress). She then transforms your wardrobe space for you, with the help of The Holding Company and their linen-lined baskets. She can also provide hangers, lavender bags, shoe trees, garment bags and acid-free tissue paper, making dressing a pleasure

and not a lucky dip.

> Should disaster strike as you put on that dream dress, if you've got time to whiz it round to Julia she can replace that zip faster than you fit your false eyelashes. And if it's bling bling you want, follow Lulu's example. When she decided in a dress rehearsal that her retro jeans needed sprucing up, they biked the jeans over to Julia who spent all day adding 400 Swarovski diamonds and had them back to her in time for the show!

> **Designer Alterations, 220a Queenstown Road, London SW8 4LP**
T · 020 7498 4360
W · designeralterations.com

For Leesa Whisker Wardrobe Management services see page 168

DEDICATED CREATOR OF FASHION

> You know that coat you bought in the designer sale that was a size too big but you couldn't bear not to have it? Well, now it will fit at last. Paul, who has been sewing since he was seven years old, will put his hand to any alteration, even the little jobs like hems and cuffs. And if you show him a picture of that to-die-for dress he can whip up a made-to-measure from scratch, too. Well used to the pressure of photo shoots, one night Paul stayed up all night knitting a black and white scarf that had been requested for the morning's shoot – and this is from a man who says he doesn't knit!

> Paul has travelled all over Britain and to America (the customer covers expenses) at the request of clients who love his consideration and concern for the work. He once saved the day for a bride who had bought her vintage wedding dress at a flea market in Paris. It was so old and fragile she couldn't even try it on, so didn't even know if it fitted – just one of those 'I have to have it' moments. Paul reworked it by sewing a new dress underneath and then laying the vintage

one on top – it looked stunning. Paul is based in Marylebone, London and is by appointment only.

> **Paul Strotton T · 07968 985 775**
E · paulstrotton@yahoo.co.uk

NO MISSION IMPOSSIBLE

> You know how some women seem to squeeze so much into their lives it makes you wonder what an earth you've been doing with your own! Well Caroline Thorpe, seamstress to the stars, is one such woman. Sewing since she was 14 and already a well-established theatrical costumier in opera, Caroline made the move into the Hollywood stratosphere when she worked with some of the cast on the first *Mission Impossible* film. Quickly becoming a darling of the fashion magazine stylists, she started working for *Vogue*, *Vanity Fair*, *Harpers* and *GQ*. Famous for her precision cutting, tucking and sewing, she has perfected the fit on Divas and movie stars among countless others.

> Used to working under pressure, Caroline once created a film premiere dress for a leading lady, from sourcing the fabric to a secret late night fitting, within a two-day turnaround, all while she was organising her own son's christening!

> Caroline normally works on fashion shoots but she will work with private clients – please call for prices.

> **Caroline Thorpe T · 07958 376 739**

COBBLERS

See Shoes and Boots page 171

DRESS AGENCIES

For Dress Hire see page 18

DON'T GET DRESSED ANYWHERE ELSE

> Rush in for a pair of Manolos, try on the latest Prada coat, or leave with the latest Fendi handbag, these are just some of the fab designer labels available at The Dresser.

> Set up in 1986, and now one of London's leading secondhand designer clothes agencies, The Dresser is the place to go for designer labels in mint condition at a fraction of their original cost. Celebrities, socialites and fashion editors sell their designer labels through the shop, which accepts men's and women's contemporary and couture clothing and accessories.

> The Dresser also offers a Private View Day when the shop is stocked with its new season collections, so make sure you get on their mailing list and bag yourself an invite.

> **The Dresser, 10 Porchester Place, London W2 2BS**
T·020 7724 7212 W·dresseronline.co.uk

PRE-ENJOYED PERFECTION

> Have you ever wished that an expert had been there in the changing room with you to say 'No, don't go there' before you made an expensive and impulsive error of judgement? If the answer is yes, you should start shopping at Bertie Golightly.

> When former Superman stunt girl Roberta Gibbs, who has also worked with Hitchcock and Shelly Winters, broke both ankles in her back garden, she set up a nearly-new, second-hand (or 'gently worn', as we like to say) boutique.

> Twenty-five years on this is still the place to buy all your top-end goodies, from Chanel to Escada. Besides the suits, eveningwear and separates, there are hundreds of accessories

to set off your outfit – they love dressing you from top to toe and are trained in actually saying 'no' when it's needed! I particularly loved the Vintage Pucci purse and their very talented in-house tailor. Having just moved from London to Wiltshire, Bertie is very happy to arrange for collection of your clothes for sale; please phone her for an appointment.

> **Bertie Golightly, 4 Kingsbury Street, Marlborough, Wiltshire SN8 1HU**
T·01672 513 318 W·bertiego.co.uk

SECRET IN THE ATTIC

> That absolutely fabulous and hardly-worn clothing from fashion and film shoots has to go somewhere right? Yep, it's put in The Loft. With a mix of wonderful second-hand and new designer clothing, stock flies out the door – so be sure to visit often. The insider secret is that they stock vintage Vivienne Westwood, but there is also a great selection for the man in your life, with suits from Ozwald Boateng and Paul Smith. I found a lovely Gucci evening bag for £70.00, so not everything will cost you a month's salary. The cheapest item I found was a lovely pair of Tsubi jeans for £5.00 (normally £180.00 retail). They also had a Chanel jacket reduced from £550.00 to £125.00. One almost wants to camp on the street outside to wait for the new deliveries. Get in the queue!

> **The Loft, 35 Monmouth Street, London WC2H 9DD**
T·020 7240 3807 W·the-loft.co.uk

A GIFT THAT KEEPS ON GIVING

> I'm not sure why 'second-hand' sounds so much more stylish in Italian – *Seconda Mano* – except that most things do. As it's only 15 minutes from where I live, I'm always popping into this great shop to browse the rails, which are bursting with designer cast-offs, not to mention a fab selection of shoes. I walked past once and saw a Missoni dress in the window. Trying to be good, I kept on

GOSSIP, GIGGLE, SWIG AND SWAP

FREE CLOTHES AND ACCESSORIES, all the girls round, a chance to clear out your wardrobe and loads of champagne - what more could you want from a party? I've attended two and hosted one, and it's really great fun. Spread the word – swapping is the new shopping.

Commonly named 'Bitch & Swap', I changed the name to **'Gossip & Swap It'** when I hosted my own party. Anyway, it involves your best friends getting together to swap their "I've not worn this for years" cast-offs and having a good old gossip and drink at the same time. Everyone will go home with bags full of 'gently-worn' clothes and accessories, all **for free**.

Now, anyone knows when it comes to free clothes there has to be a bit of order. Did you see the fight for the Anya Hindmarch 'I'm Not a Plastic Bag'? So here's some **flexible rules:**

GOSSIP & SWAP IT . . .

1 **What swaps?** Trousers, tops, dresses, hats, coats, jackets, jewellery, bags, shoes, make-up (unused) and "why-the-hell-did-I-buy-that" items.

2 Items can be designer, high-street or **vintage** (loved by all!)

3 Bring **a good selection.** If you don't have anything to swap back for an item you may want to sulk! Sometimes no one wants the stuff but you'll get over the embarrassment. Hard luck – bad buy!

4 All items must be **clean** and in as **near-perfect** condition as possible.

5 Go round the room **in turn**, showing one item each. Explain why you have brought it and want to swap it – some girls will have hilarious stories.

6 If only one girlfriend wants your offering, they have to swap one of their items for it. If more than one person wants an item, then it's up for **'Auction'**. For this, everyone offers whatever it takes to secure this **hot** item – bribes or best-piece-swap – and the girl who's offering this gorgeous number decides what they like best!

7 Make sure everyone goes home with something 'new' otherwise there will be more sulking.

A FEW EXTRA TIPS:

Set up another room with a good **full-length mirror** where people can change – the first time I was invited to one of these, most of the girls didn't know one another and we were all **too embarrassed** to try things on. Also, after a few glasses of vino I think my judgement was a bit hazy and I went home with a belt that I couldn't even buckle around my thigh, a bag with a broken zip (see rule 4 above) and a stunning green jacket that I couldn't get my arms into! For this lot I had given up a pair of vintage Gucci sunglasses, an evening bag and an Issey Miyake top – mmm, something wrong there! However, **It doesn't matter** about inviting people with similar clothes sizes – **jewellery** and **bags** go extremely well and are often the most fought-over items. When I hosted my own party, I also gave out a **goodie bag** at the end – one of the things I hand-made was an individual notebook with the girl's name printed on, decorated with Swarovski crystals and a picture of a cute little dog with a fluffy collar (naturally, it was a female dog, which was my small gesture in referring to the original title of the party). Rebecca, who hosted the first party I went to, gave a fabulous prize and certificate for the most sought after item.

Above all, enjoy **hanging out** with your friends and feeling a **shopping high** with **none of the guilt.**

walking, then thought I've just got to try it on – so I walked back and it wasn't in the window and we are talking less than five minutes here... Somebody was trying it on in the changing room. Well, I waited patiently to see if it fitted and I'm gutted to say that the other woman purchased it. I'm still not over it! Lesson One: If you see something you like, especially vintage or lightly worn – buy it now! They have just moved downstairs at Giovanni Hair, Health and Beauty Salon in Upper Street.

> Seconda Mano, 114 Upper Street, London N1 1QN T·020 7359 5284

CLICK ON A CLASSIC
> Girls, girls, girls, put Shonamac.com on your internet favourites list right now. They offer a great service if you want a complete wardrobe clear-out, and some unbelievable designer bargains if you want to rebuild it again!
> They can visit you at home (London only) if you have a reasonable number of items to sell or you decide you want a wardrobe clearance service. They'll sort through your designer or vintage clothes, before auctioning them online. You receive 50 per cent of the profits so you can then buy, buy, buy.
> Items listed for auction include covetable vintage clothes, designer jewellery and clothes and to-die-for shoes, All the items are auctioned on their ebay store with over 300 items per week, ranging from £15.00 to £1000.00. They were recently auctioning a cashmere Chanel Suit – it went for £265.00! Also up were some gorgeous Gucci velvet evening shoes, and a Moschino velvet devor jacket – that went for £72.00.
> They also offer some other great services from colour and style consultations, wardrobe weeding and personal shopping – a great gift for your favourite girlfriend.

> Shonamac.com, World End Studios, 132 Lots Road, London SW10 ORJ T·020 7349 7225 W·shonamac.com

DRY-CLEANING

Twenty years ago or so, I borrowed my flat-mate's silk blouse and skirt for a party when she was away, so didn't quite get permission to wear it... and of course, you guessed it, I spilt something horrible on it, though I can't quite remember what. I was mortified but luckily a sympathetic dry-cleaner pulled out all the stops and saved a friendship. Here are a few other dry-cleaners who have helped me out since then. For other cleaning/laundry services see page 86.

DISCOVER THE SECRET JET-SET SERVICE
> For a super-luxe laundry, dry-cleaning and alteration service, Her Majesty and well-known celebrities turn to Blossom & Browne's Sycamore. The staff are trained to a high standard in fabric care and specialise in handling antique and fine linen, as well as invisible mending, even your cashmere, and starch work, which is great for dress collars.
> You can drop items into any of their four branches or they will pick up and drop off at no extra charge if you have set up an account (to set up an account for their delivery and collection service phone T·020 8552 1231).
> If you're a frequent flyer, their Jet-Set Service is a must. Simply drop off your clothes on the way back from the airport and they will wash them all, pack in tissue and return them to you ready for the next trip – my idea of heaven!

> Blossom & Browne's Sycamore, 73A Clarendon Road, London W11 4JF T·020 7727 2635
> or 160 Regents Park Road, London NW1 8NX T·020 7722 1713
> or 8 Old Town, Clapham, London SW4 OJY T·020 7622 7171 W·blossomandbrowne.co.uk

DON'T BE AFRAID OF THE DARK

> If your light pink Joseph trousers have seen better days, but still make your bum look great, give them a new lease of life by dying them a darker colour. Chalfont offer six dark colours — bottle green, black, navy blue, cardinal red, peony and brown — and can dye all natural materials such as cotton, wool, silk or linen.

> **Chalfont Dyers & Cleaners, 222 Baker Street, London NW1 5RT T·020 7935 7316**

RAISING THE STANDARD

> Voted Best Dry-Cleaner by the *Evening Standard*, and with a raft of well-known designers who refuse to send their dry-cleaning anywhere else, you can't go wrong with Valentino. Specialists in leather and suede dry-cleaning at very reasonable prices, they also offer an alteration and repair service, and will collect and deliver on orders over £40.00.

> Maria has been referred to as the 'miracle worker', turning antique baby christening gowns (that were destined for the bin after the discovery of old yellow/brown stains) back to their original pristine white and removing stains which other dry-cleaners have not managed to remove. She takes the utmost care with every item, and treats it as her own. Customers have even sent them their dry-cleaning from Scotland!

> So, if you're worried about dry-cleaning your antique beaded dress, now you know where to send it.

> **Valentino, 56B New Oxford Street, London WC1A 1ES T·020 7436 1660**

> **or Unit 5, 125 Shaftesbury Avenue (off Stacey Street), London WC2H 8AD T·020 7240 5879**

See also Harry Berger page 78

EYE-CATCHING
EYEWEAR

LOOK NO FURTHER

> The selection of glasses and sunglasses Sveta and Ragini offer at 36 Opticians is probably one of the best I have ever seen in any opticians', including in New York. And despite its Knightsbridge location, they don't come with Knightsbridge prices, with frames starting from £40.00. The staff are wonderfully friendly and very quick to pick out the perfect frames for you from amongst the hundreds on offer. The designs include retro, vintage, new designers whose glasses will surely become collectors' items, commission and bespoke. And for all those struggling to read the A-Z, they have very fashionable loops and longettes, along with beautiful glasses' cases that you can wear as evening bags. They also offer all the other optical services, NHS testing, contact lenses and a great kids' collection, which, having worn glasses since I was two, I can really appreciate.

> **36 Opticians, 36 Beauchamp Place, London SW3 1NU
T·020 7581 6336 W·36opticians.co.uk**

ANYONE SEEN MY GLASSES?

> Steve Hudson, a co-owner of The Eye Company, has over 25 years' experience in the optical profession — there's not much this man doesn't know about eyes and eyewear, so he'll be able to help you make the best choices with your glasses or contacts.

> Fallen in love with a must-have pair of glasses in a blockbuster movie? Bring in a photo or picture and, from £180.00 for plastic frames, they can make an exact copy for you. They have a fantastic collection of vintage and antique frames in store to set off any face, and if you're looking forward not

backward, they also carry cutting-edge designer frames from the likes of Frédéric Beausoleil, Oliver Peoples, Lafont, Orgreen and Mykita.

> To use their bespoke service, make an appointment for a consultation and they will style a one-off pair that your friends will rush to imitate. If you are buying an off-the-peg pair and believe you've seen them cheaper elsewhere, they will match the price or better it. More importantly, you can take the frames home and try them on with your wardrobe, or show all your friends, before you commit to buying them.

> Steve even shared a few tricks of the trade with me which I wished I'd known about ten years ago: never use tissue paper to clean your lenses as it is highly abrasive and will damage them – always use a special micro-fibre lens cloth. And if you have coated lenses, which occasionally need to be degreased, you should never wash them with hot water as this can damage the coating – wash them with cold water and washing-up liquid.

> **The Eye Company, 159 Wardour Street, London W1F 8WH**
> **T · 020 7434 0988   W · eye-company.co.uk**

OPENING OUR EYES TO THE PAST

> Two seasons ago at London Fashion Week, I fell in love with a pair of sunglasses which didn't have any traditional sides to them – these sides looked like a necklace with a chain adorned with baubles which you just slipped round your ear and they looked amazing. Being a collector, I'm very cross with myself – actually I'm absolutely furious – that I didn't immediately go out and buy a pair. Of course, being a limited edition, now you can't get them for love nor money.

> The story is that in 1970 at the age of 23, Linda Farrow formed her own fashion label collaborating with her optician husband. They were also distributors for major brands such as Pucci, Stendhal and Sonia Rykiel. In 2003, her son stumbled across thousands of seventies and eighties classic sunglasses in their original packaging at their London warehouse and decided to revive the brand. Selling to exclusive retailers worldwide, they are also keeping their fingers on the pulse and debuting new limited-edition collections in collaboration with top designers. (For further stockists worldwide check online)

> UK stockists include the Linda Farrow Gallery at the Designer Studio in Harrods and Liberty, Harvey Nichols, Selfridges and Browns Focus.

> **Linda Farrow Vintage   T · 020 7730 1234 (Harrods)**
> **W · lindafarrowvintage.com**

A SIGHT FOR SORE EYES

> I was stopped in my tracks at a trade fair recently by the most amazing selection of glasses frames and Ready Readers. The ready-to-wear reading glasses are available in six powers (from £6.45) and the most gorgeous designs, including diamanté, animal print and floral. As my eyes continue to deteriorate, I am now the proud owner of their black floral diamanté pair which I wear in addition to my contacts when I need to read any small print – like the A-Z!

> If you need prescription spectacles, then you can choose a frame from their optical frames, enter your prescription details, and your glasses will be delivered in around 7-10 days. They make the glasses so-o-o-o affordable (from £45.00 complete); why not order a few different pairs to match different parts of your wardrobe! They kindly offer a seven-day trial service for any prescription frames, just so you can be certain they really suit you. The price also includes free anti-reflective and scratch-resistant coatings, something I've always paid a lot more for on top of my frame cost at other opticians.

> Online, they also offer a handy guide to

frame and face shape, an exclusive fashion-only range (if you don't need prescription glasses), sunglasses and accessories.

> SightStation T · 0870 850 3354
  W · sightstation.com

FABULOUS FABRICS

IMITATION IS THE SINCEREST FORM OF FLATTERY

> If the divine piece of vintage fabric you found while rummaging down the market is not quite big enough to cover your great-grandmother's Regency armchair, don't despair. Phone Alan Shaw at Glasgow School of Art's Centre for Advanced Textiles. They will scan in your design (check there is no copyright) and lovingly work to reproduce it on the right fabric, or indeed in any colour way, even if you wanted the circles changed from pink to blue, or the background from green to red. As it takes a lot of skill, the artwork is the most costly part of the service and can cost from £50.00 to £400.00, with the printing onto material costing £35.00-£65.00 per metre. They will send you the finished design on a CD so you can print more material at a later stage if needed.

> They have also been working closely with designers like Lucienne Day to recreate her old 1960s prints, which you can purchase online at **W · classictextiles.com**.

> I asked Alan if he could scan a really old piece of wallpaper I had found onto material and he told me that this is also a possibility.

> **Centre for Advanced Textiles, The Glasgow School of Art, 158 Renfrew Street, Glasgow G3 6RF**
  T · 0141 353 4742 W · catdigital.co.uk

COUTURE FRESH FROM THE CATWALK

> If you're a fabric fanatic, make the trip to Joel and Son Fabrics – they have a collection to die for. Every taste and price is catered for, with shelves brimming with cotton, silks, organza, wools, devore velvets, satins, lace and even suit fabrics from labels such as Ermenegildo Zegna. If you spot a print on the catwalk, chances are you'll find it here as they are the biggest couture fabric store in England. And if you're looking for a unique hand-beaded or hand-embroidered fabric for your wedding dress, this is definitely the place to go. The quality of their stock and service has been rewarded with a Royal Warrant to the Queen.

> **Joel and Son Fabrics, 75–83 Church Street, London NW8 8EU**
  T · 020 7724 6895
  W · joelandsonfabrics.co.uk

FASHION GUIDES & MUST-HAVE BOOKS

ONE STOP FASHIONISTA SHOP

> With fashion magazines from around the world and over 2,000 books relating to fashion, from how to illustrate for fashion, to trend-forecasting, to resource books for beaded bags, lingerie, shoe design, handbag-making and bridal couture, RD Franks is a real treasure trove. I can barely carry all my purchases when I leave and it is one of only two places I know that stocks the fabulous *White* – an Italian bridal magazine that you just have to buy for the amazing photography. They also offer a very handy subscription service and will send a book worldwide.

> **RD Franks, Kent House, Market Place, London W1W 8HY**
  T · 020 7636 1244 W · rdfranks.co.uk

GO ON, BE A KNOW-IT-ALL!

> You'll know Kate Spade for her divine handbags and social stationery, and of course her new home range. In 2004 she published three gorgeous books, *Manners*, *Occasions* and *Style* (Simon & Schuster) which are each filled with wonderful water-colour illustrations, top tips, quotes and helpful nuggets of information. In *Style* you'll find suggestions for combining colours and accessories, and sections on style in the office, at a party and while travelling. The Maintaining Style section tells you how best to organise your wardrobe, to care for your clothes, including vintage and cashmere, and look after your jewellery. Kate hopes her book will 'offer ideas and kindle a fresh sense of spirit and adventure.' Buy it for a friend – in fact, buy all three, the set would make a fantastic present. (US$20.00 each) 'Fashion changes... style remains' – Diana Vreeland.

> *Style*, Kate Spade W·simonsays.com (Simon & Schuster)
   Available in most bookshops or through amazon.co.uk

LOCATION, LOCATION, LOCATION

> I was so excited to find this vintage directory in RD Franks (*see page* 151). It was only after I bought it that I realised it only covered the USA! Of course I love travelling to New York and San Francisco, so I know it won't be under-used. Not only does it list all vintage stores by state, it also offers interesting notes on buying vintage, sizing, cleaning and caring for your vintage treasures, fashion expos and auctions.

> **The Vintage Fashion Directory: The National Sourcebook of Vintage Fashion Retailers**, Daniela Turudich & The Editors at Streamline Press (Streamline Press)

HERE'S ONE I MADE EARLIER

> Another great find from RD Franks (*see page* 151), *The Textile Directory* (*see also page* 184) is a godsend to all of you who are interested in textiles and art and craft, from education to shopping. They list some fantastic courses where you can spend a weekend in a country house learning embroidery or lace-making. Or what about zipping over for a textile course/holiday in France where you can learn patchwork, quilting, embroidery and much more. You can even stay here in the UK and try your hand at traditional Japanese embroidery/stitched beading.

> The directory also includes textile artists and designers, so you can source fantastic and talented craftspeople to stitch, knit and hand-paint or embroider – the list is endless. Finally, you can find the best sources for textiles, beads, buttons, dressmaking, craft supplies and haberdashery. This is truly one book that must be in your reference library.

> *The Textile Directory* – available at Word4Word Design & Publishing Ltd, 8 King Charles Court, Evesham WR11 4RF
   T·0870 220 2820
   W·thetextiledirectory.com

DON'T LEAVE HOME WITHOUT IT

> Even though I've shopped till I've dropped in many cities across the globe, my taste in fashion may not be the same as yours, and so, my best suggestion is for you to buy the shopping bible – the *Where to Wear* guides. I have the Paris and San Francisco ones, and they also publish guides for London, New York, Los Angeles, Florida and Las Vegas, Italy, and Australia (Sydney & Melbourne). If you're always looking for birthday presents for shopaholic girlfriends, stock up on the boxed set. The guides are available in many bookstores or you can order them direct. £9.99 or four books for the price of three at £29.99.

> **Where to Wear, 10 Cinnamon Row, Plantation Wharf, London SW11 3TW**
   T·020 7801 1398 W·wheretowear.com

HANDBAGS

For handbag repair, see Footwear page 171

GOODY BAGS HAVE NEVER LOOKED SO GREAT

> We all love parties, we all love handbags, why has it taken so long for someone to combine the two? Bagladies bring you the chicest bags in gorgeous soft leathers and they will visit you at home for a bag party where you can choose any design, colour and leather from their bespoke collection of bags and accessories. Pining after a Birkin-style? Then choose their ever-popular 'Classic' which comes in a choice of over 28 colours, depending on your choice of leather, ranging from crocodile to suede or, my favourite, the softest nubuck. And if you host a party, they'll give you a bag or percentage of sales as your gift.

> The parties, so far, have been London-based, but they will consider travelling further afield for the right kind of party, and they also sell worldwide through their website. The collection is continually expanding and your order will take up to two months to be lovingly made. They can offer the bag in any size, and travel bags are very popular — one customer ordered 10 bags in fuchsia pink but of varying sizes — jealous or what!
> Prices: bespoke bags from £295.00
> **Bagladies   T · 020 8541 0174**
> **W · bagladies.co.uk**

ARM CANDY

> Everyone needs a fashion fetish. For some people it's shoes, for me it's handbags. I have around 40 and I don't ever want to add up what I've spent on them in total, especially as some of them have only seen daylight once or twice. Luckily now, thanks to this innovative website, I don't have to buy new bags, I can just hire them. Join as a member and you can select a handbag to use for as long as you like — a day, a month or a year. When you get bored with it, just go into their closet and pick another — it's that simple. If you really can't bear to part with it, they can give you a quote to purchase it.

> If you join at the Diva-In-Training level, membership will cost you £29.95 per month. There are three membership levels, along with an Über Collection — if you choose the Fashionista premier membership level for £99.95 a month, you will have the pick of any handbag — Prada, Marc Jacobs, Dolce & Gabbana, JP Tod's, Gucci and Fendi to name a few. They even promise to try and source a bag for you if you have your heart set on a particular one (the latest Birkin was out of the closet within two days). The only problem is knowing which one to choose: one member changes her bags six times a month and buys all the season's new bags… I'd never be able to keep track of my car keys!
> **W · be-a-fashionista.co.uk**
> **E · info@be-a-fashionista.co.uk**

BAGS ARE U.S.

> Don't worry if you're not living in cool Britannia, if you're state-side log on to Bag Borrow or Steal's website to pick up a Chanel Bucket Bag, Fendi Oversized Buckle B. Bag, Gucci Tote or Prada Embossed Metallic Satchel. You can view by bag type, collection, designer or colour. They also have a great collection of designer jewellery and accessories you can borrow, and an outlet store' where you can buy their 'gently used' bags. Oh how I wish I lived in the States! Membership from $20.00 a month, with weekly rentals from as little as $6.00 (plus shipping). I love their name!
> **T · (toll free) +1 866 922 2267**
> **W · bagborroworsteal.com**

GUINNESS IS GOOD FOR YOU

> If you are a collector of bags then you simply must get your hands on the collectable and limited edition bags by Lulu Guinness.

> Lulu brings two new limited edition, numbered bags out per season, and we are talking only 200 or 500 of each.

> Past collections have included fans, houses, chocolate box, birdcage (press the base and the bird sings) and evening dresses. They are highly sought after so make sure you visit one of her shops as soon as they hit the shelves.

> Of course, while you're visiting you'll see all her other fabulous handbags, including her new couture collection, jewellery, shoes, sunglasses and bed linen. I have three of her bags and I'm sure it won't stop there. In fact just now I'm ogling one of her lip bags and the divine gold snakeskin vanity case – be still thy beating heart!

> Her website is very entertaining and full of her inspirations and designs – a must for any fan – and a permanent in my bookmarks!

> **Lulu Guinness, 3 Ellis Street, London SW1X 9AL**
T·020 7823 4828

> **Lulu Guinness New York, 394 Bleecker Street, New York, NY 10014-2453 T·+1 212 367 2120**
W·luluguinness.com

INIMITABLE STYLE

> With stores in the UK, USA, Japan, Taiwan, Singapore, Malaysia and Hong Kong, Anya Hindmarch's great bags, shoes and accessories are no longer a secret known only to the fashionistas. Her 'be a bag' and quirky crisp, coke and baked-bean bags have inspired many imitations. Anya can make up an evening bag in virtually any fabric in ten different styles, right down to choosing the antique beaded handle. These are very popular for evening functions or weddings and you can even have a monogram or

secret message added. I love the fact that this inner panel, hidden under a secret flap, is embossed with the giver's own handwriting – one man wrote his proposal this way! And it's not just her bags which are customisable; you can also inscribe luxury leather photo albums or jewellery boxes.

> And if your loved one is feeling flush, Anya's Ebury bag should be on your wish list. You can choose the size and skin (crocodile or box calf) in one of seven colours, then sit back and wait while the artisans in Tuscany produce your bag. Not only that, but your bag will be presented to you beautifully wrapped in it's own hand-tooled box, with your own unique number and your name, plus of course, your giver's personalised handwritten inscription carefully embossed in copperplate.
Prices: from £895.00 to £6,500.00 (for the crocodile Ebury). For other worldwide store locations refer to the list online.

> **Anya Hindmarch, 15–17 Pont St, London SW1X 9EH T·020 7838 9177**

> **or 63 Ledbury Road, Notting Hill, London W11 2AJ T·020 7792 4427**

> **New York – 29 East 60th Street, New York NY 10022 T·+1 212 750 3974**
W·anyahindmarch.co.uk

BUY ROYAL APPOINTMENT

> I met Nuria Gambau at the Chelsea Crafts Show, (now Origin, *see page* 187) and was drawn to her stand by the stunning feathered, beaded and embroidered creations of her 'wearable art'. Her designs have included bags covered with butterflies; lemons; sequins and even mushrooms – the Princess Bag, made with soft pink rosebuds and marabou feathers is absolutely gorgeous.

> She has made bags for celebrities and royalty and her work has been purchased by the V&A. She also makes wonderful bags on commission, for weddings, and can even

make one in the same fabric and with the same adornments as your wedding dress. Her design skills don't stop at handbags, she designs amazing fashion and home accessories – her lamps are fantastic and very unique. Handbag commissions start from £250.00 and you should allow two weeks for ordering. By appointment only.
> **Nuria London Design T · 020 8354 1361 W · nurialondon.com**

IT'S GOT YOUR NAME ALL OVER IT
> Sam McKechnie (who also makes exquisite lavender and rose-filled 'fairy' dolls, *see page* 201) makes fantastic vintage fabric totes adorned with antique brooches, lockets, flowers or shells. The bags come with a unique message, which she calls her 'Tag', which you can also wear as a necklace or charm bracelet. The tag can be made up of any letters or a name. I have one of her dolls and one of these totes is next on my 'to buy' list.
> **The Magpie and the Wardrobe T · 07770 961 362 W · magpiewardrobe.co.uk**

FORGET THE WAITING LIST
> If you take a photo, make a drawing or have a picture of your favourite 'must-have-bag' and send it to Melissa Simpson, she will make it, by hand, in any fabric, and you will have a true one-off. Prices range from £15.00 for a small purse, up to £600.00 for a larger bag. Melissa, who has over 15 years of experience, has won awards at design shows for her own leather goods and also makes briefcases, laptop bags, handbags, personal organisers or credit-card holders. She makes bags for the fashion designers and can do exclusive small runs.
> **Melissa Simpson, Zeal House, 8 Deer Park Road, London SW19 3UU T · 020 8542 6700 W · melissa.uk.com**

NO VANDA WE LOVE HER!
> What a talent! Not only does Vanda make bespoke bags, she also makes scarves, shawls, jewellery and shoes. She weaves, sews or creates a unique item just for you with imaginative special touches. Her hand-crocheted mohair shawl should top your 'to buy' list – you select a colour from the yarn chart and Vanda weaves your shawl using vintage ceramic and wooden beads plus any other little trinket or gems you may have chosen. Prices start at £300.00. Get in quick for her new range of shoes, boots, gloves, soft leather shawls and ceramics using exclusive art deco and art nouveau art-work.
> **Vanda Smith T · 020 7485 8333 / 07979 273 794 E · vanda@vandasmith.com**

HISTORICAL HAPPINESS
> Few people know as much about vintage fashion as Leslie Verrinder. Tucked away in a great space on the ground floor of Alfie's Antique Market, he sells period costume and accessories. He stocks a large range of very beautiful vintage evening bags from the 20th century.
> He particularly remembers one innovative piece which had a light on the front and inside – great for getting your key in the lock late at night. He initially thought this find was made in the 1950s, but it turned out it was made in 1938 by Elsa Schiaparelli and Salvador Dali. Sadly this bag has now been sold to a museum, but Tin Tin Collectables have plenty of other interesting ones at very good prices.
> Open Tuesday–Saturday, 10.00 a.m.–6.00 p.m.
> **Tin Tin Collectables, Alfie's Antique Market, Unit G38-42, 13-25 Church Street, Marylebone, London NW8 8DT T · 020 7258 1305 W · tintincollectables.net**

GET EMOTIONAL ABOUT BAGGAGE

> If you're going to splash out on some luxury luggage, you want something that makes a statement at the airport. Alison van der Lande's first collection was launched in January 2004 and since then those in the know have been snapping up her colourful and exciting pieces.

> I saw her collection at London Fashion Week and immediately gravitated to the Classico white leather weekend bag (also great for hand luggage), with wonderful pink stitching and matching lining.

> Her bags have also been snapped up to appear in movies and television, not to mention by numerous celebrities. Alison was commissioned to design the first ever 'Derby' Bag for the Epsom Derby and Ladies' Day events.

> Beautiful Italian and Spanish leather bags from make-up bags, handbags, wheelie cases, golf bags and the gorgeous – I had to have one – weekend bag, all come in cool white, candy floss pink, aquamarine and conker brown.

> Her bags are sold in the UK, Paris, Tokyo and New York (see online for stockists).

> **Alison van der Lande T · 01420 488 552 W · alisonvanderlande.co.uk**

HOSIERY

SOCKING IT TO EUROPE'S FANCIEST FEET

> Delphine Murat wowed the perfectly pedicured feet of the fashion world when she launched her minisock. The minisock can be worn with sandals, stilettos or ballet pumps. It comes in five different styles in Lycra, lace (dentelle) and metallic fabrics and is available in an amazing 35 different colours. I love the Coquette range which runs around your ankle and has a long tie that criss-crosses up your leg – they totally transform the look of your shoe. The minisocks are sort of a cross between a fashionable sock and a sexy stocking.

> You can purchase online, with international delivery, but check their stockists list as they're sold in top department stores and exclusive boutiques worldwide.
Prices: €20-40.

> **Minisock, Studio-Boutique Delphine Murat, 21, rue saint Roch, Paris 1er
T · +33 (0) 1 47 00 77 00 W · minisock.com**

A TIGHT FIT GUARANTEED

> I loved the Hosiery Finder on this website – you enter brand, product, occasion and denier, along with the option of a colour wheel, plus style choices such as open-toe, back seam, tall, fuller figure, and so on. The website also has hosiery advice and a top-ten product list. Mytights sells high-fashion hosiery, as well as 'old faithfuls' – well worth a click around.

> **T · 0845 004 8400 W · mytights.com**

NOT SUCH AN ODD IDEA

> We all have a sock-guzzling monster lurking in our tumble-dryers and that our favourite socks often lose their mates, so wouldn't it be wonderful to have a regular new supply sent to your front door? The innovative company SockRush will send you cotton-rich socks (size and length to suit) on a monthly, two-monthly, or three-monthly basis. The socks are currently only available in black, however the shorter-length socks can be ordered with toes in four different colours. They will send them to anywhere in the world, free of any delivery charges.
Prices: For UK subscription: £9.99 for a pack of four as a single delivery.

> **W · sockrush.com
E · helpful@SockRush.com**

SOCK IT TO ME!

> Socks as gifts have a bad rap, but I can't get enough of them and now I have a place to go

to indulge my fancy. Following the trend in Japan for socks becoming a fashion statement, Tabio has opened on the King's Road with a two-storey shop devoted entirely to men's and women's socks and tights. My favourite of all are the 'secret socks' with the most divine colour selection.

> You name it, it's there — we are talking knee-high, over-the-knee, toe socks, fishnets (in such a choice of colours), leg warmers, spats (no toes), trainer socks... In fact, with over 1,500 different styles, you could sort your Christmas present list for the next ten years in one afternoon!

> **Tabio, 94 King's Road, London SW3 4TZ**
> **T·020 7591 1960**
> **or 66 Neal Street, London WC2H 9PA**
> **T·020 7836 3713**
> **W·tabio.com**

LET YOUR LEGS LIVE A LITTLE

> When I clicked onto tightsplease.co.uk (for research purposes only, you understand), a funny thing happened. Almost without noticing, I had clicked five or six items straight into my shopping basket! They offer a fantastic selection of stockings, tights, socks and hold-ups. You can choose from: petite, maternity, wedding, partywear, brightly coloured, footless, kids, legwarmers, prints, patterns, shapewear, fishnets, lace, and so many others. They also offer a good range of lingerie products. Delivery is offered worldwide and if you're ordering from the UK you can often receive your order within two days.

> **Tightsplease T·0845 365 1221**
> **W·tightsplease.co.uk**

JEWELLERY

CHARMING STORY

> Leslie and Lisa, a mother and daughter family business, started by collecting vintage charms and making bracelets for friends and relatives. Having searched far and wide at fairs, boot fairs and shows to source wonderful charms, they are now offering a very personalised service. Phone them to tell them about yourself, or the person you want to give a bracelet to. To make the bracelet as personal as possible, they want to know all the gossip — the time your friend got drunk at a wedding on three glasses of champagne when you were 15, or passed her driving test on the seventh attempt, or lost her neighbours' dog for two days when they were away on holiday...

> The more information you give them, the more the C.H.A.R.M bracelet will mean to that special person who receives it. These gifts have proved so popular that Leslie and Lisa are now making antique-inspired solid gold charms which you can order online. They make around 80 new charms each year so you'll always have plenty to choose from.

> I had to get out the tissues when Leslie told me they had a customer who had just turned 50 and had been presented with one of their charm bracelets — 40 of her friends had each purchased a charm of their choice and Leslie and Lisa had made the bracelet up for her — what a lovely gift.

> **C.H.A.R.M T·From USA 1 800 616 6067 /**
> **From outside USA +1 212 625 0054**
> **W·charmco.com**

BEDAZZLE YOUR PRINCE CHARMING

> It's not only princesses who get to wear tiaras these days. If you think your jewellery collection is lacking a little sparkle, then you must visit the charming Count Alexander von Beregshasy. He has made his name hand-

crafting gorgeous, museum-quality reproductions of the famous Crown Jewels of England, Austria, France and Russia. His jewels are triple-plated in palladium and set with Austrian Swarovski crystals or Russian cubic zirconias. Amazingly, some of his tiaras even convert into necklaces, which is very useful.

> When I visited his Palatial Jewel Boutique I fell in love with a pair of shoe earrings that he'd made and was pleasantly surprised when I asked 'how much please'? with slight trepidation – I never would have dreamed I could afford a signed piece from a Royal Crown Jeweller.

> Count Alexander is also a period-jewellery stylist for films and brides. You've probably seen his exquisite creations while watching *Titanic* and *The Phantom of the Opera*. His boutique also includes his own designs of necklaces, earrings, chokers, rings, bracelets, cufflinks, shoe buckles and beautiful, sparkling jewelled bodice ornaments.
Prices: Tiaras £30-£5,000. Jewels from £20.00. Open Tuesday-Sunday 11.00 a.m.-4.30 p.m.

> **Count Alexander, 13 The Mall Antiques Arcade, 359 Upper Street, Camden Passage, Islington, London N1 OPD T·020 7354 0058 / 07958 132 958 W·countalexander.com**

VINTAGE TREASURE TROVE

> I first met Linda at the Battersea Vintage Fair where I just couldn't take my eyes off her exquisite and unique vintage jewellery. I admit that I did succumb and purchase a gorgeous brooch, but I assure you that was me being restrained! Her pieces range from 1890 to modern day, from Bakelite bangles to jewel-encrusted necklaces, and you will undoubtedly find a piece that will be the envy of your girlfriends.

> Linda travels far and wide searching markets, fairs and auctions to find the 'simply-must-own' treasures. And she doesn't only sell jewellery – she has a real eye for fabulous handbags, clothes and shoes, and offers a great service of advising on a complete head-to-toe look. Over the years of seeing her at her shop and fairs, she's had many fabulous things, such as a 1980s Chanel cross (£650.00) and a Paco Rabane gold-mesh handbag (£100.00). Many authors of books on handbags and perfume bottles have come to her for her expertise and she also lectures on these subjects.

> Recently she has sourced the most amazing Swarovski crystal-encrusted pens. I've just bought a bright red one from her (£45.00) – but they are available in many other colours. She offers a valuation service and also buys special pieces. You simply must visit. She is open 1.00 p.m.-6.00 p.m., Monday to Friday, and by appointment on Saturday.

> **Linda Bee, Vintage Jewellery & Fashion Accessories, 1-7 Davies Mews, London W1K 5AB T·020 7629 5921 W·graysantiques.com**

A GIRL'S BEST FRIEND... FOR ONE NIGHT ONLY

> Mention the words 'vintage jewellery' and my knees start to shake – when I pop into Bentley & Skinner my whole body shakes! They have a divine collection of vintage jewellery including art deco, Victorian, Georgian and Edwardian styles. What I love is the fact that you can hire this jewellery for a special night. So if you fancy a pair of diamond studs or you've been coveting a diamond tiara after seeing one at a high society wedding, pop down to Bond Street. Hire charges are from one per cent of the value of the item (plus VAT), with a minimum £50.00 hire charge.

> **Bentley & Skinner, 8 New Bond Street, London W1 S3SL T·020 7629 0651 W·bentley-skinner.co.uk**

DARE TO DAZZLE

> I've been coming to Eclectica for years to buy that vintage necklace or those gorgeous earrings that are guaranteed to impress at a wedding or glitzy party. Liz, the owner, has a passion for jewellery and always helps me find just the right piece. She even takes the time to give it the perfect fit by lengthening or shortening a necklace, or tightening screws or clips on the earrings. She also has a constantly changing stock of great vintage bags – snapped up sometimes even before they've gone in the window. The shop is looking to relocate and therefore is currently closed but you can still purchase her lovely pieces from her website.

> T · 020 7700 5949   W · eclectica.biz

NEW JEWEL IN THE TOWN

> Recently opened in Camden Passage is Kirt Holmes. Kirt's jewellery is quite unique, Swarovski crystal, coral, charms, curiosities, found objects, semi precious stones and sterling silver chains are blended to make stunning bracelets, rings, necklaces and earrings. I've purchased some of her lovely pieces which are greatly admired every time I wear them.

> Her jewellery has been snapped up by Erickson Beamon and Barney's New York to name but a few – and she has a long list of designers with whom she has collaborated. In addition to creating jewellery for the catwalk shows she has created special pieces for films, most notably *Gosford Park* and the film adaptation of *Brideshead Revisited*.

> **Kirt Holmes, 16 Camden Passage, Islington, London N1 8ED**
> T · 0207 226 1080   W · kirtholmes.com

HOST A DESIGNER SOIREE

> I spotted Liz at the Vintage Fashion and Textile Fair and immediately bought one of her great rose corsages with vintage faux pearls and diamantés. I thought it would look excellent hanging from one of my plain handbags – and it does. Liz is a jewellery and fashion designer based in London, and all her designs are unique and contemporary. She can come to your home with her whole collection, but get your friends around because if you show to more than four she'll give you 25 per cent off anything you buy for yourself. Liz will also make individual bespoke pieces at excellent prices. Liz actually trained as a 3D designer and also designs interiors, specialising in boutique-style bedrooms. You should see her hand-painted walls decorated with lace and jewellery – gorgeous.

> **Liz Joseph   T · 07713 774460**
> W · lizjoseph.com
> E · lizjoseph199@yahoo.com

A PRECIOUS FIND

> While shopping in Marylebone Lane, I came across this absolutely divine jewellery shop. They stock about 45 designers from around the world, offering contemporary, avant-garde and precious jewellery and couture pieces. Don't let the couture put you off, with bracelets starting at just £16.00, it's the perfect place for gifts. I purchased two lovely pieces for under £70.00. I could have bought so much more, but the corsage I did choose has had so many comments, I wear it all the time.

> They have a lower level for shoppers who are looking to spend a little more, where there's plenty of opportunity to sit back, relax with a drink and nibbles, forget that nagging VISA bill and peruse your potential purchases.

> **Kabiri, 37 Marylebone High Street, London W1U 4QE**
> T · 020 7224 1808   W · kabiri.co.uk

THE PAST IS WORTH PAYING FOR

> As I was walking through the exhibition at London Fashion Week. I was stopped in my tracks by Vanda's stunning jewellery designs. Her one-off creations include neckpieces,

bracelets, brooches and belts, and are made using restored antique artefacts, old Victorian and Edwardian photos, clear resin, glass beads, vintage velvet and lace, as well as plastic, silver, copper and brass. I wanted four of her designs immediately, but then I found that all the ones I'd admired were in the £250.00-plus range, but there's always my birthday, Valentines, Christmas – oh yes, and Mother's Day and…

> Available in top designer boutiques world-wide (for stockists contact E · info@vandaleitao.com). For bespoke pieces contact Vanda direct.
Prices: £40.00-£300.00

> **Vanda Leitão, 1 Dawnay Road, Earlsfield, London SW18 3PQ**
T · 020 8946 9927 W · vandaleitao.com

ONCE UPON A TIME, NOT THAT FAR AWAY

> If you want a glittering one-of-a-kind piece with a tale to tell, go to Paula Goodburn. This designer makes amazing one-off pieces that are either ethnic and organic, or vintage and contemporary, and each piece comes in a little pouch complete with its own story written on a small scroll telling the history of the components. Paula has collected amulets all her life and was inspired to incorporate them into her pieces along with vintage brooches and old belt buckles (which she sources from markets around Europe), semi-precious stones, Swarovski crystals, antique beads and Venetian glass.

> On her website, I saw a divine necklace called Venetian Easter, made around a vintage pink diamante brooch, and also including Murano glass beads, crystals, pearls and old glass beads from a Victorian necklace. Obviously I wasn't the only admirer as when I phoned to buy it, it had already sold. Paula told me she nearly cries when she sells her necklaces – I nearly cried when I found out I couldn't have this one! Actually that's a lie, I sobbed uncontrollably, however she can also make pieces for you incorporating some of your old treasures (I have drawers-full ready and waiting), so one day one of her designs will be all mine!

> You can buy her jewellery at Liberty and elsewhere – see her website for a list of stockists.

> **Porcupine Rocks T · 07710 322 558**
W · porcupinerocks.com

SOMETHING OLD, SOMETHING NEW

> Susan has a passion for 1930s and antique jewellery, and has been a jewellery designer for over 25 years. Not only can she design fabulous pieces, she can also give your old jewellery a new lease of life. If you don't like that diamond necklace anymore, no trouble, she can restyle it into a ring or bracelet. She can also repair and restore jewellery, remodel, or sell your diamonds and jewels at extremely good prices. She will visit you at home and you can both have fun playing around with your jewellery to up-date or restyle it.

> **Susan Walker Ltd T · 020 8969 1213 / 07778 802 712**
W · susanwalkerdesigns.com

LINGERIE

DON'T RETURN TO SENDER

> Knickerscription is the creation of the owners of the lovely boutique Coco Ribbon (*see page 187*). A year's supply of thongs or briefs will be delivered by your postman, so you need never be caught out in greying stretchy pants in the gym's changing room ever again. Prices are a minimum of £55.00 per year, which will deliver two knickers every three months, with other options offered. International delivery is available.

> **The Panty Postman / Coco Ribbon**
T · 020 7229 4904 W · pantypostman.com

FIT FOR A QUEEN

> There's not much Rigby & Peller don't know about measuring busts and getting the right fit, they've been doing it since 1939 and have held the Royal Warrant since 1960. Their extensive range of quality, ready-to-wear bras are available from 30AA up to 48K and they don't only stock their own Rigby & Peller range, but also other brands including Prima Donna, Lejaby, Gossard, Elle Macpherson and La Perla. They told me that, when they first visit, around 85 per cent of customers are wearing the wrong size bra! Basically, if you've ever experienced your bra riding up, your underwire digging in, indents in your shoulder from the straps, falling out of the bottom of your bra, or a bumpy silhouette under your clothes, then you are wearing the wrong bra size.

> Appointments are not needed for ready-to-wear, however allow up to an hour for fitting and choosing your lingerie. They offer maternity and bridal lingerie along with swimwear, nightwear and mastectomy bras. And once you've paid for the best, why not also buy their Lingerie Satin Bath wash to keep your lingerie looking its best. Remember you should always hand wash your bras, especially those with underwiring.

> They are well known for their high level of customer service and their made-to-measure corsetry. I'm told by those in the know that their bespoke basques can give you back your figure and you can still breathe! I'm saving up to buy one right now, to fight back against my post-son tummy and advancing years! Bespoke bras start at £215.00, underwear basques at £690.00, outerwear basques at £800.00. Orders can take six to eight weeks and bespoke work is by appointment only.

> **Rigby & Peller, 22A Conduit Street, London W1S 2XT**

> **or 2 Hans Road, London SW3 1RX**

> **or Brent Cross Shopping Centre, London NW4 3FD**
T · 0845 076 5545 W · rigbyandpeller.com

WHO SAYS SUPPORT CAN'T BE SEXY?

> Carol knows everything there is to know about bras – she even gives talks at clubs and shows on 'underwear over the last 60 years', accompanied by her collection of really old underwear. Carol and her colleagues like to give you a personal fitting first, so you can be sure of the perfect fit, then you can buy by mail-order worldwide or your husband or partner can buy you some sexy gift, safe in the knowledge he is buying you the right size. They are also specialists in mastectomy bras, nursing and bridal lingerie – they cater for brides with very large busts who want to wear a strapless dress and will ensure you are truly supported on the day. Sizes 30-46, cup sizes AA-JJ.

> **Sweet Dreams, 6 High Street, Cornwall Place, Buckingham MK18 1NT**
T · 01280 812 507
W · sweetdreams-bra.co.uk

LOVE YOUR LINGERIE

> Tallulah Lingerie is a lovely little shop in Cross Street (off Upper Street), offering gorgeous bras and underwear, cammies, nighties and other little treats. Nicola, the owner, is really charming and helpful and will help you find what you didn't even know you were looking for! Brands include Lejaby, Damaris, Spoylt, Princesse Tam-Tam and Huit. I've bought many smalls that make a big impression from here. Men in the know shop here when they're looking for maximum brownie points.

> **Tallulah Lingerie, 65 Cross Street, Islington, London N1 2BB**
T · 020 7704 0066
W · tallulah-lingerie.co.uk

NOT
TO BE MISSED

FROM BRIDES TO BRIGADIERS

> Hand & Lock are the longest-established bespoke hand-embroidery company in the UK. They've been creating embroidered textiles for the fashion, theatre and military worlds for over 200 years. Today their customers include collectors, military tailors, brides, interior designers and top fashion designers, and they've hand-beaded and embroidered opera costumes, couture garments, pop stars' corsets, Come Dancing outfits, and theatre and film costumes, and restored many antique dresses.

> I went to visit and was in awe at their wonderful array of designs and embroidery, including their collection of rare textiles (archives date back to 1790), which can be used to inspire your contemporary pattern – 'if you can imagine it, they can embroider it'. I only wish we could include photographs, as their beading and embroidery was completely breathtaking and I simply can't do it justice in words. I was told that, in times gone by, they used to examine the work of the embroiderers and beaders minutely, and would cut it up and tell them to start again if they saw one stitch or bead out of place!

> They design monograms and will hand-bead bridal dresses and shoes, evening wear, handbags, show pieces and one-off's, and their embroidery skills include tambour beading, Irish, appliqué, metallic thread, cornely and beading. Don't be put off thinking it will cost you a fortune – a shirt monogram starts from £40.00, and they can work within a small budget. They have an online shop where you can purchase a range of embroidery products and accessories, although many are accoutrements for military regiments throughout the world.

> **Hand & Lock, 86 Margaret Street, London W1W 8TE**
T · 020 7580 7488
W · hand-embroidery.co.uk

ON YOUR MARKS, GET SET, SHOP!

> An exclusive, invitation-only fashion event offering over 40 designer labels at wholesale prices and below. Pick up bargains from the likes of Cacharel, Roberto Cavalli, Dolce & Gabbana, Patrick Cox, and True Religion Brand Jeans. Clothes are not just sample sizes – they promise something for everyone, with sizes from 4 to 14 along with handbags and shoes. Set up over six years ago by Kate Nobelius and Shelli-Ann Couch, the Billion Dollar Babe sales are now the most anticipated seasonal fashion event in the calendar. Sales are hosted over two days in London, New York, Los Angeles, Chicago. San Francisco and Dublin.

> Join as a Platinum or Gold VIP member and you can have first dibs before the doors open to the rest of the VIP shoppers at 5.00 p.m. on Friday. Platinum Membership (£125.00) will allow you and four friends unlimited shopping from 12 noon on the Friday and complimentary cocktails. Plus when you join you'll receive a welcome goodie bag filled with luxury beauty and lifestyle products (you can also use your membership to shop at the other sales worldwide). Gold membership (£75.00) allows you and two friends to visit from 3.00 p.m. on the Friday, complimentary cocktails and priority check-in (no waiting in queues). If you're happy just to shop after 5.00 p.m. on the Friday or on Saturday, you need to register for an invitation (£2.00 towards Fashion Targets Breast Cancer). As you can imagine, I'll be going Platinum all the way. What with getting all the best bargains, I'll practically be making money!

> **Billion Dollar Babes   T · 020 7384 1110**
W · billiondollarbabes.co.uk

TINKER, TAILOR, SOLDIER, SAILOR

Roger Buffin amassed an extraordinary collection of 350,000 buttons during his fifty-year career as a 'negotiating traveller' in France from the 1930s onwards. Working with dressmakers and furriers, M. Buffin travelled the country supplying them with his wonderful buttons and haberdashery. From the great Paris couture houses such as Chanel and Fath, to the more humble dressmaker, he would leave a box or two for them to peruse until he visited them again.

The collection was bequeathed on his death, and Jackie Kilpatrick and Mary Hawkins are now owners of this astonishing treasure.

I met Jackie at the Hammersmith Vintage Textile Fair selling some of these buttons and I purchased many to update my old cardigans and coats.

By trade, Jackie is a couture dressmaker and she will remodel vintage clothes, including bridal gowns. I got very excited when she said she was thinking of offering button parties, as I certainly don't know anyone else who offers this unique service. However, she's decided that may be something for the future, as she's currently so busy with all her couture dressmaking she doesn't know how she'd fit it all in. What she will offer is a button viewing to serious button buyers (by appointment only; small charge redeemable against purchases), and she is very happy to have a group of you and your friends visit her.

Jacqueline Kilpatrick, 43 The Grove, Teddington, Middlesex TW11 8AT
T·020 8977 1439 W·jkcouture.co.uk

ONLINE FASHION

If your idea of hell is worrying about the parking meter as you try on a skimpy dress next to a 'wish I looked like that girl' in an overcrowded changing room, online shopping is the way to go.

If you don't mind not touching before you buy, don't feel the need to check the colour in the sunlight (setting off alarms as you go), and have a realistic idea of what size you are, then look at these fabulous websites. I love to sit there in my pyjamas with a delicious home-made cappuccino. In my book www = world-wide wardrobe, so log on and fill those shopping carts…

CELEBRITY STYLE WITHOUT STALKING…
> This is a site for star style and celebrity fashion trends. If you've seen something you like worn by well-known types, but have no idea where to lay your hands on it, chances are you'll be able to find something similar at ASOS.com. You can flick through their fabulous look book or shop under categories including jewellery, shoe boutique, accessories, men, women, lingerie & nightwear and swimwear. I thought the prices were really reasonable – I wanted to purchase a pair of white sunglasses for £10.00 and a pair of boots for £20.00. And talking of boots, they have a great selection of footwear for small feet. Jamilla, a friend who is such a trendy dresser always looks fabulous. When you ask her 'where did you get that it's gorgeous?' more than likely her response is…
> **W·asos.com**

DO PLAY WITH MATCHES!
> Over the last 14 years Matches has grown from a single shop into a string of eleven stores scattered throughout Notting Hill, Wimbledon and Richmond. And now, to the

delight of all of us not living in West London, Matches has launched itself onto the internet and is accessible to fashion devotees everywhere.

> With hundreds of designers, including Chloé, Marc Jacobs, Missoni, Lanvin, Bottega Veneta and Temperley, you can browse hundreds and hundreds of items, watch catwalk shows and then just click the items to add them to your wish list. Departments include Women, Men, Just In and Designers, or you can search the Lookbook and pre-order hot items. You can also browse and click on items featured in their magazine, and if you need any kind of style advice, just email their team of stylists who will get you from fumbling to fashionista in less time than it takes you to check your credit card limit online!

> T· 0870 067 8838 W· matchesfashion.com

STAY IN YOUR HOUSE, SHOP WITH YOUR MOUSE

> My-wardrobe.com is designed to offer you the latest in high-fashion clothing, shoes and accessories from the likes of 7 For All Mankind, 18th Amendment, Antik Batik, Beatrix Ong, Orla Kiely, Sass & Bide, Paul & Joe and Gharani Strok, to name but a few. Supporting UK and European designers, along with the simply must-have hip US and Australian designers, my-wardrobe.com bring you a comprehensive current-season collection.

> Delivery is worldwide and orders to most UK and European destinations are delivered the next day. So if you suddenly realise that, despite the frustrating lack of free space in your wardrobe, you have absolutely nothing to wear and no time to hit the high street, simply fire up your laptop and click your way to drop-dead gorgeous.

> The Sale section is very good – I spotted a C & C California bell-sleeve top that was originally £51.00 down to £15.00 – and the site is constantly being updated with new and fantastic items that honestly do want to come and live with you!

> My-wardrobe.com T· UK 0845 260 3880 / International +44 20 7692 0800 W· my-wardrobe.com

FLAWLESS FASHION AT YOUR FINGERTIPS

> We all owe our thanks to Natalie Massenet, Founder and Chairman of net-a-porter.com who has revolutionised the way we can shop online.

> Unless you've been living in the Arctic, you probably already know about the wonder that is net-a-porter.com, but I can't tell enough people about the pages of shopping, including top runway trends, hottest designers, the must-haves for the current season, and great little sections such as: Top Tens, What's New, Most-Wanted's and IT Lists – heart palpitations or what!

> The site is really easy to navigate; you can shop by designer, what's hot, runway trends or what's new. Best of all, there is a fantastic sale section and great city guides. I've also signed up for weekly updates to be sent to me directly by email, so as to stay one step ahead of the new season's 'must buy or my life isn't worth living'. Simply place your mouse over what you 'need' to own and click your way to contentment.

> W· net-a-porter.com T· UK 08456 751 321; USA (toll free) +1 800 481 1064; rest of the world +44 (0) 1473 323 032

TIME FOR THE ADVANCED SEARCH

> Well known for their selection of end-of-season clothing and accessories, YOOX.COM also offer exclusive lines, vintage, innovative brands and limited-edition creations. Browsing in their V.I.P. (very important pieces) section can yield the likes of a pair of Jimmy Choo's, a Prada bag and a John Galliano dress or pair of trousers. I love their search facility where you can search by over

164

- 40 designers, hundreds of items, individual colour or size.
- > They've already delivered 1 million items to customers around the world and state that they sell only prime quality pieces, with no flawed or substandard products.
- > They also sell a high quality selection of art and design products, hard-to-find books and magazines.
- > **W·YOOX.COM T·Customer service 0800 1699 735 (Monday–Friday 8.00 a.m. – 8.00 p.m.)**

For Online Vintage Fashion see page 177

For Online Vintage Fashion see page 177

PERSONAL
SHOPPING

Do you ever feel that you're lacking in that mysterious Bond Street boutique etiquette? Do you worry you'll be ignored by the oh-so-chic sales staff because of the dog hairs on your several-seasons-old winter coat and your 'should have worn a hat' hair? Perhaps you're cash rich but time poor, and never quite have that free afternoon to hit those sales? If traipsing around the shops to find that drop-dead party dress or suit for that make-or-break presentation doesn't float your boat, then it's time to get yourself a personal shopper. He or she will save you time and money with a safely-guarded contact book and all the sale information you could wish for. Or why not have one of the boutiques visit you at home, so that they can help you make the most of your precious purchasing time, not to mention how much you'll save on parking!

SERVICE WITH A STYLE
- > You can't get more chic than Chanel, and as if we didn't love them enough already for their stunning clothes, they really do put us, the customers, first. This to me is the epitome of class – everyone who comes through their doors is important, no matter if you're buying a lipstick or a suit. For example, you don't have to be a film star to ask them to stay open late if you can't get in to pick out that suit till after work. If that's not going to work for your schedule, they can bring a selection from the boutique and meet you at the office, your hotel or some other suitable venue. They've even sent clothes to a woman who was house-bound with a broken leg!
- > If you're a regular customer you get all sorts of treats, from flowers for your birthday to invitations to Christmas lunches and sample sales. My favourite service, however, is that if you have some previous-season Chanel, they can revamp the outfit by re-shaping, fitting a new lining or even changing the buttons, thereby bringing it right up to date. For clients visiting from overseas, they can arrange hair appointments, restaurant bookings or an appointment at the doctor. They will even arrange for your shopping to be sent to your home or hotel so you don't have to carry it around town. Their service really is second to none – who would want to shop anywhere else?
- > And it's not just clothes; they bring out fabulous limited-edition make-up collections, and with consultations that are always free why not enjoy a complete makeover?
- > Visit the charming Monica Daniels Hoveyda, the Manager at Brompton Cross, and not only will she find you the perfect outfit to wear, she'll open up her little black book of top facialists and hairdressers to complete your red-carpet treatment.
- > **Chanel Brompton Cross, 278–280 Brompton Road, London SW3 2AB T·020 7581 8620**
- > **also Chanel, 26 Old Bond Street, London W1S 4QD T·020 7493 5040**
- > **Chanel, 167–170 Sloane Street, London SW1X 9QF T·020 7235 6631 W·chanel.com**

SPLASH OUT ON A STYLIST

> Whatever your reason for wanting a fashion makeover, a new career, post baby, a special occasion or simple boredom with your own lack of confidence, imagination and style know-how, you don't have to wait for Trinny and Susanna to come knocking. Coathanger offer two fantastic and affordable services.

> The first is the Wardrobe Co-Ordination Service where your personal stylist will come to your home, go through every piece in your wardrobe, giving it and you a new lease of life, right down to your shoes and accessories.

> You'll be given a whole heap of new ideas on how to buy the perfect capsule wardrobe, how to accessorise your way to happiness and discover new outfits within your existing wardrobe. Photos of these are taken and uploaded for your private online reference. This costs £350.00 for three to four hours and is a very popular gift.

> The other service is my favourite – shopping, shopping and more shopping. Prior to your shopping day a personal profile will be compiled of you according to your life style. Research is then conducted on all the shops specifically suited to you. You will then meet up with your personal stylist for approximately six hours of shopping bliss. Within that time you will try on many different styles, learning about different shapes and colours as well as how to complement the new outfits with the right shoes and accessories. As above a complete photo reference will be taken. During your day you'll be given some honest and friendly advice as to what suits you best and how to make dressing for every occasion a pleasurable experience.

> If time is of the essence this can all be done for you and delivered to your home or office.

> This service costs £450.00 for a full day; £275.00 for half a day. And the great thing is, the stylists can work to any budget.

> **Coathanger T · 0870 460 6194 W · coathanger.net**

BECOME AN INTERNATIONAL WOMAN OF STYLE

> Always keeping her finger on the pulse of new trends and next season's fashions, Olivia will work with you to put together a fantastic wardrobe that fits your budget, lifestyle and work commitments. Chanel-trained, with 13 years' fashion experience and having advised as a wardrobe consultant on *Cyrano de Bergerac* and *Nikita*, you really will jump to the front of the Eurostyle queue when you shop with Olivia.

> She can visit you at home or work to find out your likes and dislikes before the two of you go off shopping. She'll know exactly where to take you and will save you loads of time, heartache, and 'why did I buy that?' night sweats when the credit card bill comes through. Olivia has now relocated to South Africa but continues to work within the UK, France and South Africa and she also arranges escorted shopping trips in London, twice a year. Prices: initial consultation £250.00; personal shopping £285.00 for four hours; £570.00 for a full day and thereafter £75.00 per hour.

> **Olivia Davidson T · +27 (0) 21 794 7006 / +27 (0) 72 411 8079 W · fashionstylist.co.za**

DON'T SET OFF WITHOUT A SHOPPING SHERPA

> If you're new to Knightsbridge (for that matter, even if you're an old hand), the sheer magnitude of the shopping experience can be a little overwhelming. That's why the Parkes Hotel offers a 'shopper special' that not only includes your accommodation and chilled champagne on arrival, but an insider's guide to the area, a one-hour consultation with a personal shopper, great discount deals at local shops and a free bag pick-up service from the stores themselves, so you can literally shop till you drop. Then, at the end of the day, come back for a complimentary tea and biscuits and let them organise a massage in the privacy of your room – bliss!

> You can enjoy this absolute luxury safe in the knowledge that you are making the best of your time and money by being lead straight to the hottest labels and the best deals. During the free consultation your personal shopper, stylist and wardrobe consultant, will find out exactly what you want and need, what you dream of and what you can afford, what's in your wardrobe already and what should be in there. She will then use her expert knowledge of the area to make sure you're pointed exactly in the right direction. If you would like to have her shop with you after the consultation, she is available at £40.00 per hour and, for an additional charge (per hour), Parkes can provide you with your own limo and driver – just in case you suddenly feel the urge to shop further a field or are so dazzled by your purchases that you can't remember the way home!

> **Parkes Hotel, 41 Beaufort Gardens, London SW3 1PW**
> **T·020 7581 9944 W·parkeshotel.com**

LOOKING TO FIT YOU UP

> Renowned for their excellent personal service, Paul & Joe will hold your measurements – from shoes to waist – then order your perfect fit from each designer stocked in the boutique. They will bring a selection of clothes to your home, including Paul & Joe collections and other brands including the fabulous Mamie (re-worked vintage clothing), True Religion Brand Jeans and Lejaby underwear. Of course they will also come armed with handbags, jewellery, hats and belts. A whole new look dropped at your doorstep.

> They cater for the men in your life too, and indeed any little ones – they can bring along their menswear collection and their range of children's wear (Little Paul&Jo for 4-12-year-olds). No-one will feel left out!

> The personal shopping service is available from £50.00 per hour.

> **Paul & Joe, 39–41 Ledbury Road, London W11 2AA T·020 7243 5510**
> **or 309 Brompton Road, London SW3 2DY T·020 7589 2684**
> **or 134 Sloane Street, London SW1X 9AX T·020 7824 8844**
> **Paul & Joe Men, 33 Floral Street, Covent Garden, London WC2E 9DJ T·020 7836 3388 W·paulandjoe.com**

TALENT, TASTE AND TACT

> Amanda Platt is such a popular personal shopper you will need to book her about a month in advance. Clients who have been using Amanda for years love her for her discretion and tact; she loves to dress business ladies, and is known for producing a great look for a great price. Although slightly more expensive than other personal shoppers at £700.00 a day, you can ring her for advice for up to a year after, at no extra charge which is fabulous. It's great that she will travel anywhere in the country, you just have to cover her travel costs.

> She can visit you at home or you can just meet and shop. Amanda says, 'The most common mistake women make with their wardrobe is buying the same thing over and over again.'

> **Amanda Platt T·020 7229 8109 E·amandaplatt.co.uk**

TAKE-OUT TOPSHOP

> Did you know that if you book an appointment and give the Topshop style advisors your wish list, they will pick suitable items from the shop floor, hop in their liveried Jeep, which has on-board sat-nav so they won't get lost, and will turn up at your home, office or hotel with the goodies, which you are under no obligation to buy? Better still, if you book a party for three or more (maximum six), the hostess gets 20 per cent off her purchases.

> As you can imagine, there is quite a waiting list for this convenient service, especially as they can only fit in a few appointments a day, so if you need it for a special 'do', make sure you phone well in advance.
> I invited Topshop and four friends round to my house and we had a great time. Our stylists were charming, friendly and gave good advice, and we had a lot of fun. Naturally we also purchased quite a few pieces between us. Unfortunately we tried the service in the very early stages and they did have a few teething problems with their admin and delivery — I'm sure that is now all rectified!
> Currently the service is only available within the M25 area for the London shop and Glasgow, Manchester and Dublin.
> There's also Topshop Express, where they'll wiz your clothes round to you on a Vespa (within London zones 1-3 only). Call the Express team and they'll try their hardest to get the clothes biked on the same day. For details online see the Style Advisor section.
> **TopShop to Go – London T· 0845 124 1144**
> **Glasgow, Argyle Street T· 0776 447 1243**
> **Manchester, Arndale Centre**
> **T· 0773 989 7771**
> **Dublin, St Stephen's Green**
> **T· +353 (0) 87 294 6961**
> **W· topshop.co.uk**

GET A LITTLE EXPERT ELEGANCE

> Susie Faux is a font of knowledge, after all she's been in the business of making you look good since 1973 and has also written two books. If you visit her shop, which is known as 'the shop of firsts', not only will you find the latest exclusive Italian fashions, you'll also find charming stylists who will lavish their experience and skills on you. Susie and her small, but expert, buying team try every piece on before they buy it, to ensure the cut is right and will give you just the right look, allowing you to leave full of confidence and style.

> They also offer an appointment-only consultation for a fee of £500.00 (redeemable against any purchase), where you will receive undivided care and attention, secret tips and styling advice. Most of all, you will have a fun-filled shopping experience in finding just the right clothes and accessories for your perfect look. Well known for their skills in assembling a cleverly co-ordinated wardrobe for middle to top management from sizes 8 to 18, we love the fact they can offer flexible hours by arrangement for all of us time-conscious women. They can also arrange in-house beauty treatments and reflexology.
> **Susie Faux, Wardrobe, 42 Conduit Street, London W1S 2YH**
> **T· 020 7494 1131 W· wardrobe.co.uk**

HOMEWORK HAS NEVER BEEN SO MUCH FUN

> Leesa offers five personal services: image consultation, wardrobe planning, personal shopping for men and women, personal styling and the New York Shopping Experience (see page 195). We love her Personal Shopping service where you can try on a fantastic selection from the cream of London's boutiques, designers and high-street retailers as well as get the inside track on sourcing an elusive piece of vintage or bespoke tailoring. You can shop with Leesa (or one of her stylists) or she can shop for you and then meet at a designated venue so you can go through the selections. Personal Shopping costs £400.00 per day.
> Image Consultation (£300.00) is a three-hour one-to-one session ending in a set of fashion guidelines to fit your lifestyle and make the most of your figure and colouring. It includes a colour and body-shape analysis, a make-over, colour swatch wallet and personal style guide.
> Wardrobe Planning (£250.00) weeds the nasties from your existing wardrobe with

a comprehensive plan of recommended additions. An eBay service is available for off-loading unwanted designer items, as are wardrobe accessories including hangers, moth repellent and shoe trees, all to keep your clothes in perfect condition.

> Personal Styling (£250.00) involves a two-hour home visit to help you look at your wardrobe in a new light. New outfits are created from old by suggesting different ways of using existing items in new combinations. Each new outfit is photographed to create your own handy reference 'look book' and you'll end up with around 20 new outfits. This is a very popular service and a great gift.

> **Leesa Whisker T·0870 043 4126 / 07966 311 880 E·leesa@whiskeragency.co.uk**

SEE IN STORE FOR PERSONAL DETAILS

There are some fabulous services to be had at some of the major stores and you don't have to have a vast budget to make an appointment. You do have to book in advance though and some have quite a waiting list, so it's not for that impulsive retail therapy fix or last-minute panic buy.

GET YOUR KICKS AT HARVEY NICKS

> A favourite with lovers of luxury and style around the world, Rebecca Haynes and her team of personal shoppers at Harvey Nichols offer the most fantastic service, not only for men's and women's fashion, but for cosmetics, home ware and gifts too.

> Some of their challenges have included tracking down the last pair of a particular Jimmy Choo shoes in the world, then having them shipped to the customer ready for them to wear the next day. Another customer simply had to have a dress from a particular designer, but the last one in the shop was not her size. Rebecca and her team were able to source the last bit of material left from the designer and then had it made in Paris – now that really is customer service!

> For maximum brownie points this Christmas, simply send them a list of the people you need to buy presents for, their likes and your budget. Rebecca and her team will shop throughout the store and give you a list of suggestions. They can then gift wrap the chosen gifts and send them to the lucky recipients, leaving you free to hit the party circuit with a clear conscience. By appointment only.

> **Rebecca Haynes at Harvey Nichols, 109-125 Knightsbridge, London SW1X 7RJ T·020 7259 6638 W·harveynichols.com**

TAKING LUXURY TO A NEW LEVEL

> As you might expect from one of the world's most famous stores, Harrod's personal shopping service is probably one of the best there is. Dedicated staff have tracked down the last Chloé Python Bag in the world and delivered it to their client in time for Christmas. They have furnished a private jet for a foreign prince in 24 hours, including cashmere blankets and fine dining crystal. They've sourced a limited edition back-gammon set and shipped it to a boat in Barbados, and sold a Rembrandt original to a fashion client. Even more impressive, they've flown an entire new season's wardrobe to a client in India, whom they had never met, and the client was amazed that of the 40 pieces of Moschino, Dolce & Gabbana and Chanel, every one fitted and looked 'as if it were made for her'.

> If you could want for more, their newly launched By Appointment service is a fantastic bespoke premium shopping experience covering the wealth of products available at Harrods, from fashion to beauty, accessories, fine jewellery, furniture, crystal, art, antiques, sports and international designer collections. It truly is an indulgent,

individual way to shop the entire store, run by the most fashion-savvy people in the industry. Your own personal shopper will spend time getting to know your needs so they can suggest and find precisely what you want. They can also offer a world of exclusives – products, previews, shows and launches. A vintage chauffeur-driven Rolls Royce is available, by invitation, and the service is available internationally and is entirely complimentary. Oh, I almost forgot to mention that you will be offered Champagne and wonderful petits-fours by Laudurée...

> **Harrods By Appointment T·020 7893 8000**
> **E·byappointment@harrods.com**
> **W·harrods.com**

THEY'LL CHANGE THE SHIRT ON YOUR BACK

Next to the wrinkle-free cotton, the thing I love most about Eton Shirts is their one-hour delivery service (London only). Imagine spilling red wine down your shirt at lunch with no time to go home or get to the shops before a make-or-break meeting in the afternoon. Eton Shirts will deliver a brand new shirt to your office from their fantastic collection, including their wrinkle-free range, trendy, fashion styles or their evening wear – disaster averted.

Eton Shirts, 65 Kingsway, London WC2B 6TD
T·020 7430 1433 W·etonshirts.co.uk

SHIRT MAKERS

THE SWEET SMELL OF STYLE

> This lovely shop is very popular with the girls for choosing a bespoke shirt, from over 500 fabrics, for the men in their life. Perfect if you're not the type to plan for his birthday three months in advance (who is that type?), a Charlie Allen shirt can be measured, made and boxed up all within three weeks (from £120.00).
> Charlie is also well known for his bespoke suits (from £1,200.00.) I particularly loved the fact that when you unwrap the suit they include a Creed tester, so he'll not only look good but smell good too!
> **Charlie Allen, 1 Coopers Yard, 181 Upper Street, Islington, London N1 1RQ**
> **T·020 7359 0883 W·charlieallen.co.uk**

MADE IN ENGLAND – WORN EVERYWHERE

> Matilda Aspinall offers made-to-measure shirts for women and her business partner, the highly respected Sean O'Flynn, offers the same service for men. Matilda is happy to come to your office or home with a pile of swatches and work through the shirt designs, or of course you can visit her at their shop in the West End. The compliments roll in and her clients keep coming back for more of these gorgeous, well-made shirts. Matilda likes to support English cloth and mills, but also uses Italian fabrics – from cotton to silks, floral to voile. Each design can be customised and takes three to four weeks for delivery. Prices: from £150.00
> **Matilda Aspinall T·020 8450 9923 / 07876 470 565**
> **Sean O'Flynn, Shirtmakers, 7 Sackville Street, London W1S 3DE T·020 7437 0044 W·seanoflynnshirtmaker.co.uk**

ALL THE BEST FOLK GO BESPOKE

> For a beautiful shirt that doesn't gape at your chest or show off that roll on your tummy, and we're talking men and women here, you

must visit New & Lingwood. Only the experts know how to put the fabric where you need it and take it away from where you don't. Choosing from over 700 different fabrics, they will endeavour to create whatever you want, even down to a bit of hand embroidery. The minimum order is four shirts and prices range from £165.00 each.

> The first shirt is made up as a sample (six weeks) which you try on and from which they then make the other three (another six weeks) – you'll never go back to off-the-peg again. Naturally they are too polite to mention by name any of their celebrity client list of well-known pop stars and nobility.

> **New & Lingwood, 53 Jermyn Street, London SW1Y 6LX T · 020 7493 9621 W · newandlingwood.com**

For Ede and Ravenscroft see page 198

SHOES
AND BOOTS
(INCLUDING SHOE REPAIR)

THE SECRET SHOE DOCTOR

> Broken strap, hole in the sole, snapped heel – anything your shoe throws at you can be fixed at this hidden Chelsea gem. Their reputation for always doing their best to help their customers, including a well known shoe maestro, has meant they have not only mended shoes but have been bought some more unusual things to mend, including a teapot, camel seat, pushbike and even an electric iron! The shop is tucked away, but go down Markham Street (opposite M&S in King's Road) to the village green and you'll find them in Elystan Street.

> **Chelsea Green Shoe Company, 31 Elystan Street, London SW3 3NT T · 020 7584 0776**

BEST OF A LOAD OF COBBLERS

> When it comes to cobblers, Joe Holmes is at the top of the list. In the business since he was 14, Joe Holmes and his team at Mayfair Cobblers repair shoes and boots for clients, with all the work done by hand. Joe also recently visited a 'movie star' on set, just to make her boots fit perfectly. If you're more impressed by loyalty than celebs, he has a client who has brought him the same pair of shoes to be mended for over 40 years, and the oldest pair he has fixed was made in 1916! So there's no excuse for suffering with blisters in the name of fashion anymore. They can also do great repairs on that matching handbag.

> **Mayfair Cobblers, 4 White Horse Street, London W1J 7LG T · 020 7491 3426**

FEET THAT STAND OUT IN A CROWD

> Terry de Havilland is a name synonymous with platforms and wedge sandals – he just lo-o-o-oves high heels – in fact, the highest pair he made were eight inches and they had to be sold with a cheeky 'government health warning' label. His shoes are stocked worldwide (see stockists online), but I wanted to tell you about his custom-made shoes – he's made them for top models and celebrities, a Harry Potter film and even Tomb Raider.

> Terry has been making footwear since the 1950s after taking over his family business. In the 60s, his three-tiered snakeskin wedge sandals rocketed to stardom and were spotted on the most famous feet of the rock 'n' roll set.

> During the 1980s, when young people shocked their parents by looking after their feet in Doc Martens and other low-heeled style statements, Terry started making specially commissioned shoes for the cognoscenti.

> In 2004, Terry re-launched his brand and took the fashion, press and retailers by storm with his range of funky shoes.

> If you're ordering a custom made shoe (you must, you must), you can choose from a wedge, stiletto, platform, thigh boot or ankle boot, in snakeskin, leather or hand-printed silks and satins. He can also embellish with Swarovski crystals. The fabric is hand cut and all footwear is proudly made in London, with Terry personally closing (footwear-speak for sewing /finishing off) every shoe.
> Custom-made shoes take approximately two weeks to make, with prices from £250.00 to £800.00.
> **Terry de Havilland, Ground Floor Studio, 336 Kingsland Road, London E8 4DA T · 020 7254 4445 W · terrydehavilland.net**

SAY IT WITH SHOES

> Customers just can't get enough of Olivia's quirky, original shoe designs that give women's feet their own identity. Her past collections have included the famed blank canvas shoes sold with a DIY paint kit, fluoro pumps made from ultra-violet reacting leather, boots covered in hundreds of antique mother-of-pearl buttons, and shoe jewellery with clip-on bows. Olivia designs shoes 'for the modern contemporary who loves fashion' and her shoes are sold in boutiques across the world.
> The shop is open by appointment only.
> **Olivia Morris, 355 Portobello Road, London W10 5SA T · 020 8962 0353 W · oliviamorrisshoes.com**

IF THE SHOE FITS... BUY FIVE PAIRS

> After an extremely pleasant morning spent with shoe expert Karen at Selve, I am at long last the proud owner of a pair of winter boots that fit my size-two-and-a-half feet perfectly and don't have five-inch heels, which I can't walk in!
> My appointment at Karen's private studio started with a great chat and coffee, then moved on to the science stuff. My feet were measured by their high-tech 3D scanner, then measurements were taken of my legs so that the semi-bespoke boots would fit exactly – and then came the fun part. It took a while to choose between a high heel or wedge, chocolate-brown suede with a pink lining or zebra print with a green lining and black sole – the choices are unbelievable and the results very individual. Each season Selve offer around 20 shoe/boot designs. The footwear is made in Italy and usually takes around 28 days to make, although I got mine much quicker. I received my boots in a clear box with a Polaroid of the style on the outside – great for stacking in my wardrobe. In Autumn 2007 they will be launching their new men's shoe collection. Prices: shoes £250-£295.00; boots £450.00
> **Selve, First Floor, 93 Jermyn Street, London SW1Y 6JE T · 020 7321 0200 W · selve.co.uk**

YOU CAN GO TO THE BALL

> Last year, I bought the most perfect pair of fairytale silk pumps in a tiny side street in Paris. On their very first outing my delicately clad feet were splashed by an evil motorist while we waited for a taxi and I thought my spectacular slippers were ruined. Then I heard about Julia Taylor. Julia offers an exclusive service for shoe dying, shoe cleaning (silk or satin), or beautiful beading for evening or bridal wear. She hand-sews her beads onto the shoes rather than glueing them – which is rare these days. Julia can also add exquisite beading to handbags, or repair vintage beaded bags. Prices: shoe dying from £70.00; shoe cleaning from £60.00 (also *see page* 56)
> **Julia Taylor T · 020 7289 3966 by appointment**

SHOE
ACCESSORIES

CURE THAT SINKING FEELING

> I remember attending a very swish garden party and noticing my brand new stilettos were sinking further and further into the grass. The lawn was so soft it made walking very difficult and in the end I had to remove them — thereby loosing four inches in height and ruining my complete look! So, I was delighted to hear about the stoppers from Clean Heels that you pop on the bottom of your heels to stop that sinking feeling. The tubing also protects your precious heels from being covered in mud but can also be cut down if you're wearing kitten heels. They're reusable and are available in clear glitter, diamanté or bridal designs. They also prevent heels getting stuck in decking, so are great on patios, yachts and cruise ships. Shipping is available worldwide — allow 7 days delivery for the UK.
Price: Clear glitter £3.50; Diamanté £4.99; Bridal with pearls and diamanté £14.99
> T· 01329 317 390 W· cleanheels.co.uk

SUMMER TIME AND THE WALKING AIN'T EASY

> The thing that often lets down a pair of shoes is how quickly the inner sole looks shabby, or the dye from the writing rubbing off onto your toes and feet once they get a little sweaty! And we all know the sound when you're wearing sandals on a hot day — 'slip, squish, smack'.
> So thank you to Shannon McLinden, creator of 'suede soft' summer soles. These practical, peel-and-stick fabric strips cover your shoe sole, are completely removable and leave no sticky residue. They come in a variety of patterns — the zebra- and leopard-print insoles are popular with fashionistas and celebs — colours, widths and fabrics, and are available up to size 11 (snip the heel to size). Not only will they keep your feet soft and dry but they can give a favourite old shoes a new lease of life, too.
Price: US$7.95 per pair, or three pairs for $21.00 (plus shipping — they will ship worldwide)
> **Summer Soles**
  T· (toll free in the USA) +1 888 773 9626 / (from outside the USA) +1 972 786 5412
  W· summersoles.com

TAILOR-MADE

Tailoring has made a big comeback in women's wear and now feels fresher, smarter and more grown-up than it has in years.

WHAT'S MERE CASH WHEN IT COMES TO CASHMERE?

> Pamela Blundell specialises in high-end, one-off suits, tailored evening wear and coats. With a long list of celebrity clients, she's made lovely things for Kylie, including a gorgeous cashmere coat — I'm so jealous!
> Prices start at £2,500.00 — for this you will receive a perfectly fitted, modern but sexy, flattering suit, made with the utmost personal attention. Pamela prides herself on sourcing the best French fabrics, which she updates regularly, and every suit is lined with 100-per-cent silk.
> The first fitting and order takes six to eight weeks, but once she has all your measurements, you can ring up to find out what's new this season and order another outfit which Pamela can make for you within two weeks. Pamela is based in Soho and is available by appointment only.
> **Pamela Blundell Bespoke**
  T· 020 7289 1062

WHEN IN DOUBT, FOLLOW THE STARS

> If you, like me, can't live without your monthly fix of the fashion mags, then you're bound to have read about Richard James' personal tailoring services and he's already the tailor of choice for A-list celebrities.

> On London's Savile Row, the home of the finest bespoke tailoring in the world, you'll find his modern shop offering his ready-to-wear, accessories, shirts, ties, knitwear and sportswear and just opposite in Clifford Street, his other shop offering the bespoke tailoring (along with personalised socks and dressing gowns). Richard offers a classic but very 'now' look. He uses exclusive fabrics in unusual colours, patterns and textures, and, for a very individual look, you can choose from his archive of luxury fabrics, which buttons and lining you want and which pocket shape and trouser cut. If the classic navy chalk stripe isn't what you're after, why not choose a soft denim or camouflage? Prices: from £1,175.00 for his personal tailoring service

> **Richard James, 19 Clifford Street, London W1 3RH T·020 7434 0171**
> **or 29 Savile Row, London W1S 2EY T·020 7434 0605 W·richardjames.co.uk**

ISN'T IT TIME YOU LEARNT TO DRESS YOURSELF?

> Not only does Imtaz create exclusive garments for men and women, she can also teach you the art of tailoring with one-on-one lessons from beginners' to advanced. Imtaz is completely flexible on format and times, and will quickly have you making all your own clothes at half the price. The tailoring lessons are just £27.50 per hour – cheaper than a session with a personal trainer and with much quicker results on the figure-flattering front! If you would prefer that she did all the sewing, she can make you a stunning suit from £700.00, or a wedding dress or that lovely evening dress you've always wanted. She will also source amazing materials for that unique piece.

> Too lazy to sew? Too lazy to travel? She also offers a visiting tailoring service. She has been named as one of the top four tailors in London, has been featured in numerous magazines and has a client base that includes pop stars, supermodels and movie stars.

> **Imtaz Khaliq 7 The Walk, Independent Place, Shackwell Lane, London E8 2HE T·020 7503 3537 W·imtaz.com**

Paul Strotton (see under Alterations, page 145) – Bespoke tailoring from £500.00
T·020 7262 2771

VINTAGE FASHION

PASSAGE TO THE PAST

> Annie Moss has been in Camden Passage for 26 years. This shop is absolutely fantastic and is filled to the brim with the most divine dresses, wedding dresses, beautiful beaded bags, accessories, shawls, tops and lingerie, plus other gems dating from 1880 to 1960.

> Annie scours all the best fairs and auctions in the UK and overseas to bring you the most beautiful things. The oldest dress she has sold was an 1805 empire line and her favourite favourite buy (which is still currently for sale) is a divine 1930s pale cream, pink and blue sequin ball gown. The sequins are in the pattern of leaves and flowers and the dress has a gorgeous low back. Prices can start from as little as £9.00 for jewellery and tops, with a 1940s day dress at £85.00 and a 1930s beaded evening dress around £150.00.

> **Annie's Vintage Clothes, 12 Camden Passage, Islington, London N1 8ED T·020 7359 0796 / 0796 803 7993**

BEAT THE IN-CROWD

> I often visit this little shop as they have some great vintage buys, including beaded cardies, bags, shoes, dresses, jackets and coats. The magazines are always calling Cloud Cuckoo Land for clothes for shoots, so get down there and beat those stylists to it! Open Monday to Saturday, 11.00 a.m-5.00 p.m.

> **Cloud Cuckoo Land, 6 Charlton Place, Camden Passage, Islington, London N1 8AJ**
  T·020 7354 3141
  E·cuckoolandmail@yahoo.co.uk

WELL WORTH THE TRIP

> Once you find this shop, you will return again and again. Vintage clothes, shoes, bags and a great selection of jewellery — along with some new looks, including one-off's — await your sharp eye and honed antennae. Rellik stock clothing and accessories from the 1920s to the mid-80s, and designers include Pierre Cardin, Pucci, Ossie Clark and Vivienne Westwood. Expect to lose hours of your life browsing and to leave with a heavy bag and a lighter purse. This is the shop were some top celebs go for their unique look. Open Tuesday to Saturday.

> **Rellik, 8 Golborne Road, London W10 5NW**
  T·020 8962 0089 W·relliklondon.co.uk

THE ART OF DRESSING BEAUTIFULLY

> Step inside the door of this Aladdin's cave and you enter a secret world of clothing and accessories spanning two floors. It is run by brother and sister Tracy Tolkien and Mark Steinberg — Tracy has written a fabulous book, *Vintage — The Art of Dressing Up* (Pavilion), which is a must-read for any collector.

> The staff are very knowledgeable and they can point you in the direction of an original Pucci, Givenchy or Schiaparelli, not to mention show you the most fantastic vintage jewellery and handbags. Actually, they currently have for sale a fabulous pale lilac and dove-grey chiffon Schiaparelli evening gown delicately embroidered with sequins that comes with a dusky pink wrap — simply divine. Their most fabulous find was a Fortuny silk gown with devorée jacket (sadly now sold for £12,000.00).

> Some say the items are a little pricey, I say it depends what you're looking for — they have earrings from as little as £15.00. Anyway, these days it's getting harder and harder to buy original, well-maintained vintage pieces. And remember, they've travelled the world to bring them to you, so don't grumble about paying that little bit extra — you really do get what you pay for.

> **Steinberg & Tolkien, 193 Kings Road, Chelsea, London SW3 5ED**
  T·020 7376 3660

TA RA TUPPERWARE, SALUT VINTAGE STYLE

> If you dream of hosting a soirée to remember for all your super-stylish friends, then give the lovely Tara a call. She will come to your home, or a venue of your choice, with a beautiful selection of very reasonably priced vintage items. Brooches start from as little as £5.00 and dresses are usually in the £100.00-£150.00 bracket, with vintage couture costing slightly more of course. Tara has a passion for helping her clients put together a stunning vintage look, and with her excellent reputation based on word-of-mouth, you can rest easy that she has your complete satisfaction and not her next sale in mind.

> If you fancy a jaunt to Paris, she can even set up a venue and you can host your party there. Tara charges a small amount towards her travel costs and passes on to you any additional catering or venue fees. So round up your girls onto the Eurostar or pop the champagne, get out the old Edith Piaf records and invite la belle Paris chez vous!

> **Tara Munro, Ooh la la Vintage, 9 Avenue St Exupery, Chatillon, Paris 92320**
  T·+33 14 25 35 234 W·oohlalavintage.com

AUTHENTIC GENIUS

> Rachel Spencer studied fashion at Central Saint Martins and trained in couture embroidery at the House of Lesage in Paris. She designed embroideries for well-known shoe and fashion designers before setting up her own company, Heirloom Couture.

> Rachel's passion is to unearth beautiful wedding dresses locked away in attics and antique shops and restore them to their former glory – perhaps adding a new silk lining, handmade silk flowers or embroidering delicate designs. Recently she restored a client's grandmother's bridal dress so the bride could retain the romantic and nostalgic memory of her beloved grandmother but also show her own unique style by adding her favourite flowers, embroidery and trim. Rachel is currently hand-beading an exquisite double georgette dress with Calla lilies. This was the request of a bride whose mother (a garden designer) has cultivated a lily especially for her daughter's big day, and also named it after her honeymoon destination – how beautiful.

> Rachel will help you source vintage accessories to complete the look, but you may not need to go far as she also hires out Schiaparelli jewellery from the 1920s and 30s, vintage Manolo Blahnik and Vivienne Westwood shoes, and handmade veils with vintage jewellery. She can also embroider (or make) anything to go with your existing dress, including accessories. Allow about three months to work on designs so everyone is as stress free as possible!
Prices: Dresses £850-£6,500.00.

> **Heirloom Couture T · 020 8969 4013
W · heirloomcouture.com**

SOMETHING OLD AND SOMETHING NEW

> Charlie Brear has an enviable life as a fashion stylist working with top photographers and models. As a celebrity stylist and accessories designer, she has now launched a bespoke vintage wedding dress service, for which she has sourced beautiful pieces from both sides of the Atlantic. Charlie searches all over the USA and Europe to find anything from a 1920s to a 1960s dress which she can restore or tailor for a new bride.

> As well as finding your dream dress, Charlie can help style your complete look to guarantee that you'll be stunning head-to-toe on your big day. The Vintage Wedding Dress Company is open by appointment only.

> **The Vintage Wedding Dress Company
T · 020 7328 1398 / 07951 866 896
W · thevintageweddingdresscompany.com**

For further vintage wedding dresses and accessories see pages 177-180

VINTAGE
FASHION FAIRS

GET HIP TO FASHION HISTORY

> Held bi-monthly, this lovely London fair is great for vintage finds. Set up by Anita Bott who was fed up with everything being branded vintage as soon as it was a few years old, so she set up the fair, vetted the stall owners and now nothing gets past the door that is not true vintage. And what does she say is vintage – 'Vintage fashion to me dates before the 1970's where it exudes style, quality and uniqueness drawing from the rich influences of past eras, with a variety that is difficult to acquire today.' Here Here I say.

> What a wonderful way to spend your Sunday, hunting through the rails of dresses and skirts and trying on period hats and shoes, not to mention all the amazing handbags. Also offers textiles, trimmings, jewellery and other vintage delights. I saw the most beautiful wedding dress I have ever seen c1910 – teensy weensy waist – diet one year – and all for £400.00. I wanted to buy it just to hang it up as a piece of 'art'. This is a

popular fair so get there early, you may even spot a top model or celeb.

> £4.00, (students £2.50 with valid id)
9.30 a.m. - 4.30 p.m.

> **Anita's Vintage Fashion Fairs, Battersea Arts Centre, Grand Hall, Lavender Hill, London SW11 5TN**
T · 020 8325 5789
W · vintagefashionfairs.com

FROCK-ME, IT'S FANTASTIC!

> Frock Me is a great little fair held in the Chelsea Town Hall around five times a year. Run by Adams Fairs, there are around 60 specialists selling an array of vintage clothing, accessories, jewellery, handbags, shoes and other lovely things from a wide range of periods and styles.

> Shoppers are a mixture of models, fashionistas, stylists, students, collectors and costume designers for stage and film. Items can be a little more pricey than at some of the other fairs, but you do get very good quality and there is certainly something to suit all tastes and budgets.

> Held on a Sunday, 11.00 a.m.-5.30 p.m. Entrance charge £3.00 (students with card £1.50)

> **Frock Me, Chelsea Town Hall, King's Road, Chelsea, London SW3 5EZ**
T · 020 7254 4054
W · frockmevintagefashion.com

ALL IS FAIRS IN LOVE AND SHOPPING

> The London Textiles, Vintage Fashion and Accessories Fair is my absolute favourite and if I miss one I suffer tremendous anxiety, thinking I have missed out on a superb find. I didn't even want to write about it as I tremble to think you may beat me to that must-have buy. However, with such a huge choice available, I know there's something for everyone, so I mustn't be selfish!

> The prices are great and you can buy from a range of private dealers (many of whom only sell at fairs) and shops. You'll find an array of textiles, trimmings, lace, embroidery, linen, shoes, handbags, jewellery, beautiful vintage clothes, scarves and hats, and you can be sure that every time you go, there will be something you just have to buy. They are held every five to six weeks, with over 100 stands. Doors open at 10.00 a.m. and close at 5.00 p.m. for an entry fee of £5.00. For early birds in pursuit of that vintage worm, there is a £10.00 fee to get in between 8.00 a.m. and 10.00 a.m. – I'll see you there!

> They also hold an Antique Textiles, Vintage Costumes and Tribal Art Fair three times a year, which has more than 50 dealers and promises genuine antique textiles and costumes from 1600 to 1930, tribal art and some decorative antiques. (11.00 a.m.-5.00 p.m.)

> **Paola Francia-Gardiner, The London Textiles, Vintage Fashion and Accessories Fair, Hammersmith Town Hall, King Street, London W6 9JU**
T · 020 8543 5075 W · pa-antiques.co.uk

ONLINE
VINTAGE FASHION

MAKE EVERYDAY A RED CARPET DAY

> Original antique and vintage clothing from 1800s to today – I can sit for hours looking at all the lovely vintage fashion on Antique Dress's website, wishing I'd managed to score an invitation to the BAFTAs or the Oscars this time round! I know I would stand up to scrutiny by wearing one of these fabulous gowns.

> Deborah has some simply gorgeous wedding gowns – some lucky bride-to-be had just purchased a 1910 ecru satin trained gown with lace, wax orange-blossom decorations and original veil – unbelievably stunning and I've certainly never seen one like it.

> Deborah writes great copy for each item. Look at the entry for a Manolo Blahnik Black

Velvet and Satin Shoes with Rhinestone Buckles: 'Easily retail over $600. Buy these quick before I decide to keep them!!!! Really... this is one of those tough calls... 'To keep or not to keep... that is the question'! I wonder if Shakespeare had these kinds of dilemmas? Gorgeous shoes! Excellent condition. Expect tons of compliments. Oh god, this is tough!!! If I cry when you buy them... be kind to me! These are the kind of shoes you can wear with the simplest black dress and small rhinestone purse and you will be smashing! Measures: Marked 6.5 B ($345.00).'

> Having collected antique clothing for over 25 years, Deborah has finally run out of room to store them all and so now we are lucky and privileged to be able to buy some from her. She also has a section for memorabilia, where you can own gowns, costumes or items from the likes of Barbra Streisand or Liza Minnelli.

> **Deborah Burke, Antique Dress, PO Box 3535, Stamford, CT 06905 T· +1 203 351 0639 (only between 10.00 a.m. and 7.00 p.m. EST) W· antiquedress.com**

A NEW WORLD OF GLAMOUR

> Enokiworld has great vintage clothing with excellent write-ups for each item, some so funny that you'll barely flinch as you tap in your credit card details. They had a Black 1970s Hermes 'Kelly' bag ($4.750.00), a 1960s Emilio Pucci printed bikini in pink ($435.00) and a stunning 1930s peach silk charmeuse gown ($305.00) which I would have fought a duel at dawn for. They also have a Lifestyle section that includes retro items for your kitchen and a great Accessories department. Vintage fashions include classics from Halston, Ossie Clark, Yves Saint Laurent and Chanel, to name but a few.

> Taken straight from the horse's mouth: 'You can't be unique if you copy from head to toe,

so find inspiration from everywhere but make the extra effort to put your own spin on things with a few amazing vintage enokiworld things.'

> **T· +1 314 991 5775 W· enokiworld.com**

CAN YOU DIG IT?

> This enterprising site is made up of a group of vendors offering a great collective of vintage fashion, ephemera and accessories. I love that you can shop for items by decade, designer, individual shop or keyword.

> The Fashiondig's store locator will help you find selected vintage clothing stores by zip code, city and state, or country – a great vintage shopping resource for travellers and collectors alike. When I knew I was heading to the Big Apple, I looked up New York and it gave me listings for 127 shops. On most entries, it doesn't tell you what the shop specialises in but does give you the name and address and a handy map link (telephone numbers would have been useful). You can also Ask Janet, Fashiondig's resident style expert, any question on vintage fashion, style or beauty.

> **W· fashiondig.com**

BYGONE GOWNS TO WED FOR

> This is a divine site with gorgeous, gorgeous fashion that you can very easily own. There are six categories: Victorian-Edwardian; Flapper-WWII; Mid-Century; Designer & Couture; Bridal; and Celebrity Wardrobe & Memorabilia. When I visited the bridal section, there were over 18 pages of stunning gowns, including two dresses I would love to own: an absolutely stunning c.1935 candlelight ivory bias-cut peau-de-soi satin gown, with ecru lace inserts, cut in a unique art-deco pattern ($2,500.00); and a gorgeous Adele Scott pink satin and ivory lace gown with pearl beads, iridescent sequins and rhinestones ($425.00). The celebrity wardrobe included a Chanel coat owned

by Liza Minnelli (with certificates of authenticity). If you need a fabulous frock then look no further than this fabulous site.
> W·thefrock.com E·queries@thefrock.com

SHAKE OR STIR UP YOUR WARDROBE
> Be prepared to spend hours browsing through the wonderful clothing and accessories on Vintage Martini. The vintage clothing dates from pre-1900 to the 1960s, and ranges from ladies' clothing, hats, accessories, men's clothing, lingerie, ephemera, patterns and transfers, to vintage barware and vintage photos. On offer when I looked were some really funky sunglasses, gorgeous wedding gowns, and some fabulous evening dresses: 1950s black wool Christian Dior suit ($485.00); peacock-blue velvet 1920s evening coat ($265.00); early 1930s ivory cotton acid-lace wedding dress ($475.00); and a 1950s cocktail dress in white netting with silver Mylar stripes ($225.00). They also have some fantastic hats — I really wanted the wonderful beehive hat made of black and green iridescent coque feathers that looked exactly like a beehive hairdo ($125.00).
> They often hold sales with up to 50 per cent discount on some items. I purchased some lovely old wedding photos and they arrived from the USA within eight days. E-mail them if you're interested in an item.
> W·vintagemartini.com
  E·cecilimose@aol.com

DIOR-TO-DOOR SERVICE
> Vintageous have a lovely selection of dresses, suits, skirts, pants, blouses, outerwear, lingerie and accessories. The descriptions really pull you in — rustling teal taffeta, shimmering gold lace & lamé, liquid satin, sultry black, head-turning — how on earth could you resist?
> They have the most fantastic collection of gorgeous formal and cocktail dresses, including designs by Bill Blass, Oleg Cassini

and Christian Dior. . . you are bound to find your next party dress here. What's great is they do update their site regularly, so you are not tortured by looking at the most divine dress ever and then finding it's sold!
> Very interesting links as well.
> W·vintageous.com

THEY DO MAKE THEM LIKE THEY USED TO
> This is a fabulous service. The Vintage Pattern Lending Library houses around 3,000 antique sewing and needlework patterns, vintage fashion publications and other related historic print materials from the 1840s to the 1950s. As they believe their wonderful collection 'should be shared used, and not merely stored away', members may borrow patterns (only in USA, for $5.00 per pattern). However, anyone can buy a high quality, historically accurate reproduction. When they digitise the patterns from the original source they always include all the markings and symbols, and also add additional information to clarify any antiquated terms or vague instructions, which is very helpful.
> **Vintage Pattern Lending Library, 869 Aileen Street, Oakland, CA 94608 T·+1 510 655 3091 W·vpll.org**

LOOK, LONG AND LEARN
> This is one of the most amazing vintage fashion websites on the internet and has been on my favourites list for quite a while. One wonders where Linda Ames finds all these wonderful fashion items, many of which are in remarkable condition considering their age. I logged on time and again to pine after a divine, handmade, Irish crocheted lace coat c.1900 ($3,300.00). Categories extend from Early, Victorian, Edwardian, 1920s, 1930s, Designer, Shawls/ Textiles and Jewellery, to a wonderful Gallery section showing a sample of the best items sold by Vintage Textiles over the last seven years. I sat and simply stared and sighed in

wonder for way too long a time! Also on offer is a great Treasure Hunt section filled with lace, lingerie, trimmings, buttons, hats, hair adornments and other little gems. Best of all, Linda shares her incredible expertise with informative articles on collecting vintage clothing.

> **Linda Ames, Vintage Textiles, 18 Lee Street No. 10, Keene, NH 03431**
> **T · +1 603 352 6338 W · vintagetextile.com**

19TH CENTURY CHIC

> This is a great site, full of ladies' and gents' vintage fashion, including hats, shoes, coats, bridal, lingerie, accessories and purses. They also sell sewing patterns, cookbooks, textiles, fashion magazines, sewing notions and vanity table items. The women's fashion items range from pre-Civil War (American) to the 1960s, and when I last looked, they had some truly beautiful designer pieces including Dior, Nina Ricci and Pucci. I would have loved the c.1890 stunning black French lace dress with sequin accents and jet beading ($900.00), not to mention a very unusual 1950s hand-painted felt skirt with appliquéd hand-painted rose petals set with rhinestones ($125.00). They often offer items at sale price, with up to 30 per cent discounts. Their Graveyard category is also worth a look.

> **W · woodlandfarmsantiques.com**

SHOPPING AND PRESENTS
ANTIQUEFAIRS GUIDES TOURS
ONLINESHOPPING JEWELLERY
VINTAGE CHINA FASHIONFAIR
WINE BESPOKEGIFTS COOKIES
BOOKS GIFTWRAPPING SILVER
ART DIVINEPRESENTS CRAFTS
GREATSHOPS THANKYOUGIFTS

SHOPPING

SHOPPING GUIDES

To get the most out of a hard day's shopping there are three things to remember: plan ahead, take emergency chocolate rations and plan ahead some more. Forget your best friend or your beloved; one of these fabulous books or guides is the only shopping companion you need to worry about.

BAG YOURSELF SOME EXTRA BEAUTY

> Another gem from Josephine Fairley and Sarah Stacey: in *The Handbag Beauty Bible* all the best beauty products from 280 brands across 70 categories are tried by over 2,400 women. No more will you puzzle over what product will clear up your spots quicker, which are the best tweezers to buy, or which cleanser will give you the biggest bang for your buck. The guide is also filled with time-saving tips for beauty shopping and best beauty secrets from top make-up artists, hair pros and nail gurus. After reading it from front to back I had immediately written down 15 products I simply have to have. Beautifully illustrated by David Downton, it would make a lovely gift to give to your girlfriends. (£8.99)

> **The Handbag Beauty Bible**, **Josephine Fairley and Sarah Stacey (Kyle Cathie Limited) W·beautybible.com**

GO DIRECT TO GORGEOUS

> If you're interested in craft, fashion, interiors or art, look out for the latest edition of *The Textile Directory*. It gets bigger and better every year and lists artists, designers, makers, organisations, art galleries, museums, study centres and courses, shows and magazines, to name just a few of the categories. I love the shopping section which is chock-a-block full of where you can buy textile art

and craft supplies, including beads, buttons, dolls, embroidery, dyes, knitting, lace, ribbons, *passementerie* and soft furnishings. You'll also find out exactly who you can call on when you want to commission a piece of bespoke jewellery, a unique fabric, knitwear, corsetry, curtains, a couture outfit or a rug. You can purchase it through Word4Word (£9.99) or at RD Franks (*see page* 151).

> **The Textile Directory**, **Word4Word Design & Publishing Ltd, 8 King Charles Court, Evesham, Worcestershire WR11 4RF T·0870 220 2820 W·thetextiledirectory.com**

SAVE TIME, SPEND MONEY

> The *Time Out – London Shopping Guide* is a fantastic guide to over a thousand of London's shops and services. It's an absolute must if you shop regularly in London or are planning a big spree on your next visit. Sections include fashion, children, food & drink, home & garden and health & beauty. You'll discover all sorts of new shops and services and be so organised that you will have plenty of time left for coffee and cake! Available in most bookshops or online (often discounted). I can't recommend it enough. (£9.99)

> **Time Out – London Shopping Guide W·timeout.com**

HIT THE STREETS WITH CONFIDENCE

> When it comes to a day of well-earned retail therapy, the *Where to Wear* guides (*see* full entry on *page* 152) are *the* shopping bibles and should be as important to you as your credit cards. Compiled by fashion journalists to make shopping fun and easy, they include hard-to-find boutiques, shopping secrets and many other little gems, all listed in a reader-friendly way, alphabetically, by category and geographically.

> Buy the boxed set and you get four books for the price of three, so you might be able to

spare one for a girlfriend, but then again...
(£9.99 each or boxed sets £29.99).

> **Where to Wear, 1st floor, 571 King's Road,
London SW6 2EB T·020 7371 9004
W·wheretowear.com**

GO NATIVE IN NEW YORK

> Well known for their wonderful worldwide restaurant guides, Zagat also publish a fantastic shopping guide to New York. I read this book front to back, twice, before hitting New York for a five-day shopping, sorry, research trip. Written by 7,500 candid New York shoppers, the entries are honest, refreshing and often highly amusing.

> Two thousand shops in over 50 categories; no wonder they say there's no place like New York. The guides are available in book form ($14.95), or for your Palm, pocket PC, Blackberry or mobile phone.

> You can also buy a NYC Shopper's Pack ($22.90) which includes the shopping guide and the *New York City Gourmet Marketplace*, featuring 1,654 top food and entertaining resources. You can scoff yourself around the city's best bakers, visit the best butchers, caterers, florists, wine shops, as well as entertain or find the perfect party site. I ordered my set online and it arrived in 14 days from the USA. I thought I'd also mention that four of the restaurant guides are available in deluxe leather bound editions and would make great gifts for a friend who dines out a lot.

> **New York City Shopping, Zagat
W·zagat.com**

Here are some other great books that have helped me on my shopping quests; perfect for your bookshelf, your friend's birthday present, or both.

> *Antique & Flea Markets of London & Paris*, Rupert Thomas and Eglé Salvy (Thames and Hudson Ltd) – Great markets, inspiring photos, find all those bargains and collectibles.

> *A Shopper's Guide to Paris Fashion*, Alicia Drake (Metro Books) – My copy is thick with Post-It notes marking those must-visit shops. Also includes where to stop for coffee and croissants.

> *Suzy Gershman's **B**orn to Shop New York* and *Suzy Gershman's **B**orn to Shop London* The Ultimate Guide for People who Love to Shop (Frommer's Born to Shop) (Hungry Minds Inc, U.S.) – Two great books that are straight talking, highly informative and funny, with fantastic entries. It includes the best gifts, buys, quickie lunches, secret finds and much more.

> *Exploring the Flea Markets of France*, Sandy Price (Three Rivers Press) – If you're one to rummage, like me, this is a must-have book with comprehensive entries on more than 200 markets around the French countryside. It includes invaluable information on quality of goods, price range, scenery, amenities, history and cultural aspects of each market.

> *New York's 100 Best – Little places to shop*, Eve Claxton (City & Company) – Lists chic little boutiques and unique speciality stores in New York.

> *The Paris Shopping Companion*, Susan Swire Winkler and Caroline Lesieur (Cumberland House Publishing) – I love this book, as it not only offers advice on the best buys at each establishment, it's also sectioned into *arrondissements* (districts) and points out things to see along the way. Use it and you'll definitely find the best that Paris has to offer.

> *Crown Guides: Unique Places in San Francisco* (Zeitgeist Books) – Lovely guide to the city's more unusual speciality shops. From bars to hair salons, vintage shops to art galleries. Great photos throughout encourage you to make a visit.

All books mentioned can be purchased at W·amazon.com

FABULOUS FAIRS

Whether you're looking for valuable vintage or contemporary chic, you can pick up some amazing goodies at a fair. Here's a selection of some of the ones that I never miss. For fairs that combine fashion with accessories and textiles see:

- *The London Vintage Fashion, Textile & Accessories Fair, page 177*
- *Anita's Vintage Fashion Fairs, page 176*
- *Frock Me, page 177*

A PALACE FULL OF TREASURES

> The Alexandra Palace Antique & Collectors Fair is promoted as London's largest antiques fair with over 700 stands. You can weave your way through aisles and aisles of jewellery, furniture, toys, china, books, silver, textiles and all manner of collectibles. An absolute shopper's paradise, as long as you're wearing comfy shoes! It's held approximately five times a year and I always manage to fill a bag or two! If you love jewellery you'll find some great finds here. Currently, with the new management restructuring, the fair has been put on hold, but they are hoping to re-start the fairs from November 2007 – the website will inform you of all the goss!

> **Alexandra Palace Antique & Collectors Fair, Great Hall, Alexandra Palace, Alexandra Palace Way, London N22 7AY**
> **T · 020 8883 7061**
> **W · pigandwhistlepromotions.com**

TEXTILE TALES

> Elizabeth Baer has an enviable job with regular jaunts to France to foray in the markets and chateaux, to stock up on her wonderful collection of linens, textiles, trimmings and other treats. Her antique linen and hemp sheet collection is unrivalled and buyers come from around the world. Her finds have been used in royal palaces, stately homes, ocean villas and historic house refurbishments.

> You can visit her home by appointment only, so please telephone first. But what I love is Elizabeth organises a fantastic Talent for Textiles fair (by invitation) where you find superb deals – in fact, I almost didn't put this bit in as I wanted to keep it all to myself!

> Email her for details – she organises other vintage fairs throughout the year in various venues.

> **Elizabeth Baer, Talent for Textiles, Church House, 29 Church Street, Bradford on Avon, Wiltshire BA15 1LN**
> **T · 01225 866 136   E · dbaer@onetel.com**

FIVE-DAY FAIR FEVER

> Held twice a year in spring (March) and Christmas (November), this fair attracts thousands of visitors, including many from overseas. They also hold a spring fair in Glasgow in March. The London fair is on from Wednesday till Sunday, so you've got no excuse to miss it. The Christmas fair is my absolute favourite and I always come away laden down with bags. You could buy all of your Christmas presents here, as well as some gorgeous and unusual Christmas decorations. They have a growing number of vintage stalls where I will fight with the best to snag those highly sought after one-offs. Many products you won't see in the stores as they're from small British businesses or independent designers, makers and producers who buy or make all year round to sell at the fairs.

> The best thing about the fair is that all the stands are strictly vetted and are all of the highest quality. They also have a scrummy food section where all manner of 'tastings' will delight your senses. Try to book online as you'll save pounds off the £14.00 door price. Put it in your diary now! Ticket order line

number is released nearer to fair date (see online for details)

> *Country Living Magazine* Fair, Business Design Centre, 52 Upper Street, London N1 OQH W · countrylivingfair.com

AL FRESCO BARGAINS

> The Ardingly and Newark fairs are run by DMG Antiques who also hold fairs in Detling, Malvern and Shepton Mallet. So with 49 events spread over five venues you're bound to be able to visit one of them.

> **Ardingly** is held around six times a year with up to 1,700 stalls inside and out. Great finds are to be had, from furniture to textiles, collectibles to ceramics. Some great French dealers attend which makes it even more inviting. I don't think anyone has ever come away empty-handed. It can get a little chilly nearer October, so wrap up warm if you intend walking around the outside pitches. Tuesday is the trade day (£20.00) and Wednesday is for public entry (£5.00).

> **Newark** is billed as Europe's largest antiques event with up to 4,000 stalls over 84 acres – yikes! There's no way you'll cover it all in a day, but there are six fairs a year with lots of outside pitches. Shoppers and stallholders flock from around the world for these great events. Thursday is £20.00 and allows entry on Friday as well and Friday £10.00 before 10.00 a.m. and £5.00 after 10.00 a.m. I needed a truck to transport everything once I'd finished shopping! Their website gives you all the dates, times, useful maps and travel information.

> **DMG Antiques Fairs, PO Box 100, Newark, Nottinghamshire NG24 1DJ**
  T · 01636 702 326 W · dmgantiquefairs.com

ORIGINAL FLAIR

> This used to be the Chelsea Crafts Fair but has now moved to Somerset House and has been renamed Origin. They moved venue to allow more designers/makers to show and

sell their work and there were over 300 UK and international vendors at the inaugural Origin event. Held over two weeks (usually in October), this is a great place to shop for wonderful jewellery, ceramics, glass, fashion textiles and furniture, and you can also commission one-off works. I know October is quite early to be thinking of Christmas shopping but I usually stock up on a few Christmas presents here – or at least I tell myself that I'll be giving them away!

> **Origin, The London Craft Fair at Somerset House, Strand, London WC2R 1LA**
  T · 020 7806 2512 W · craftscouncil.org.uk

For wedding shows see page 61.

For wedding shows see page 61.

GREAT SHOPS TO VISIT

And now I can't resist putting in some of my all-time favourite shops – shops that are the perfect places for buying presents for the bottom drawer, if you can bear to part with anything you buy. Some of these shops may seem randomly placed around the UK, but you never know when you might be visiting or just driving by. Take a visit and I'm sure you'll be hooked too.

COCO POPS TO MIND FOR LUXURY

> Absolutely gorgeous things in this lifestyle shop – I simply adore Coco Ribbon (even down to their packaging). Lingerie drapes over French armoires, books sit atop classic furniture and jewellery lies on glass dressers. The shop resembles a beautiful boudoir where nearly everything is for sale.

> The founders, Alison Chow and Sophie Oliver, source products from around the world, especially Sydney, Alison's hometown. I've purchased many a gift here, from French-milled soap to a stuffed cat called Uggy. It's an absolute treasure-trove, with luxurious throws, silky lingerie and nightwear,

handbags, their signature butterflies, candles, exclusive designer fashion and other 'don't-need-it-but-simply-must-have-its'.

> Another couple of gems they offer are W·pantypostman.com (*see page* 160) which delivers pretty new knickers to your door every three months (delivery worldwide), and an event-styling service.

> **Coco Ribbon, 21 Kensington Park Road, Notting Hill, London W11 2EU**
T·020 7229 4904 W·cocoribbon.com

THE ECLECTIC'S SHANGRI-LA

> If I'm in the King's Road area, without a doubt I visit Couverture to see what little gem I might find. Initially the owner, Emily Dyson, specialised in hand-finished bed linen and bed clothing, but now her products include all sorts of original, desirable and vintage pieces for the home. For example, over time I've purchased five vintage coloured serving dishes for dips and snacks which together form a petal, an antique rag doll which took me back to when I was five, a knitted, hand-embroidered rabbit, meant as a gift but still sitting on my shelf three years later, and loads of birthday presents which I've managed to actually give away. Several designs have been developed exclusively by Emily, including soft lambswool throws, a children's knitwear collection and accessories for the home. Next time you're reading a gift list suggestion or 'what's new' list in something like *Vogue* or *Elle Decoration*, invariably the stylists/editor will have been to Couverture to source a unique item. Don't be left out.

> **Couverture, 310 King's Road, London SW3 5UH T·020 7795 1200**
W·couverture.co.uk

SHED YOUR SHOPPING INHIBITIONS

> Philippa just loves to shop for anything vintage, but luckily for us she also likes to sell it again. When her husband Richard could

hardly get through the door of their house for all the bags of ribbon and textiles, he put his foot down and went and built her a wonderful garden shed. This is where you'll now find her treasure trove of vintage textiles, quilts, blankets, ribbon, linen, tea sets etc. She also supplies props for magazines; so the lovely floral china jug you saw in that photo may well be for sale!

> Philippa travels all over the UK to source her goods. They're all one-offs and she doesn't sell repro. Philippa also offers personalised advice on decorating your home and she can source individual items for you. Visiting is an absolute treat – refreshments are served in her wonderful garden and then you can shop at leisure. By appointment only.

> **Philippa Lloyd, Fountain House, Helmdon, Brackley, Northamptonshire NN13 5QA**
T·01295 768 288 / 07801 860 739
W·philippalloyd.co.uk

ONLY IN LALA LAND

> I absolutely love this little shop. It's really girlie, with super present potential, not to mention the strong possibility of finding a little something for yourself! Gorgeous lingerie, designer clothing, handbags to make you weep, vintage jewellery, unusual greeting cards and delicate china vintage tea sets are nestled among hosts of other lovely things. I've seen this shop described as 'wonderfully indulgent' – I tend to agree.

> **Miss Lala's Boudoir, 148 Gloucester Avenue, Primrose Hill, London NW1 8JA**
T·020 7483 1888
W·misslalasboudoir.co.uk

BURIED TREASURE

> You simply have to visit Ollie where old dresses hang from chandeliers and vintage textiles drape over gorgeous furniture and lovely *objets d'art*. There is a really wonderful selection of well-chosen antiques on two floors and treats hiding in every nook

and cranny, so take your time and have a good rummage. Well known for his wonderful lights and furniture.

> Ollie, 69 Golborne Road, London W10 6RD
  T · 07768 790 725

PRAY YOU'VE GOT ROOM ON YOUR CREDIT CARD

> In this wonderful, two-storied lifestyle store, the owner Geraldine Sanglier has put together a fantastic collection of products exclusive to the area — from designer clothes and accessories, to an eclectic mix of gorgeous smellies, homeware, fab jewellery, footwear, furniture and other surprises. She's just opened a second branch in Cardiff.

> Prey, 3 York Buildings, George Street, Bath
  BA1 2EB T · 01225 329 933 W · preyuk.com
  Cardiff Store, 6/8 Morgan Arcade, Cardiff
  CF10 1AF T · 02920 233 293

CHOOSE A HAPPY ENDING

> I had to wander around this shop four times because I was so amazed, not only with the stock and shop design, but that such a shop existed tucked away in this street and I hadn't known about it before. They class their shop as... 'an eclectic mix of old and new, art, objects, textiles and furniture, clothing, jewellery, a little nature and some junk.'

> If you do buy something, note how they wrap your purchase — it's unique! I won't spoil it by telling you. The owners said to me, after I purchased a 1960s evening handbag (among other things!), 'If you take it home and then think 'Why did I buy this?' then we will take it back with a no-quibble guarantee.' I bet you never do!

> Only open Sunday, 12.00-6.00 p.m. or by appointment.

> Story, 4 Wilkes Street, London E1 6QF
  T · 020 7377 0313

BARNSTORMING IDEAS FOR DECORATIVE LIVING

> Charlotte's barn in South Northamptonshire is full of a mix of English and French furniture, antique cupboards (Georgian and Victorian), painted furniture and a lovely collection of decorative accessories. I met Charlotte at the *Country Living* Fair when she was exhibiting some of her lovely things. Unfortunately, almost everything had sold stickers on by the time I reached her display, but I did manage to buy a beautiful fine bone china muffin dish *circa* 1890. Her decorative accessories include vintage toys, cushions, old English china, rustic garden accessories, a good selection of French linen sheets and some vintage fabrics. Charlotte can also source individual items for you. You can visit most days, by appointment only.

> Charlotte Supple, Elm Lodge Farm, 1 High Street, Wappenham NN12 8SN
  T · 01327 860 955 or 07976 406 641

TANN OUT OF TANN FOR STYLE

> Once you get past the odd numbering of Regents Park Road, you'll find this divine lifestyle store. (Go to the end of Regents Park Road, over the little bridge.) Robert designs and builds gorgeous sofas, lampshades and other bits. I've already started saving for the divine shocking pink and gold settee. He also sells a real mix of antique and contemporary interior pieces, and when I visited he had a great selection of chandeliers. He 'loves buying old furniture and making it sexy' and offers some lovely vintage fabrics for sale by the metre or to upholster your favourite piece of furniture. The shop features a fantastic fish tank set into the wall, which Robert has surrounded with a Venetian mirror frame — I simply must have one!

> Tann Rokka, 123 Regents Park Road, London NW1 8BE
  T · 020 7722 3999 W · tannrokka.com

AN ANGEL'S NOT JUST FOR CHRISTMAS

> I get up really, really early to get over to Barnes for the Tobias and The Angel (and The Dining Room Shop – *see page 2*) Christmas Sale, where Angel Hughes sells her wonderful Christmas decorations. The rest of the year the shop sells their own and antique furniture, wonderful vintage textiles (another reason I visit), vintage knick-knacks, linen, antique jugs, china and glassware. They now also make their own block-printed fabrics and offer an interior design service.

> But back to my annual early-morning pilgrimage; Angel is obsessed with old Christmas decorations and has a huge personal collection, which flamed a desire to start making her own decorations. All of them are handmade using antique textiles, silks, ribbons, beads, sequins, semi-precious stones and old treasures.

> She's famous for her Christmas fairies – she creates only 18-20 a year, with each one beautifully made from antique lace, silks, ribbons, beads and bows, and gives each one a wand, necklace and very good knickers! The angels and fairies are numbered and dated and some are even reserved by July. I don't dare write the price here in case my husband sees how much I paid for one...

> **Tobias and The Angel, 68 White Hart Lane, Barnes, London SW13 OPZ**
> **T·020 8878 890**
> **W·tobiasandtheangel.com**

FOLLOW THE PAPER TRAIL

> If you're a hoarder like me, then get out your 1960s' *Vogue* magazines as they are worth around £30.00 each now. If you are looking for a vintage copy of your favourite magazine for fashion ideas, or perhaps an issue from the year of a friend's birth for an original gift, then head for the Vinmagco shop in Soho (or E: piclib.vintage@ndonet.com which takes you to The Vintage Magazine Co). I just bought an October 1960 edition of *Vogue* to

frame – it's fabulous. Their stock includes fashion, glamour and popular culture magazines from 1900 onwards, mainly in English, but they do stock some French and Italian titles.

BAG BOYS

And if you're shopping in the Seven Dials area (Covent Garden), why not bag yourself a hunky bag boy? These men have been chosen for their brawn, patience and charm, and are available to accompany you on four-hour shopping stints. They'll carry all your heavy bags and will be honest enough to tell you that if those clingy white trousers really aren't doing much for you... Register as a Friend of Seven Dials (W·sevendials.co.uk/friends) and this complimentary service is offered on a first-come, first-served basis. Just click on your chosen man – mmm, Clinton or Gunther, couldn't decide between the two, or you can also book Murray or Terri.

While you're in the Seven Dials area, be sure to pop into French Touch which offers top brand used handbags and accessories with vintage and new handbag styles, along with designer costume jewellery. Brands include Chanel, Louis Vuitton, and Hermès with handbags starting from £150.00 and costume jewellery from £100.00. You could even get your hands on a limited edition Hermès Kelly bag. Other shops not to miss include The Loft at 35 Monmouth Street (see page 146);

W·sevendials.co.uk/bagboys
French Touch, 11 Shelton Street, London WC2H 9JN T·020 7240 2680
W·frenchtouchshop.com

> The shop began life as The Vintage Magazine Shop in 1974 but growth has led to changes and now Vintage Magazine Co and Vinmag Archive operate from 10,000 sq ft in East London, barely enough space to house their vast collection.

> The archive offers commercial and collectors' sections and includes many more titles/genres than the shop, including newspapers, posters, programmes, photos and general ephemera. They hire magazines for window displays and film props, and also offer a great picture library service. TV and fashion companies go there to do their research (by appointment only). They will sell their very old magazines if they have a duplicate, will buy your vintage mags and can also offer a framing service if you want to frame your purchase.

> **Vinmagco, 39–43 Brewer Street, London W1R 9UD T·020 7438 8525**

> **The Vintage Magazine Co and Vinmag Archive Ltd, 84–90 Digby Road, London E9 6HX T·020 8533 7588 W·vinmag.com**

Caroline Zoob (see pages 194 and 283).

ONLINE SHOPPING

Online shopping is booming, according to IMRG who have just announced British shoppers have spent more than £100 billion since online shopping began 12 years ago.

I'm afraid I'm completely hooked. With my NBF – Google, I can shop my way around the world sitting in my pyjamas, no make-up, no parking fees and no pressure, shopping to my heart's content buying from some lovely, unique businesses. Click On!

JOURNALS IN SEARCH OF AN AUTHOR

> If you love writing in journals and notebooks, then this is the site for you. Pamela Barsky has made unique journals for recording all manner of occasions such as dinner parties, travel, therapy, or a film lover's journal. She has also designed blank journals with fabulous sayings on the cover such as *who'd have thought I'd turn out to be the creative one in my family; horribly misspelled words and atrocious grammer; sometimes I think life would be easier if I weren't so fabulous; lots of bad ideas; and I will not date unavailable men.*

> Pamela also designs cosmetic bags, teddy bears, buttons, magnets and journals, all made from vintage scarves, and disposable, leather-like luggage tags with witty sayings like *I'm pretty sure this isn't your bag.*

> Pamela says she spends her time practising yoga, designing new products and watching the plants in her backyard grow. She's also writing a book about the fine art of complaining.

> **Pamela Barsky Boutique T·USA +1 323 935 9140 W·pamelabarsky.com**

BOLSTER YOUR HOME IMAGE

> Charlotte's gorgeous home items are in high demand at the fairs. You can purchase all her lovely offerings on her website, alternatively, you can phone her at the number below and arrange a good time to visit her in London. She makes contemporary textiles from antique French linens – monogrammed cushions, sheets, fabulous bolsters, lampshades, floral appliqué and ticking cushions, peg bags, laundry bags and lavender bags decorated with ribbon, crystals or flowers.

> Her ribbon cushions are made with muted vintage velvet and silk ribbon decorated with diamanté brooches and buckles on a linen background.

> **Charlotte Casadejus T·020 7378 9755 / 07814 146 577 W·charlottecasadejus.com**

FAIRWEATHER FINDS

> Oh my goodness, I wanted so-o-o-o many things from this gorgeous site.

> Philippa Fairweather sources an ever-changing collection of vintage and weathered furniture and architectural pieces. You'll find original pieces for your home, garden or office, but if you can't see what you're looking for, then Philippa will help you source a certain piece, even visiting your home to advise on what would look perfect.

> Philippa travels widely, from Moroccan deserts to Borneo, and comes across wonderful finds that are unusual, beautiful or quirky. She loves gentle distressing and elegant weathering. When I went online, there were some gorgeous Eastern European chests of drawers, dressers, old Hungarian panelled and box benches and a gorgeous, round, glass-fronted cabinet – things like this can be colour-matched and re-distressed for you. If your garden is lacking that certain something, look at her garden ornaments, birdhouses and vintage beehives.

> **Philippa Fairweather, Jeddah House, New Village, Freshwater, Isle of Wight, PO40 9HU T · 07979 593 096 W · fairandweathered.com**

WARNING: ONE HOME MAY NOT BE ENOUGH

> Imogen is passionate about interiors and, like me, l-o-v-e-s gently shabbily painted furniture and soft furnishings in faded colours. I met her at the *Country Living Magazine* fair (*see page* 186) where she had a selection of decorative and antique items for the home and garden.

> I quickly grabbed the beautiful antique glass sundae dishes with gorgeous old shell-shaped spoons and a delicate china tea set. I had to restrain myself from also taking a 19th-century French mirror, a wooden toy and a set of French enamel canisters.

> Imogen scours the French and English

countryside to find lovely things to give our homes unique style and identity. She offers an interior design consultancy and will also source items on request. Her website offers a constantly changing selection of stock and she's very happy to email pictures of any items you're interested in.

> Interior consultancy by appointment only (Wimbledon area).

> **Imogen Jamieson T · 020 8942 2108 W · imogenjamieson.co.uk**

RE-MARKABLE

> Not only is RE a fabulous shop to visit, I'm addicted to their website. Simon Young and Jenny Vaughan travel worldwide on a mission to shop and bring you the most fabulous selection of old and new goodies. They also offer an eclectic mix of crafts and one-offs, often sourced from local craftspeople, like their knitters and welders.

> Their shop (closed on Mondays), just 30 minutes drive west of Newcastle upon Tyne, was an old workshop which they've filled with furniture, garden delights, textiles, pressed glass (salts, glasses, vintage cake-stands), stationery, pre-1950 vintage quilts (£65.00) and other desirable products. Here's my shopping list:

- Hand crocheted cotton coat hangers (£9.50)
- Folding wooden 'peggy' (£12.50) – traditionally to hang smalls to dry but also a great way to display your Christmas cards and decorations.
- Dove garland for summer garden party (£6.00)
- French glass milk bottle (from £4.50)

> They offer a worldwide mail-order service (on everything except their furniture) and have even mailed their wonderful French products (which they bought in France) back to French customers! They also offer a very handy interiors sourcing service, very useful if you're doing a bit of renovation.

> RE, Bishops Yard, Main Street, Corbridge,
  Northumberland NE45 5LA
  T · 01434 634 567 W · re-foundobjects.com

RURALLY USEFUL STUFF

> Really Rural Inspirations produce a wide
  range of both decorative and practical
  furniture along the lines of Shaker and
  French rustic style. A large proportion of the
  work is carried out by hand to produce
  unique, natural-looking pieces. I saw their
  wonderful items at the *Country Living
  Magazine* Spring Fair and wanted at least
  four of them.
> Something every hectic home should have is
  a noticeboard and one of their Classroom
  Chalkboards puts a classy twist on this
  functional family friend. Four school
  chalkboards are fitted in a row with a
  traditional card holder above each board for
  the person's name and a tiny shelf with a
  handy row of shaker pegs on the bottom.
  They also make wall shelves, boot racks, peg
  shelves, wine cupboards, step boxes, plate
  racks and bookcases. Beautiful work in a
  choice of fantastic colours.
> **Really Rural Inspirations, Head Office, The
  Old Apple House, 37 Kings Hey Drive,
  Churchtown, Southport, Lancashire
  PR9 7JB T · 01704 222 721
  W · reallyruralinspirations.co.uk**

LOOK TO THE PAST FOR THE
PERFECT PRESENT

> Janet Gaynor, owner of AZillion Sparklz,
  offers an absolutely fabulous website full of
  antique and vintage costume jewellery,
  including bakelite, Victorian, plastic, sterling
  silver, fine estate and rhinestone. I collect
  vintage brooches and they have an amazing
  collection along with cufflinks, compacts,
  charms, perfumes, mesh and beaded bags,
  watch fobs, buckles and many other
  great finds.
> Azillion Sparklz has over 1,500 items of

vintage, contemporary, fine estate and
accessories, and has a very easy-to-use
search facility where you can browse by
category, era or designer's name.
> A great idea for a present: say your friend
  has a passion for butterflies or dogs, type
  your keywords in and Bob's your uncle, a
  selection of perfect gifts. There are some
  divine things under the section Critters and
  Figurals. Janet also offers a really interesting
  information and reference section with tips
  and guides to cleaning and repair, replating
  and storage. If you're looking for a specific
  piece you can add it to their 'Want List'. They
  also buy. $25.00 minimum order.
> **AZillion Sparklz Vintage Jewelry, PO Box
  35038, Tucson, AZ 85740**
> **T · From USA +1 877 380 4726 or
  mobile +1 520 907 2839 W · sparklz.com**

LOST IN TRANSPORTATION

> Have you ever lost your baggage while
  travelling? Thousands of us do, but do you
  know what happens to all the items that
  never get reunited with their owners?
> After around 90 days of intensive tracking by
  airlines, Unclaimed Baggage buy it by the
  truckload and then sell it from their store in
  the Appalachian Mountains, or online.
> They reckon about one million items pass
  through the store annually, with about 60 per
  cent of the items falling under the category
  of clothing. Other items are cameras,
  sporting goods, jewellery, glasses, books,
  electronics and, of course, luggage. They
  have some interesting things on their site –
  I loved the *Lost Treasures from Around the
  World* section, which lists some of the more
  unique items people have left behind...
  a Gucci suitcase filled with Egyptian artefacts
  dating back to 1500 BC; a suit of armour;
  a 5.8 carat diamond ring; a guidance system
  for a F16 fighter jet; a rattlesnake; an
  unpacked parachute and a 40.95 carat
  emerald!

> What they can't do is find *your* lost item – but they can sell you someone else's. If you can't get to the store in Scottsboro, Alabama, then shop online where items are updated daily. Oh, and they also have a very useful section on travel tips and how to keep your own belongings secure in future.

> **Unclaimed Baggage Center, 509 West Willow Street, Scottsboro, Alabama 35768 T· USA +1 256 259 1525 W· unclaimedbaggage.com**

CURIOUSLY SCRUMMY SECRETS

> I love WhippetGrey for the creative way they present their products to you on their website. Once you click on one of the four categories, a pop-up image appears (like when you open a child's 3D pop-up book), then you click on the coloured items.

> The four categories, *Curious Objects*, *Secret Garden*, *The Den*, and *Scrummy Treats*, have an assortment of wonderful things for the home, accessories, collectable art, toys and books, garden treasures and tempting delights sourced from around the world. Their catalogue is full of 'must-buy' products, I immediately fell in love with their linen 'numbered' tea towels, tea lights, life-size lead birds and their adorable Liberty print animals. Present problem solved!

> **WhippetGrey, Old Village Stores, Little Missenden, Buckinghamshire HP7 0QX T· Order Line 01494 890 400 W· whippetgrey.co.uk**

LET LOOSE IN LEWES

> I first saw Caroline's lovely handmade collection at the *Country Living Magazine* Christmas Fair about four years ago. When the doors open at 10.00 a.m., everyone in the know rushes to her stand to buy her divine goodies. Throughout the day when you pass her stall you'll see a constant crowd at least four deep. She stocks a wide range of vintage items as well as beautifully crafted, handmade collectables. Her tiny hand-embroidered, vintage linen framed pictures are snapped up quicker than you can shout 'I'll take three, please'. She has a gorgeous shop in Lewes (open Wednesday-Saturday only) filled with decorative accessories, collectables made with vintage textiles, specially commissioned crockery, antiques, vintage ribbons sold by the metre, quilts, lovely hand-knitted presents for newborns, lavender-filled vintage linen pillows, hand-carved wooden birds and furniture.

> You can also commission personalised items like a child's name picture, hand-embroidered on antique linen.

> Luckily for us she has an online store where you can see and buy all these gorgeous things. I've purchased so much from her over the years and given many of her things as very well-received gifts.

> **Caroline Zoob, 33a Cliffe High Street, Lewes, East Sussex BN7 2AN T· 01273 476 464   W· caroline-zoob.co.uk**

SHOPPING TOURS

TOO GOOD TO KEEP QUIET ABOUT

> Usually if you say you're going to Florence it will draw sighs of envy at the chance to see the Ponte Vecchio and Uffizi Gallery and re-enact scenes from *Room With A View*. However on this trip you'll leave the traditional city sites behind to the other three million tourists. For just outside Florence you can shop to your heart's content at the outlets of top designers, at low, low discount prices. Hush Hush Traveller offers trips to The Mall, one of Italy's most exclusive outlet centres, lined with shops of the world's top designers – Armani, Gucci, Burberry, La Perla and many more. You'll also visit Space, Prada's discount outlet which sells Miu Miu, Helmut Lang, Jil Sander and, of course, Prada. And finally, if you haven't already

maxed out your credit card, a trip to Dolce & Gabbana.

> Prices include return economy class flights to Florence, two nights' hotel accommodation with continental breakfast (based on two people sharing), transfers and fully-escorted fashion trips within Italy. You'll travel in air-conditioned comfort from £415.00, or you can go for just one night/two days from £225.00. They can also tailor-make a trip for you if you want to go with a group of friends or just your best friend. Great present idea – they'll even gift wrap the voucher – definitely top of my Christmas list this year.

> **Hush Hush Traveller T·0870 062 3418 W·hushhushtraveller.com**

YOU CAN'T AFFORD TO STAY AT HOME

> With the catchy motto 'for people who live to shop and love to travel', Shop Around Tours was set up by Deborah Mayer, a serious shopper who craves the thrill of a great buy. It was while she was shopping at the designer outlet of Prada, in Italy, stocking up on a few can't-resist bargain handbags, that Shop Around Tours was born.

> She noticed that these nondescript ware-houses are located in the middle of nowhere and unless you had a car and spoke the lingo you probably wouldn't ever find them.

> Her tours combine group meals and shopping excursions with loads of free time to do what you want. You stay in four-star hotels with many meals included (three tours are currently available). Two of these tours are:

> *Shop Around Italy* includes Milan, Florence and Rome, where you visit two outlet malls and the Prada outlet. You'll be able to buy brands like Dolce & Gabbana, Bally, La Perla, Missoni, Gucci, Fendi, Alexander McQueen, Stella McCartney and Emilio Pucci, to name a few – Six nights including round-trip economy airfare (from the USA) $2,195.00. If you're living in another country and wish to

join for the land-only part of the tour, the cost is $1,600.00.

> The other tour on offer is *Shop Around Tuscany*, where you have a fabulous shop-till-you-drop day at the new Barberino outlet centre offering 150 brands, another day at the Prada outlet, where you can get some bargains from Prada, Miu Miu, Helmet Lang and Jil Sander, and a final shopping outlet mall including Salvatore Ferragamo, Bottega Veneta, Balenciaga, Emillio Pucci and Armani. From the USA $2,095.00; land only $1,600.00.

> Check their website for tour dates and itineraries but book early as when I looked in May their October tour was already sold out.

> **Shop Around Tours, 305 East 24th Street, Suite 2N, New York, NY 10010 T·USA +1 212 684 3763 W·shoparoundtours.com**

NEW YORK, NEW YORK

> Whisker is your official guide to reaching Shopping Heaven. For a fee of £600.00 you can shop with one of their stylists for the day or (if you don't mind sharing!) the stylist can take a group of you and your friends (*see* her personal styling services on *page* 168).).

> The fee covers planning your customised itinerary and the stylist's advice and time on the day. You can discover cool vintage boutiques in the Lower East Side, visit top designer boutiques, have personal changing suites reserved at famous up-market department stores or hit the exclusive shops on Fifth Avenue.

> They can also arrange an array of amazing treats like walk-in manicures and pedicures, appointments with the best celebrity hairstylists in New York, massages at Bliss Spa or pre-booked tables at hip restaurants.

> Imagine enjoying breakfast at a great people-watching brasserie in the Meatpacking District, blow-dries and manicures at a favourite celebrity-spotting salon, shopping

at a selection of fantastic boutiques and vintage shops - breath - lunch in a fabulous restaurant, more shopping, a pit stop to taste divine little cupcakes at a tiny West Village bakery made famous by Sex & The City, and finally finishing with post-shopping cocktails to celebrate. How will the rest of your life ever live up to such a day?

> **Leesa Whisker, Whisker Agency**
  T · 0870 043 4126   W · whiskeragency.co.uk

You may also like to look at:

> **W · 10vendôme.com   T · +33 1 53 45 66 83**
  for the finest personal shopping service in Paris.
> **W · shopgotham.com** – for a selection of private and scheduled shopping tours

PRESENTS
COVETABLE, GORGEOUS
AND UNIQUE PRESENTS

FREE THE COOKIE MONSTER!
> The B & G Cookie Company in Los Angeles was started by two sisters, Beverley and Grace. They make delicious chocolate chip cookies, white chocolate chip cookies with coconut and macadamia nuts, and amazing brownies. The cookies are individually wrapped, packed into a gorgeous little brown valise which is then tied with a pink, light blue or white bow. You can order The Overnighter, which is a case of half a dozen cookies for $18.00, or go all out and order To The Moon — three dozen cookies packed into three tiered suitcases for $108.00. They only offer nationwide delivery in the USA, but I've included them because this is a nice gift to send as a thank-you to someone in the US instead of flowers.

> **B & G Cookie Company, 916 S. Olive Street, Los Angeles, CA 90015**
  T · +1 888 77 YUMMY /+1 888 779 8669
  W · bandgcookie.com

THREE CENTURIES OF EXPERTISE
> Berry Bros. & Rudd is Britain's oldest wine and spirit merchant. It was established in 1698 and is still a family-run wine merchant today. I love the idea that you can lay down a fine wine for a recipient until something like a tenth anniversary or a twenty-first birthday. When using their cellars for storage you must buy a minimum of one case, however they are very happy to deliver a single bottle as a gift. With choices from over 3,000 wines they advise that for laying down, red wine or ports age better and increase in value — they have a 1927 vintage port which has been in one of their customer's private reserves since 1930! Their website is really informative offering vintage charts, wine storage information and a pronunciation guide where you can actually hear the correct way to pronounce a wine's name. They offer many services to their customers from wine investment, cellar plans, wine clubs, wine courses and wine tasting.
> They have shops in Dublin and Hong Kong and a factory outlet in Basingstoke with at least 25 per cent off single bottle prices.

> **Berry Bros & Rudd, 3 St James's Street, London SW1A 1EG**
  T · 0870 900 4300   W · bbr.com

GIFT OF A LIFETIME
> Jonathan Maitland, the founder of Bespoke Films, has worked in TV and film for over 20 years. He has produced many programmes for the BBC and his team is drawn from a pool of BAFTA and Royal Television Society award-winning producers and directors. For the ultimate gift, they will work with you to create a tailor-made documentary film of a lifetime. You can include celebrities, music,

historic newsreel footage, wonderful locations and even secret filming.

> Currently, they've been commissioned by three daughters to create a film of their father's life for his sixtieth birthday. They're also working on a film celebrating a fortieth wedding anniversary, intermixing it with 28 old cine films of the family – I'm sure there won't be a dry eye in the house when they show that one.

> Allow around eight weeks to research and film; once completed, your film arrives luxuriously packaged in a handmade leather case. Prices: from £5,000.00

> **Bespoke Films   T·020 8834 7293 W·bespokefilms.com**

ALWAYS JUDGE THE CHOCOLATES BY THEIR COVER

> I love this service from Charbonnel et Walker. Their oval chocolate boxes can be customised using a choice of your favourite fabric, be it vintage, designer or 60s psychedelic. A beautiful chocolate box will be handcrafted to your individual style, then filled with a selection of truffles or plain and milk chocolates. You could order one for a special friend, as they can send the box, with a personal message, worldwide. Delivery takes about five weeks from receipt of fabric, but do allow longer for busiest periods (i.e. Valentines, Easter and Christmas).

> Prices: from £20.00, depending on the size of box and weight of chocolates

> **Charbonnel et Walker, One, The Royal Arcade, 28 Old Bond Street, London W1S 4BT   T·020 7491 0939 W·charbonnel.co.uk**

WHY STOP FOR COFFEE?

> For those of you who are always on the go, the gorgeous Connolly's travel espresso machine that plugs into a car lighter will revolutionise your day. Simply fab, it comes in a leather travel case in a choice of black,

tan, chocolate brown and red, and contains two cups, two leather-covered containers for your coffee and sugar, two horn teaspoons, two linen napkins and, of course, the travel espresso machine. No more queuing up for your coffee again, and at £650.00 after just two cups a day it will have more than paid for itself in the first six months!

> I popped in to have a look at this and noticed all sorts of other little gems – the clothing is fabulous, not to mention their leather jump-lead kit and their champagne case – all part of life's gorgeous little luxuries...

> **Connolly, 41 Conduit Street, London W1S 2YQ   T·020 7439 2510 W·connollyretail.co.uk**

BEAUTY IN A BOTTLE

> Every girl must have one – a bottle of DIVA vodka that is. It's not just any vodka; this is a multi award-winning vodka bottled with a unique column of crystals – each bottle has been hand-assembled, so no two are alike. This oh-so-glamorous tipple hails from Blackwood, a distillery in Shetland, where the vodka has been triple-distilled, ice-filtered, filtered through purifying Nordic birch charcoal, then finally passed through a fine sand of crushed diamonds and gems. You can purchase a bottle for £35.00 with CZ gems from Harvey Nichols, Selfridges, House of Fraser and a long list of other stockists (see online), or you can opt for the bespoke range with real jewels. What about the heart-shaped rubies for £540,000.00? You can also commission your own special edition using a cubic zirconia for a special occasion, a wedding or party. Whatever you choose, the Divas on the DIVA hotline will be happy to consider any request.

> And if you're really quick, you may be able to purchase exclusively from Harvey Nichols (nationwide) their limited edition, hand-labelled and individually numbered Kirsten Goss bottles (£65.00). Each bottle's wand is

filled with Swarovski crystals that Kirsten and her team will make up into her signature cluster ring. Make one Diva very happy.

> **DIVA Vodka T·01595 696 082**
> **W·divavodka.com**

PUT THE SHIRT ON HIS BACK

> For any man who's difficult to buy for, this is a fantastic service started about two years ago by Ede and Ravenscroft, robe makers and tailors since 1689. First you choose the shirt length from over 80 different materials. They beautifully wrap the cloth in one of their boxes and you present it to your man. He then visits one of their stores to choose his collar and cuffs, and has a personally tailored shirt made. He can also go into the store and choose the fabric himself, or even swap your gift if he dares to doubt your judgement!

> Just to mention, they do advise that this service offers a better fabric selection from November as they gear up for the Christmas rush. Very good value at £95.00. Three stores in London with additional branches in Cambridge, Edinburgh and Oxford.

> **Ede and Ravenscroft, 8 Burlington Gardens, Savile Row, London W1X 1LG**
> **T·020 7734 5450**
> **or 93 Chancery Lane, London WC2A 1DU**
> **T·020 7405 3906**
> **or 2 Gracechurch Street, London EC3V ODP**
> **T·020 7929 1848**
> **W·edeandravenscroft.co.uk**

IT'S ALL ABOUT THE LABEL

> Any celebration falls flat without a bit of champers, but you can take it to the next level with one of these incredible, personalised, engraved bottles. You can choose from the house champagne or Lanson, Moet, Veuve Cliquot, Bolinger, Dom Perignon, Krug, etc., then write your message (20 words max) select a typestyle in silver or gold, and they'll engrave the

message above the original label on the bottle. You can even include a monogram, clip art or your own signature. Great gift for congratulations, new baby, house-warming or just because. From £32.41 including VAT and carriage. They can also offer this service for spirits and wines.

> **Engraved Champers T·0870 190 0072**
> **W·engravedchampers.com**

OPEN A BOTTLE AND TURN THE PAGE

> Sara Hurn had the idea for this great company over three years ago and I think it makes a fabulous present. Order a vintage wine, port, claret or brandy, and a newspaper, from the date of birth of the recipient, will be included in the silk-lined presentation case. If you opt for the connoisseur gift, it will also include a vintage summary of the chosen wine and a hand-engraved plaque with your personal message. They have over 3,500 bottles of mature wines dating back as far as 1890, stored in carefully controlled conditions. I sent a 1959 bottle of red wine to my husband and he was thrilled.

> If you can't see the year you need online, email Sara and she'll let you know what she has available and at what prices. She's just presented someone with an 1898 bottle of wine and the oldest bottle she's recently presented for a birthday was a 1921 brandy. If your budget doesn't stretch to the vintage, you can order a newspaper from the year of birth and she can present that with a more contemporary bottle of wine. She offers a great wedding gift with three bottles of wine, which the couple are to drink on their first, their fifth and their tenth wedding anniversary – what a nice way to be remembered! Naturally prices are dependent on the vintage and producer of the chosen wine (from £45.00).

> **Sara Hurn, Fine Wine of the Times**
> **T·0845 644 0720**
> **W·finewineofthetimes.co.uk**

THYME FOR A NOVEL GIFT

> Choose from a great selection of original plant and food gifts that are beautifully packaged in rustic wooden crates and hand-tied with raffia. The lovely House Warming Crate consists of four terracotta pots filled with sage, thyme, oregano and rosemary and another three pots with seeds to plant French parsley, basil and coriander, together with a bottle of champers to toast the occasion. The equally charming Pesto Lover's Kit has a stone pine tree (which will produce the pine nuts to make the pesto), basil seeds, a packet of Italian egg tagliatelle, a bag of pine nuts (to use while you're waiting for the tree to produce them!), and of course an easy-peasy recipe to follow. I absolutely love the Winter Chills & Misery Kit, the essential first-aid crate to banish gloomy winter colds containing a small bottle of whisky, fresh lemons, cloves, cinnamon, honey, a toddy glass and recipes for the perfect hot toddy!

> **The Gluttonous Gardener, Vitis House, 50 Dickens Street, London SW8 3EQ
T·0207 627 0800   W·glut.co.uk**

OH THE POSH POSH TRAVELLING LIFE...

> If you're thinking of arranging a romantic getaway to remember, or a special gift for a wedding then read on. My friend Christine once bought her husband Ian the following trip, all organised by Gourmet Touring.

> They flew to Bordeaux where they were met by a representative who took them to their hire car, an original E-type 1967 soft-top Jaguar. Then, after a quick talk about how they operated the car and the satellite navigation system, they set off to their chateau travelling through stunning 8th-12th century Bastide villages and rolling countryside. Christine and Ian wanted to visit some vineyards and so GT had arranged appointments and programmed the car's sat-nav so they didn't get lost en-route!

> On arrival at their accommodation (Christine had taken an optional upgrade to a chateau), their luggage and a bottle of champers were waiting for them. Their time was their own, they could go where they wanted, when they wanted, but they could also select from a range of topics including cultural interest and local festivals. To help them find local points of interest and avoid the crowds, Gourmet Touring had prepared a personalised guide for them. They could have also included other packages such as spa treatments, golf, cooking lessons and delicious gourmet hampers for a picnic.

> On one of the evenings they drove the Jaguar to a Michelin starred restaurant (again already pre-booked/paid) and had a sumptuous meal. At the end of the meal, Gourmet Touring chauffeured them back to the chateau so they didn't drink-drive (and returned the sports car ready for the next day's adventure). Christine and Ian had the most fantastic time and highly recommend the experience.

> From £550.00 per person for three nights (exclusive of travel to Bordeaux). You have the option of hiring a Fiat Barchetta, Porsche Boxster or a 1967 E-type Jaguar. I loved Gourmet Touring's quote: 'Celebrating an occasion by experiencing shared indulgences will bring more smiles and leave more memories than any material gift.'

> **Gourmet Touring   T·+33 (0) 632 800 474
W·gourmet-touring.com**

YOU NAME IT, SHE'LL MAKE IT

> One of my friends commissioned the most gorgeous children's canvas nameplate from the very-ever-so-talented Michele Gudino and it immediately became the must-buy item for every mum I know. Michele has created several adorable characters she calls Mooki – monkeys, rabbits, frogs and chickens which are painted in lovely soft pastels – and then she attaches the child's

name. You won't have seen anything like it.

> Although Michele has immersed herself in a number of children's projects since becoming a mum herself, whomever you're buying a present for she should be your go-to gift guru. Not only is she accomplished at painting murals and furniture, she's made stage props, themed parties and also turns her hand to bespoke invitations. Prices: from £25.00; allow two weeks from ordering to delivery.

> **Michele Gudino T · 020 8368 7039
E · sendusamessage@tiscali.co.uk**

KEEPSAKES BY KATE

> This is a family-run business by Susi and Kate (mother and daughter) who, after completing a bookbinding course, started to produce photograph albums for family and friends. The albums proved so popular that in 2004 they decided to set up their business, Kate Books.

> They produce handcrafted photograph albums made of Italian archival, acid-free paper, tissue interleaved, covered with a gorgeous selection of Japanese silk-screen-printed papers and with spines of Japanese silk. They offer a very personal service and quick turnaround time (10 days), and have been chosen to exclusively work with several prestigious wedding photographers – an accolade indeed! Prices: Albums £25-£85.00 depending on size; notebook £14.00.

> **Kate Books T · 01243 780 786 /
07931 688 161 / 07717 153 521
W · katebooks.co.uk**

LIGHT YEARS AHEAD OF
THE COMPETITION

> For over ten years Light Monkey have been taking stunning photos at weddings and presenting the bride and groom with an amazing bound book in the newlywed's choice of covers and text (*see page* 55 in the wedding section). They now offer other

services and if you provide the photos, text, mementos, etc., they can make up a book for any special occasion. I can't wait to get one done of my son's first year. If you have a landmark birthday for a parent or grandparent coming up, why not consider a *Your Life* book? They're currently working on a family history for a client; what a fantastic way to preserve the photos, memories and history to be passed on to future generations.

> **Light Monkey T · 070 2092 1184
W · lightmonkey.co.uk**

GIFTS FOR WHEN WORDS FAIL YOU

> Jeannine from Lost for Words is one of the most charming, 'I can do anything for you', ladies you'll ever meet. She has set up a business offering fantastic personalised presents that quite simply will leave the recipient speechless.

> All the gifts contain photographs and a story tailored to your friend or loved one. They are perfect for every occasion – anniversaries, weddings, new baby or just to say 'I Love You'. You can commission your very own gift book, booklets, cards, calendars (and we are talking a very unique calendar) and chocolates.

> Visit Jeannine at her studio or just chat over the phone and, depending on what you want, she can have your gift ready within two weeks. (Last-minute panic buys may also be possible!)

> You don't need to give her pages and pages. She likes to keep it simple for you, and so just needs 10 or so facts about the person – basically, she can make anything work wonderfully.

> Your unique gift will earn you so many brownie points, not just for its beauty but also because they will *never* have received anything like it – *ever*!

> Gift books start at £250.00, calendars £110.00, chocolate box £175.00 and Wishing

Cards from £20.00. Her most amazing party crackers (*see page* 45) with teeny personalised booklets for each individual cost £175.00 (for four) – I simply must order some.

> **Lost for Words, Lancaster House,**
> **237 Sussex Gardens, London W2 3UD**
> **T·020 7262 2292 / 07802 815 336**
> **W·lostforwordsonline.com**

I BELIEVE IN FAIRIES

> Sam specialises in making beautiful things from genuine antique and vintage treasures sourced in England and France. I find it hard to express just how lovely her little English rose's fairy dolls are without showing a photo (there is a great photo of them on her website). I first saw them at the Chelsea Antiques Show and wanted five immediately. They're made from vintage fabrics and adorned with flowers, beads and trinkets, and can be filled with lavender and rose petals. She also offers a bespoke service where she will make a fairy looking like your daughter, wife or friend. They're so exquisite and not just for children – I have mine on a shelf – and she receives loads of delightful comments. Sam also makes bags, T-shirts and jewellery (*see page* 155).

> **Magpie and the Wardrobe**
> **T·07770 961 362**
> **W·magpiewardrobe.co.uk**

PETACULAR DESIGNS

> Clare Fraser draws quirky, cartoon-like images of dogs and cats, then uses textiles, screen printing, hand and machine embroidery, and transfer printing to create a range of one-off bags, scarves, coin purses, magnets and cushions. She uses a large variety of fabrics, including velvets, mohair, silk, ginghams and cottons. You can visit all Pin Pin stockists online. I love her bespoke items. All you have to do is choose your fabric, colour and finish and send her a picture of your favourite cat or dog, and you'll receive a wonderful one-off piece that will be the envy of your friends, even if they are your pets!

> **Clare Fraser, Pin-Pin   T·020 8286 2559**
> **W·pinpin.co.uk**

MUSIC TO OUR EARS

> I remember just how much time and trouble it took my not-so-techno-savvy husband to get his music library on to the iPod I gave him. So I'm delighted to tell you about Jeff Underwood who offers a simply fantastic service of loading all your music onto your iPod

> There are three very easy steps.
> • Call Pod Serve - they'll drive round, daytime or evening, and pick up your CDs and discuss your music requirements. (If you're outside the M25, Jeff may be able to work out something with couriers.)
> • Sit back and wait while they expertly convert ('rip') your CDs to Apple iPod format, adding comprehensive album, artist, track, genre data and artwork.
> • Finally your CDs are returned in person, plus a new digital version on secure DVDs. They load your music onto your iPod and will even spend time explaining how iTunes works.

> Other services for your iPod include scanning of photos and converting movies or transferring all the songs from the iPod to your hard drive. They can also safeguard any pre-loaded songs already on your iPod. Allow one week for the service and they support all MP3 players and all file formats. I now know what my husband is getting for Christmas – that's one I can cross off my list! Price: £1.00 per CD (minimum charge £100.00), plus £15.00 travel costs.

> **Jeff Underwood – podServe**
> **T·01277 222 398 / 07960 325 207**
> **W·podserve.co.uk**

SAY IT WITH FLOWERS

> I saw Hanne's beautiful work at the Chelsea Crafts Fair. If you know someone who adores roses, flowers generally or polka dots, then look no further than Hanne's wonderful handmade collection of cups, jugs, bowls, dinner plates and tea pots. I absolutely adored her two-tiered cake-stand that would sit proudly on any armoire and the floral cup that sits neatly on its own tray – divine! She also does an amazing technique of stitching and embroidering the porcelain with silk threads to make distinctive little pots, boxes and dishes. Prices from as little as £4.00

> **Hanne Rysgaard, Blaze Studio, 84 Colston Street, Bristol BS1 5BB**
> **T·07976 327 958 W·hannerysgaard.com**

SOMETHING TO SING ABOUT

> The lovely Kay from A Soap Opera makes wonderful bespoke soaps that contain no harmful chemicals, animal derived ingredients or preservatives, including an organic and sodium laurel sulphate-free range.

> She creates designs so beautiful that you probably won't want to use them at all as they'll make your bathroom or kitchen look so elegant.

> I've purchased her cupcake soaps, a car for my son, the chocolate soaps for guests and the fantastic Rock Star, a pyramid-shaped soap with a lovely gem effect. She also makes Jewels Of The Sea - a selection of pearls and shell-shaped soaps, lovingly hand-crafted in sandy, layered colours and displayed on a plate of gold or white capiz shell - and Soapsicles which are fun iced-lolly soaps for the children. I personally can't wait for her Christmas bauble soaps. One customer purchased two bars from her at a fair and then came back two weeks later and purchased 12 more - he was so thrilled with them he wanted to give them as presents to everyone he knew.

> A Soap Opera can create soaps specific to your requirements (they would make lovely favours) and if you fancy a girl's night in, then she'll hold a soap party in the comfort of your own home (sorry, London region only).

> **A Soap Opera T·020 8556 5654 / 07956 129 480 W·a-soap-opera.com**

DELIGHT YOUR FAVOURITE BOOKWORM

> I saw a gorgeous photo in *Elle Decoration* of a pile of old books re-covered in bold, richly patterned fabrics. Of course my radar went up and I immediately phoned Shepherds to order one for a friend. The spines are leather embossed and the book has a luxury satin ribbon marker. For a unique present, find out from the recipient what their favourite book is, then have it covered in a luxurious fabric. Prices start from £55.00, but please check with Shepherds on your fabric choice as some fabrics are not suitable. Or you could choose one of their fabulous Japanese papers for the cover – it will really stand out on a bookshelf.

> If you're looking to spend that little bit extra, their classic novels are bound in the finest goatskin leather and hand-finished in gold leaf with a gorgeous matching slipcase made from decorative Japanese paper. You can even have these personalised with gold initials. Poetry anthologies, children's books and non-fiction are also available from £195.00.

> Naturally, they also provide all the traditional book-binding services, including gold finishing, leather onlays and gold blocking, restoration and conservation, as well as offering albums, stationery and accessories.

> **Shepherds, 76 Rochester Row, London SW1P 1JU T·020 7620 0060 W·shepherdsbookbinding.com**

FOR THE STATIONERY-AHOLIC

> Smythson of Bond Street makes gorgeous A5 leather-covered floppy notebooks, which you can have embossed with gold or silver letters. Choose one of their fab colours and emboss a personalised title such as *Samm's Brilliant Brainstorms*, *Michelle's Must-Have List*, *Jo's Genius Log* or *Kay's Little Pink Book*, and give them to your delighted girlfriends. Embossing from £5.95 per letter and notebooks from £115.00. If this is a little more than you wanted to spend, you can pick up one of their adorable little notebooks (from £28.00) with titles such as: *Happiness is Shopping*; *IT List*; *Fashionista*; and *Princess Notes*. I have six of them!

> **Smythson of Bond Street, 40 New Bond Street, London W1S 2DE T·020 7629 8558**
> **135 Sloane Street, London SW1X 9AX T·020 7730 5520**
> **(They also have concessions in Selfridges, Harrods and Harvey Nichols in London, Manchester and Edinburgh and Heathrow Airport Terminals 3 & 4)**
> **4 West 57th Street, New York NY 10019 T·+1 212 265 4573**
> **For Mail Order: T·08705 211 311 W·smythson.com**

I'LL TAKE AN ARK FULL

> Jeff Soan refers to his work as Wobbly Wood – if you look at his site you'll get the picture. His playful sculptures and toys have won him the title of Toymaker of the Year (and other accolades).

> It's not only toys he carves, but beautifully articulated creatures, including fish, seals, pigs and dogs, from reclaimed and found timber, or wood from sustainable sources. He uses the wood's natural forms and features to achieve the most remarkable markings, feathers and textures. My husband gave me a beautiful fish when we first started dating, and it still has pride of place in our sitting room. It is so-o-o-o tactile and

I've told so many of my friends where they can get one too, that I'm contemplating asking for a commission! I love the spiky fish that he now makes, but also long for one of his rocking chickens. If I hint long enough, I may get one for Christmas. Prices start at £12.00 and go up to £1,750.00 for a very tall giraffe. I think this customer comment on his site sums it up beautifully: 'I was actually in search of a new sofa and ended up buying the octopus and a full-sized crocodile – not very comfortable, but very much more interesting.'

> **Jeff Soan T·020 8691 1332 W·wobblywood.co.uk**

HONOURABLE MENTIONABLES

> Star Treatment Gift Services compiles wonderful gift baskets for the Hollywood entertainment industry. They've sent gifts to entire casts and special gifts to the likes of Jody Foster, Julia Roberts, Elton John and Robert DeNiro. But don't let that intimidate you; they're very happy to give you the star treatment as well. You can choose from categories including Candles, Bakery, Fruit, Gourmet, Floral, Fun, For Her, For Him and For Baby, or you can ask their design department to create an original basket based on personal tastes or hobbies. They can get individual items monogrammed and offer a personal shopping service.

> When my girlfriend Samm was travelling the USA writing her book, I wanted to send her a nice birthday present. Knowing she couldn't cart around any large items, I found a wonderful range of pack-happy clothes bags (in the For Her section) for keeping track of belts, shoes, jewellery, underwear and make-up. They were all labelled with titles such as Bejewelled, In Your Clutches, To Have And To Hold, The Great Unwashed, Unmentionables and Goody Two Shoes (from $18.00). I knew Samm loved keeping everything neat and tidy, so I sent her Unmentionables and The

Great Unwashed for her clean and dirty underwear, and she absolutely loved them. More exciting still, they don't just send the items in a basket, you can have them sent in things like a doctors' bag, beach bag, or leather suitcase (for an extra cost, of course).

> **Star Treatment Gift Services, 15200 Stagg Street, Van Nuys CA 91405**
> **T·USA 800 444 9059 or +1 818 781 9016 W·startreatment.com**

REFLECT OVER A RETRO CUPPA

> Tea with Alice is a lovely new venture set up by husband and wife team, Alison and Simon Jones. Alison and Simon source vintage china and pottery, which is then luxuriously packaged in their exclusively designed Tea With Alice box, to make a timeless and unusual present. Each set is individually named and numbered, and comes with a handmade card describing each item.
> The Vintage Retro range is made up of complementary combinations of vintage or retro teaware – china or pottery teacups, saucers and plates. Together, these china trios make expertly blended 'harlequin' sets, perfect for a beautiful and individual tea-time occasion. Designs range from pretty, traditional, floral fine bone china, to the stronger and funkier earthenware or pottery retro sets from the 1950s through 1970s.
> You can choose from their completed sets or order a custom selection. You can also order a gift box, containing just one cup, saucer, and plate. I think that would make a perfect birthday, thank you, get well soon or 'just thinking of you' gift. A mail order service is offered, just make your choices online and reserve your one-off box prior to sending payment. Gift box (one trio) from £20.00; boxes of four trios from £95.00; plus p&p.

> **Tea With Alice, The Village Farmhouse, Hanchurch Lane, Hanchurch, Staffordshire ST4 8RY T·01782 659 453 W·teawithalice.com**

DARLING, YOU SHOULD HAVE!

> Give someone you love the gift of learning. From the art of cocktail making to learning a circus skill, from cooking a curry to playing golf, they're all gifts that keep on giving. The sky's the limit; you can give them the experience of recording their own CD, a personal shopping day, or the chance to feed a tiger or drive a steam train. Naturally, Thanksdarling also have all the sporty, daredevil-type activities from Formula One racing to zorbing. And if none of those ideas appeal, they have a good selection of gifts such as a share in your friend's favourite football club, or even a Freedom gift voucher that lets the recipient choose.

> **Thanksdarling Ltd, Unit 3, Omega Works, Roach Road, Fish Island, London E3 2PD T·0870 606 6666 W·thanksdarling.com**

FED UP WITH YOUR VIRTUAL FAMILY?

> There's nothing better than a stunning photo album to persuade us to finally get our digital photos off our computer. Kathleen Takushi's charming handstitched, felt appliquéed, 4in. x 6in. photo albums will hold 24 of your favourite family pictures. Choose from a selection of themed appliqués including dogs, cats, fashionable coats, stilettos, flowers and baby prams. She also offers a range of journals and larger photo albums. They come beautifully packaged in pink tissue in a chocolate-brown gift box. Refer to the website for comprehensive USA store list or where you can buy online. Prices from $30.00.

> **Kathleen Takushi W·ktnewyork.com**

DO NOT PASS, GO RIGHT IN!

> Known as the perfect home for life's luxuries, with a level of service second-to-none, William & Son can provide you with wonderful bespoke gifts. Twenty-first century sterling silver iPod cases nestle next to a generous selection of men's cufflinks,

timepieces, jewellery, cashmere, christening gifts, backgammon sets and lovely leather goodies, such as their passport covers. These are available for over 20 countries in everything from gold leather to pink ostrich or green lizard. You can order the covers in a choice of wonderful pastels, 'brights' or gentlemen's colours (from £90.00). I would love to be given their handmade leather Monopoly set with sterling silver pieces, roof-tiled houses and hotels and a leather money-holding wallet for each player – they can even make you a bespoke one with all the properties, etc., personalised – what a gift!

> **William & Son, No 10 Mount Street, London W1K 2TY T · 020 7493 8385 W · williamandson.com**

PLAY THE NUMBERS GAME

> If you remember the fun you had painting by numbers when you were a child, you'll love this unique gift idea. Send your photo to 1-2-3 Art and you'll receive a paint-by-number canvas or textured paper of your image, plus 42 acrylic paints, and brushes to paint with. A really fun idea for any age. Prices: $49.95 (+$15.00 outside the USA)

> **1-2-3 ART, P.O. Box 24814, Louisville, KY 40224 T · USA +1 (502) 225 4006 W · easy123art.com**

IT'S THE THOUGHT
THAT COUNTS

· For a friend who's going off on a beach holiday, buy a large beach towel and roll it up with fabulous holiday must-haves such as: an i-shuffle loaded with their favourite tunes (*see page* 201 , sunscreen, flip flops, a good holiday read, a stylish beach bag, a sarong and a sunhat.

· I love collecting vintage teacups with roses or beautiful designs, and you'll always find them at antique and car boot fairs. For a lovely thank-you present when you stay with friends, fill a pretty teacup with the finest drinking chocolate or ground coffee, wrap it in coloured cellophane and tie it all up with vintage ribbon.

· Buy a beautiful antique spoon from a market and engrave it with words of endearment. My friend was given a jam spoon for Valentine's Day with *I love you* inscribed on it – I thought it was a charming gift and I yearned for one too. Just before Christmas each year we have a group of friends over for dinner- I always love planning their presents and last year I presented them each with an antique napkin ring with their initial engraved on it – it did take me a while to locate each letter at the markets but it was fun looking for them.

· When I sent a round-robin email to find out what was the best present anyone had received, my friend Kay wrote back that she had purchased an authentic signed and framed photo of Al Pacino for her nephew who was a huge fan of the actor. She said his expression was priceless and she had never seen such excitement – 'It was as though he had won the lottery and he told me it was the best present he had ever received, so to me, it was worth every penny spent!' And she means every penny, as some of these are not cheap. Make sure you buy from a reputable dealer, there are many listed online. You can buy photos of sports figures, models, movie and pop stars and often their value will increase over time.

· I once gave a friend who was known for her lovely thank-yous a beautiful selection of blank correspondence cards, note cards and the stamps to send them, all wrapped up with vintage ribbon. This saved her shopping around for them every time she needed one. She thought it was a uniquely fab present – in fact, I got one of the cards back with a lovely note of appreciation.

GUEST WHAT I'VE BOUGHT YOU

For me, the very best bit about giving dinner parties or having people to stay is buying little gifts for my friends, or decorations for the dinner table or guest bedroom. If you've been invited for a weekend stay or a dinner party and don't want to give the usual bunch of flowers or box of standard chocolates, perhaps you might be inspired by a few of these ideas – all gifts I have received, given or made:

- Mini trugs of vegetables (especially if you have home-grown)
- Home-made organic body scrub (combine sea salt, olive oil and fresh lavender) in a beautiful container
- Designer chocolates – I especially love the box of handbag chocolates from **W·chocochocohouse.com** (*see pag*e 255).
- An after-dinner game – **W· cheatwell.com** do a fun tin called Host Your Own After-Dinner Games which includes 16 games. 'Snatch', from **W·pedlars.co.uk**, is also great fun for those who like word games (*see pag*e 278).
- Anything from Harvey Nichols Food Hall – the packaging is divine!
  W·harveynichols.com
- Good champagne (Cava or sparkling wine just doesn't cut it!)
- Guest soaps and vintage linen guest towels
- A bundle of the latest magazines or bestseller books, all tied up with velvet ribbon
- Download great dance music and compile your own CD; print labels using pictures of you and your friends
- A case of wine (with a packet of painkillers)
- A lovely old vintage book on entertaining/etiquette – you can bet if they like to entertain they'll enjoy reading it

- A wicker basket (antique ones are great) full of goodies that make up an easy-to-cook meal – naturally Italian springs to mind as you can fill the basket with home-made pasta sauce, fresh pasta, pesto, fresh herbs, ciabatta, organic olive oil and parmesan. You could even write a little thank-you in Italian (*Grazie mille!*).
- One of every flavour in Green & Black's range of chocolate – dark, white, mint, caramel, ginger, cherry, raisin & hazelnut, etc, all wrapped up in vintage trimmings. The butterscotch is so yummy it took me mere weeks – days – who am I kidding? – hours, to eat it all.
- Gift certificate for a massage therapist to visit them (*see page* 237) – I also made a sign that read 'Do Not Disturb – no partners, pesky kids, pets, peeking or phones' and tied it with ribbon to hang on their door while they were getting their massage.
- If you want to send flowers, do so ahead of the event as this will stop the host/ess from having to find a vase and arranging them in a last-minute panic.
- Particularly as a thank-you for a long visit, or holiday, take photos during your stay, buy a lovely album, arrange the photos and write memorable inscriptions.

And here are some more gift ideas for…

- **The Traveller:** 'Pack happy clothes bags' (*see page* 203) W·startreatment.com
- **The New Parent/s:** Bags of groceries with quick, simple-to-prepare and healthy things to eat and cook, such as fresh pasta and sauce, lots of organic fruit, chocolate, milk and fresh bread. Also newborn nappies and wipes, and a lovely bath product – shop online and have it all delivered.
- **The Movers:** Swish note cards with their new address and phone number – you can

The perfect book for any hostess, *A Gracious Welcome – Etiquette and Ideas for Entertaining Houseguests*, Amy Nebens (Chronicle Books) is full of great ideas, from preparing your home to welcoming touches. I loved the Hanging Door Sign and the Bath Salt Mix. And there are lovely photographs – including a very sweet vintage teddy sitting on a tray with a glass of milk and two home-baked biscuits!

easily make them yourself using A4 card (you can buy a great selection now for your inkjet printer) – design the layout then cut them to A5 size. Buy a nice packet of envelopes (tissue-lined would be great) and tie with vintage ribbon, or buy a nice box, and *voilà*!

LOVELY ILLUSTRATED BOOKS

PICTURE THE PERFECT GIFT

> Laura Stoddart is one of the illustrators I admire most. You may well have seen her work in magazines such as *World of Interiors*, *Gardens Illustrated* and *Vogue Entertaining*, or her wonderful line of stationery. The people she draws are very distinctive, long and thin with tiny heads. She has compiled and illustrated two wonderful books filled with her illustrations and quotes and poems: *Off the Beaten Track – A Traveller's Anthology* and *Up the Garden Path – A Little Anthology* which would be great for a housewarming present. Both titles are published by Orion Books.

> **The Orion Publishing Group**
> **T·020 7240 3444 W·orionbooks.co.uk**

THE ART OF LIVING WELL

> Artist Sara Midda has written some delightful books – two in particular I've given to several friends as gifts:

> Her first book *In & Out of the Garden*, which was three years in preparation, is a fantastic present for anyone who likes gardening, watercolours, or script and calligraphy. Filled with garden lore, quotes and advice, not to mention good old folk remedies, I searched high and low for my copy and ended up using a book-finding service to find a copy to give as a gift. (This was before the days of the internet). I'm delighted that they have now reprinted it.

> The other book I simply adore is *South of France – A Sketchbook*. I can lose myself in this book for hours. It takes you through a year's sojourn in the South of France – a journal crammed with images, notions and day-to-day discoveries. The wonderful watercolours capture French life at its most glorious and even on the greyest, dampest day they can transport you to lying in a hammock underneath an azure sky, surrounded by lavender fields, sipping on a glass of wine and relishing a rustic sandwich of fresh baguette and camembert.

> **Workman Publishing Company, New York**
> **W·workman.com**

PERSONALISED PHOTO ALBUM

If you have a special birthday or wedding anniversary coming up for a family member or dear friend, then why not make them a personalised photo album? Buy a lovely leather-bound photo album, (Smythson's would be my choice) then collate and copy special photos onto each page and write your own messages and comments. They will be sure to treasure it for the rest of their lives.

INCLINED TO PERFECTION

> If you're a lover of beautifully printed and illustrated books, take a look at Incline Press. Kathy and Graham use a combination of metal type and a 19th-century hand press that allows them to print, hand-sew and bind their own unique books. The illustrations are often wonderful lino or wood cuts as they are in *Marco's Animal Alphabet*, where each lino cut is coloured using the art of *pochoir*, the stencil method of hand colouring. They produce a limited number of special editions of each title and then a further 100-200 numbered copies. They can also design and hand print bespoke invitations, business cards and writing paper.

> **Incline Press, 36 Bow Street, Oldham OL1 1SJ T·0161 627 1966 W·inclinepress.com**

HELPFUL GIFTS

It's a rare day that we don't hear someone complain that they don't have enough time to do everything they want or need to do. So instead of buying things for those special people in your life, why not give them a gift of a person who does things? If you hear someone with one of the following common life stresses, for example, you'll know exactly how to go about helping them out...

'I ran out of good ideas for my husband's birthday in 1997, what on earth should I get him this year?'

> For a bespoke and creative present look no further than Apt Wrapped. They'll have you fill in a questionnaire about the recipient and then create the perfect one-off gift for you. They made a mini camper van for one lady's husband whose dream was to explore the UK countryside in a camper van. When he opened the door to his van, he saw his life in miniature inside, complete with all his favourite things. There was a cut-out photo of his wife and daughter sitting on the sofa, books on pubs, gadgets, and weekend supplements with covers showing his favourite music and football team, condiments, beer, cooking, shopping for food and camping. There were 12 scenic backdrops and even a route finder on the dashboard. It was made from walnut, beech plywood, cotton materials, foam, Perspex, acetate prints and customised miniature objects.

> Other gifts they have made include personalised board games, and they've also created some really funky and unique wedding invitations. Your friend/partner won't have ever received a present like it. Petra tells us that she's had grown men cry when they've received one of her gifts! Of course, they also make them for ladies, too.

> **Petra Johnsson, Apt Wrapped, 108 Stapleton Hall Road, London N4 4QA T·020 8374 5790 W·aptwrapped.com**

'I have four wardrobesfull of clothes and nothing to wear!'

> If your wardrobe is uninspiring and cluttered with clothes you seldom wear but can't bring yourself to throw away, then it's time to call Suzanne, Coathanger's chief stylist. She'll reorganise your closet and give your clothes a completely new lease of life. Suzanne will co-ordinate your existing wardrobe and show you how to accessorise, advise on colour and body shapes, and inject new life into old favourites.

> Having styled for many years, working with celebrities in TV, film and magazines, she certainly knows what's hot and what's not, and will give honest and friendly advice.

> 'She loves working within fashion, and even after all these years still gets very excited when she sees her clients 'look amazing' after they have been 'coathangered'!

> You can order a gift certificate online or phone Suzanne to discuss details.
> **Suzanne Bernie – Coathanger**
> **T·0870 460 6194 W·coathanger.net**

'I'm so bored with my house I hate going home after work!'
> If you want to transform your home but simply don't have the funds to buy all new stuff, buy a gift certificate from the fabulous interior design store, Lipp. They offer a 're-dress your home service' where they will come over and use their expertise to move things around to give your home a new look, whilst working with the furniture and accessories that you've already got. I guarantee that the wonderful Therese can help find you space in your home that you didn't know existed.
> They also offer an interior design service (central London only), involving a consultation followed by a presentation of the new look including colour charts, samples of materials and a detailed cost breakdown.
> The gift certificate is also valid in their lovely shop, where new stock is introduced every four to six weeks and staff really do go out of their way to help you fall in love with your home all over again.
> **Therese Dempster, Lipp, 118a Holland Park Avenue, London W11 4UA**
> **T·020 7243 2432**

'The nanny's just quit, winter's coming and the garden's a tip, the crack in the living room wall is growing by the day, the dry-cleaning is piling up behind the kitchen door, the car's filthy, it's my husband's birthday next week, I want to get a deal on our flights to NZ and try to buy tickets to the rugby, I've got to type up instructions for the temp who's coming in while we're on holiday, book a manicure and pedicure, and keep my own business on track…'
> Is it just me who lives with a constant 'To Do'

list running on a loop through my brain? I wish I'd found out about Ten UK earlier. It's a lifestyle and home-management service that can handle all the daily stresses for you. The company was set up in 1997 by Alex Cheatle who wanted to help people get the most out of life by renting someone else's time, sort of 'a cross between a butler, pa and trusted friend'.
> They have a special 'Gift of Time' Christmas package – you can give a present of a lifestyle manager for three months, six months, or even a year (£200.00 per month). The recipient will meet their own dedicated lifestyle manager and can delegate as many tasks as they like to them within the set time period.
> What sort of things, you may well ask. They've had people ask for help with loft conversions, getting a table in that exclusive restaurant, scoring great tickets for top shows, tracking down a certain car licence number to buy, finding out the number of a well-known football manager, and even finding a plumber to fix an emergency leak on a bank holiday (the problem was that the house was in the middle of the festivities of the Notting Hill Carnival and the plumber had to walk a mile to get there – no cars were allowed – carrying all his tools!). They've even purchased new cars for members – they are one of the only lifestyle management or concierge services that offer an in-house specialist motoring team with industry contacts and great buying power.
> You can also join from £75.00 per month for unlimited time, but you won't have a dedicated lifestyle manager (£12.50 per half hour if they have to leave the office). This would have to be my ultimate gift.
> **Ten UK, 30 Market Place, London W1W 8AP**
> **T·07000 101 999 W·tenuk.co.uk**

'My garden is so messy and full of weeds, I can't find my shed!'
> Get in Woodhams Landscapes who offer a blow-and-mow service (cut grass and clear leaves and debris) or full garden management from £55.50. And while they're there, they can offer planting ideas and garden advice. They can even power-wash the driveway. However, if you want a divine garden design plan, expect to cough up £700.00 plus VAT for a terrace or small garden. If you want a garden designer to visit for a design brief, it costs £100.00 (plus VAT) within the M25.
> **Woodhams Landscapes, 45 Elizabeth Street, London SW1W 9PP**
> **T · 020 7346 5656   W · woodhams.co.uk**

GIFT WRAPPING

It doesn't even matter what's inside, a beautifully wrapped present is always a joy to receive. Here are some shops and services that will help you shame the other gifts under the tree!

Ribbons & Trimmings

HEAD DOWNSTAIRS FOR UP-TO-THE MINUTE IDEAS
> Tucked away in a basement in Little Portland Street, you'll find Barnett Lawson Trimmings' rows and rows of shelves brimming with exciting trimmings, ribbon, flowers, feathers, buttons, cords and braids. With over 10,000 items in stock, they supply to the film, TV and theatre trades and are also hugely popular with party/event organisers, not to mention the well-known fashion designers who occasionally pop in. Thankfully the public can also wander in and purchase their wonderful stock at very good prices. They will custom-print ribbon in a great selection

of colours (printing usually takes two weeks), can dye any trimming to match your fabric, hand-make custom corsages, and offer many other services.
> **Barnett Lawson Trimmings, 16–17 Little Portland Street, London W1W 8NE**
> **T · 020 7636 8591   W · bltrimmings.com**

WEAVE IT TO THE EXPERTS
> At last I've found a great company who offer personalised occasion woven ribbon at a very reasonable price. You can order the 8mm, white, cream or pastel ribbon with a choice of five font styles and numerous choices of colours for the text. Your message can include up to 50 characters, spaces and/or motifs, with a minimum order of 20 metres.
> You could order ribbon announcing the arrival of a new baby with the date, name and birth weight, or messages like *Happy Birthday Finn*, *Merry Christmas with all my love Beverley*, *I Love You*, or *A Present From Lottie*. Allow up to ten days for delivery, although mine came much quicker and Peter is so helpful I'm sure if you needed it in a rush they would pull out all the stops to help.
> **Peter Gregory, GB Nametapes. Unit 53, Honeyborough Industrial Estate, Neyland, Pembrokeshire SA73 1SE**
> **T · 01646 600 664   W · gbnametapes.co.uk**

WRAPPING UP MEMORIES
> You can buy all manner of ribbon and trims online through Nostalgia. They offer a wonderful colour selection of silk ribbons, not to mention French jacquard, hand-dyed, organza, velvet and wire-edged ribbons, flower and leaves trims, and other great embellishments.
> **Nostalgia, 147a Nottingham Road, Eastwood, Nottingham NG16 3GJ**
> **T · 01773 712 240 W · nostalgiaribbon.com**

ADD PIZAZZ TO ANY PARCEL

> I can't keep away from this shop and every time I visit it my bank balance takes a serious battering. Not only does it stock an enormous selection of the most beautiful ribbons and trimmings, like feather fringing, crystal drops, shell and suede, handmade tassels, velvets, satins, and exquisite little flowers sewn onto ribbon, but you can also buy corsages, flowers, butterflies, and an ever-changing stock of little treats that you can sew or glue onto anything. They have four shops – two in London, one in Glasgow and one in Newcastle-upon-Tyne.

> **VV Rouleaux, 54 Sloane Square, Cliveden Place, London SW1W 8AX T·020 7730 3125**
> **102 Marylebone Lane, London W1U 2QD T·020 7224 5179**
> **94 Miller Street, Merchant City, Glasgow, G1 1DT T·0141 221 2277**
> **38 Brentwood Avenue, Jesmond, Newcastle upon Tyne, NE2 3DH T·0191 281 3003 W·vvrouleaux.com**

Wrapping Paper

THE CHERRY ON THE CAKE

> This is a fantastic site where you can choose from a lovely range of wrapping paper and ribbons, then order your own message to be printed across it – *A Gift From Kay*, *Birthday Wishes from Rebecca*, *Lots of Love from Mum & Dad*.

> The Merry Cherry Red paper with white text looks fabulous. Based in the USA, but they do ship overseas.

> **Name Maker Inc, P O Box 43821, Atlanta, GA 30336 T·in the USA 800 241 2890; or from outside USA + 1 404 691 2237 W·namemaker.com**

BECOME A WRAP STAR

> Why not have your own bespoke wrapping paper made up? I saw this on a present my friend was given and it looked fantastic. Send a photo, drawing or whatever to Wrapsody and they will create a full-size, high-quality sheet of multi-image wrapping paper for £3.75. It would be nice to wrap a wedding or anniversary present with a photo of the couple. Allow three working days for ordering.

> **Wrapsody T·01522 869 737 W·wrapsody.com**

LIVE FOR THE PRESENT

> Rachel Ashwell of the Shabby Chic fame has written a gorgeous book called *The Gift of Giving*. With sections on searching for treasures, theming presents, colour inspiration, vintage gifts, and one-of-a-kind gifts, it inspires you to immediately go out gathering gifts just so that you can follow her advice on how to present them beautifully. There are also tips on table decoration and flowers if you're throwing a baby shower or other little themed parties.

> ***The Gift of Giving**, Rachel Ashwell, Regan Books*

For fabulous gift wrapping classes with Jane Means – see page 52
See page 54 for a very useful book on the art of gift wrapping
Also see page 53 for The Wrapping Company

BEAUTY AND PAMPERING
GROOMING
HAIRCUT EXTENSIONS
PEDICURES
ATHOMETREATMENTS
TANNING
MAKEUP BROWS

In this Beauty section I wanted to tell you about all the lovely individuals who give a great personal service and have a natural talent, as opposed to beauty institutions who have a top reputation but have many therapists (although I've mentioned a few of those too!).

To keep things consistent I didn't have 50 different testers try out a few treatments each, just one very thorough person (that's me!). What's more, I paid for every treatment, hair cut, colour and blow-dry (except four) and most of my visits were in disguise!!

I've spent thousands of pounds on facials, waxing, manicures, pedicures, hair colouring and cutting, make-up and beauty products, but I've obviously not been able to test everyone I've mentioned due to financial and time constraints and partly for the sake of my poor hair. I've also included some I haven't used, but my friends have, or because you simply just had to know about them.

A quick word of warning: it's often been hard keeping up with great therapists who move around quicker than I can type their phone numbers. I did a last-minute check on their contact details just before going to print but please check before you turn up on their doorstep...

EYES
PERFECT BROWS
Waxing, Plucking, Threading, Colouring

BROWS THAT ARE WORTH THE OW!

> Blink Eyebrow Bars, set up by Vanita Parti, offer a walk-in service for eyebrow threading. Threading is a highly specialist skill with many of the top practitioners learning it in childhood. As more and more people recognise the merits of threading, these drop-in bars have become increasingly popular, so if you're on a tight schedule you may be better off making an appointment. They do try and keep one chair for appointments and one for drop-ins though, so you should get one on the day you need.

> Currently they have three drop-in bars, at Fenwick, Harvey Nichols and Selfridges, and Vanita only picks the top threaders with years of experience. She says 'one hair can make all the difference to a perfect arch'.

> The only downside is that the chairs are in the main beauty hall so everyone can see you having your brows fixed. This lack of privacy didn't worry me, as when I had mine threaded by Rekha at Selfridges she was so quick and professional it literally was Blink and it's all over.

> **Blink Eyebrow Bars W·blinkbrowbar.com**
> **Fenwick, 63 New Bond Street, London W1A 3BS T·020 7629 9161**
> **Harvey Nichols, 109–125 Knightsbridge, London SW1X 7RJ T·020 7235 5000 x2322**
> **Selfridges, 400 Oxford Street, London W1A 1AB T·020 7318 3538**

ANTICIPATE SATISFACTION

> It took me eight months to get a facial with Vaishaly (*see* main entry, *page 218*), but her treatments are well worth the wait. I'd never had threading done before, so didn't know what to expect. Vaishaly is an expert brow shaper and though it brought tears to my eyes when she threaded my eyebrows, it also brought a smile to my face when I saw the results. I stayed hair-free for months and friends loved my new look.

> **Vaishaly, 51 Paddington Street, London W1U 4H T·020 7224 6088 W·vaishaly.com**

SEMI-PERMANENT PERFECTION

> I have a friend who accidentally shaved her eyebrows off (don't ask!) and they didn't quite grow back. It's a shame she didn't know about Sophie, one of the leading permanent

make-up artists in the country. She has perfected micro-pigmentation, a technique that uses a pen to tattoo one of 25 realistic-shades onto your brows. Sophie works with clients who have lost their eyebrows through chemotherapy or radiotherapy, suffer from alopecia, need correction work or just want her service for cosmetic reasons.

> Your first visit will consist of a consultation and treatment, after which you may need a quick touch-up; otherwise you won't need to retouch for 12-18 months. Naturally, as one of the best she works closely with many celebrities and pop stars.

> Sophie Thorpe, 106 Draycott Avenue, London SW3 3AE T·020 7589 5899
W·sophiethorpe.co.uk

FACE FACTS – IT'S ALL IN THE BROWS

> Kamini has been developing her technique for over 20 years and is said to rival the best eyebrow threaders in New York. She has a fantastic eye for how your eyebrows should be shaped. To say she's fixated by eyebrows would be an understatement – she even admits to walking down the street and looking at women's brows, not their clothes. She says the right brows can alter a face dramatically and told me mine were all out of shape. She promised she could get my eyebrows to the perfect shape with about three threading sessions. I have to say that even after my first session they looked simply fantastic and the effect lasted for ages before I got even a hint of regrowth.

> Kamini Vaghela, 14–16 Lancer Square, Kensington Church Street, London W8 4EP
T·020 7937 2411

> or at Claridge's Olympus Suite
T·020 7409 6565 on Thursdays

Also see page 216 for Arezoo Kaviani

LUSCIOUS LASHES

MAKE A PERMANENT IMPRESSION

> If you compiled a list of iconic eyelashes, sixties super-babe Twiggy would have to come near the top of the list. Friend of the stars, Rhonda Beattie, not only tints but can add extra lashes or even perm them to really open up your eyes. Yes, that's right – she's renowned for her eyelash perm, which she's been doing for over 10 years. The treatment's fine for sensitive eyes, but Rhonda recommends removing contacts, so don't forget your solutions. The perm will last a good two months, often three if you look after them well. £72.00 for eyelash perm (one hour), £88.00 for eyelash tint and perm (90 minutes).

> Rhonda Beattie at Michaeljohn, 25 Albermarle Street, London W1S 4HU
T·020 7629 6969

GO TO LUNG FOR LONG AND LAVISH

> After visiting Susie for her wonderful Facial Dynamics (*see page* 217), I had to go back and try her Fantasy Tan treatment (*page* 226) and her Lavish Lashes. These synthetic lashes come in various lengths and Susie can masterfully create different looks, from long fluttering lashes to shorter ones with more volume. It's a complicated process and you should allow a good two hours. An individual synthetic eyelash with a specially formulated bonding agent is applied to your own natural eyelash, so you can shower and swim, no problem, and if you want to wear mascara as well (although I find you don't need to) you can use the Lavish Lash mascara or any other non-waterproof mascara.

> Susie is a perfectionist and you will love the results. Great for your honeymoon. Full set £130.00.

> Susie Lung, 50 Manchester Street, London W1M 5PB T·07957 771 503

W·lavish-lashes.co.uk – gives you further information, and great before-and-after pictures. It also has a list of salons that apply Lavish Lashes if you're not able to visit Susie Lung. Also see Pout (page 42).

FACE

FAB FACIALS

TRUST EWA TO HAVE GOOD SKIN

> With her wonderful healing hands, intuition and genuine love for her work, Ewa took me to another place. I had a divine massage as part of my facial. Ewa offers Anne Semonine 'couture' facials that can last from one to two hours depending on the client. She's happy to give you tips on how to look after your skin and is particularly good if you have problem skin – she read my body/skin really well. Ewa has such a fount of knowledge and knows so many people in the health and beauty world, that no matter what your problem, she can probably recommend you to the right person. It was a lovely, lovely experience. Ewa can be found at the Olympus Suite, Claridges, and prices are from £110.00.

> **Ewa Berkmann   T· 020 7937 3837**
  E· ewaberkmann@hotmail.com

GO WITH THE GLOW

> When you visit Arezoo you're immediately cocooned in lovely warm towels and blankets while she makes her skin assessment. She then cleans, tones, exfoliates, extracts, steams and uses other treatments as is deemed necessary. When your skin is glowing, next comes the best bit. I was floating while her warm hands got to work giving me one of the best facial massages ever. She can leave you to relax or she'll quite happily chat away – we had a great laugh.

> Not only was her facial superb, she even

phoned round some of her contacts to try and sort out the origins of a skin reaction I was suffering at the time. It turns out most reactions at skin level are related to our internal organs. I thought it was lovely of her to try and help me. She uses Ayur-medic products which feature both Ayurvedic herbs and proven anti-aging compounds.

> Arezoo was also among the first to introduce both threading and the Brazilian to the UK over 15 years ago. She's famous for her Playboy and has also commissioned an exclusive range of J Maskrey body jewellery. Actually, this was one of the first things to catch my eye as I walked into her salon – wonderful Swarovski crystal body art sparkling in the sunshine. I wanted to buy at least six – the dragonfly is superb! I digress; after she has stripped you bare, you can have Just Married, Happy Birthday, Just Divorced, Happy Anniversary or one of her own exclusive range applied. She told me at least two girls are now blissfully married after being sent home with a new look and 'Marry Me' on their privates! Of course, you can also apply them to other parts of your body if you're feeling slightly less adventurous. Her clients fly in from all over the world to see her, and include a raft of celebrities (so until you book, her address remains closely guarded).

> Having moved into her Knightsbridge salon in 2001, she works seven days a week, along with her lovely assistants Liria and Irene. Her work is her passion and it really shows – she'll always have time to see you. I'm booked in with her again for my eyebrows and a little (yes, I said a little) waxing. If you're visiting for your first facial, allow two to three hours. It's unbelievable value, with prices from £150.00 for a facial, £35.00 for threading and £65.00 for a Brazilian.

> **Arezoo Kaviani, Hans Crescent,**
  Knightsbridge, London SW1 OLL
  T· 020 7584 6868 / 07768 903 090
  W· arezoo.co.uk

A IS FOR AMAZING RESULTS

> Known as *the* facialist, with women flocking from around the world for her signature treatment, Amanda offers a chic service in a private, scented setting so divine there's quite a waiting list.

> She uses her own gorgeous products and I adore her cleansing pomade. Experience your skin being massaged with lovely things like camellia oil and Persian rose water, and leave feeling beautiful without your make-up! Prices from £200.00.

> **Amanda Lacey T · 020 7351 4443**
  W · amandalacey.com

WE'RE ALL ABOUT EVE

> There's a big difference between having an Eve Lom Facial and getting a facial by Eve Lom, one can be done as far afield as Miami, the other can only be done in London. When I phoned for an appointment, I was delighted to be told that I would only have to wait for six weeks. I was then devastated to realise that I couldn't make it on the day I was offered. However, despite not having first-hand experience, I do know others that have had the luxury of one of Eve's facials and they simply adored it.

> The preparation (and finishing off) is carried out by one of Eve's assistants, while Eve herself performs the lengthy, healing massage, including her renowned cranio-sacral work. My friend headed for home not only feeling more relaxed than she had in years, but all revved up to start the new diet and take up the lifestyle tips which Eve imparts during the treatment. Eve Lom fans include many celebrities, and pretty much anyone who has ever experienced her magic hands. Prices: £245.00 for the first treatment then £195.00.

> **Eve Lom, Eve Lom Clinic, 2 Spanish Place,**
  London W1U 3HU T · 020 7935 9988
  W · evelom.co.uk

THE BEST OF BOTH WORLDS

> The lovely Susie has devised a new form of facial, called Facial Dynamics, incorporating the best of Eastern and Western therapies and massage techniques to really restore your face. It works on releasing years of built-up tension and stress in the face, neck, head and scalp. Susie stimulates your lymphatic system to give you an all-round boost and improve your circulation. She also focuses on nasal congestion, which she says can manifest itself in puffiness around your eyes and forehead.

> Thai massage, stimulation of acupressure points and deep tissue work are the core elements of Facial Dynamics. Susie uses the best organic Argan oils from Morocco mixed with sandalwood and jasmine, so don't plan on going out anywhere straight after, as your hair will be lavished in oil. Susie lets you in on lots of beauty secrets during your treatment and you'll come away feeling absolutely wonderful – I certainly did. She also offers Organic facials using Dr Hauschka, Fantasy Tan spray and Lavish Lash eyelashes (*see pages* 215 and 226). Tucked away in a basement, she doesn't have a waiting area, so don't arrive too early for your appointment. Facial Dynamics costs £75.00 for a 75-minute session.

> **Susie Lung, 50 Manchester Street, London**
  W1M 5PB T · 07957 771 503

MULTI-TASKING AS ONLY A WOMAN CAN

> After 14 years' experience in New York working with renowned companies, Kirsty discovered a winning facial treatment. Upon returning to London she became the resident beauty expert at *The Times* and then set up her own treatment rooms with an exclusive client list. She's now the name on everyone's lips for the best in skincare. With her holistic background and study of Chinese therapy, you're in very capable hands as she cleanses, exfoliates, extracts, massages and

moisturises. Lie on her heated table and enjoy a pampering customised facial and a whole lot more: while your skin is soaking up the benefits of your face mask, you'll receive a wonderful hot-stone neck and shoulder massage and a soothing foot treatment. Kirsty loves to pamper you but she also ensures she makes a difference to your skin and you will see results. She uses her own line of multi-tasking products with anti-aging ingredients which are paraben and petrochemical free. Prices for her facial start at £95.00, and her products are available by mail order and at Selfridges, London.

> **Kirsty McLeod, 34 Moreton Street, London SW1V 2PD T · 020 7834 0101 W · kirstymcleod.com**

JOIN THE A-LIST IN LINDA'S SANCTUARY

> Once you're cocooned in one of Linda's lovely warm beds you won't want to leave. She offers an haute-couture facial with the most amazing light touch. Coupled with her vast knowledge and professionalism, the little bit extra she offers to all her clients will leave you with not only glowing skin but also a wonderful feeling of being really cared for.

> Her walls are filled with photos and words of gratitude from top celebs and she's also a favourite with high-flying men in need of a bit of pampering. Don't let that intimidate you; prices still remain some of the most reasonable in London for someone with such a reputation and you won't have to wait too long to get an appointment.

> Linda's philosophy is to maintain the highest standards and give the best treatments using the finest products and equipment. She works with the wonderful Yon Ka products, (amongst others) giving excellent facials and is great at eyebrow shaping, and there's nothing she doesn't know about make-up. What I particularly loved about Linda was her concern for your overall well-being. Using her wide-ranging knowledge, she pointed me in

the right direction to a man who could help me with my frequent migraines. Prices from £85.00.

> **Linda Meredith, Health and Beauty Clinic, 36 Beauchamp Place, Knightsbridge, London SW3 1NU T · 020 7225 2755 W · lindameridith.com**

NO-NONSENSE GURU GETS RESULTS

> After waiting eight months for an appointment, I was very excited to meet the woman American *Vogue* named as one of London's 'most sought after beauty gurus'. I was really surprised when I saw how young Vaishaly is or at least looks – I don't know her age, but when someone looks this good you know they take care of themselves and will in turn take good care of you. I've had two facials from her now and she certainly hasn't aged in the last two years.

> I've had facials in my time which felt like a butterfly was dancing on my skin and had no beneficial effect at all: I left Vaishaly's with probably the cleanest and softest skin I've felt in a long time. Personally, I didn't find it particularly relaxing as she really gets on with the extractions, lymphatic drainage, micro-dermabrasion and ends with her special Indian head massage, but the results were impressive.

> She also had threaded my eyebrows for the first time, which was amazing. She's an expert brow shaper (*see page* 214). Clients include a raft of celebrities, so put your name down now. Prices from £120.00.

> **Vaishaly, 51 Paddington Street, London W1U 4HR T · 020 7224 6088 W · vaishaly.com**

ON A QUEST FOR THE BEST

> I've known Maggie at Beauty Works for over 10 years and she continues to astound me with her passion for providing the best products and treatments for her clients. She scours the world trying out new treatments,

OH LA... **LA PRAIRIE!**

Now, I know there's a lot of talk about price versus product versus "does it actually do anything?", but I can reassure you that after using **La Prairie skin care** you'll know that it was money well spent. There's no getting away from the fact that it's expensive, but hey, so are those £300.00 pair of shoes which are actually really uncomfortable and do nothing much for your feet, not to mention your posture. So, no argument really, everyone sees your face all the time, so just forget about buying those shoes or latest handbag and treat yourself to some of this fabulous range of products instead.

La Prairie has turned my skin around in the last year, and it all started with a free sample of the **Skin Caviar Luxe Cream** given to me by my dear friend Beverley. We were at a girlie party and she gave us all a sample – four of us are now using nothing else.

They have such a fabulous range – especially their cellular, anti-aging treatments. The exclusive **La Prairie Cellular Complex** is only found in La Prairie products, and these age-fighting ingredients deliver nutrients essential to the health, vitality and overall appearance of your skin, helping to combat premature aging, environmental hazards and the stresses of everyday life.

As everyone's skin is different, there's no point in me telling you what's great for me, as you'll be different. So book an appointment with your nearest **La Prairie consultant** (at well-known department stores) and she'll work out a skincare programme for you. More importantly, you'll be able to try the products and experience the feeling of the creams on your skin. You can also do a personal skincare consultation online.

Tip: Every summer, just in time for your holiday, they launch a little travel kit with a lovely selection of their products in a very smart cosmetic bag. Don't miss it.

In the year that I've been using La Prairie, my close friends have made comments like "**Your skin's so radiant**", "Gosh, your skin is so lovely, you don't need any make-up" and "Your skin is beautiful". I've never had comments like this before, and I had used other expensive products. My skin was very, very dry and prone to breakouts (I never had spots as a teenager!). Now it's renewed, I hardly ever get a spot and it feels like velvet. Put some on your dressing table now – the packaging is divine too!

W· laprairie.com

equipment and products, and she always goes that extra mile to secure not just the latest but the best in the industry. Her work in semi-permanent make-up is rapidly developing an international reputation, and clients, including overseas royalty, fly her out to their homes just to enjoy her skillful techniques.

> Her skincare treatments are brilliant. I once went to Maggie with a patch of awful, dry, flaky skin on the side of my face (think fish scales) for which I'd had different diagnoses from three different doctors, with no improvement. When Maggie had completed my treatment, the improvement was remarkable. She's trained in a wide variety of treatments, so she can combine all sorts of techniques to achieve the best result.

> I particularly like the complimentary treats, such as a hand or foot massage, which she offers while your skin masque is working its magic. Best of all, Maggie works on Sunday, which is my favourite time to pop out for some 'me time'.

> **Maggie Smyth, Beauty Works, 23a Topsfield Parade, Tottenham Lane, London N8 8PP T · 020 8340 8069 W · beautyworksonline.co.uk**

MAKE-UP HAVENS

PAMPER YOURSELF PARIS STYLE

> Learn the tricks of the trade by make-up artists who work regularly on magazines, fashion and music shoots. You can either have a one-on-one lesson (£100.00 for an hour) or you can sit back and enjoy your make-up being applied. This is very popular with ladies on their way to castings, special occasions, or that special job interview. Their make-up artists have tended to a long A-list of celebrities. And if you can't get to the salon, they can come to your hotel, office or home in central London (from £200.00 –

they will travel further for additional travel costs).

> Their nail therapists are in high demand with celebs and of course work on the shows at London Fashion week. They give a fantastic manicure for a very affordable price. I'm definitely booking in.

> I love that you can book the salon for private pamper parties. Bring all your friends, enjoy pizza and wine, and party while being pampered.

> **The Beauty Lounge, 2 Percy Street, London W1T 1DD T · 020 7436 8686 W · beautylounge.co.uk**

GET THE FACE TO MATCH YOUR WARDROBE

> When I made my appointment with John Gustafson I had to wait nine months, but it was well worth it. If patience isn't your strong point don't be put off, add your name to the cancellation list and you may well be seen a lot sooner.

> John works as an independent beauty and make-up consultant at The Beauty Studio in Fenwick. He's also resident beauty guru on **W · handbag.com**. A salon consultation of one and a half to two hours cost £100.00 with £50.00 redeemable against any products purchased.

> First John talked with me about what I was comfortable with in regards to my make-up and skin care routine, what I felt I needed, my preferences and lifestyle. Then he tailor made a skin care and make-up regime for me, considering all those things we'd talked about, the time I felt I could spend on getting ready each morning and my budget.

> My old brown eye-shadow, which I'd been wearing for I don't know how many years, was swiftly replaced and my soft pink lipstick was promptly relegated to the this-does-not-suit-you bin as he showed me how to freshen up my look. He also gave me tips and guidance on how to change the look for

evening before a night out. I guarantee you'll emerge a new you, looking younger, fresher and extremely 'now'.

> John Gustafson, The Beauty Studio,
  3rd Floor, Fenwick, New Bond Street,
  London W1A 3BS T·0208 409 9823

WHO IS THE MAYFAIREST OF THEM ALL?

> Mathew Alexander is one of the leading hair and make-up artists in the UK. If you visit his newly opened and extremely chic Hair & Make-up Boutique in Mayfair, you can rest assured that you'll be treated to a very personal experience in gorgeous surroundings

> You may have to wait your turn with his A-list clientele requiring beautification for the red carpet, but you too can book either a two-hour make-up lesson which will guarantee a younger, more updated look, or a fabulous new hair cut that will have your friends' jaws dropping!

> Or if you receive the invite of the year and looking stunning is a complete necessity, then let him apply your make-up. He'll make you look better than you ever thought you could. Mathew is also available for bridal make-up or personal visits to your home. Prices: cut and blow-dry £125.00; make-up lesson £250.00; make-up application £150.00; express 30-minute make-up application £75.00.

> Mathew Alexander, 12 Lancashire Court,
  London, W1S 1EY T·020 7495 1122
  W·mathewalexander.co.uk

Also see page 236 for make-up artists that visit in the comfort of your home.

BODY

MANICURES AND PEDICURES

Also see pages 237 and 239 for therapists that visit in the comfort of your home.

TRANSATLANTIC TREATS FOR YOUR TOOTSIES

> I know I said I wasn't going to recommend a salon, but I have to make another exception. I've had fabulous manicures at the Bliss Spa in London and an even more wonderful pedicure in their New York salon. The only trouble is choosing which treatment you're going to treat yourself to.

> Their pedicure is known as a 'facial for your feet' and includes buffing, scrubbing, soaking, clipping and filing … deep breath … pummelling, paraffin-ing, pruning and polishing to perfection. You'll enjoy 90 minutes of foot fantasy (£80.00). They also offer a double-choc pedicure for those who adore chocolate or a hot milk and almond pedicure. Can I have one of each, please?

> Bliss London, 60 Sloane Avenue, London
  SW3 3DD T·020 7590 6146

> Bliss New York, 2nd floor, 568 Broadway,
  NYC, NY 10012 T·+1 212 219 8970
  (see online for other Bliss Spas in New
  York, Los Angeles & San Francisco)
  W·blissworld.com W·blisslondon.co.uk

RING THE CHAPPLE BELL

> Discreetly tucked away, with a tiny sign on the bell button, you'll find the Grande Dame of manicurists. I had the best manicure ever and we'd been chatting so much that I was amazed to find that it had taken over an hour and a half. I left feeling I'd made a friend for life. Iris is a favourite with beauty journalists – you've probably read her tips and quotes for great nails (she's very big on sweet almond oil), as she's always featured in the

magazines. Prices: Manicure £35.00; pedicure £55.00.

> **Iris Chapple at The Nail Studio, 3 Spanish Place, London W1U 3HX**
> **T · 07956 307392 / 020 7486 6001**

DOUBLE DELIGHTS WITH THE BEST IN THE BIZ

> Leighton Denny won the Nail Technician of the Year award so many times he was voted into the Hall of Fame and is now one of the judges!

> I've never had a mani and pedi at the same time and was lucky enough to have two men at once!, a manicure from Leighton and a pedicure from Paul Foster. But as Leighton is concentrating on his new product range now, juggling his A-list of clients and fitting in all the fashion shoots, I hear it's quite hard to get an appointment with him. Still, no harm in trying. You can buy his great range of nail colours and products at **W · shop.helenmarks.co.uk** – I've purchased a lovely chocolate brown colour, 'Not Tonight' and 'Golden Girl' a stunning gold nail colour and they arrived next day!

> **Leighton Denny Nail Team, Urban Retreat at Harrods, 87-135 Brompton Road, Knightsbridge, London SW1X 7XL**
> **T · 020 7893 8333**

> **or Urban Retreat Manchester at Harvey Nichols, 21 New Cathedral Street, Manchester M3 1RE   T · 0161 828 8856**
> **W · urbanretreat.co.uk**

ARE YOUR FEET FANTASTIQUE?

> If there's anything better than relaxing propped up on big soft pillows on a comfy bed in an exclusive hotel, it's being joined there by Bastien Gonzalez. The famed French pedicurist will treat your feet to an hour of pampering they'll never forget. With his training as a podiatrist and years of experience, there isn't anything he doesn't know about the feet and skin. He's quick to point out that your feet have 56 muscles, 26 bones and 103 ligaments, and the majority of the time they are stuffed into shoes deprived of oxygen. He says that not many people look after their feet properly on a regular basis and that if they did it would prevent a lot of the problems he sees (mobility problems, calluses, corns and dry skin).

> His innovation was to develop a pedicure as a global concept of well-being, while still retaining the luxury and glamourous touch. In his own words, his concept of a pedicure 'combines the treatment in itself, pedicure, 'pedi' meaning foot, 'cure' meaning treatment, with a more holistic approach.'

> His technique includes three stages: a medical pedicure, beauty treatments, then well-being, with around 20 minutes spent on each stage. Your nails and skin are cut, buffed and rubbed using a scalpel (you won't feel a thing, I promise), a dentist drill (rather ticklish!), his wonderful range of products (more on those later) and his divine massage technique. He does not paint your nails but instead applies a buffing paste and rubs with a chamois leather nail buffer (a secret from his grandmother), leaving you with naturally shiny nails. (I did notice that his own hands and nails were immaculate!)

> He works in exclusive hotels in Paris, London and New York, and is often flown around the world in private jets by his clients. You can also receive a treatment with one of his 'ambassadors' whom he has trained at the One&Only resorts in Mauritus, Maldives, Dubai and Mexico.

> His extra special customers receive treats like a pot of his Sensitive Feet Balm with their name engraved in gold on the sides of the pot – what a lovely touch. Around 32 per cent of his clients are men, so if your partner needs his feet attended to, you know whom to call.

> As he is so highly sought after and splitting his time between three countries, you need

to book well in advance — in fact, book right now! It will be the best £110.00 you'll ever spend, your feet will thank you and you'll have the most natural, healthy-looking feet ever to grace a pair of sandals this summer!

> If you can't wait for the appointment, start by trying the products he has created under his brand Révérence de Bastien. They include essential oils and smell heavenly, as well as having great therapeutic benefits.

> The Sensitive Feet Balm in a tube (€35) or pot (€58), Silky Talcum Powder Cool Veil (€25) and the Unguent for Nails & Cuticles, can all be bought online or at Colette in Paris (for other stockists refer to the list on his website). My lips are sealed at the moment, but he is announcing an exciting, new venture very soon so stay tuned.

> **Bastien Gonzalez**
  For London: T · 020 7565 0869
> **For Paris: Autour de Christophe Robin,**
  9 rue Guénégaud, 75006 Paris
  T · +33 01 42 60 99 15
  W · bastiengonzalez.com
  E · contact@bastiengonzalez.com

10 GOOD REASONS TO BOOK THE BEST

> Recently named Nail Technician of the Year, with an ever-increasing celebrity list, Jacqui is a huge hit on fashion shoots and at London and Paris Fashion Week. Heavily involved in nail-treatments training and education, including the new nail NVQs, it's surprising she has anytime left to attend to your nails, but thankfully she does. What's more, if you visit her at Creative Nails, the prices are exceptional, with a luxury manicure from £25.00 and nail enhancements from £75.00 (for prices for a personal visit please discuss with Jacqui).

> Her experience is phenomenal, with over 21 years spent creating stunning nails all over the world. More impressive still, some of her current clients have been with her almost since the beginning of her career. She's

written four books on nails and her fashion-show work threw her into the limelight when she created diamond-encrusted and six-inch-corkscrew nails. And who could forget the fabulous nail art when she matched the models' nails to the fashion designer's clothes with striking snakeskin nails — that was some 10 years ago and it's still being talked about!

> She does fabulous bridal nails by embedding lace in the acrylic nail, which looks fantastic. Shame I didn't know about that for my wedding! She truly believes that 'finger nails are a fashion accessory'.

> **Jacqui Jefford, Creative Nail Academy,**
  37-38 Downtown Business Centre, Batten Road, Downton, Hampshire SP5 3HU
  T · 01725 512 552 / 07740 862 916

SIGN UP WITH AN UNBEATABLE TEAM

> Widely considered one of the world's top nail technicians, with 18 years' experience, Marian has, of course, worked on all the big fashion shows and fashion shoots. Not only will you be in the best of hands, but you'll have the best hands (or feet) too! Marian and Charles Worthington have joined forces at the flagship Percy Street salon and the new House of Charles Worthington, and launched Marian Newman Nails at Charles Worthington. Marian and her team offer a great nail service with a Nails to Go menu including just a quick paint, and a Nails on Prescription menu, including the full-blown Custom Blend Manicure offering enhanced natural nails to match and compliment your skin tone.

> Marian is available personally at the salon approximately one day a month (£100.00 per hour), otherwise book one of her team (I visited Zoe Pocock who unfortunately has now left).

> Your nails are assessed and then you're advised which treatment would be best for you. I originally went in wanting longer nails,

as my nails were all at different lengths – and don't you just hate it when you're due for your manicure and you break a nail right off? Anyway, I digress – I was soon convinced that my nails would look very chic and natural at the shorter length, so I spent the next hour having a very thorough manicure.

> Finally my nails were buffed and shined until they looked absolutely fabulous. Each step of the manicure is fully explained, so you can keep up the maintenance of your nails at home with your own nail-care programme and maintain fab-looking hands and nails. A week later they still look great.

> Oh, and I must tell you the treats are on Charles, so while you sit having your treatment you can enjoy champagne, brownies, fairy cakes, tea, coffee…mmm, unbelievably generous! The whole experience was great. Prices: £10.00–£95.00

> **Marian Newman Nails at Charles Worthington, 7 Percy Street, London W1T 1DH T·020 7631 1370**

> **or The House of Charles Worthington, 28 Great Queen Street, Covent Garden, London WC2B 5BB T·020 7831 5303 W·charlesworthington.com**

And now your feet are looking ever-so lovely, why not go online and order some of the best toe rings I've seen at **W·kissmytoes.com**. You'll find butterflies, hearts, lips and more in 14K yellow and white gold, adorned with rubies, diamonds or sapphires.

HAIR REMOVAL

SOMETHING FOR THE WEEKEND

> For those of you who are slightly more adventurous, visit Paula Bedwell at the organic Green Hair Beauty salon, and ask for her unique Candibox (hairstyling down under!). Using a combination of natural green-tea wax and unbleached cloth strips, which she says is near-painless and gives a neater and smoother finish, your pubic hair is waxed into a shape, be it a heart, arrow, star or beautiful butterfly. It's then coloured with fudge spray-paint in various colours (which will wash off), and finally your new look is decorated with crystals. You need to book a consultation a week before your treatment, when you will choose your design, so that Paula can order your template, and you'll also have a patch test for any allergies. (She hasn't found anyone allergic to the spray yet.) On the day, allow at least an hour for your appointment. Prices: Candibox £75.00

> **Paula Bedwell, Green Hair Beauty, 330 Old Street, London EC1V 9DR T·020 7729 5707 W·greensalons.co.uk**

PAIN-FREE SMOOTHNESS IS OH-SO-SWEET

> Maryna offers hair removal by sugaring (using a mixture of sugar water and lemon juice) which is 100 per cent natural and she says less irritating to skin and more effective than waxing.

> Well known for her Brazilian and Hollywood, she offers male and female treatments. Prices: from £18.00 for half-leg; works within SE1 area (Vauxhall/Lambeth Bridge), but can also visit your home elsewhere for a minimum call-out charge of £100.00.

> **Maryna Hurford T·07947 485 788**

DARE TO GO BARE

> People wax lyrical about her Playboy – all off…eek! Arezoo offers fantastic waxing and threading, along with J. Maskrey body

jewellery to add that extra sparkle. She even works Sundays. I had my eyebrows threaded and Arezoo has such a great technique I didn't feel any discomfort at all, and the result was stunning (*see page* 216). Prices: £65.00 Brazilian, £35.00 threading

> **Arezoo Kaviani, Hans Crescent, Knightsbridge, London SW1 OLL T·020 7584 6868 / 07768 903 090 W·arezoo.co.uk**

PRACTICE MAKES PERFECT

> Otylia will have you laughing so much you won't even notice she's given you a Brazilian. Known as 'the waxer to rival the New York J Sisters', she's renowned worldwide for her skill. Otylia claims her hot-wax method is much less painful than strip waxing, and much gentler if you have a tendency to suffer from in-grown hairs.

> Hailing from Poland and with a background in nursing, Otylia has now been working in the beauty field for over 25 years. As one of the first beauticians to do Brazilians really well, word of mouth has now created an enormous clientele. Although she won't name names, her faithful fans flock from around the world to visit her and as the queen of waxing, she's seen and done it all, so don't be shy!

> Her clinic also offers laser hair removal and if you can't get an appointment with Otylia, ask for Cassie who is also excellent. Prices: waxing from £20.00; Brazilian from £49.00

> **Otylia Roberts' Beauty Centre, Greenhouse, 142 Wigmore Street, London W1U 3SH T·020 7486 5537 W·otyliaroberts.co.uk**

MARVELLOUS MASSAGE

SISTERHOOD LENDS A HEALING HAND

> I first met Stefania at London Fashion Week when I tried out a massage for my bad back. (I think it was Phylis Diller who said 'I'm now of an age when my back goes out more than I do.') Stefania and I have kept in contact over the years; she has worked as a practitioner at Claridges, and with her twin sister, Donata, at The Dorchester Hotel.

> Now, Stefania and Donata are working together at the Hale Clinic in London. Both sisters have been involved in several fields within the health sector since 1998, including Swedish, remedial massage, sport, myofascial release, aromatherapy and reflexology. Stefania and Donata are currently studying the Feldenkrais method to aid body awareness. They believe that we need to communicate to our being as a whole – body, mind and spirit. They use only the highest quality, organic aromatherapy and massage oils.

> They want you to keep fit as you age, and the twins have a contagious optimism that rubs off on all those they meet.

> They also work with the wonderful Alessandra Capponi, at the Hale Clinic, whom they introduced me to for my migraines and other complaints. Alessandra, originally a physiotherapist, worked with children with cerebral palsy and later studied Shiatsu, macrobiotics and natural healing techniques. She has also studied the Zilgrei pulsing method, infant massage, Ayurvedic massage, aromatheraphy, manual lymph drainage (MLD), chromotherapy, crystal therapy, somatic craniosacral therapy, visceral manipulation, autogenous training and Synapsis wave. I bet you're exhausted just reading what she can do, so lie back and let her weave her truly magic touch.

> Alessandra dedicates a lot of her time to working with pregnant women to prepare

them for a natural birth. She also works with people who have unresolved, long-standing problems. Contact Alessandra through Stefania or Donata or at the Hale Clinic.
> They try to 'make possible what seems impossible'. Treatments start from £80.00.
> **Stefania & Donata D'Addetta, Hale Clinic, 7 Park Crescent, London W1B 1PF
T · 07930 481 869
E · gemelle@hotmail.co.uk**

Also see page 237 for therapists that visit in the comfort of your home. For pregnancy massage see page 273

THERE'S ALWAYS TIME TO BE FABULOUS!
> Finally, a service I've long been waiting for: instead of booking individual treatments, you book a package in which two beauty therapists work on you at the same time for up to an hour. If you have little time and have been neglecting all your usual waxing, plucking, cleaning and preening, then book the Weekly Groom, which includes a manicure, pedicure, brow tidy and a facial, all for £105.00. They offer a variety of combinations of treatments, from the Zone-Out Hour if you're feeling really stressed, to a Beach Babes' Hour just before you jet off to the sun. Other packages include: Face Lifter Hour, Urban Renewal Hour, Skin Blitz Hour, Combined Power Hour, Double Digits Hour; and new, due to popular demand, the Half-Hour Zoom Groom for those of us really short on time. Prices: from £60.00
> **Groom, 49 Beauchamp Place, Knightsbridge, London SW3 1NY
T · 020 7581 1248**
> **Selfridges, 400 Oxford Street, London, W1A 1AB T · 020 7499 1199
W · groomlondon.com**

TANNING

SPRAY GOODBYE TO SUNBURN
> So what if you have to stand naked posing in a Charlie's Angels-style pose — this spray-on-mystic tan will be worth it! Heidi was one of the first to introduce the tanning booth which sprays a fine mist of colour that dries in seconds. A few tips: any hair removal must be done at least two days before tanning; don't apply any body creams or perfumes on the day; and, lastly, don't shower for at least eight hours after the tanning session. Colour emerges gradually through the day and lasts for up to seven days. After the treatment my friend looked as if she had just come back from a lovely holiday. Prices: One treatment £25.00; course of 5 treatments £100.00
> **Heidi Klein, 174 Westbourne Grove, Notting Hill, London W11 2RW T · 020 7243 5665
W · heidiklein.com**

NOT-SO-PALE BUT INTERESTING
> After visiting Susie for her wonderful Facial Dynamics (*see page 217*), I had to go back and try her Lavish Lashes (*see page 215*) and her Fantasy Tan treatment. Susie says, 'It's one of the quickest ways of reinventing yourself and perks up your whole wardrobe.'
> This was one of the first airbrush spray tans in the UK and has a choice of six to eight colour shades, including a very light one. Susie is so quick she can apply all over in 15 minutes and the colour lasts up to six days — more if you refuse to wash (because you look so 'gorgeous'). Perfect for brides going on their honeymoon. You can't be self-conscious with Susie as you stand there in paper knickers with a paper hat covering your hair, a paper mask and little else, as you're made to turn left, right, stand tall, bend over, stretch up etc., but then it's all done. I was amazed at my new look — I never tan and so as a virgin Fantasy Tanner I couldn't stop lifting up my top and gazing at my brown

tummy. I would highly recommend it prior to going on holiday, as it would make you feel fab in your swimmers right from the first day and avoids that unpleasant pink tone on days two and three! Susie can achieve great effects by blending the colours and sculpting. Price: £45.00

> Susie Lung, 50 Manchester Street, London W1M 5PB T · 07957 771 503

Also see page 238 for Becky Howard, who will visit you at home.

HAIR

Whether it's the latest cut, colour, hair extension, blow dry, or hair-up, these are my favourites, or those that offer a little something different for the weekend. Be warned, they may not be the cheapest and you may have to join the queue but it will be worth it.

GORGEOUS COLOUR

VOTED BEST-IN-SALON

> If you're an avid follower of the fashionistas' lists of beauty secrets, you'll probably already be familiar with the colourist Sibi Bolan. Sibi works her colour magic to revitalise and rejuvenate your look and Daniel Hersheson himself called her 'the best salon-based colourist ever' – an accolade, indeed! Forget stripes and regrowth, she creates such a fabulous, natural look you'll have people wondering if you colour your hair or not. Prices: tints £75.00, half head £160.00, full head £190.00

> Sibi Bolan at Daniel Hersheson, Harvey Nichols, Knightsbridge, London SW1X 7RJ T · 020 7201 8797 W · danielhersheson.com

MORE FUN, GUARANTEED

> Nicola's work history is enviable, working with top photographers and celebrities, films and theatre, and for top magazines and advertising campaigns. Word spread and the secret was out – you can't beat her 'blondes'. Her celebrity client list is a veritable who's who of light-haired lovelies. Prices start from £180.00.

> Nicola Clarke at John Frieda, 4 Aldford Street, London W1K 2AE T · 020 7491 0840 W · johnfrieda.co.uk

> or John Frieda, 75 New Cavendish Street, London W1W 6XA T · 020 7636 1401

BECOME YOUR MOST FABULOUS SELF

> It was great to meet colour supremo to the stars, Carl Dawson, who is highly sought after for his colour technique and has tended the tresses of many a celebrity, not to mention working on films and photo shoots.

> He's hugely talented and knows exactly what colours are right for you. He highlighted my hair with fabulous toffee and golden tones and it looked so-o-o-o natural, shiny and fabulous. All my friends remarked on how great I looked – one even asked if I'd had surgery, as she couldn't pinpoint why I looked so good. How's that for natural highlights?! Prices: tint £90.00, half head £220.00, full head £270.00

> Carl Dawson at The Nicky Clarke Salon, 130 Mount Street, London W1K 3NY T · 0844 884 8888

THE COOL CHOICE

> Rebecca is famed for creating natural, gorgeous colours with organic colourings and is in high demand with society babes and Hollywood A-listers. She is one of Hari's senior colourists and is considered one of the top colourists in London. Book at least a month in advance. Prices: tint £60.00, half head £180.00, full head £250.00

> Rebecca Frost at Hari's, 305 Brompton Road, London SW3 2DY T · 020 7581 5211 W · harissalon.com

For Jo Hansford see page 235

SIGN UP FOR SPANISH STYLE

> Lupe has an excellent eye for colour and, although she lives in Spain, she does two-week stints in London at Michaeljohn. Prices from £85.00

> **Lupe Longuiera at Michaeljohn,
> 25 Albemarle Street, London W1S 4HU
> T· 020 7629 6969 W· michaeljohn.co.uk**

YOU PAY TO TURN HEADS

> Richard is one of the best colourists I've ever been to and I'm always being complimented on my lovely colour. No bones – it is expensive. If you want a real treat, ask for the private room and book the legendary Daniel Galvin (Snr).

> We also love the wireless internet connection, so you can work away during your colour – let's face it girls, looking beautiful takes time; let's not waste it! Prices: Half-head colour with Richard from £226.00; Daniel Galvin Snr from £300.00.

> **Richard Newman at Daniel Galvin,
> 58–60 George Street, London W1U 7ET
> T· 020 7486 9661 W· danielgalvin.com**

POPPY'S NOT JUST ABOUT REDHEADS ...

> If you're a bit nervous about trying a new colour, treat yourself to a trip to see a true expert with over 23 years' experience in colouring. Lovely, bubbly Poppy worked in top London salons for over 12 years before moving to Michaeljohn. She's renowned for her great highlights, especially on blondes, and is consequently in hot demand. Prices: tint £85.00, half head £140.00, and full head £180.00

> **Poppy Parr at Michaeljohn, 25 Albermarle Street, London W1S 4HU
> T· 020 7629 6969 W· michaeljohn.co.uk**

TRUST HER WINNING WAYS

> Winner of the British Colourist of the Year 2005 (she's now won it three times), and crowned British Hairdresser of the Year 2005,

Lisa is hailed as a natural talent who can make even the worst head of hair look a million dollars. With over 15 years' experience in salons, stage, television and magazine shoots, she's coloured the hair of many celebrities. Her speciality is colour correction, so no need to go round with that scarf on your head sobbing uncontrollably!

> Her salon offers a great relaxation area where you can lounge about while your colour is developing, help yourself to refreshments (including alcohol), paint your nails at the DIY manicure bar, touch up your make-up, or use their Mac computer to catch up on your emails – I might move in! Other salons are planned soon, so watch this space. A personal appointment with Lisa costs £250.00, which includes a cut and/or colour.

> **Lisa Shepherd – Midlands, Town Mills, Mill Street, Kidderminster DY11 6XG
> T· 01562 748 833 W· lisashepherd.co.uk**

CUTTING EDGE CUTS

NEVER SAY NO TO A SQUEEZE

> Known as one of the top ten hair gurus in the UK, Antoinette is Global Creative Director of Aveda and spends a lot of her time jetting around the world demonstrating her skills to other professionals. However, if you time it right you can still book her for a fantastic style/cut at the salon. Acclaimed for her creativity, vision and originality, she has worked with numerous celebrity clients and has styled for loads of magazine editorials and for TV. She has been nominated for and received numerous awards, including London Hairdresser of the Year for two consecutive years. Known for her directional cutting techniques, she is famed for the Clippertwist giving hair the just-got-out-of-bed look; the Squeeze, which creates tousled curls and lift; and the Backslash, which adds gentle layers to fine hair making it look full and sexy. Prices: £225.00 for your first cut with

Antoinette, £175.00 thereafter.
> **Antoinette Beenders at Aveda Institute,
174 High Holborn, London WC1V 7AA
T · 020 7759 7355
W · antoinettebeenders.com**

CATWALK CUTIE
> Elliot is great for his ability to translate high-fashion trends into sexy hair and has women walking away from the salon feeling absolutely gorgeous. Price: from £100.00
> **Elliot Bute at Daniel Hersheson, 45 Conduit Street, London W1S 2YN T · 020 7434 1747
W · danielhersheson.com**

FAB BUT NOT FOR THE FAINT HEARTED
> If you visit Michael, prepare for a few home truths. He's not at all shy about telling you your haircut is wrong, your hair colour's off, and your eyebrows and eyelashes need colouring. Luckily he's just as happy to tell you about all the celebrities' hair he tends to. In fact, he reeled them off so quickly I couldn't write them all down. He says although his cut is expensive, you will look fab and it will last you for months. Not only that, his manner is such that you'll be in stitches and will be thoroughly entertained! Price for a cut with Michael £250.00.
> But don't just stop at the haircut, his salon Nyumba is a one-stop-shop offering many wonderful treatments, including reflexology, nutritional advice, manicures, pedicures, facials, massage, and make-up lessons and/or application.
> The best bit is that as a first-time client, if you book a beauty or nail-care treatment you receive a complimentary blow-dry. And another complimentary service is the valet parking service offered by the doormen (you just pay the meter charge). Expect VIP service!
> **Michael Charalambous at Nyumba,
6-7 Mount Street, London W1K 3EH
T · 020 7408 1489 W · nyumbasalon.com**

GET MORE THAN YOU PAY FOR
> There aren't many places left where you can get a good haircut for under £45.00, so I thought I'd try out Zoo in Islington. That was over two years ago and John is so good that now I won't go anywhere else. It's been a long time since I've been called a 'Babe' and that's exactly what happened as I walked down the street after I had my hair cut by John (who incidentally does great colour as well). I tried to sleep face-down in the pillow for a week so I wouldn't mess it up!
> **John Cunningham at Zoo, 267 Upper Street, Islington, London N1 2UQ
T · 020 7226 1865**

UP WITH THE BEST OF THEM
> Joel leads a team of 30 stylists at John Frieda and is their UK Creative Director. Always in demand as the favoured stylist for a raft of magazines and photographers, he has also worked with top fashion designers. He's tousled the hair of numerous celebrities, so if you have to wait a few weeks for an appointment, do – you won't be disappointed. His skill at hair-up styles is so well known that I heard about it from another top hairdresser – a rare endorsement. Prices from £160.00
> **Joel Goncalves at John Frieda, 4 Aldford Street, London W1K 2AE
T · 020 7491 0840 W · johnfrieda.co.uk**

LUKE THE PART
> Highly regarded by the fashion and beauty media for his constant innovation, Luke is great at giving models a new look and so is always in demand by the world's top photographers, designers and magazines. He'll treat you just the same and you'll come out looking gorgeous, gorgeous, gorgeous. Prices: from £120.00
> **Luke Hersheson at Daniel Hersheson, 45 Conduit Street, London W1S 2YN
T · 020 7434 1747 W · danielhersheson.com**

BY GEORGE, HE'S GOT IT

> When models want a career-launching haircut we've been told they head for the super-talented, all-round-stylist, George at Daniel Hersheson. As a key member of their artistic team, he helps create the looks that grace the runways. Naturally, I had to book in immediately. Not only talented but extremely charming, he gently persuaded me to lob off about four inches of my hair (gulp!) and created a very chic, falls-into-place look that has been much admired. He's a perfectionist and won't let you leave until the last hair is in place. My husband loved my new look and commented on it as soon as he saw me, without prompting! George absolutely loves styling hair as well and is in constant demand for those hot dates and other must-look-good occasions. And despite all of George's fashion credentials, he's still a lovely down-to-earth guy. Prices: cut £100.00, blow-dry £50.00

> **George Northwood at Daniel Hersheson, 45 Conduit Street, London W1S 2YN T·020 7434 1747 W·danielhersheson.com**

THE FIRST CUT IS THE DEAREST...

> I was told Lee offered the most expensive cut in London – he told me 'probably in the world', so I was intrigued. This is of course if you ask for his couture cut as part of his at-home design service for the grand total of £1,000.00. If Lee comes to your home, he will spend the time getting to know you, looking at your wardrobe to understand your sense of style, and having a really good look at your facial features.

> You can of course visit him at his salon and have a cut there for the slightly cheaper price of £200.00. If you go to his place, you'll be showered with the most expensive champagne and chocolates. Lee will then start to find out all about you, including your taste in clothes and lifestyle, before cutting your hair.

> He believes a lot of haircuts go wrong in the consultation stage as most salon appointments are 45 minutes, consultations usually take 15 minutes and that only leaves 30 minutes for the hair cut!

> In 2002 he was chuffed to be named Most Influential Hairdresser of the Year as voted by other professionals in the industry. Although he has a raft of celebrity clients, he's very discreet. He says he's as 'committed to creating a good look for any client, whether A-list, B-list or shopping list, and so are the people who work with me. We care about what we do, not who we do. Let's just say I've been known to style a celeb or two, and leave it at that.' His very informative website offers a great glossary of 'hairdresser speak'.

> **Lee Stafford, Lee Stafford Salons, 155a Wardour Street, Soho, London W1F 8WG T·020 7494 1777 W·leestafford.com**
> **or Leigh on Sea T·01702 471 954;**
> **or Brighton T·01273 729 305**

BEST BLOW-DRIES

INDUSTRY INSIDERS KNOW WHERE TO GO

> Jesus is known as the 'Blow-Dry King' of Hari's and his appointment booking sheet is full of women who know they'll leave the salon with a head turning, glossy and natural looking style. When he's not at Hari's, he's not only making the models look fabulous on magazine shoots, but he's also the man that many of the industry's top journalists flock to, and they're a tough crowd to please! Prices from £55.00

> **Jesus Olvera Garcia, Hari's, 305 Brompton Road, London SW3 2DY T·020 7581 5211 W·harissalon.com**

FROM PARIS WITH LOVE

> Highly recommended, the charming, Parisian-trained Frederic says he loves to make women look fabulous. Having worked

in Paris for over 10 years, including teaching and session work, Frederic certainly knows a thing or two about styling and blow-dries. Naturally, he's also wonderful at cutting and loves to style fab new looks. Prices: cut £110.00, blow-dry £65.00

> **Frederic Gielly at Michaeljohn,
25 Albemarle Street, London W1S 4HU
T· 020 7629 6969 W· michaeljohn.co.uk**

TIME FOR A RED CARPET RESTYLE

> Always in demand on shoots and even at the Oscars, I guarantee that Clifford will make you look absolutely gorgeous. He has a fab reputation for cutting and styling but unfortunately I have only experienced his blow dry which I have to say was one of the best I've ever had, and so quick – friends told me I looked like I'd just stepped off the page of a fashion magazine – can't get any better than that! My next cut is his! Book in immediately. Prices: £100.00 cut and blow-dry; £150.00 restyle

> **Clifford McDavid at Sejour, 3–5 Bray Place, Chelsea, London SW3 3LL
T· 020 7589 1100 W· sejour.co.uk**

LONG-TERM SATISFACTION

> The ever-so-lovely and very French Jean-Marc has people lining up, not just for his haircuts and wonderful blow-drying but because he absolutely loves giving his clients very manageable, natural looks. You know, the kind that still look great three weeks later! The Windle team are regulars backstage at shows in London, Paris and New York, and Jean-Marc is no exception. Having worked on the fashion shows, he knows all the up-to-the-minute looks for cutting and styling. Prices: blow-dry £40.00, cut £80.00. Available by appointment Wednesday to Saturday.

> **Jean-Marc Vrezil at Windle, 41–42 Shorts Gardens, London WC2H 9AP
T· 020 7497 2393 W· windlehair.com**

DIY LESSONS

You know how it is – you get a lovely haircut that is beautifully blow-dried, then after you wash and style it, it never looks the same. Well, here are some salons that offer excellent blow-drying master classes:

TRACK DOWN SOME TRADE SECRETS

> If you'd like to feel salon-great every time you step out of your front door, it's well worth spending a couple of hours learning a few tricks of the trade. At the Aveda Institute you can book a hands-on, 90-minute session with an expert. First they'll look at your style of hair and talk through your lifestyle, and then it's over to the backwash to show you how to wash your hair correctly and the best products to use. Next you knuckle down for some practical lessons in blow-drying using different brushes, whether you want to create curls, hair-up or just want your hair looking casually fabulous. Available Monday to Saturday for £40.00.

> **Aveda Institute, 174 High Holborn, London, WC1V 7AA T· 020 7759 7355
W· avedainstitute.co.uk**

BE A DO-IT-YOURSELF DIVA

> Darren says his salon was one of the first in London to offer blow-drying lessons to his clients. After you've completed your hour's lesson with him, you'll wonder how you ever did it before. Bring along all the tools you use when drying your hair at home and he'll take you through a 10-point programme to have you drying your hair like the professionals. Lessons can also include using straightening irons, curling tongs, up-dos, and some hot tips on changing from 'office hair' to 'GAT' hair.

> You'll find all the tips and lessons time-friendly and informative. Clipso's team have won many awards, including Artistic Team of the Year. Prices: from £45.00 per hour with a

stylist; £80.00 for a lesson with Darren.

> **Darren Fowler, Clipso Salon, 42 Windmill Street, London W1T 2JZ T·020 7580 3449 W·clipso.co.uk**

MASTER THE ART OF STYLING

> At any of the four Charles Worthington salons you can have a one-hour master class in blow-drying. Your stylist will teach you great techniques, show you the best products and tools to use and give you top styling tips. You'll also go home with a goodie bag, all for just £45.00 — a complete bargain. And with any treatment you have at the salon, you're lavished with complimentary champagne and nibbles!! Thought I'd better tell you that. Visit the new House of Charles Worthington in Covent Garden for added luxury.

> **The House of Charles Worthington, 28 Great Queen Street, Covent Garden, London WC2B 5BB T·020 7831 5303**
> **or Charles Worthington, 7 Percy Street, London W1T 1DH T·020 7631 1370**
> **or The Dorchester, Park Lane, London W1A 2HJ T·020 7317 6321**
> **or The Broadgate Club, 1 Exchange Place, London EC2M 2QT T·020 7638 0802 W·charlesworthington.com**

AMAZING EXTENSIONS

PERFECT WEDDING HAIR'S A PIECE OF CAKE

> Every bride wants to be a wow on her wedding day, and sometimes we've got to improve on what we've inherited! If you think your crowning glory could do with a bit of a boost on your big day, Joanne Brown, Style Director and Wedding Hair Specialist at the Canary Wharf branch of Toni & Guy is the woman to see. She's the queen of catwalk hair, including dressing models for London Fashion Week no less. Pop into the salon and she'll snip a few bits off your hair and then in

around a week you'll get a perfectly matched hairpiece. This can be incorporated into your own hair for a stunning look and is yours to use again for any other special occasion. Prices: from £90.00

> **Joanne Brown at Toni & Guy, Canada Place, Canary Wharf, London E14 5AH T·020 7987 6222**

NO-RISK KNOCK OUT

> For a fear-free, fabulous new look that you can use again and again, pop along to Cobella's for one of their ponytail extensions. The ponytail, which is made from human hair, is matched by colour, length and texture to your own hair and attached around your own ponytail using Velcro. It adds such incredible volume that you'll wonder why you haven't done it sooner. Prices start from £90.00.

> **Cobella, Cobella House, 5 Kensington High Street, London W8 5NP T·020 7937 8888 / 0870 900 0440 W·cobella.co.uk**

EUROPE'S BEST-KEPT BEAUTY SECRET

> The lovely tri-lingual Elena specialises in hair extensions with a difference: instead of using glue, she sews the European human hair into your hair, so your own hair will grow normally and you can brush, blow-dry, highlight and even colour it without using special products.

> Elena has clients come from around the world, but I can't name names as their extensions are so good they do not own up to them! The initial visit is the most costly, as you are paying a one-off fee for the hair extensions. After that you visit every two months or so as your own hair grows and the extensions need to be repositioned. If you look after them well they will last for years. Prices from £250.00 to £1,000.00 depending on hair length, volume and colour, with adjustments £50.00-£150.00.

By appointment only.

> **Elena Lachuer, 19 Cadogan Gardens, London SW3 2RW**
> **T · 07774 741 440   W · elenalachuer.com**

WHY WAIT FOR LONG HAIR?

> Those in the know go to Sebastian at Cobella who has been applying hair extensions for over six years. He's dressed the hair of many a pop star and can use human hair which is pre-bonded or monofibre which is plaited into your own hair – no glue and easy to remove. Lasts about three months. Prices: Signature (8 strands) £50.00, Enhancer (20 strands) £120.00, full head from £750.00

> **Sebastian Nabeth, Cobella, Cobella House, 5 Kensington High Street, London W8 5NP**
> **T · 020 7937 8888 / 0870 900 0440**
> **W · cobella.co.uk**

GLAMOROUS UP DO's

SOCIETY SECRET

> Two great stylists from Hari's are Jesus Olvera Garcia (*see page* 230) and Benjamin Ahrens. Benjamin, their Creative Director specialises in chignons and putting hair up. He is called on to do many society weddings (he is an expert at securing veils and tiaras) and London's well-heeled clientele. Having been in the business for over 20 years he has worked with top photographers, models and celebrities on all the best magazines. Prices from £80.00.

> **Benjamin Ahrens, Hari's, 305 Brompton Road, London SW3 2DY**
> **T · 020 7581 5211   W · harissalon.com**

GET THE MAX FACTOR

> Limp-haired ladies come from around the country to Parisian-trained Max for his hair-up and styling! Extremely creative, he's also a big favourite with brides-to-be searching for the look of a lifetime. He can create

remarkable styles, even with shortish hair, so if you want to look sexy, funky, young, coutured, stunning, or all of the above, then book an appointment immediately. Prices from £80.00.

> **Max Coles at Michaeljohn, 25 Albemarle Street, London W1S 4HU**
> **T · 020 7629 6969   W · michaeljohn.co.uk**

SOMETHING BORROWED, SOMETHING HUGH

> If you thought, as I did, that the Duchess of Cornwall looked radiant on her wedding day, you may already know that her hair was styled for that special occasion by Hugh Green. Hugh is highly sought after for his bridal/tiara work and even travels internationally to attend to brides (p.o.a). Hairdressing since the age of nine, (yes, 9 years old!), he not only transforms women on the biggest day of their lives, but does great haircuts, too. Naturally, with his skills, he has tended the hair of many a celebrity. Prices from £52.00 (blow-dry), cut £110.00

> **Hugh Green at Hugh & Stephen, 161 Ebury Street, London SW1W 9QN**
> **T · 020 7730 2196**

SUPER SALONS

BE READY FOR YOUR CLOSE UP

> Cobella at Selfridges is known as a mega salon for good reason: with over five pages of treatments listed, you'll be hard pushed not to find one to your liking. The salon is arranged in a series of zones, each offering specialised services or treatments. The Colour Zone alone has over 120 coloured hair wefts on the wall to help you choose your perfect shade.

> I loved their innovative treatment packages: the Diva consists of a shine hair treatment and blow-dry, glossy make-up and French manicure (£100.00), while the Starlet

includes a sexy hair-up, diamante manicure and pedicure (£150.00). If you go for the SOS Red Carpet Emergency, in one hour they will give you a manicure, pedicure, eyebrow shape and hair-up or blow-dry (£85.00). They also have three great beauty package possibilities for Mother's Day, Father's Day and Grandmother's Day, where your loved ones will be truly pampered (from £100.00).

> At the original Cobella Akqa in Kensington High Street the hairdressing is superb and you can also get great hair or pony-tail extensions (see page 232). Their spa offers lovely treatments and make-up design, as well as an extensive list of men's grooming treatments. You can also book in for their Cobella Retreat for Two, which includes a champagne lunch, or hire out the whole place for a relaxing spa party.

> **Cobella at Selfridges, 3rd floor, Oxford Street, W1A 1AB T·020 7659 5000**
> **Cobella Akqa Day Spa & Salon, Cobella House, 5 Kensington High Street, London W8 5NP T·020 7937 8888 W·cobella.co.uk**

HURRY TO HARI'S

> Famous for fantastic highlights, fab natural tints, hair-up and bridal hair, you can certainly find all the stylists you need at Hari's (see pages 227/230/233). With over 30 years in the business, and a great reputation, they also offer lovely treatments such as Ole Henriksen facials, caviar hair treatments, (see page 41), pit-stop party makeovers for a big night out, and – an excellent pressie for the man in your life – the Man-i-cure package.

> Everything is in place for top-class treatment: the range of fantastic products, more than a dozen top stylists, the special lighting for the colourists, the VIP room, tasty energy-giving juices and, most luxurious of all, waxing with 24-carat gold leaf to leave your legs shimmering. With four floors, a mix of modern and antique decor and lovely calm

spaces there is no need to go on – just get yourself down there to be truly pampered.

> **Hari's, 305 Brompton Road, London SW3 2DY T·020 7581 5211 W·harissalon.com**

TAKE YOUR HAIR TO SALON HEAVEN

> Now this is what a salon experience should be about... I'd been told that I'd experience great hairdressing at Sejour, but I was still surprised at how much I loved my trip there. Swathed in a silk Kimono with a fuchsia-pink sash, I was taken upstairs to the colour studio. I was immediately struck by Tara Bernerd's salon design, including Osborne and Little wallpaper, wooden floors, pink and canary-yellow lacquered benches, and burgundy pony-skin surround mirrors.

> I chose some goodies from the in-house chef's special detox menu, which includes raw nuts with fruit, veggie sticks with humus, and homemade organic soup. There are also some not so light things on offer, such as Diane's popcorn, home-made lemonade and cappuccinos.

> I was told my 'hair needs a little love' – a nice way of saying it looks crap! In no time at all the colour is ready and I am taken down to the basement and the nicest backwash area I've ever experienced. Lying down flat on a massage chair surrounded by candles, flowers and soft music, I sink back into the hugely relaxing Chroma Perfect deep-conditioning treatment, expertly carried out by Jade A. It takes the promise of a blow-dry by the fantastic Clifford McDavid (normally found on the set of pop videos, awards shows or society weddings) to persuade me to move at all! (See page 231.)

> It's now that I get to see the fabulous, but oh-so-subtle colour, the soft toffee and golden tones catch the light beautifully. Clifford then applies his finishing touches and I saunter out of the salon, the envy of every female friend I meet for many weeks to come (cut

and blow-dry with Clifford from £100.00).
And there's so much more I could have tried:

> *The Sejour Sterling Service* – the ultimate
VIP day of top-to-toe pampering: chauffeur,
champagne breakfast, colour, cut, manicure,
pedicure, make-up, eyebrow shape, and your
own assistant for the day. (£1,000.00)

> *It's All About The Eyes* – night and day looks,
including an eyebrow shape and make-up
techniques. (p.o.a.)

> *Girlie Parties* – Exclusive use of the salon for
you and your friends: turn up after work,
shower, change, then have your hair, make-
up and nails attended to ready for some
serious partying. (p.o.a.)

> They'll open late for you, and even visit you
at home or at your office. However, as I have
neither a pink kimono nor a massage chair,
an in-house chef or a pony-skin surround
mirror in my miniature home office, I know
where I'll be heading for my next
transformation!

> **Sejour, 3-5 Bray Place, Chelsea, London
SW3 3LL T·020 7589 1100 W·sejour.co.uk**

FOR DIVAS WITH DEADLINES

> Already mentioned for their master class in
blow-drying (*page* 232), Charles Worthington
salons really want you to feel relaxed and
pampered. Of course, we weren't swayed by
the complimentary champagne and nibbles
which you get with any treatment, or the
goodie bag for first-time customers!

> The Percy Street flagship salon offers a
fantastic colour clinic where you can book a
30-minute colour consultation appointment
in the colour clinic with the very talented
Colour Director, Carolyn Newman. For a small
charge of £20.00 (which is redeemable
against further colour treatments), you'll go
through a personality profile test, full-face
shape and colour analysis using Charles
Worthington colour fans, wigs and pieces
to show you how you can achieve your
perfect colour.

> If time is money, the Express Highlights
service has two colour therapists work on
your hair in under 90-minutes and you can
also have a wonderful Marian Newman Nails
treatment. If you're also due for a cut, book
in with the talented Adam Reed, their
Creative Director, for gorgeous results.

> **Charles Worthington, 7 Percy Street,
London W1T 1DH T·0207 631 1370
W·charlesworthington.com**

IN THE COMFORT OF YOUR HOME

HEAVENLY HAIR

INDULGE IN A SUPERSTAR MAKEOVER

> Jo Hansford is synonymous with beautiful
bespoke colour and well-conditioned hair,
and also offers a wonderful pampering
session in your home. Jo has been called to
tame the tresses of many a celebrity, but
says that all her clients are VIPs to her.

> Jo and her assistant will colour your hair
beautifully and her top stylists will then cut
and style a new you. You'll also experience a
divine manicure and pedicure whilst enjoying
a glass or two of champagne. Prices: from
£2,000.00 with Jo or £1,200.00 with 'just'
her top styling team (also depends on your
location, travel expenses). Book early as
there's usually a three-month waiting list
for Jo.

> **Jo Hansford: Book through Joanna
Hansford T·020 7409 7020**

ENJOY THE ULTIMATE GOOD HAIR DAY

> Highly recommended by Toni Jade (*see page*
237) Heidi does all the big fashion shows and
shoots, and absolutely adores dressing hair
for a special occasion. She can visit you at
home and offers cuts and/or blow-drying. If

you want your hair really glam, she'll look at your outfit and talk to you about the occasion, then wow you with a fantastic look. She can work early mornings, late evenings and weekends. And it's not only females who vie for her services; she's also styled well-known male actors for their West End theatre performances. Prices from £110.00

> **Book Heidi Stanton through John Frieda Salon   T·020 7636 1401**

COME ON OVER TO MY PLACE

> The lovely Lisa will whiz round to your home and give you a great colour, cut, perm or blow-dry. She's also fabulous at putting hair up and has styled many weddings. Having worked in the top London salons for over seven years, she knows all the tricks to give you a 'you won't even look like you've had a colour' colour. I often have her come over and just blow-dry my hair as it always looks so fab and I feel a million dollars afterwards. Prices: from £16.00 (but she may add travel costs if travelling a long distance).

> **Lisa Tsindides
T·020 8505 9799 / 0779 919 6241**

HEAD-TO-TOE TREATS

> In 1990 Linda left a well-known London salon to set up business working in the comfort of her clients' homes. Although based in Islington, she will travel all over London and offers very flexible hours and weekend visits. For half-head colour, expect to pay £80.00. She's also a fully-trained aromatherapist offering wonderful massages (£60.00 for one and a half hours). Due to her established clientele (she's even been flown out to Brunei to colour hair), you'll need to book at least a week or two in advance.

> **Linda Williams
T·020 7278 6219 / 07956 331 044**

COVER GIRL MAKE-UP

GOOD MEN AND WOMEN ALL

> When I worked on magazines, we often used Joy Goodman's editorial make-up and hair teams. They've worked with some of the best photographers, personalities and magazines for the last 22 years and they know a thing or two about the right look and the latest beauty and hair trends.

> As they don't restrict their talent to the media world, they will also visit you at home (from £250.00). Phone the agency and give them a brief and they will send along one of their top artists or stylists. And if you're looking for a bit of body painting for that very special occasion, ask for Rozelle Parry, she's amazing.

> **Joy Goodman Make-up Agency, 21 Kingswood Avenue, London NW6 6LL**
> **T·020 8968 6887   W·joygoodman.com**

YOU'LL ALWAYS REMEMBER YOUR FIRST TIME

> Sarah has built her professional reputation for her fantastic work beautifying the stars for glamorous high-fashion shoots. But don't worry, if you book well in advance for your glam night out or your special day, Sarah will definitely make time for you. Despite her love of working on famous faces, she gets her biggest buzz from transforming the make-over virgins! She'll leave you looking naturally gorgeous, younger and fresher, and with a host of little tips and tricks of the trade. She'll teach you how you can apply your own make-up and she'll even go through your make-up bag, throw out and recommend. Now be honest, who was Prime Minister when you bought that electric pink lipstick?! She's bubbly, lots of fun, knowledge-able and passionate and will not only sort out your make-up bag but probably your life, too! Prices start from £350.00, but so worth it.

> **Sarah Reygate   T·07956 481 429**

DON'T DELAY, BOOK HER TODAY

> You'll need to book in advance for the lovely Marina, but she will effortlessly make you look naturally gorgeous. Marina has worked at all the shows, darling, and now has a raft of celebrity clients and GATs. So as soon as you set the date or that invitation pops through the door, book her immediately for your wedding day or that big night out. She also offers a very special manicure that lasts for days. Prices: Make-up applications start at £120.00 in and out of London; A manicure starts at £50.00 within London.

> **Marina Sandoval T · 07740 623 120
E · marinasandoval@gmail.com**

LUXURY MANIS & PEDIS

ONE WOMAN WONDER-WORKER

> Toni will have your hands and particularly your feet in tip-top shape after she's worked her magic. She gives a wonderful foot massage using products sourced from around the world and is always up-to-date with the latest trends, tips and tricks. Her signature look includes applying diamantes to your tootsies; perfect for a beach holiday.

> Actually, she's a complete one-stop beauty shop, not only will she give you a luxurious mani and pedi (1 hour 45 minutes), you can also catch up on your waxing, eyebrow tidying and eyelash tinting. She's available for weddings and recently pampered a bride for three days prior to her big day. She can also bring with her some top stylists who attend to your hair and make-up, give you divine massages and facials and even yoga to keep you centred.

> Word of mouth has her constantly booked, but she'll always make time for you. Her fee for central London is £100.00 for the manicure and pedicure. She'll travel further, but expect to pay travelling costs.

> **Toni Jade T · 07931 718 667**

For other manicures and pedicures at your home see page 239

MARVELLOUS MASSAGE

SUREFIRE WAY TO RELAX AT HOME

> I've had Rebecca visit me at home for massages on a regular basis for over three years and they're always fantastic. I'm particularly fond of the way she massages my ears! Rebecca specialises in deep-tissue massage, but can use oils if preferred. There's nothing better than having a massage and then going straight to bed – no getting dressed again or going out in the cold. Rebecca also has many corporate clients and can visit you at the office or home. London only, I'm afraid. Prices from £35.00.

> **Rebecca Bruce T · 07749 935 963
E · brucerebecca@hotmail.com**

FIT A HOLIDAY INTO AN AFTERNOON

> As a practising masseur and therapist in Southern Australia since 1982, John has incorporated into his massage the ancient wisdom he has been privileged to share from the Aboriginal people. John offers a Kiradjee (Aboriginal word meaning healer) massage that has to be experienced to be believed. He's the resident Kiradjee consultant to the Body Experience in Richmond, works at the Ritz Hotel in Paris and will also come to your home to treat you with his unique technique.

> After putting you into a dream-like state, he will seduce the tone of your muscles into surrendering their knots with a deep-tissue massage that will be not only sublimely relaxing but also deeply healing. Your body will feel as though it's been rewired. He suggests you opt for the home visit, as the treatment often induces feelings of euphoria and lightness, resulting in a prolonged post-treatment state of relaxation. John says one of his clients told him having his treatment

was like 'being on a beach holiday for three weeks'. Prices: Treatment of 90 minutes £130.00; two hours £150.00. (Listed prices cover central London area, but he will travel further with travel costs extra.)

> **John Odel T·07766 044 121**
> **W·kiradjee.com.au**
> or at **Body Experience T·020 8334 9999**

TOUCHED BY GENIUS

> You can visit the wonderful Nari at his modest basement room in Human Nature, one of London's oldest health-food shops, or he can visit you at your home, office or hotel. Nari started massaging at Human Nature over 17 years ago and glowing recommendations have drawn well-named devotees. His luxury three-hour massage is quite unbelievable. It starts with an intense dry skin brushing and then a deep body massage, alternated with light feathery strokes, finishing with a face massage and optional Indian head massage, leaving your body feeling firm and your skin extra-smooth and glowing for days.

> Nari claims to give the 'best massage in the world', he says 'someone has to'…and with his natural health expertise he can also give in-depth advice on nutritional supplements. I thought his massage was fantastic, and not only that, he's a thoroughly nice, genuine person. Prices: Luxury massage – three hours £200.00, £300.00 if visiting you; regular massage – 60 minutes plus 15-minute consultation £80.00, £130.00 if visiting you.

> **Nari Sadhuram, Human Nature, 13 Malvern Road, London NW6 5PS**
> **T·020 7328 5452**
> **W·thismassageworks.co.uk**

See also pages 273-274 for:
Beatrice Palazzo
Leona-Stephens-Ofner
Erika Tourell

TANNING

STREAK-FREE GUARANTEE

> Becky has been tanning bods with the original St Tropez tan for over six years now and she still believes it gives one of the best tans ever. All she needs is an hour to exfoliate your body, moisturise, apply the tan and brush off the excess. You then have a good night's sleep, jump in the shower in the morning and – ta da! – your wonderful new tan is revealed. Easy peasy, and Becky will travel anywhere within M25. Price: £100.00 for a full-body tan.

> **Becky Howard T·07880 548 211**

For other therapists that offer this service see below

ALL-ROUND TREATS AT HOME

The worst thing about any in-salon treatment is having to leave the cosiness of the salon and a) getting your newly blow-dried hair rained on, b) getting all stressed again fighting your way home through the rush hour, and/or c) feeling you have to put all your make-up back on your newly scrubbed face that should actually be left make-up free after a facial. Well, instead of schlepping to the spa, let the spa come to you. Then you can jump straight into bed after that long massage and have your best night's sleep ever!

NAIL THAT WORK-LIFE BALANCE

> Fed up with their busy and stressful corporate careers, Rebecca and Clare Hopkins founded Balance being, a five-star service offering bespoke packages in London, daytime or evening, or at the weekend. Although London-based they can be flexible regarding location.

> Focusing on relaxation and well-being, they

come and do absolutely everything for you. On offer are yoga, beauty treatments, reflexology and makeovers. We particularly love their party packages where they hand out a timetable for the day, bring magazines, goodie bags, cook gorgeous meals, make tantalising cocktails and can even offer wine-tasting, salsa dancing and tarot-card reading. And it's not just for the girls; Rebecca and Clare have hosted a detox weekend for five men and left them comatose and converted. Prices: from £60.00 (plus VAT) for each therapist; or £200.00 per person for the party packages.

> **Rebecca & Clare Hopkins, Balance being**
  T · 07880 551 808 (Rebecca) or 07799 881
  214 (Clare) W · balancebeing.com

INVITE ANGELS INTO YOUR HOME

> Heaven at Home's pampering parties are hugely popular. You can choose any number of therapists to come to your house. Their 'pamperologists' will pamper you and your party into a 'blissed-out state of gorgeousness'.

> Choose from a range of pampering packages such as Perfect for Partners, Mum's the Word or Heavenly Hands, and you'll also receive a pamper hamper full of goodies. We love that they can also send over a Heavenly Helper who will take care of all the catering (£75.00 for three hours). Either you can buy all the supplies from your local supermarket and she will prepare, serve and even wash up (you won't have to lift one of your manicured hands!), or they can do all the catering for you.

> If you just want a bit of 'me-time', you can also book individual treatments – they will arrive and set about transforming your room by lighting scented candles, dimming the lights and offering you a fluffy bathrobe, before weaving their magic on your weary body. Therapists are available countrywide. Prices: individual treatments from £75.00 per

hour; pamper parties from £100.00.
> **Heaven at Home T · 0871 200 1282**
  W · heavenathome.net

MAKE-OVER YOURSELF AT HOME

> Perfectly At Home can send you lovely therapists offering all manner of treatments from beauty, make-up, massage, grooming for men and bridal, to hair and pre/post-natal. We love the fact that they can send senior stylists from Michaeljohn to cut and blow-dry your hair for only £90.00; great value for an at-home treat.

> We also love their Party Treats: your friends will be lining up at your front door to try out the Feast for Hands, Back Smoothie and Headonism. Appointments can be made up to 10.00 p.m., seven days a week. All treatments are London-based, but they will travel further for bridal treatments and spa parties. Prices: £75.00 for one hour.

> **Perfectly At Home T · 020 7610 8000**
  W · perfectlyathome.com

BEAUTY QUEEN OF THE NORTH

> I hate to tell you about Justine as I want to keep her all to myself. She's my all-time, all-round favourite therapist, with a special passion for feet – she'll give you the most thorough pedicure you'll ever have. You can have a manicure, pedicure, half-leg wax and and still have change from £55.00, which is remarkable for an at-home treat.

> As her diary is so booked up with appointments from her regular clients, and she has a new baby, she will now only travel within the North London area. You may want to consider moving!

> **Justine Podemsky T · 07967 821 868**

HARD TO FIND BETTER

> Unlisted London say they 'provide the solution for those with busy lives and those who demand unconditional privacy'. I say they offer one of the most imaginative

selections of treatments available at home, in a hotel room or at the office. Order one of their brochures and you will find it hard to choose from their extensive menus, which include treats under headings like Unspoiled Luxury, Unexpected Euphoria and Unprecedented Pleasure. This team of London's most sought after hairstylists, colourists, make-up artists, beauticians, manicurists, masseurs, fitness professionals and complementary practitioners also offers a great selection of treatments for men. There are discounts for package deals, for example, six deluxe pedicures in eight months for £235.00 instead of £270.00. You can also purchase the products they use in their treatments, which include some quality names.

> **Unlisted London, Davies House, 33 Davies Street, London W1K 4LR**
> **T · 0870 225 5007   W · unlistedlondon.com**

GROOMING

BRING OUT THE GENTLEMAN IN HIM

> A gift certificate for your man to try out the treatments and products at the fabulous Gentlemen's Tonic will put you in his good books for a long time to come.

> Apart from the usual haircut and shave, you can book individual treatments for hands, feet, hair, face, neck and shoulders, or you can book one of their packages: The Hemingway for 'after a heavy night of drinking and bull-fighting' sounds great – love the name! Or why not The Rubio 'for the ultimate Playboy' – this includes a haircut and finish, wet shave, express facial, hand treatment and Swedish massage (£165.00 for 135 mins). He can even get have his teeth whitened from £300.00.

> I love that you can book a Father and Son Haircut and Finish – they'll give Dad a Bloody Mary while the little one watches cartoons. How sweet!

> They also stock one of the largest ranges of men's grooming products in London that can be purchased at GT or online. They have just opened in the private members club, Eight, however GT is open to non members.

> **Gentlemen's Tonic, 31a Bruton Place, Mayfair, London W1J 6NN**
> **T · 020 7297 4343**

> **or Eight, 1 Change Alley, London, EC3V 3ND (T · as above)**
> **W · gentlemenstonic.com**

THE PERFECT GENTLEMAN

> Geo. F. Trumper is known throughout the world for its range of gentlemen's fragrances and grooming products, Trumper has also been serving the grooming needs of London gentlemen for over 125 years. They have been honoured with the Royal Warrant of Queen Victoria and five subsequent monarchs. Not only do they offer hair styling

and cutting but also facial cleansing and massage, manicures and pedicures.

> They are also renowned for their traditional wet shave with open razor and even offer a shaving school where your man can have a one-to-one on the best shaving technique for his skin (£50.00). Many men just do not shave correctly and this can cause numerous problems from in-grown hairs to redness.

> If he thinks he's got shaving down to an art, I'm sure his feet need attention, so buy him a gift certificate to visit the fab Marc Metcalfe, their resident Chiropodist, who works on feet to relieve ailments all over the body as well as treating any 'nasties'. The consultation concludes with a foot massage and a lesson on cutting toenails properly, all for a very reasonable £40.00. I gave my husband, Marcus, the shaving lesson and feet treat for a birthday present and after we had a divine, leisurely breakfast at The Wolseley, he strolled over to Geo. F. Trumpers for his treatment and lesson which he thoroughly enjoyed.

> **Geo. F. Trumper, 9 Curzon Street, W1J 5HQ T·020 7499 1850 W·trumpers.com**

IT'S ONE SMALL CLICK FOR MANKIND

> If you're tired of your man stealing your products, get him linked up with Mankind Direct. Their website offers over 60 brands of wonderful grooming products, including DKNY, Phytomer, Ren, Anthony, and N.V. Perricone. There's also an excellent FAQ section and a Grooming Clinic where he can get to know his skin type. We love the Problem/Solution section offering products for dry, flaky skin, wrinkles, razor bumps, etc. They also offer a free sample service as it's hard to tell just how good these things smell online.

> **Mankind Direct, Unit 25, Invincible Road, Farnborough, Hampshire GU14 7QU T·Orders 0844 557 4902; Enquiries 0844 557 7060 W·mankind.co.uk**

PERFECT FOR YOUR METROSEXUAL

> Come on ladies, why should we have all the pampering? The Refinery offers a great one-stop, head-to-toe grooming and spa experience exclusively for men, with the atmosphere of a modern gentlemen's club.

> Men can visit the barber, have a facial, a massage, manicure or pedicure, reflexology, tan or wax, and they can also get their clothes pressed and shoes shined. They also offer some unique and exclusive treatments. Your man can lie back and enjoy LCD entertainment during treatments and, for the boys who like toys, they even have games consoles. For those in a rush they offer The Pit Stop for 15-minute treatments. If your man has got all day – they can enjoy the club lounge, which has internet, email and financial market access, along with yummy snacks and drinks. Great retail, too.

> **The Refinery, 60 Brook Street, London W1K 5DU T·020 7409 2001**

> **or 38 Bishopsgate, London EC2N 4AJ T·020 7588 1006**

> **or at Harrods, Knightsbridge, London SW1X 7XL T·020 7893 8332 W·the-refinery.com**

FOR WHEN YOU DON'T CARE TO SHARE ...

> Nicky Kinnaird pounded the pavements of the world so she could bring us Space.NK, the very best, most original, most fantastic selection of beauty products, including aromatherapy, bath, fragrance, make-up, hair-, skin- and sun-care products. No doubt, like me, you will spend ages shopping here. Well, the good news is that now they've opened a branch for the man in your life. Yipee! No more sniffing your guy's hair to find out why your favourite shampoo is half empty, hiding your very expensive moisturiser with SPF 30 at the first sign of summer, or picking decidedly non-female hairs out of your exfoliating soap!

> This concept store carries over 30 brands of

men's prestige grooming products, including Frederic Fekkai, Anthony Logistics, Ren, Kiehl's, Marc Jacobs and Lancaster. There's also a fab treatment room where he can have wonderful facial and body treatments.

> **Space.NK.Men, 8 Broadwick Street, Soho, London W1F 8HW**
> **T·020 7287 2667 W·spacenk.co.uk**

And if you're in London and your man fancies a haircut or wet shave, tell him about one of these other well-respected establishments:

RELIVE THE ROARING TWENTIES

> This transformed, world-famous, 1920s Art Deco barber shop now offers all manner of hair and beauty treatments, including teeth whitening. A wet shave with hot towel costs £26.00 and, whilst they can usually offer drop-in appointments, it's best to book. If you have a spare couple of hours why not treat your man to the Male Retreat – a wet shave with hot towel, hair wash and cut, and a neck, back and shoulder massage.

> **Austin's Grooming and Beauty Salon at Austin Reed, 103-113 Regent Street, London W1B 4HL**
> **T·020 7534 7719 W·austinreed.co.uk**

FOR THE SMOOTH OPERATOR

> For a traditional wet shave with hot towels, try The Refinery at Harrods (see above) – £35.00 for 30-40 minutes. It's not always necessary to book an appointment and naturally you can also have all the other usual treatments, from haircutting to massages and facials.

> **The Refinery at Harrods, Knightsbridge, London SW1X 7XL T·020 7893 8332**

EAT

EATINGIN CUPCAKES HAMPERS
DIVINEBESPOKECHOCOLATES
AFTERNOONTEA INGREDIENTS
HEALTHYFOOD PICNICS CAKES
BREAKFAST HOMEDELIVERIES
EATCOOKERYLESSONS SPICES

TEA TIME

Much as I'd love to give you a list of all the restaurants I find most worthy, there's no point when you have such great guides as **Zagats** *and* **Hardens**. *However, the one thing restaurant guides don't do justice to is the great British cuppa! Whether you just need to rest your weary legs after a long day's shopping, or you're planning a fancy tea party (very now), wouldn't you love to know where to find a delicious morning or afternoon tea? Instead of a boozy hen night, why not round up your friends, order a cup of Earl Grey or Lapsang Souchong, stick your little pinkie in the air and get ready for some classy gossip? There'll be no vodka-induced faux pas to regret the morning after and think of all those empty booze calories you can replace with as many* millefeuille, *éclairs and scones smothered in clotted cream as your sweetest tooth desires.*

LEGENDARY
LONDON HOTELS

LET THE GUILD BE YOUR GUIDE

> I'm sure you've heard of mystery shoppers, well, what about mystery tea inspectors? Did you know there is a Tea Guild (*see page* 250) whose members travel around the country incognito, visiting tea venues and hotels to find the best morning/afternoon tea? They rate them on 17 criteria, ranging from crockery and décor to the variety of tea. Their Top London Afternoon Tea award in 2006 went to Claridge's.

> Claridge's offer a huge choice of over 30 different teas, along with finger sandwiches, French pastries and freshly baked scones. A truly delicious experience; I quite agree with Spencer Tracy's quip: '...I don't want to go to heaven, I want to go to Claridge's.'

> Afternoon tea is served from 3.00 p.m. until 5.30 p.m., from £30.50 (plus service). Reservations are essential.

> **Claridge's, Brook Street, London W1K 4HR**
T · 020 7629 8860 W · claridges.co.uk

PUTTING THE TEA IN GLITZY

> If you're really out to impress your tea companion, it would be hard to beat the winner of the Tea Council's Award for the Best Afternoon Tea in London. Afternoon tea doesn't get much fancier than at the Dorchester, you can even combine it with a chilled glass of champers. Soak in the opulent atmosphere of the refurbished Promenade Room and indulge in a sinful selection of finger sandwiches, scones and French pastries. Tea is served at 2.30 p.m. and 4.45 p.m. daily and booking is essential. High Tea is served a little later, so you can go straight on to the theatre. Set tea price(s) £28.50, £34.50 and £38.50.

> **The Dorchester, 53 Park Lane,**
London W1K 1QA
T · 020 7629 8888 W · thedorchester.com

TURN OVER A NEW LEAF

> Buttery crumpets, delicate sandwiches (with their crusts cut off, if you please!), scones with clotted cream, and a choice of champagne or Darjeeling. Mmm, tough decision. As you sit in the glass-roofed conservatory with a Chinoiserie theme at the Lanesborough, the resident pianist will play softly in the background or, during the Christmas period, you may well be serenaded by a festive choir. Happy to talk you through their large selection, their new tea sommelier service will help you sort out your preferences, so you can get the most from this winner of The Tea Guild's Top London Afternoon Tea Award 2005 and a coveted Tea Guild Award of Excellence in 2006. Tea is served every day from 3.30 p.m. until 6.00 p.m. (from 4.00 p.m.

on Sundays), and booking is essential. Prices start from £28.00.

> **The Lanesborough, Hyde Park Corner, Knightsbridge, London SW1X 7TA**
  T · 020 7259 5599 W · lanesborough.com

A RUNAWAY SUCCESS

> With savouries in miniature mouthfuls for the figure conscious, and cakes and pastries inspired by the latest season's catwalk designs, the traditional afternoon tea has had a serious makeover at The Berkeley. Who wouldn't be tempted by an Yves Saint Laurent frou-frou berry mousse, a Balenciaga monochrome-striped chocolate éclair, or an Oscar de la Renta evening dress biscuit? If you're feeling a little daring, an Elizabeth Hurley Beach fuchsia vanilla bikini biscuit or white swimsuit chocolate biscuit might be the way to go. All come served on a bespoke collection of Paul Smith fine bone china, or in a Baccarat flute if you opt for the champers.

> And if your eyes are bigger than your stomach, fear not – your unfinished delectables can be taken away in one of their little Prêt handbag-style takeaway boxes in pale mint green with pink handles. You can also purchase lovely gift cards and notelets, with pink tissue-lined envelopes, designed by Anzu (*also see page* 29). Prêt-à-Portea is served in the Caramel Room of The Berkeley between 2.00 p.m. and 6.00 p.m. every day, priced at £33.00 per person, £41.00 with a glass of champers, or £48.00 with a glass of 'couture' champagne. Reservations are recommended.

> **Prêt-à-Portea, The Caramel Room, The Berkeley, Wilton Place, Knightsbridge, London SW1X 7RL**
  T · 020 7235 6000 W · the-berkeley.co.uk

MEMORIES ARE MADE OF THIS

> Afternoon tea at the Ritz is more than a holiday treat, it's a London institution. However, it's not something you can do on a whim. You need to book in advance, often up to six weeks ahead, and don't turn up in jeans or trainers as you'll probably be politely shown the door. Gentlemen are requested to wear a jacket and tie. There are five sittings every day at 11.30 a.m., 1.30 p.m., 3.30 p.m., 5.30 p.m. and 7.30 p.m. The last sitting may seem a little late for afternoon tea, but it is extra special: it's called Champagne Afternoon Tea and you're offered a complimentary glass of champers, which you don't get at the other sittings. Served in the Palm Court, with sophisticated piano music setting the scene during the week and the romantic playing of a harp serenading you at the weekend, you're treated to a choice of over 17 teas, finely cut sandwiches, freshly baked apple and raisin scones with jam and clotted Devonshire cream, and a range of mouth-wateringly divine fruit compote pastries. At a set price of £35.00 per head, it really is a very affordable thing to tick off your 'To Do Before I Die' list.

> **The Ritz Hotel, 150 Piccadilly, London W1J 9BR**
  T · 020 7493 8181
  W · theritzlondon.com/tea/

SAME GLAMOUR, NO CORSET

> We can thank the Victorians for introducing afternoon tea. It became a time for the ladies to gossip and show off their finest china and linens, and when The Savoy hotel opened its doors in 1889 it offered sumptuous teas from day one.

> Almost 120 years later you can still treat yourself to a variety of freshly filled sandwiches, mouth-watering French pastries, teacakes, and scones with clotted cream and strawberry preserve, all served on delicate Royal Doulton china, while listening to the pianist gently tinkling the ivories. For an additional drop of luxury, opt for the Champagne Tea and enjoy a glass of bubbly. Served in the Thames Foyer surrounded by

a wonderful collection of Art Deco mirrors, tea is served at 2.00 p.m. with seatings every 15 minutes until 5.00 p.m. They also offer a Theatre Tea served between 5.30 p.m. and 7.30 p.m., with some light hot dishes to prevent your tummy grumbling during the second act!

> Bookings are recommended. The traditional tea costs £31.50 per person and the Champagne Tea £38.50.

> **The Savoy, Strand, Covent Garden, London WC2R OEU**
T·020 7836 4343 W·fairmont.com/Savoy

A FABULOUS PLACE
FOR TEA

SUDDENLY PARIS

> Once you could only have visited this gorgeous tearoom in Paris, now they have crossed the Channel and opened in Harrods. With a passion for the splendour and refinement of the 18th and 19th centuries, the Ladurée tearoom comprises different salons spread over two levels. The Boutique boasts a seven-metre counter filled with the most wonderful religieuses, millefeuilles, cakes, éclairs, croissants and their divine macaroons, not to mention their wonderful signature gift boxes, which I'm starting to collect! You can take tea and light snacks in the Neo-Etruscan Salon or upstairs in the Orange Salon.

> Now, back to those wonderful macaroons! Each season brings new flavours, such as gingerbread, liquorice or orange blossom, but you can always pick up the chocolate, vanilla, coffee, rose petal, pistachio, lemon, salted butter caramel or red fruit flavours. They make a lovely staying-with gift or wedding favour when they're packaged in those gorgeous gift boxes.

> **Ladurée at Harrods, 87/135 Brompton Road, London SW1X 7XL**
T·020 3155 0111 W·laduree.com

HAPPY LIKE YOU'VE JUST STEPPED OUT OF A SALON

> An oh la la slice of Paris in the heart of London! The fruit-filled pastries at Maison Blanc's Salon de Thé certainly had me coming back for more. I could have eaten another thirteen and not felt at all guilty. Nice cappuccinos, too.

> Maison Blanc can be found in London (Holland Park, Chiswick, Chelsea, St John's Wood, Hampstead, Kensington Church Street, Fulham, Putney and Muswell Hill), as well as towns in the South East, including Cobham, Farnham, Chichester, Guildford, Richmond and, the original shop in Oxford (see their website for addresses).

> **Maison Blanc**
T·020 8838 0848 W·maisonblanc.co.uk

THE PARLOUR'S GOT GAME

> Step into this converted 18th-century townhouse and you're spoilt for choice with the restaurants, bars, tea room and art gallery. Sketch is well known for its upstairs restaurant, The Lecture Room and Library, which has been referred to as a 'temple to fine dining'. Downstairs is The Parlour, a rather apt name for a place to take afternoon tea. Choose your cake, or more likely cakes, from the glass counter – these are simply divine – tiny works of art with explosive flavours. My hot chocolate took a very long time to come, but I was told it was being especially made in the kitchen. I thought perhaps they were melting the chocolate pieces with the hot milk, the proper way to make hot chocolate – yum – so I didn't mind waiting. Anyway, if you do have to wait you can always visit the unbelievably glamorous ladies' room (Note to self: buy Swarovski crystal for downstairs bathroom.)

> **The Parlour at Sketch, 9 Conduit Street, London W1S 2XG**
T·0870 777 4488 W·sketch.uk.com

A CELEBRATED QUINTET

> Now with ten locations in London (see online for addresses), you've no excuse to miss out on the wonderful patisseries while you're relaxing with a cappuccino at Patisserie Valerie. You can order fabulous bespoke celebration cakes at their Marylebone branch, where they also make their own chocolate and offer wonderful Easter and Valentine's goodies. Weekends are very popular, especially around lunchtime when everyone queues to get a table.

> **Patisserie Valerie**
  W·patisserie-valerie.co.uk
  105 Marylebone High Street, London W1M
  3BD T·020 7935 6240

SAINT PAUL OF DELICIOUS THINGS

> Mmmmm, yum, yum, yum – that's all I need say. OK, I'll also say that they're open from 7.30 a.m. during the week, to catch all you early birds (9.00 a.m. at weekends).

> I mention their lovely breads in the picnic section (*see page* 262). If you pop into their newly refurbished Covent Garden branch you can order your bread and then sit and have your refreshments whilst watching your bread being baked (up to 4.00 p.m.). Rather lovely – I can just smell it...

> **PAUL UK, 115 Marylebone High Street,**
  London W1V 4SB T·020 7224 5615
  Covent Garden – 29 Bedford Street,
  London WC2E 9ED T·020 7836 3304

> **for the other 18 branches see their website**
  W·paul-uk.com

FIT FOR A QUEEN

> Winter Whispers, White Monkey, Japanese Cherry, Margaret's Hope and Iron Goddess of Mercy – these are all teas you can order at the rather elegant tearooms at the Tea Palace. This is the place to go to experience a Palace Tea or Champagne Tea (they also do breakfast and lunch), where you can choose from over 160 teas to accompany your hot scones, strawberry jam and clotted cream. You can also visit their traditional tea counter and order loose leaf teas in gorgeous tea caddies, which make a lovely gift. If you need advice, speak to their master tea sommeliers who are happy to share their expert knowledge. They even offer their own blended Ayurvedic infusions.

> **Tea Palace, 175 Westbourne Grove,**
  London W11 2FB
  T·020 7727 2600 W·teapalace.co.uk

DECOR AND DECORUM

> The Wolseley is a lovely place to enjoy a sumptuous menu of assorted finger sandwiches, scones with clotted cream and pastries in Art Deco surroundings.

> I've been here for several lovely dinners, and for breakfast, and the service is second to none. It's been awarded a Tea Guild's Top London Afternoon Tea Award, and quite rightly so. Tea is served from 3.30 p.m. until 5.30 p.m. Monday to Saturday and from 3.30 p.m. until 6.30 p.m. Sunday. Best to make a reservation, as it's very popular. Cream tea is from £8.25; Afternoon Tea from £19.50.

> **The Wolseley, 160 Piccadilly,**
  London W1J 9EB
  T·020 7499 6996 W·thewolseley.com

FANCY A VINTAGE CUPPA?

> I loved my visit to Alan Yau's (creator of Wagamama and Hakkasan) serene tearooms Yauatcha, and was spoilt for choice with a huge selection of teas and divine petits gateaux, tartelets and pastries. I let my taste buds loose on a Fennel crème brulée and a Shanghai Lily (almond rose biscuit, gewurtzraminer, lychee compote, rose confit) and I was delighted with the experience. If you're not quite up for the 35-year-old Puer tea at £46.00, you can choose from more than 150 teas on the menu, or try a tea cocktail, tea smoothie or iced tea. Coffee and

TEA FOR TWO

If you're travelling around the UK and can't get by without your four cups of tea a day, you're not alone. According to Food from Britain, more than 163 million cups of tea are drunk in Britain every day; what they don't say is how many of those are good cuppas!

If you don't want to be let down by tea on your travels, you must purchase the new book from the Tea Guild/AA, *Afternoon Tea - Perfect Places for Afternoon Tea*. It lists over 300 places, by region, to enjoy afternoon tea, from luxurious hotels to charming village tearooms. Also includes recipes for cakes and scones, and tips on how to make the perfect cup of tea. It's available directly from the Tea Guild's website (£9.99) or from bookshops.

W · tea.co.uk

wines are also available for those who prefer something a little stronger.
> Pink Champagne Afternoon Tea (12.30 p.m. - 6.00 p.m.), £26.50 or Yauatcha Afternoon Tea, £19.00.
> **Yauatcha, 15 Broadwick Street, London W1F ODL**
   T · 020 7494 8888

STRESSED FROM SHOPPING?
> If you've shopped till you're ready to drop, or just feel like a quick pick-me-up before hitting the next store, pop into Relax and unwind while they give you a refreshing massage in their massage chairs (from £10.00). Choose from a range of options, from the Relax Energiser – a 15-minute classic – to the Relax Unwinder – pure bliss with 30 minutes of chair massage, including non-acupressure techniques.

> You get a complimentary tea or coffee included in the price, and if you fancy a longer treatment you can sign up for a full-body massage or other natural body treatments. You can also purchase gift vouchers and fabulous flowers. Open all year, except Christmas Day, Boxing Day and New Year's Day.
> **Soho: 10.00 a.m. - 9.00 p.m., Monday–Saturday; 12.00 p.m. - 8.00 p.m., Sunday.**
> **BBC White City: 10.00 a.m. - 7.00 p.m., Monday–Friday.**
> **Relax Soho, 65–67 Brewer Street, Soho, London W1F 9UP T · 020 7494 3333**
> **Relax BBC White City, 2–3 The Media Centre, London W12 7TS**
   T · 020 8811 8844 W · relax.org.uk

BREAKFAST
IN BED

Having breakfast in bed cooked for you by your significant other is pretty fantastic, but wouldn't it be even better if you could both stay cosy under the duvet? All you have to do is decide who is going to answer the front door to hear the wonderful news that 'breakfast is served'.

WAKING UP'S NOT HARD TO DO!
> Rosslyn Deli in Hampstead offers breakfast in bed for red-letter days like Valentine's Day and Mother's Day, or for a special birthday treat. Breakfast includes a scrummy assortment of mini croissants with strawberry jam and orange juice, plus either Valentine's chocolates and a rose, a Mother's Day cake, or a birthday cake. They can put together other treats if you wish, for example, a Lover's Box or a picnic. Prices include local delivery to NW3, NW8, NW5, NW11 and NW6. Outside these areas, you need to add £5.00

plus £2.50 per postcode crossed, so phone for a quote.

> **Rosslyn Delicatessen, 56 Rosslyn Hill, Hampstead, London NW3 1ND**
> **T · 020 7794 9210   W · delirosslyn.co.uk**

ABSURDLY DECADENT — AND WHY NOT?

> Iona Grant provides a breakfast-in-bed service, from the most traditional smoked salmon, scrambled eggs, wholemeal toast, champagne and fresh coffee for you and your partner, to the 'full English' for any number of guests, with a whole range of continental, fusion, kippers and croque-monsieur falling somewhere in between! She'll pre-prepare wherever possible and come to your home to add the finishing touches in your own kitchen before serving and clearing up. Any Central or West London address is possible and her prices range from modest to the absurd (her words, not mine) depending on your requirements!

> **Iona Grant   T · 07720 443 132**
> **E · iona@macunlimited.net**

See also Sophie Douglas-Bate page 13

SPECTACULAR CAKES AND CUPCAKES

See page 278 for more yummy cakes
See page 55 for wedding cakes

MAKE TODAY A RED LETTER DAY

> Don't even try sticking to your list when you pop into this shop. Besides offering mouth-watering lunches and tasty goodies, Konditor & Cook offer a great cake selection. I particularly love the Red Letter Box, which is a long thin box with 15 or 17 little square cakes. You can decorate these mini treats

with whatever message you fancy and it costs just £40.00 (plus postage). Their Magic Cakes are also very popular, especially for weddings. The little square, bite-size cakes, decorated with text and pictures, look fantastic piled high on different-sized cake stands (from £2.80). With five shops in London you're never far from these delights. Their website opens with a quote from Nigella Lawson (Vogue): 'fabulous cakes … the sort you'd make yourself if only you had the time, energy or inclination.' I couldn't say it any better myself.

> **Konditor & Cook, 22 Cornwall Road, London SE1 8TW**
> **Branches at London Bridge, Grays Inn Road, Shaftesbury Avenue and at The Gerkin (see online for addresses)**
> **T · 020 7261 0456**
> **W · konditorandcook.co.uk**

SWEET SAVOIR FAIRE

> Amazing cakes by cake maker to the stars and two-time winner of Continental Pâtissier of the Year award, Eric Lanlard. I was first amazed by the beauty of Eric's cake designs at a wedding show — once I had battled my way through the brides who were surrounding his booth. I then had the pleasure of tasting his divine patisseries at a party and have since become hooked — and fat! — just kidding.

> Don't let his being a pâtissier to the rich and famous put you off — cakes start from as little as £40.00. If you're throwing a party and want scrummy mini puds and pâtisseries, prices start from £5.00 per serving. They look divine and taste unbelievable, and the team can create any cake design you require. As they say, 'the only limit is your imagination.'

> **Savoir Design, 2 Kingfisher House, Battersea Reach, Juniper Drive, off York Road, London SW18 1TX**
> **T · 020 7978 5555   W · savoirdesign.co.uk**

COUTURE
CUPCAKES

Cupcakes, cupcakes, cupcakes (or fairy cakes if you're sitting in the parlour). Here are some great companies who can supply you with freshly baked, divine, colourful, designer cupcakes.

ON THE MARKET FOR DELICIOUS TREATS

> When this gorgeous shop opened its doors in the middle of Portobello Market, I'm sure the stallholders were very worried. Not about competition, you understand, but simply because the cakes were so delicious and tempting they worried they'd leave their stalls unattended and expand their waistlines not their businesses! Tarek Malouf wanted to bring high-quality American home-baking to London and everything is baked in their kitchen using only the best ingredients. Once a week they offer a very popular cupcake-of-the-day, which includes such scrummy flavours as lavender, mint chocolate, carrot, peanut toffee and cappuccino. They also make a tempting range of cakes, pies, breads, cookies and bars.

> The cupcakes are available with a chocolate or vanilla sponge with chocolate or vanilla buttercream icing (icing can be plain or pink, green, blue or yellow). As I write, they are about to open a new shop in South Kensington and I'd better point out that the Portobello Road shop is closed on a Monday.

> They also deliver, although unfortunately only to a small part of West London. Don't sulk, buy in bulk because they make up for it by offering a free cupcake for every 12 you buy (two days' notice required). Prices: Cupcakes from £1.55; adorable mini-cupcakes from 95p

> **the hummingbird bakery, 133 Portobello Road, Notting Hill, London W11 2DY
T · 020 7229 6446
W · hummingbirdbakery.com**

NOT SO EASY TO STOP AT ONE!

> The Little Cupcake Company's cakes are baked fresh to order and I love it that they come in 'Little' and 'Not So Little', and are elegantly packaged in beribboned gift boxes.

> They cater for picnics, garden, dinner, birthday and children's parties, as well as weddings, anniversaries and new arrivals. They offer three collections – Signature, Chocolate and Seasonal. They can print guest's names, characters or pictures in edible ink onto fondant discs which sit on top of the cakes. This personal touch is becoming very popular and I can see why. They can also provide individually boxed cakes for favours and presents.

> Mail order (they are currently developing their online ordering) they require 48 hours' notice for a standard order, slightly longer if you require customisation. Delivery is to mainland UK only.
Prices: Little cakes £12.00 per dozen (minimum order 3 dozen); Not So Little £18.00 per dozen (minimum order of 2 dozen)

> **The Little Cupcake Company, Carpenter Court, 1 Maple Road, Bramhall, Stockport, Cheshire SK7 2DH
T · 0845 296 9188
W · thelittlecupcakecompany.co.uk**

CAKES WORTH CELEBRATING

> Peggy Porschen has been baking and decorating cakes from early childhood. She has completed a Cordon Bleu course in French patisserie and has now set up her own business making cakes and cookies for events. (She's baked goodies for many a celebrity wedding and party.) Peggy is without doubt the queen of cupcakes, they are simply exquisite and not a single cake leaves the premises without Peggy giving it her own personal touch. The cupcakes have a minimum order requirement of 24 with prices starting from £5.50 each.

> She does not offer a mail-order service, but cakes can be couriered or you can pick them up yourself. I ate her gorgeously decorated cookies at a product launch and simply had to buy her first book *Pretty Party Cakes – Sweet and Stylish Cookies and Cakes for all Occasions* (Quadrille). Not only is the book beautifully designed, with fabulous photography, but the basic cake recipes are so easy to follow. And when I used the sponge recipe for my son's birthday, one of the dads told me it was the nicest cake he had ever eaten at a party.

> Peggy is renowned for her spectacular wedding and party cakes, and achieves perfect results for each of her creations. She likes to meet you first for a personal consultation (by appointment, Monday-Friday, 10.00 a.m.-6.00 p.m.) where she will guide you through her creative process and, best of all, you get to taste the delicious cakes. Her portfolio is extensive and you will be so amazed at her divine cakes you'll be hard pushed to choose just one – she's also happy to create something unique for you. Peggy has been awarded 'Best Wedding Cake Maker' in the Wrapit Wedding Industry Awards 2007 and her book Pretty Party Cakes won the Gourmand Award for the 'Best Book for Entertaining in the World'.

> She has recently published her second book, *Romantic Cakes – Cookies and Cakes to Celebrate Love* (Quadrille). I have just purchased it and found it even more fantastic and inspiring than I had anticipated.

> **Peggy Porschen Ltd, 32 Madison Studios, The Village, 101 Amies Street, London SW11 2JW**
> **T· 020 7738 1339**
> **W· peggyporschen.com**

HIT A SEXY SUGAR HIGH

> Amanda from the Utterly Sexy Café bakes the most delicious, soft pastel fairy cakes decorated with gorgeous handmade sugar roses and leaves. As if that wasn't enough, for a small extra cost she will add butterflies and even a dusting of glitter. All her cakes are made to order, so it is possible to choose size, design, colour and flavour. And talking of flavour, you can feast on Tangy Lemon, Coffee, Vanilla, Chocolate, Cardamon and raisins soaked in Earl Grey Tea. Her UK-wide mail-order service offers the fairy cakes in a presentation box (which opens up like a lotus flower) and four cupcakes will cost £20.00 (plus £3.00 p&p).

> I love it that Amanda also offers a full catering service, providing beautifully prepared, creatively decorated food. If you're hosting a teatime party or reception, you can also hire her 1930-50s vintage china. She has a huge selection of sets or you can use mismatched designs, which I think looks lovely. Or why not just relax and allow Amanda to take care of the entire party. She offers a Pink and Lace and China Tea party with waitresses serving in 1950s' aprons, lace tablecloths, birds, butterflies, vintage china, pink sugar cubes with silver tongs and vintage cake stands overflowing with delectable cakes and tarts. Her Quintessential Teatime Menu starts from £20.00 per person.

> Naturally she is called upon to style and cater to many a wedding and can also provide you with tiers of beautifully decorated fairy cakes. When she exhibited at the Designer Wedding Show (*see page* 61), her fairy cakes were so gorgeous they had brides flocking to her stand – they taste scrummy too!

> **Utterly Sexy Café**
> **T· 01725 511 146 / 07968 868 860**
> **W· utterlysexycafe.co.uk**

OTHER LOVELY CUPCAKES

FOR THE BEST NAME

> **Crumbs and Doilies** – Isn't it great? Of course, so are their mouth-watering cakes. Great ideas for gifts and parties with fabulous decorations: £20.00 for 2 dozen mini cupcakes; larger cupcakes also available.
> **T · 07772 281 457**
> **W · crumbsanddoilies.co.uk**

FOR CELEBRITY CRED

> **Paparazzi at the Primrose Bakery** – The cake on the lips of rock stars and models. Three different flavours, coloured butter-creams and two sizes – regular (£1.75) and mini (£1.15). Decorations can be made to suit any occasion. (Hand Delivery in London only)
> **T · 020 7483 4222**
> **W · primrosebakery.org.uk**

DIY CUPCAKE COUTURE

PICTURE YOUR PERFECT CAKE

> I was inspired to visit this shop after 'attempting' to follow a recipe for cupcakes decorated with sugarcraft and printed frosting sheets.
> The printed frosting sheets are fab. You send Jane Asher's shop an image (photograph, text or drawing) by post, or email as a jpeg file, and they will print it onto edible sheets, either as one big image, multiple copies, or loads of individual characters to cut out and use on cupcakes – perfect for my son's birthday party.
> The printed frosting can be sent worldwide and costs £25.00 for a small sheet or £35.00 for the larger sheet. Visit the website for a great selection of mail order items.
> As well as this fantastic service, what an unbelievable shop! It offers everything a cake maker could possibly need – beginner or advanced. They sell cutters, decorations, books, cake tins in all sorts of wonderful shapes and sizes, and all manner of things that I didn't even know you could use in baking!
> If you aren't the type to bake your own, then order one of their personalised cakes, safe in the knowledge that they use GM-free and organic produce wherever possible.
> **Jane Asher Party Cakes & Sugarcraft, 22-24 Cale Street, London SW3 3QU T · 020 7584 6177 W · jane-asher.co.uk**

PATTER CAKE, PATTER CAKE, BAKER'S MAN

> I was searching the internet trying to source chocolate brown and pale pink cupcake holders when I came across Sweet Celebrations and hit the jackpot. They also have a fantastic selection of cookie cutters, including handbags, stilettos, bikinis, butterflies, hats, dresses, sunglasses, dogs and hugs and kisses – I couldn't possibly list them all here, the catalogue goes on for pages and pages. You can then decorate your cookies or cupcakes with their wonderful stencils, transfer sheets, dusting powders, edible sprinkles and icing and sugar decorations.
> They also sell sugar-paste decorations, cake toppers, plastic decorations and inspiring books and, of course, all bake-ware and accessories (although I wouldn't necessarily buy those from overseas as you often end up paying hefty duty).
> I simply had to have their neon, scalloped cups with gold rims ($3.29 for 60) in bright pinks and greens, as they look gorgeous filled with little sweets. Their delicate favour cups ($15.99 for 200) with lovely prints, look like fresh blossoms and leaves when empty and look wonderful scattered on a table – great for parties and weddings.
> They have been in the mail-order business for over 50 years and ship worldwide.

My dear friend Kay, who went more 'mad' than me ordering, received her crate within 10 days.

> **Sweet Celebrations Inc, 7009 Washington Ave S, Edina, MN 55439**
> **T · USA (toll free) 1 800 328 6722**
> **Outside USA +1 952 943 1508**
> **W · sweetc.com**

CATERERS

As many of the caterers also offer a party planning or designing service you will find them within the Celebrate and Entertain section (see pages 11-16)

CHEFS

For Private Chefs see pages 3 and 15

DIVINE BESPOKE CHOCOLATES

EDIBLE ACCESSORIES

> Can't stop buying handbags? (I have 50!) Look no further than these simply divine little mini handbags in edible chocolate with decadent fillings. Made with the best chocolate from France and Belgium, with no chemical additives or preservatives, they make a lovely gift if you're going to stay somewhere as a house guest. The bags come in many different designs and you can buy in boxes of six or 12. Although shipped from America my order came within a week ($32.00, plus $15.00 shipping).

> They've just opened a fabulous Chocolate Boutique where you can also buy chocolate rings, boots, truffles, and even a five-and-a-half-inch-high Aphrodite.

> **Choco Choco House Boutique, 83 Pembroke, Boston, MA 02118**
> **T · +1 (617) 718 0946**
> **W · chocochocohouse.com**

THE ULTIMATE IN SWEET NOTHINGS

> Get creative and personalise a novelty chocolate bar with your own pictures or text or choose from a gallery of images. The image or message is actually printed on the chocolate, not on the wrapper. You can send a Groovy Card for a birthday, congratulations, Valentine's or Christmas.

> They have a mail-order service, and you should receive your order within three days, but unfortunately delivery is only within the United Kingdom. If you are ordering under 50 pieces you need to order through Flying Flowers and if you order over 50 pieces, say for a wedding or party, you do this through Groovy Chocolate.

> **Groovy Chocolate Limited, 5 Bank Street, Elie, Fife KY9 1BW T · 01333 331 166**
> **W · groovychocolate.com**
> **W · flyingflowers.com T · 0870 191 3400**

CHOCOLATES TO MAKE YOU MELT

> Artisan du Chocolat is probably the best chocolatier in London. Lovingly made by hand with no preservatives, theirs are memorable and exceptional chocolates. The flavours are fantastic, the designs are fabulous and the packaging divine. I love the Couture Collection, which are made with rare cocoa beans, pure or infused with fruits, nuts, seeds, flowers, herbs and spices ranging from vanilla and fresh mint to the more exotic sechuan pepper, banana and thyme, coriander praline or Lapsang Souchong tea.

> The couture chocolates are beautifully decorated with gold swirls, chequer boards, stripes, leaves and flowers, and look stunning arranged in the box. You can also commission a word, initials or saying on the chocolates which would be great for a wedding or party – they will even post worldwide. Their tasting sessions have turned into a bit of a cult event, and they

won the *Observer* Food Award 2004 for Best Producer.

> **Artisan du Chocolat, 89 Lower Sloane Street, London SW1 W8DA**
> **T · 020 7824 8365**
> **W · artisanduchocolat.com**

TWO'S YUMMY, TWELVE'S A WOW

> Exquisitely packaged and delicious hand-made truffles, chocolates, glazed chestnuts, pralines, chocolate bars and fruit pastes; you'll be hard pushed to choose. I love La Maison du Chocolat's hat boxes filled with delicious goodies, which would make a lovely thank-you present, and their new chocolate pearls, which you make into a divine hot or cold chocolate drink. All their chocolates can be delivered, however, to taste their delicious pastries, biscuits and cakes you'll have to visit one of their five boutiques in Paris, Cannes, London, New York or Tokyo. They make special cakes and tarts for Valentine's, Easter and Christmas, and for anyone with food intolerances they offer chocolates with no sugar, milk or dairy ingredients.

> They want to awaken your senses and taste buds, so offer a Parcours Initiatique session (chocolate tasting) that you can book by phone. You can buy a little box of two choco-lates from as little as £2.50, but somehow I think you may go for the box of 12!

> **La Maison du Chocolat, 45–46 Piccadilly, London W1J 0DS T · 020 7287 8500**
> **W · lamaisonduchocolat.com**
> **Also at Harrods, 87–135 Brompton Road, Knightsbridge, London SW1X 7XL**
> **T · 020 7730 1234**

A DELIGHT FOR ALL SEASONS

> These chocolates are so exquisitely dressed in flowers, silver, gold or jewellery that you'll want to keep them all for yourself. With over 52 different types of chocolate, including almond, praline, dates, pistachio, coffee grain and even light chocolates, their chocolates change with the seasons, trends and for special occasions. Extremely popular for weddings, Christmas, Valentine's and new-baby gifts, these handmade premium chocolates can be decorated with little items such as safety pins, dummies, teddies, butterflies, charms or diamante buckles.

> Patchi also manufacture silver art pieces and tableware, decorative items and toy figures, which can accompany the chocolates to make a stunning gift. Chocolates from £1.90 per item.

> **Patchi, Harrods Chocolate Room, Brompton Road, London SW1X 7XL**
> **T · 020 7893 8606 W · patchi.com**

YOU MAY NOT CARE TO SHARE

> Forget fighting for the next 'It' bag, today's must-have item is the newest collection of chocolates produced by Plaisir Du Chocolat. They produce two collections a year, with an artist commissioned to design particular themes each time. Last Christmas they made a gorgeous, limited-edition collection of round chocolate balls that looked exactly like Christmas baubles. They sold out within minutes — even I wasn't quick enough! They also produced a collection of chocolates with rare alcohols, including 50-year-old rums and an ancient cognac.

> The chocolate collections are presented in a Celadon green box and look so lovely it can be hard to bring yourself to eat them. Not that hard though, as they taste as good as they look, and remember, you have to eat them within about a week as they're made with the freshest ingredients and no preservatives. Flavours include prune and Armagnac, Chinese gunpowder tea and fresh mint leaves, lavender, rose flowers, bitter orange, liquorice — oh, my mouth is watering...

> They also offer great chocolate workshops for children, and hold chocolate parties for adults. I love the idea of the chocolate and

champagne soirée. You can try some of their famous hot chocolate at their Salon or book one of their monthly tasting evenings. Shipping is available worldwide and you can also purchase the chocolate collections at their concessions in Harvey Nichols in Manchester and Edinburgh, and a small selection in Selfridges, London. Online, the chocolates are priced from £3.70 (box of four). I suggest you buy the wonderful L'Invitation au Voyage, a box which fans out over four levels and includes 64 chocolates of your choice – divine! (£52.00)

> **Plaisir Du Chocolat, The Shop: Melrose, High Street, Melrose TD6 9PA**
  T· 018969 820 202
  W· plaisirduchocolat.com
> **The Salon: 251-253 Canongate, Edinburgh EH8 8BQ T· 0131 556 9524**

COOKERY LESSONS

FROM NOODLES TO KNIVES

> I'm sure most of you have heard of Leith's cookery school. My sister did a professional course with them and cooks the most divine meals, not to mention mouth-watering desserts. Apart from the professional courses, they offer all manner of courses to help you hone your culinary skills. These range from Saturday morning to special interest courses including Italian Cooking, Thai Cooking for Beginners, Chocolate, Knife Skills, Sauces, and Carving Demonstrations – so something for everyone. Prices are very reasonable from £50.00 for a half-day course. Currently they are at 21 St Alban's Grove, London, W8 5BP, but in January 2008 they are moving so I've listed their new address below.

> **Leith's School of Food and Wine, 16-20 Wendell Road, London, W12 9RT**
  T· 020 7229 0177 W· leiths.com

YEAR-ROUND EXPERTISE

> The Raymond Blanc Cookery School offers one-, two- and four-day courses which cover: great tips for creating the perfect dinner parties; making bread with one of the leading artisan bakers in Britain; creating wonderful vegetarian dishes with produce from their own organic garden; and a look at Fusion Cuisine. During the holidays they offer a one-day cookery class for children, which keeps the budding chefs busy cooking up a storm along with herb-tasting competitions and making floating islands.

> The courses don't require vast prior experience, just a love of learning – and food! You'll discover the secrets of producing the finest foods, in a lovely environment. Course prices start from £275.00; £200.00 for the children's course.

> **Le Manoir aux Quat'Saisons, Church Road, Great Milton, Oxford OX44 7PD**
  T· 01844 278 881 W· manoir.com

SEX UP YOUR CULINARY REPERTOIRE

> Just three months after it opened, the Novelli Academy was placed in the top 25 cookery schools in the world. The Novelli Academy is run by Jean Christophe Novelli at his restored 14th-century Hertfordshire farmhouse. Jean Christophe is a Michelin and 5AA Rosette award winning French chef whose attributes include, AA Chef's, Chef of the Year, European Chef of the Year finalist (representing Great Britain) and the prestigious Egon Ronay Desert of the Year. He's also won Restaurant of the Year on numerous occasions and many other awards. So you will be in excellent hands when you take one (or both) of the new courses (although more are in the pipeline) that are on offer.

> The one day Tasting and Demonstration Day is designed for novice or experienced cooks (£495.00), watching Jean Christophe prepare his famous signature dishes.

> Or partake in the Hands-on Masterclass

(£995.00) with personal tuition by Jean Christophe. He will enhance your cookery skills and you'll be cooking sumptuous dishes from a specially designated menu. You'll have a day of fun, entertainment and also enjoy a champagne reception, not to mention you'll walk away with a Novelli Academy Masterclass Certificate, a signed copy of the new Jean Christophe Novelli cookery book and a DVD with highlights of your day. Also included is a night's stay at the 4 star hotel, Sopwell House, in nearby St Albans.

> You may also be tempted by the fact that he was recently voted 'World's Sexiest Chef' and in the 'Top 50 Beautiful Men' poll.

> **Novelli Associates Ltd, Crouchmore Farm, Tea Green, Hertfordshire LU2 8PS**
  T· 01582 454 070
  W· jeanchristophenovelli.com

NO ONE COOKS LIKE LA MAMMA

> I was originally attracted to Mamma Agata's cookery courses as I thought it would be a wonderful gift to give newlyweds. You get your own private cooking lessons with Mamma in her home in the town of Ravello, and after cooking you eat on her terrace overlooking the Amalfi coast.

> This is a demonstration cookery course where you learn the art of homestyle cooking with regional ingredients, cooking traditional Italian dishes like antipasti, pastas, breads, seasonal vegetable dishes and meat dishes – and, last but not least, cakes and marmalades. All the recipes will be clearly demonstrated in a warm and relaxed atmosphere and, after the class, participants share in the beautiful meal and enjoy the local wines of the Amalfi region. In a land where limoncello is famous, Mamma Agata also prepares liqueurs made from lemon, tangerine and fennel.

> Mamma Agata has cooked for Humphrey Bogart, Fred Astaire, Richard Burton and Elizabeth Taylor, to name but a few. Chiara,

her daughter, who works alongside Mamma Agata, is a fount of local knowledge and will help with any other requests if needed, such as day trips to local islands, shopping or even painting courses.

> Or if you don't want to partake in the cooking demonstration, why not just book an exclusive, romantic dinner prepared by Mamma Agata on her terrace? (p.o.a.)
  Lessons cost €180 per person.

> **Mamma Agata, Piazza S. Cosma, 9, 84010 Ravello (Salerno), Italy**
  W· mammaagata.com
  E· info@mammaagata.com

DINNER PARTIES
For Dinner Parties see Celebrate & Entertain page 2

INGREDIENTS

CUT OUT THE MIDDLEMAN

> Food from Britain produce this fantastic online guide to over 3,000 regional food and drink producers in the UK. It will tell you who produces what and offers a link to their website (if they have one). You can search by product or region, and can also use their shopping market facility and buy the goods directly from the producer. A good search facility if you're looking for that key component for your next dinner party.

> **Food from Britain, 4th Floor Manning House, 22 Carlisle Place, London SW1P 1JA**
  T· 020 7233 5111 or 020 7233 9515
  W· regionalfoodanddrink.co.uk

ADD A LITTLE MYSTERY TO YOUR MAIN COURSE

> If you like to spend your evenings browsing through vintage or obscure cookbooks planning mouth-watering meals, but don't know what half the ingredients look like,

let alone where to buy them, fret no more. Long gone are the days of phoning round every deli or specialist food store in the phone book.

> Offering specialist and gourmet products from around the world, including herbs and spices, oils and vinegars, pickles and preservatives, pasta, rice, dried gourmet products and pulses, stocks and sauces, plus speciality food items and unique gifts, Hard to Find Foods has done all the hard work for you.

> **Hard to Find Foods, PO Box 96, Radlett, Herts WD7 8YX**
  T·0870 383 4670
  W·hardtofindfoods.co.uk

HOT TO TROT (ROUND TO YOUR HOUSE)

> If you can't get to Notting Hill to visit The Spice Shop then visit their website and, providing your order is over £10.00, they'll deliver worldwide, right to your door. Not only do they offer a huge variety of herbs and spices, they also have things like dried mushrooms, essential oils and natural food colourings.

> Birgit Erath travels the world learning about cooking methods, spices and herbs – in fact she was just leaving for Bolivia when I spoke with her and was also attending a course on Inca cooking. She only buys from carefully selected growers (she actually mixes them all in London) and none of the herbs and spices contain any artificial colouring or preservatives.

> Browsing their website I found out that Devil's Penis is a chilli, but I do wonder what recipe I might use it in!

> **The Spice Shop, 1 Blenheim Crescent, London W11 2EE**
  T·020 7221 4448 W·thespiceshop.co.uk

HOME DELIVERIES

EATING IN

SOFA DINING FOR SOPHISTICATES

> Fancy a chilli & coconut prawn curry from Deya, a Monterey Jack & bacon cheeseburger from Hamburger Union, or Cantonese chicken in black bean sauce from Mr Wing? No problem, phone Room Service and they'll deliver freshly prepared, made-to-order dishes directly from over 80 of London's top restaurants. You pay the same as if you were eating in the restaurant (except you can sit in your pyjamas), plus a nominal delivery charge (£4.95), and as they also offer a mobile off-licence, you can order the perfect drink to accompany your meal. And, if you spill it all down your front, don't worry – they also offer a laundry and dry-cleaning service with free pick-up and delivery from/to your home, office or hotel. Currently delivery is limited to central London (see list of available postcodes online).

> **Room Service Deliveries Ltd, 65 Maygrove Road, London NW6 2EH**
  T·020 7644 6666 W·roomservice.co.uk

Also see Effortless Eating page 4 and Model Catering page 284

HEALTHY OPTIONS
DELIVERED TO YOUR DOOR

You used to wake up, open your front door and find your milk and maybe a newspaper. Now you can get three perfectly balanced and delicious meals (plus two snacks) delivered each morning. No longer need you worry about what to buy, what to cook or how to stick to a healthy, balanced diet.

A MODEL DIET AT YOUR DOOR

> The Pure Package was set up in 2004 by

Jennifer Irvine and has already won her a string of awards, including being voted one of 2005's top 50 entrepreneurs. Along with her nutritionists, dietary therapists and chefs, and in full consultation with you, she will work out your own personal programme of daily meals. Whether you want to lose weight or increase energy, suffer from food intolerances, or just want to ensure you're receiving a healthy, balanced diet, The Pure Package will deliver three gorgeous meals, plus snacks and a menu card, by 6.00 a.m. each morning.

> They have catered to supermodels, athletes, frantic city workers and those with a mission to get thin! As they're based right next to New Covent Garden Market, they can pick what's in season, ingredients are free range, many organic, and none of the products are genetically modified. They incorporate any food allergies and as a matter of course avoid sugar and wheat. And just in case you're thinking it's all going to be terribly boring and dull, here's what you might receive for a couple of days:

Day One
Breakfast – mixed berries, live yoghurt and granola muesli

Lunch – cob salad and char-grilled swordfish

Dinner – Thai green curry

Snacks – pineapple and black sesame seeds, dairy-free dark chocolate mousse

Day Two
Breakfast – apricot granola

Lunch – seared soy-glazed salmon, baby spinach and Asian herb salad

Snacks – crudités and guacamole, and a date and walnut muffin

Dinner – corn-fed chicken and mixed mushroom barley risotto

> How could you resist? The Pure Package programme costs £33.95 per day for a minimum of 10 days (£26.95 per day for 90 days); these prices include delivery within the M25.

> **The Pure Package, Arch 40, New Covent Garden Market, London SW8 5PP T·0845 612 3888 W·purepackage.com**

EAT YOURSELF DELICIOUSLY SLIM
> Silhouette Chefs deliver three meals plus two snacks a day, based on the tested Zone diet by Dr Barry Sears (**W·drsears.com**) which works on a fully balanced diet programme of 40 per cent carbohydrates, 30 per cent favourable fats and 30 per cent protein.

> These gourmet meals and healthy snacks promote weight loss and, on average, people on the programme lose between one and a half and four pounds per week (although it's not guaranteed). Clients also report lower blood sugar levels, considerably reduced cholesterol and body fat, and increased energy levels. They can cater for any food intolerances, and can also supply kosher as well as halal diets.

> Several packages are available, including weight loss, healthy eating, standard, tailored, corporate and partner's package, depending on your specific requirements. Prices from £27.00 per day (7-days/week package for 3 months).

> **Silhouette Chefs, 100 Clements Road, London SE16 4DG T · 020 7394 8899 W · silhouettechefs.com**

PERFECT PICNICS

There's something about picnics that's very romantic and relaxing: finding a lovely setting, laying out the picnic rug with cushions and sipping a glass of chilled champagne while you savour your cold Game Pie. (Sorry, I think I'm confusing my life with a Merchant Ivory film!) We went to Glyndebourne to see Cosi Fan Tutte *– they really know how to picnic in style there. We saw tables fully laid with lace tablecloth, silver tableware, linen napkins, candelabra and lovely flower arrangements, not to mention all the delicious food.*

So, first, here are some great picnic accessories, hampers and backpacks.

PICNIC ACCESSORIES

AL FRESCO FANTASY

> This is a gorgeous, gorgeous kitchen shop opened by June Summerill and Bernadette Bishop 12 years ago. June and Bernadette discover all sorts of lovely goodies on their relentless quest for new stock and I love their combination of old and new pieces.

> Apart from all the useful kitchen objects, for your picnic you could pick up old Provencal table linen, coloured glassware, vintage cutlery, cheeseboards, gorgeous baskets, not to mention one of their antique picnic hampers. Their shop is a delight to browse, and I'm sure you won't leave without a few select purchases.

> **Summerill & Bishop Limited, 100 Portland Road, London W11 4LN**
> **T·020 7221 4566**
> **W·summerillandbishop.com**

FROM RETRO TO REGAL

> This website offers a great selection of picnic hampers, from mini marvels for two to luxury baskets for four complete with Wedgwood fine bone china. PicnicShop also offers the Cath Kidston blossom-design hamper, which I love, but hurry as they only have a limited number. If you don't manage to get your hands on one look at the traditional, natural range, they are their best- seller. They also have backpacks, cool storage, rugs and furniture.

> The website includes picnic tips and a picnic locator telling you all the top places in the UK to have your picnic.

> **PicnicShop T·0845 867 4196**
> **W·picnicshop.co.uk**

DON'T LOOK BACK, IT'S PACKED

> Simply Picnic offers a great selection of backpacks, including ones for children so they can carry their own picnic (which they love to do). I drink so much tea I may even buy their coffee-and-tea backpack and have it permanently attached to my back! Their all-singing, all-dancing ultimate picnic back-pack includes a blanket, gingham napkins, melamine plates, acrylic wine glasses, cutlery, bottle holder and corkscrew, cheese board and knife, salt and pepper pots, and a wine stopper for £59.50. They also offer a choice of 14 hampers, deluxe picnic cooler on wheels, seats, wine and champagne carriers, and a portable cheese board folder. Delivery costs range from £2.95 to £9.95 depending on weight of the package.

> **Simply Picnic T·0871 990 6253**
> **W·simplypicnic.co.uk**

WILD ABOUT THE SAFARI

> The Safari Picnic Box (£79.00) is very, very stylish. It's covered in khaki-green canvas and includes two wine glasses, melamine plates, cutlery, salt and pepper shakers, napkins, napkin rings and a tablecloth. Each item is buckled in securely with brown mock-leather straps, but the best thing is it comes with its own table. Simply unfasten the flap-down table, flip out the attached feet, et voilà!

> **I Want One of Those T·0870 241 1066**
> **W·iwantoneofthose.com**

PICNIC
MUST HAVES

TWO HUNDRED YEARS OF CHEESE

> No picnic would be complete without a fantastic selection of cheeses and who better to go to than Paxton & Whitfield who have been selling cheese for over 200 years.

> And they don't only offer fabulous cheeses, their pickles, relishes and biscuits ensure a perfect pairing.

> They also sell fine food, from ham, pâté, fruit cake and Florentines to hampers, and wine. No need to go anywhere else really, and with three shops and an online store, ordering couldn't be easier.

> **Paxton & Whitfield**
> **London – 93 Jermyn Street, London**
> **SW1Y 6JE T·020 7930 0259**
> **Stratford-upon-Avon – 13 Wood Street,**
> **CV37 6JF T·01789 415 544**
> **Bath – 1 John Street, BA1 2JL**
> **T·01225 466 403**
> **W·paxtonandwhitfield.co.uk**

THE TRUE HOME OF HAMPERS

> Fortnum & Mason hampers have been oohed and aahed over at Ascot, the Boat Race, Henley, Wimbledon, Lord's and Twickenham as far back as the late 1800s. And I bet you didn't know that it was they who first recognised a future staple when they were shown one by a travelling salesperson back in 1886 and so introduced the baked bean to Britain. Don't worry, you won't get any baked beans in your Piccadilly Hamper. This picnic tea hamper arrives in a willow basket stamped with the F&M logo and is just perfect for a spring or summer picnic, containing cutlery for four, four champagne glasses, rose champagne, lemon drizzle cake, strawberry preserve, Jersey clotted cream, four scones and a punnet of strawberries. The Piccadilly Hamper is priced at £75.00, with UK delivery £7.00. Many other choices

of hampers are available (not all suitable for picnics) and several can be delivered worldwide!

> **Fortnum & Mason plc, 181 Piccadilly,**
> **London W1A 1ER**
> **T·020 7734 8040**
> **W·fortnumandmason.com**

USE YOUR LOAF – PICNIC WITH PRIDE

> If you want bread, don't go anywhere else but PAUL, who offers 140 different styles of bread with no hidden nasties (artificial additives or preservatives). PAUL has invented his collection of what he calls ephemerals: 'different kinds of bread, designed to highlight the flavour, the fruit, or the special occasion of a particular season or even month.' That means they're all limited editions and only around for a short time. I'd get your order in.

> I was tempted by the bread with figs and bread with hazelnuts and immediately headed off to the nearest of their 20 UK stores (check online). There's no better accompaniment to a picnic of French cheese and wine. They now offer a quick delivery service within London, with a minimum order of £25.00. Phone your order to 0845 6120 401. (*Also see page* 249)

> **PAUL UK, 115 Marylebone High Street,**
> **London W1V 4SB T·020 7224 5615**
> **Covent Garden – 29 Bedford Street,**
> **London WC2E 9ED T·020 7836 3304**
> **W·paul-uk.com**

LUXURY PICNICS

DRIVE ON PARKER

> This is a lovely treat or a romantic gift on offer from Antique & Hollywood Limousines in South Devon. 'Parker' will pick you up from Exeter station in one of his 1930s American cars — you have the choice of a Buick, Packard or Oldsmobile. After a quick tour of Exeter, it's off to see some of Devon's lovely

little coastal fishing villages, thatched cottage villages and forgotten by-roads, with stunning views over old towns. Parker is a veritable fount of knowledge about the area and has a few surprises up his sleeve for you during his four-hour tour.

> Once at your picnic spot, Parker will set up the picnic, pop the bubbly and start the old gramophone playing some classic 78s. He'll then retire gracefully, while you enjoy your set-menu picnic of assorted quiches, pâté, scotch eggs, salads and coleslaw, assorted cheese and grapes, baguettes, strawberries with clotted cream and, of course, the bubbly. (£225.00 for up to four people)

> And if you're looking for accommodation in the area, Stuart from Antique & Hollywood Limousines recommends the Victoria Hotel in Sidmouth (T · 01395 512 651), where they filmed *Jeeves and Wooster*, or The Hotel Barcelona in Exeter (T · 0118 983 1348).

> **Antique & Hollywood Limousines,**
  7 Pollybrook, Town Lane, Woodbury,
  Exeter EX5 1NF
  T · 01395 232 432 W · limohireuk.co.uk

PICNIC WITH YOUR OWN FOOTMAN

> The Mandarin Oriental Hyde Park is a dab hand at providing sumptuous picnics. The tradition began when the hotel was still called the Hyde Park Hotel and they arranged picnics for débutantes post-war and until the 1950s. They offer a selection of picnic hampers, each bursting with delicious homemade delicacies to suit every occasion. Menu highlights include poached lobster, chicken and mango croquette, wasabi tuna tempura, and coronation chicken, along with a variety of afternoon tea pastries, summer pudding and carved fruits.

> A hotel footman will carry and arrange the picnic in the park, whether you want to be on the banks of the Serpentine or tucked away in a leafy glade. If you wish to go further afield, order the picnic and a limousine, and relax in chauffeur-driven comfort. If you're having a picnic party and require a butler to serve your champagne, this can also be arranged (at an extra cost). The hotel has even organised a picnic with a horse and carriage, along with cashmere blankets, a silver bucket filled with the most delicate meringues and a bottle of the finest Cognac. They have also prepared sumptuous picnics for surprise engagements, for example, the gentleman who invited his girlfriend to meet him for a quick lunch out of the office on a Friday: She found a car waiting to pick her up and it whisked her to Hyde Park where he was waiting with the picnic laid out and a bottle of champagne. He had also called her boss and secretly organised for her to have the rest of the afternoon off, and he had booked a romantic weekend at the hotel. What a guy! Has he a brother?

> Picnics priced from £70.00 per person (based on two sharing) with champagne optional, and not included in that price. Hampers are available from May to September only and should be booked at least 24 hours in advance.

> **Mandarin Oriental Hyde Park, 66**
  Knightsbridge, London SW1X 7LA
  T · 020 7235 2000
  W · mandarinoriental.com

GRAB A GREAT IDEA

> We went for a great breakfast in Oliver Peyton's restaurant and café Inn the Park and discovered they will pack you a luxury takeaway picnic, including rug and cutlery. You need to book 24 hours in advance and you can choose from their 'Grab and Go' menu selection. St James's Park has some wonderful picnic spots – my favourite is the Duck Island and Lake – and offers deckchairs from April until September. Picnics from Inn the Park are available from April to August.

> **Inn the Park, St James's Park,**
  London SW1A 2BJ
  T · 020 7451 9999 W · innthepark.com

OH, I DO LIKE TO BE BESIDE THE SEASIDE...

> If you're heading off to the beach at Brighton, then book your picnic through the award-winning The Real Eating Company (*see also page* 50). They provide divine goodies either in wicker hampers or hand-held disposable boxes, which are just perfect when sand is involved. The fare ranges from freshly made sandwiches, charcuterie, cheeses, homemade cakes, olives, wine, champagne, beer and organic soft drinks.

> You can order online from the beginning of May through to the middle of September for a minimum £25.00 spend, and they require 48 hours' notice. It's a local service only and you need to collect the hamper, or for a £10.00 charge they will deliver within a 10-mile radius. The wicker hampers incur an extra charge of £20.00 for a large hamper with leather straps (for four people) or £13.00 for a medium hamper (two people). Hampers can be collected from either of their shops – Hove, if you're heading to the beach, or Lewes if you're heading to Glyndebourne.

> **The Real Eating Company, 86/87 Western Road, Hove, East Sussex BN3 1JB**
  T· 01273 221 444

> **or 18 Cliffe High Street, Lewes, East Sussex BN7 2AJ**
  T· 01273 402 650 W· real-eating.co.uk

WHO SAYS ROMANCE DOESN'T COME IN A BOX?

> You can either order your Villandry picnic by phone, fax, e-mail or online, or you can pop in and choose all your own goodies, although be warned, there is such a divine choice you may find yourself buying slightly more than you bargained for. All the food is homemade in the Villandry kitchens by their wonderful bakers and chefs. The picnic feeds two people and the standard version comes in a Villandry box with everything packaged separately, so you don't need plates. All other items that come with the picnic – the napkins, cutlery and glasses – are also disposable. If you want a traditional picnic hamper they can rent you one (price on application).

> They also offer a wonderful three-course Valentine's Hamper, the contents of which you can choose from a menu including grilled tiger-prawn skewers with grilled fennel salad, grilled half-lobster with tarragon mayonnaise and keta, a heart-shaped white-chocolate marquise with crème Anglaise – not to mention the heart-shaped cheeses, bread and table decorations.

> If you want to pre-order your picnic, they require 48 hours' notice and the service is not available on a Sunday. For the first time this year, you can order online, otherwise phone, fax or e-mail your request. Delivery charges are £8.00 in central London and £15.00 outside London for all dry/non-fresh hampers. Fresh hampers (three-course meals you can prepare at home) are only delivered in central London, delivery charge £8.00.

> **Villandry, 170 Great Portland Street, London W1W 5QB**
  T· 020 7631 3131 W· villandry.com

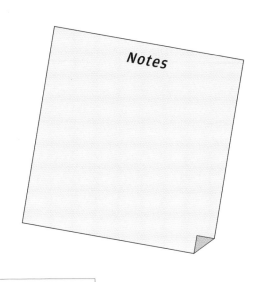

FAMILY

TODDLERS

CELEBRATIONCAKES

PARTYBAGS

USEFULSERVICES   CATS

ADVICE

CHILDRENSPARTYIDEAS

PETSHOPS

PREGNANCYMASSAGE

NINE MONTHS AND COUNTING!

USEFUL PREGNANCY BOOKS & DIRECTORIES

BEYOND THE BIG DAY

> *Birth and Beyond* is the ideal book to take you through pregnancy, birth and parenthood. It's written by Dr Yehudi Gordon, one of the world's leading obstetricians, with the help of a wonderful team of midwives, medical professionals, complementary therapists and parents. Yehudi founded the birth unit at the Hospital of St John and St Elizabeth in London, regarded as the model for integrated care in pregnancy, birth and beyond. My sister had her babies delivered by him, and we sought his advice after suffering our fourth miscarriage. When I needed anything answered during my pregnancy, or after the birth of our son, I found everything in this book. The book recommends integrated holistic healthcare and combines up-to-date medical knowledge with traditional wisdom. Keep it by your bedside for day-to-day practical advice.
> *Birth and Beyond: Pregnancy, birth, your baby and family – the definitive guide*, **Dr Yehudi Gordon (Vermilion) W· randomhouse.co.uk**

THE FAT LADIES CLUB

> This started with five women comparing notes on pregnancy at antenatal classes, then deciding to write them down, truthfully, bluntly and humorously. They self-published the notes as a book which also included their experiences in the first few months. The book sold out and is now published by Penguin.
> *The Fat Ladies Club: The Indispensible 'Real World' Guide to Pregnancy*, **Andrea Bettridge, Hilary Gardener, Sarah Groves, Annette Jones and Lyndsey Lawrence (Penguin) W· penguin.co.uk**

ALWAYS BOOK A GUIDE

> If you're having your first baby, you must buy yourself the *London Baby Guide* or the *UK Baby Guide*. I found them indispensable when sourcing products and services, and for days out and activity groups. They have many great sections, including 1,000 shops and mail order businesses, over 500 suggested books, 1,500 websites, support groups for every kind of issue, details of different birth options, and obstetric intervention statistics. I'm still using mine three years on. Available at most bookshops or online.
> *London Baby Guide* or *UK Baby Guide*, **Kate Calvert (Hardens) W· hardens.com**

THE NEW CONTENTED LITTLE BABY BOOK

> You can either go with Gina Ford's fairly strict regime (one of our postnatal group followed it word for word and her children all sleep from 7 p.m. till 7 a.m.!), or just pick up some little gems. She has also written *From Contented Baby to Confident Child (Problem Solving in the First Three Years)*, which will help you with feeding and sleeping, potty training, tantrums and preparing for nursery.
> *The New Contented Little Baby Book: The Secret to Calm And Confident Parenting* and *From Contented Baby to Confident Child*, **Gina Ford (Vermilion) W· contentedbaby.com**

SECRETS OF THE BABY WHISPERER

> If you've ever had that frustrating feeling that your baby is trying to tell you something important, but you've no idea what it is, turn to Tracy. She's had more than 20 years' experience looking after some 5,000 babies and has successfully taught parents how to 'understand' what their babies are saying. I found this book useful and informative,

but also reassuring. Her opening chapter title says it all really: 'Love the baby you gave birth to'.

> ***Secrets of the Baby Whisperer: How to Calm, Connect and Communicate with Your Baby***, Tracy Hogg and Melinda Blau (Ballantine Books)

THE (DISTRICT) BABY DIRECTORY

> Each district-specific edition of *The Baby Directory* has over 200 pages holding all you need for pregnancy and life with babies and children under five. I bought the London edition back in 2001 (this one has been going for nine years) and I have been delighted with it. They also offer East, Central, South-East, West Midlands, South West, North West and North East England directories.
> Their website offers a useful encyclopaedia of pregnancy and a nanny finder service.

> ***The (District) Baby Directory***
> T · 020 8678 9000 W · babydirectory.com

FASHION

DRESS TO THE NINES FOR THE WHOLE NINE MONTHS

> 9 London opened its doors in 2002 offering one of the best and most exclusive selections of designer maternity-wear and they were also one of the first to customise maternity jeans. Celebrities, in a quest to look their best throughout pregnancy, have loved their stylish range (you can see all the comments online, including Gwen Stefani, Elizabeth Hurley and Kate Winslet's).
> Pick up a fab pair of the hugely popular Citizens of Humanity maternity jeans, Tankinis from Melissa Odabash, stunning clothes from Dalai Mama and their own stylish range – 9 London.
> They also offer a fab service called 9-to-go, which means you don't even have to step outside your door – they bring it all to your home. They'll even do pregnancy parties,

where you get all your pregnant girlfriends together and all shop till you drop – well, not literally! – bliss, especially in those later months. Private appointments are available outside normal shop hours and they will ship worldwide using Fed-Ex for a next-day delivery. They have even customised a wedding dress for a pregnant bride. Fantastic service from Emily Evans, 9 London's owner and lovely customer care.
> And you'll be thrilled to know you can also buy Tiny 9 their collection for newborns to nine-year olds.

> **9 London, 8 Hollywood Road, London SW10 9HY**
> T · 020 7352 7600 W · 9London.co.uk

TAKE A TRIP TO MUMMY HEAVEN

> Blossom is renowned for being a fantastic one-stop shopping haven and a great resource centre for all the needs of expectant mums and dads. They stock maternity apparel from non-maternity designers like Matthew Williamson and Missoni, and have also commissioned designers such as Alice Temperley and Gharani Strok to make clothes exclusively for the shop. They have a fantastic selection of designer jeans, including Seven for all Mankind, True Religion Brand Jeans and Citizens of Humanity.
> They also offer health and beauty products – many organic – exclusive gifts, useful books, and clothes and cuddlies for babies 0-12 months, not to mention the stylish Anya Hindmarch and Storksak Nappy Bags.
> They're also the exclusive UK stockist of the Swiss luxury children's furniture range, Castor & Chouca.
> So drop in, enjoy a soothing herbal tea, and join a long list of celebrity shoppers who have visited. If you can't get to London, don't fret – you can shop at Blossom online.

> **Blossom, 164 Walton Street, Brompton Cross, London SW3 2JL**
> T · 020 7589 7500 / 0845 262 7500
> W · blossommotherandchild.com

NO PERSUASION REQUIRED

> Great name, great shop, great fashion! Push opened in Islington after I had my baby – grrrr – but I still had to go in and have a good look as the window was a magnet. They offer a wonderful personal service and will soon have you kitted out looking fashionable and comfortable, not to mention sexy! Stocking a range of designer maternity wear, including Citizens of Humanity jeans and Juicy Couture, they're also the exclusive stockist of Australian frock queen Leona Edmiston. I wanted to get pregnant again just to wear the lace kaftan from Hommemummy.

> Handy evening appointments are available by arrangement, and they also offer products (Zita West, Active Birth Centre), accessories and loads of great advice. Put it on your 'must visit' list.

> **Push, 9 Theberton Street, Islington, London N1 0QY**
> **T · 020 7359 2003 W · pushmaternity.com**

MATERNITY SHOPPING
ONLINE

W · apeainthepod.com
With over 18 shop categories, from designers, career looks, casual and special occasion, to hosiery and intimates, and a great accessories section including a stunning red and pink patent diaperbag by Cynthia Rowley, this US-based online store proudly lists the host of celebrities who have worn their stylish maternity wear! Luckily for us, they also ship worldwide.

W · bumpessentials.com
This is a fantastic idea – buy one box and get four basic but perfect, black stretch-jersey items. The cami, A-line skirt, top and slim-leg trouser will take you right through your pregnancy – not bad for £90.00.

PREGNANCY WISH LIST

In the earlier months go to **TopShop** and buy everything two sizes bigger than you would normally wear – chances are they will last throughout the pregnancy – and of course they also have a maternity range.

Seven stylish treats to buy, buy and buy:

1 *Wrap dress* – **Diane von Furstenberg T · 020 7221 1120 W · dvflondon.com**

2 *Maternity jeans* – James Jeans, True Religion, Seven for all Mankind **Blossom T · 020 7589 7500**

3 *Suit* – 9 London **T · 020 7352 7600 W · 9London.co.uk**

4 *Juicy Couture tracksuit* – **W · duematernity.com**

5 *Shoes* – semi-bespoke any colour, any heel, any lining, any style. Your ankles with thank you for it. **Selve T · 020 7321 0200 W · selve.co.uk**

6 *Maternity bra* – it's vital that you're fitted properly, but not before your third/fourth month (do not buy an underwire bra) – **Selfridges T · 0870 837 7377** or **M&S T · 0845 302 1234**

7 *Baby bag* – fashionable designs with fantastic removable compartments which means it can be used for laptop or overnight bag as well – **Hennabecca T · 0845 009 7866 W · Hennabecca.co.uk**

W·duematernity.com

Stylish maternity wear, nappy bags, lingerie and beauty products fill these lovely stores in the USA. If you're not planning a trip soon then just log on and shop to your bumps content.

W·figleaves.com

Once you know your new bra size (which may change up to three times, so don't buy too many bras in one go!), you can order from this online lingerie store that stocks trendy maternity and nursing bras , amongst others, Elle Macpherson's Intimates, Emily B Maternity and Blossom Mother & Child. They also have a nice selection of maternity swimwear, briefs and hosiery.

W·isabellaoliver.com

This site was set up by Vanessa and Baukjen, two friends with backgrounds in fashion and marketing, who were frustrated by the lack of stylish and simple maternity clothes. Their collection includes soft jersey fabric pieces that are easy to dress up or down.

They've divided their collection into usefully themed lists: Evenings Out, Wedding Ideas, Work and 4th Trimester Line which is for your pre-bump clothes. Stylish, stylish and stylish.

W·net-a-porter.com

When pregnancy fatigue hits and you can't face a stressful drive to the shops, this has to be the ultimate place to shop to your heart's content. With a host of fab designers (many of their designs fit until the later stages of pregnancy), you will surely have the most fashionable bump in town. All you have to do is wait for the doorbell to ring, then start unwrapping those beautifully wrapped boxes.

HEALTH, ADVICE & SUPPORT

DON'T SUFFER IN SILENCE

> A UK-based charity that provides free telephone and internet support, along with a whole host of useful information. I wish I'd known more about positioning and attachment – very important that you get it right. I didn't and it caused weeks of misery and pain and I almost gave up. However, once it was finally sorted (I went and saw a breastfeeding counsellor) it was brilliant and I absolutely loved breast feeding – I felt it was a great time to bond.
> **The Association of Breast feeding Mothers (ABM) T·08444 122 949 W·abm.me.uk**

WAS THAT ONE PINT OR TWO!

> If you're going back to work and still wish your baby to have your breast milk, or you want your partner to be able to help with the night-time feeding, one breast pump friends and I can highly recommend is the Ameda-Lactaline Personal dual electric breast-pump. (It has also been awarded 'Best Buy' by parenting magazines.)
> I got in a bit of a state when I tried a hand-operated breast pump and failed miserably. Once I'd purchased the Ameda electric pump, I never looked back. Our friend Maria who is now expecting baby number four has used it for every one of her babies – I think she's even called in some spare parts to cope with the overload!! She purchases everything through Amber Medical who offer excellent customer service and advice. They are the exclusive distributor of some of the world's top Mother and Baby care products and along with the Ameda breastpump you can also buy a handy backpack, cooling elements and many accessories. If you don't want to purchase the pump (£85.00), they offer a useful hire service.
> **Amber Medical Limited, Unit 1, Belvedere Trading Estate, Taunton, Somerset TA1 1BA T·01823 336 362 W·ambermed.co.uk**

RELAX UNDER THE GENTLE TOUCH

> Dr Gowri Motha is a fully-qualified medical doctor and obstetrician, and an expert in many complementary therapies. By mixing the best of conventional medicine with the best of the alternative, she created 'The Jeyarani Way' Gentle Birth Method to make expectant mothers 'Birthfit', ultimately working towards a shorter, natural labour. I would recommend this to anyone who has any fears about the whole process or who would just like to approach their pregnancy in an holistic, ayurvedic way.

> I had suffered four miscarriages before hearing about Gowri and luckily my fifth pregnancy went full term. I am sure it was the marvellous help and support of Gowri, as she kept me centred, relaxed and positive, and Bill Smith, Clinical Diagnostic Services, who scanned me right from the start and reassured us throughout the pregnancy that things were going well.

> Gowri and her team of gentle birth practitioners offer one-to-one treatments in reflexology, creative healing, Bowen therapy, Reiki and craniosacral therapy. She has helped many well known mothers to give birth to their precious bundles!

> **Gentle Birth Method, Jeyarani Centre T·020 8530 1146 (All bookings are made through this number)**

> **or Viveka, 27a Queen's Terrace, St Johns Wood, London NW8 6EA T·020 7483 3788**

> **Bill Smith, Head of Ultrasond, Clinical Diagnostic Services T·020 7483 3611**

MAKE SOPHIE YOUR NEW BEST FRIEND

> If you suddenly realise that you've left it too late to enrol at your local antenatal class (which book up months in advance), don't panic check out New Baby Company. This independently-run organisation provides professional, practical and personal advice during and after pregnancy. The lovely Sophie Durlacher set the company up after realising that mums and dads needed help not only in the antenatal but also in the postnatal period, which a lot of parents find is the most nerve-wracking time. Their course is called Birth & Beyond and they also offer first aid and weaning classes.

> Sophie is full of information and her team can help you in all areas of pre- and post-pregnancy. The course includes what they call 'confident care' which is invaluable in those first few days after the birth when you're suddenly responsible for your tiny baby and perhaps feel you don't know how to do the right thing. Start thinking about going to classes around four to five months into your pregnancy, as some people book much later and find they don't have time to complete the course as the baby arrives early!

> Unfortunately, their classes are currently only held in Notting Hill Gate, Wandsworth and Chelsea, but they do offer private one-to-one sessions in your home and can set up the course around what you want to know — this is fab, fab, fab.

> **New Baby Company T·020 7751 1152 W·newbabycompany.com**

THE ULTIMATE FAMILY-PLANNING SOLUTION

> Help move a family from overseas to London, settling in the children with nannies, nurseries and schools; host a meet-a-mum party with wonderful beauty treatments followed by dinner; help a mum and dad 'escape' for a romantic spa weekend; organise Lucy's sixth-birthday party with Mickey Mouse and organise dad's business trip to Paris via helicopter. It sounds like a tough job for a whole team of personal assistants, but actually this was all in a day's work for The Essential Darling Company.

> This parenting company will offer you a dedicated lifestyle management and concierge service, and help you to organise and manage your home and family life, no matter where you are in the world. They offer

over 30 years' experience in midwifery and maternity, and can provide professional and discreet assistance to married, divorced and single parents, looking after all the day-to-day, non-stop running and planning of family life. They can cover medical care, maternity, child- and baby-care, health and beauty, entertainment, children's activity planning, shopping, special events, party planning, and home and domestic. You don't even have to become a member to enjoy their personal and friendly service, as they can offer their services on an *ad hoc* basis for one-off tasks. Alternatively, you can pay a monthly fee for unlimited access.

> **The Essential Darling Company, 35 Hill View Gardens, The Hyde, London NW9 OTE T · 020 7323 9621 W · essentialdarling.com**

SPEED-DIAL CONFIDENCE TRICK

> Vicki has a private practice offering best feeding guidance (breast or bottle), newborn support and advice. Vicki is a registered midwife and NNEB-certificated nursery nurse, and she has also completed the UNICEF Baby-Friendly Breastfeeding Management course. She'll help you with any queries you have about your baby-care routine, visiting you either at home or in hospital, or via a telephone consultation. She's happy to help with any query, and still gets calls from clients who had their baby two years ago.

> **Vicki Scott T · 07960 611 987 E · vickiscott@babyconfidence.co.uk**

THE COMPLETE A–Z OF BABY SUPPORT

> Zita West has an enormous fan base and has helped a lot of happy pregnancies, couples and babies. She has been involved in childbirth for over 20 years as a midwife, acupuncturist, nutritional advisor, author and consultant specialising in fertility and pregnancy. She offers pregnancy programmes, treatments and products, and is one of Europe's leading experts on how couples can

improve their fertility through natural means. Zita can help with male reproductive health, gynaecological problems, preparation and support for IVF, pre-conception care, ante-natal and postnatal, nutrition, breastfeeding and hypno-birthing classes.

> **Zita West T · 020 7224 0017 W · zitawest.com**

MASSAGE

I absolutely swear by massage – it can bring about a lovely sense of relaxation and fix those stiff muscles and various aches and pains. I'm a huge fan of having it done at home as you don't have to get dressed after, go out in the cold or fight your way home in traffic, rather defeating the object of relaxing!

I've used Rebecca Bruce (see page 237) for years now, even during my pregnancy. (My osteopath told me about her, so she came well recommended.) I've included some other massage therapists here as well, as there is nothing worse than wanting a massage and finding the therapist you want is fully booked for the next three weeks. These other therapists are known to me through word of mouth; I've had long chats with them but I've not tried them personally.

LET BEATRICE HELP YOU BOND WITH YOUR BUMP

> Beatrice is recommended by Sophie at the New Baby Company who had yoga sessions with her, as well as massage. Beatrice believes it's essential to connect with your baby and body during the months of pregnancy, and tells me that some of the things she can help you with are lower-back pain, and visualisation and breathing techniques. She's been a massage therapist, specialising in therapeutic massage, for over seven years, and has also done a specialist pregnancy

massage course. She offers one-to-one yoga sessions in your home, which can be very beneficial, but unfortunately she only works in central, NW and west London.

> **Beatrice Palazzo T · 07747 685 190**

SHE'S GOT THE WHOLE WORLD IN HER HANDS

> Leona has travelled the globe to learn the art of massage and incorporates techniques from India, Japan and Australia. She offers many kinds of treatments including remedial, shiatsu, reiki, reflexology, Thai and cranial sacro-therapy, adapting each treatment to the individual. Leona can help you get in touch with yourself physically and emotion-ally, work on your physical aches and pains, or work on your energy levels. With over 10 years' experience, you'll be in great hands. She makes home visits at £50.00 per hour (or you can visit her for £35.00); she's based in north London, but will travel further (extra cost).

> **Leona Stephens-Ofner T · 020 7254 1713 / 07906 265 261**

MASSAGE THOSE NEW-MUM WORRIES AWAY

> 'With all the necessary physical and emotional adjustments during pregnancy and motherhood, massage can bring comfort, support and a wonderful sense of nurturing. It can help to lower blood pressure, improve circulation, and alleviate back pain, headaches and tight muscles, as well as providing you with a much needed peaceful space to allow you to connect with yourself and baby.' Wise words from Erika Tourell and reason enough to go on one of her courses, visit her studio, or invite her to work with you at your home.

> Erika has over 17 years' experience as a massage therapist combining many tech-niques including deep-tissue, acupressure, shiatsu, Swedish, holistic and sports massage, lymph drainage, aromatherapy and, more recently, craniosacral therapy. She's also been teaching hatha yoga for 10 years.

> As a mother of two, Erika has become more involved with working with pregnant women and new mothers, and provides wonderful nurturing support. She also regularly teaches on weekend residential retreats for mothers and babies, and mothers-to-be (for details, check out **W · mamaheaven.org**).

> Erika works at Lambton Place Health Club and Triyoga in Primrose Hill, north London, but will also make home visits to west, north-west and south-west London.

> **Erika Tourell T · 020 7229 8562 / 07720 576 173
E · erikatourell@hotmail.com**

ELECTRIC SCREAM!

One thing we found we missed when we had a baby was going to the movies. A fairly cheap night out got to be rather more expensive once you factored in a babysitter for three to four hours. Thankfully, some cinemas wised up to this and have set up times when you can go along with your baby and watch a movie.

The Electric Cinema in west London is one of these – they offer *Electric Scream!* sessions for parents or carers with babies under one year old. You can sit back and enjoy a full-length feature, jiggling baby on your lap without worry-ing about disturbing others.

It's run every Monday (except bank holidays) at 3.00 p.m. – the only requirement being that you're accom-panied by a baby.

**The Electric Cinema, 191 Portobello Road, London W11 2ED
T · 020 7908 9696**

BABIES, TODDLERS AND TWEENIES

I did a survey amongst all my friends who had had a baby and asked them what was the best gift or help someone had given them after the birth of their children, or, in hindsight, what would have helped them the most. These two replies were my favourites – they just seem to sum it all up.

From Jackie

1. My absolute number-one present was friends arriving with food, feeding me and then leaving (after clearing up)!

2. An air-conditioned car (I really struggled, and so did Alex when he was tiny, in the hot sun in our non-air-conditioned car)

3. My Mum and/or one of my sisters living around the corner instead of 170 miles away

4. Husband to work part-time – but still earn the same money – so that we could both share in the pleasure of the baby's first six months

5. Environmentally friendly disposable nappies – Alex's will still be around in the landfill site in a thousand years time!

6. A housekeeper – just for a couple of hours a day – to clean, wash and iron!

7. A baby seat designed so that they can lie down when they are tiny instead of sit up

8. Annabel Karmel's invaluable *Complete Baby & Toddler Meal Planner* – definitely worth having

9. A digital video camera

10. For your husband to say he still loves you/fancies you when you are looking exhausted, covered in breast milk, vomit and poo!

From Lottie

1. An Anya Hindmarch baby/nappy bag

2. One of those sporty jogging buggies with big wheels to roll over our gravel and for me to run (pant!) behind

3. An XL wrap dress by Gloria von Furstenburg that would expand and shrink with me

4. An Allegra Hicks kaftan to hide the baby fat and swan around in when people came to peek at baby

5. A Trip Trapp baby chair

6. A top-of-the-range Polaroid camera and a fabulous Smythson album to instantly record baby's first hours/days

7. A fabulous hand-held tape recorder to record baby's first gurgles/sounds – we still have the kids on tape somewhere...

8. Amongst all the gorgeous fluffy bunnies, teddies, etc, one of the best pressies I received after Max was born was a mini bottle of Moët and a box of Fortnum & Mason violet crèmes just for me!

BABY BAGS

Having tested many kinds of nappy bags just to find the right one, I feel that the designer ones should be more than just a very expensive bag with a changing mat and some pockets. I think you're better off buying one that has been specifically made for all the paraphernalia you will need to carry around. However, some of you will like functional and some of you will like fashionable, while some are looking for a combination of the two, so I've split my finds into three categories: the functional (and I think the best), the stylish and the designer.

FULLY FUNCTIONAL

GO OUT HAPPY WITH YOUR NAPPY
> I love, love, love the selection at
  W·happybags.co.uk. Not only do they stock

stylish and fab bags from the likes of Storksak, OiOI and Diaper Diva, but they also stock the wonderful Skip-Hop range which clips on to the buggy. And for stylish and active dads buy the Diaper Dude range.

> Something else I just had to buy was the VIP – the Very Intelligent Pocket. With nine pockets of its own, it's an inner pocket which you can insert into whichever bag you choose to go with on any given day (I have over 50), so all your essentials travel with you from bag to bag – inspired. Actually they have a whole heap of fabulous products including the very new baa-baa blinds – a travel blackout blind that fits to all shapes and sizes of windows using suckers to fasten directly onto the glass – a great invention. Start filling that cart now.

> **Happybags, Heath House, Threadneedle Street, Bergh Apton, Norwich, Norfolk NR15 1BJ**
  T·01508 480 249 W·happybags.co.uk

PICK OUT A POCKET OR TWO

> Designed by Rebecca Walker and Helena Sampson, two mums who discovered a gap in the market for a baby bag that offered the flexibility of detachable internal compartments and loads of space, but still looked fashionable and stylish, the Hennabecca gets my vote for one of the most useful baby bags around, with a pocket for absolutely everything. But it isn't only a baby bag – just pull out all the compartments and you have a stylish laptop, in-flight or overnight bag. So versatile it practically pays for itself!

> There are lots of great designs, including the canvas limited edition or the classic leather. Prices start from £85.00, although they sometimes have great sales.

> **Hennabecca T·0845 009 7866**
  W·hennabecca.co.uk

PRACTICAL NEVER LOOKED SO GOOD

> Popular with celebrity mums, Storksak have a great choice of stylish and practical bags. These all-in-one wonders all include thermo-insulated bottle holder, changing mat, key-ring clip and detachable mirror, and individual compartments for nappies, phone and purse which you can pop out to make room for your laptop or other items when your little one is safely potty-trained. I really liked the chocolate 'Gigi'.

> They're all available online, or at Harrods, John Lewis or Selfridges (with more stockists listed online).

> **Storksak T·0207 482 8883**
  W·storksak.co.uk

SUPERB STYLE

PICTURE IT NOW

> Want to stand out at the Mummy and Baby Group? What could be better than having your own baby's photo on your personalised Nappy Be a Bag (£375.00)? It's a canvas bag including changing mat, bottle storage and a nappy compartment, all set for a stylish day out.

> **Anya Hindmarch T·020 7838 9177**
  W·anyahindmarch.com

CAN YOU DIG IT?

> For a lovely selection of Stateside diaper bags (from $195.00), look no further than Kate Spade who currently offers ten designs. Trouble is she offers all sorts of other goodies too so you may end up spending way more than you budgeted.

> **Kate Spade W·katespade.com**

DESIGNER DEALS

EVERYONE LOVES LOUIS

> From their Mini monogrammed range, the Louis Vuitton nappy bag (£925.00) comes in either blue denim or khaki. It has a baby

section with three pockets, a machine-washable, detachable changing mat, and a mum's section that includes a mobile-phone pocket. Go online to find your nearest stockists.

> **Louis Vuitton T · 020 7399 4050**
> **W · louisvuitton.com**

TUNEFUL TIP

> And talking about Nappy Bags ... here's what Amy Allen had to say in her wonderful book *This Little Piggy went to Prada* which is full of nursery rhymes for the Blahnik Brigade. I've bought several copies for my friends – it makes a lovely, fun gift, and every copy bought in the UK will see a donation made to Save the Children. Another little gem from Spy Publishing (*also see page* 118)

> **Spy Publishing**
> **W · thislittlepiggywenttoprada.com**

To be sung to the tune of Frère Jacques ...
Louis Vuitton, Louis Vuitton,
Mulberry, Mulberry?
Nappy bag dilemma – Lulu, Kate or Anya?
Shopping spree, buy all three.

BABY BLANKETS

Even though knitting is cool again (and wonderfully stress-relieving), some of us just can't K2 P2, or indeed don't have the time. One of the most useful things a mum can make or receive as a present is a cot or pram blanket.

YESTERYEAR STYLE FOR FUTURE GENERATIONS

> I wish I'd known about Charlotte when Finn, our son, was born – I certainly would have ordered one of her beautifully designed, handmade, personalised, reversible cot blankets. Made from wool or cotton, with inspiration taken from early American patchwork quilts and Victorian samplers,

these blankets will make great family heirlooms. Allow 28 days for delivery, with prices from £60.00.

> **Charlotte, 11 Heigham Road, Norwich, Norfolk NR2 3AT**
> **T · 01603 627 448**
> **W · charlottecotblankets.com**

LITTLE GIFTS, BIG TEMPTATIONS

> From the founder of the White Company comes The Little White Company, with the most adorable accessories, bedding, furniture and clothes for newborn babes and children. I guarantee that if you visit the shop you'll walk out with a lot more than you went in for. They offer several great baby blankets that will be treasured for years to come: a gingham (blue or pink), super-soft, pure lambswool blanket (£30.00); a satin-edged pram or cot blanket (£12/£15.00); a pure cotton, knitted, patchwork-design blanket in white (£25.00); and my top choice, although more pricey, a pure cashmere, lace-knit baby-shawl (£100.00). You'll be spoilt for choice.

> **Little White Company, 90 Marylebone High Street, London W1U 4QZ**
> **T · 020 7486 7550**
> **or 261 Pavilion Road, London SW1X 0BP**
> **T · 020 7881 0783**
> **Order by phone: 0870 900 9555 or online**
> **W · thewhitecompany.com**

Also see Baby Dior page 280

CHILDREN'S BOOKS

BEDTIME FUN FOR LITTLE LINGUISTS

> My Little Adventure Personalised Children's Books is a great little site where I've ordered several books for my friends' children. Each book can be personalised with the child's name and names of family and friends. They have a good selection of adapted children's

FABULOUS PRESENT

If you need to buy a child a present then you should definitely buy one of these pop-up books for their amazing paper engineering. I'm sure in years to come these books, with their exquisite art by Robert Sabuda, will become collectors' items. Be amazed by colourful, detailed, stunning pop-ups with all manner of treats – spinning wheels, little miniature books, iridescent pieces, 3D glasses for viewing the Emerald City – no, I mustn't spoil *all* the surprises! Two titles currently available from Simon & Schuster are *Alice's Adventures in Wonderland* and *The Wonderful Wizard of Oz*. Both priced at £19.99. My son is whisked into their worlds and transfixed every time we open one.

books, including *The Lion Cub and Me* which is a hot favourite.
> **My Little Adventure, P.O.Box 674, Camberley, Surrey GU17 0BW**
T·01252 409 383
W·mylittleadventure.co.uk

LASHINGS OF VINTAGE ENID BLYTON
> Pedlars is a small family business that prides itself on choosing products with real love and care. They hold an ever-changing stock of collectable children's books, with beautiful old covers, in very good condition. You could give the gift of an Enid Blyton book you loved as a child, or you may like to look through their other categories, as they have some little gems. I couldn't resist the really great word game called Snatch, not to

mention the Giant Pirate Diamond which is fantastic for a themed party. Their customer service has won them the Orange 'Small is Beautiful' Award.
> **Pedlars T·01330 850 400**
W·pedlars.co.uk

PUT YOUR LITTLE PERSON ON THE PAGE
> Penwizard's little personalised books are cute – although the choice of titles is limited. The website allows you to change the appearance of the main character (hair, skin and clothes) so it will look more like your own child, and you can also add personal friends', pets' and siblings' names. The sheer delight you see on your child's face when all his family and friends' names are read is priceless. Would also make a nice gift for a friend or grandchild. Prices start from £13.99.
> **Penwizard W·penwizard.co.uk**

CAKES

For further cakes see pages 55-56 and 251-255

BE A BASKET CASE
> This mail-order company delivers the finest American baked goods in gift baskets or tins – the new baby and Christmas selections are fantastic.
> I love that they're all made without artificial flavourings or preservatives, using fresh fruit juices, organic flour, Belgian chocolate and free-range eggs, and all recipes are unique and exclusive to the Bakery. They also bake six days a week. so you'll definitely be eating the freshest tasting goodies on your block! My friend received a lovely basket full of baked delights when she had her first child and she said it was one of the best presents she received.
> **Beverly Hills Bakery T·020 7586 0070**
W·beverlyhillsbakery.com

KOSHER CAKES

> We had to include this company because they use all natural ingredients and a friend of ours was delighted that there was someone that offered kosher ingredients. Established for over 15 years and one of the leading suppliers of kosher home-made patisserie, The Cake Company offer a free design service and can scan any picture or photo onto your cake −ideal for birthdays or anniversaries.

> **The Cake Company, 2 Sentinel Square, London NW4 2EL**
> **T · 020 8202 2327**
> **W · thecakecompany.co.uk**

LOVE YOUR CAKE AND EAT IT

> If you want to shop online and have your cake delivered anywhere in south-east England, The Cake Store has hundreds of novelty cakes to choose from. Frankly, I can't wait for my son's next birthday party so I can order one of these fabulous works of art. Look at the children's category and you'll find it pretty tough to narrow it down to one of their huge selection. They would like three days' notice to make the cake (but can do it quicker in an emergency), and you also have a choice of fillings, along with choosing the colour of your inscription/icing. They've already won 32 gold and silver medals at international exhibitions, an impressive accolade indeed.

> **The Cake Store, 111 Sydenham Road, London SE26 5EZ**
> **T · 0800 052 0058 or 020 8778 4705**
> **W · thecakestore.com**

LET THEM EAT CAKE!

> Treacle is a lovely shop in Columbia Road, right in amongst the famous Columbia Road Flower Market, selling gorgeous little cupcakes. Unfortunately, they're only open on Saturday from 11.30 a.m.-5.30 p.m. and Sunday from 9.00 a.m.-3.00 p.m., however you can order from them and pick up anytime or have them deliver. The minimum order is 48 mini cakes for £28.00. Try to get to the shop if you can, as they also have wonderful retro and vintage china for sale, as well as other baking-related treasures. My son Finn spends ages choosing which coloured cake he wants to eat. We usually end up buying more than one and having a nice cuppa to wash them all down.

> **Treacle, 110-112 Columbia Road, London E2 7RG**
> **T · 020 7729 5657 W · treacleworld.com**

CHRISTENING / NEWBORN PRESENTS

If you're stuck for ideas to give new parents, or you have to buy a christening present and need a little inspiration, get Googling. You'll get 67,600,000 hits when you enter baby 'gifts' and will be overwhelmed with choices − some of them not so good! Some that I have listed here I have used myself, the others came from many hours of looking at some of those 67,600,000 hits. When I came across a shop in the USA selling a Harley Davidson rocking motorcycle, I knew I had seen it all. Happy shopping!

UNUSUALLY USEFUL PRESENTS

> After having a child of her own and realising the need to be able to send lovely gifts, Simran Foote set up Baby Celebrate. She searches far and wide to source the items on her site which are in many cases not available in the high street. I particularly liked the useful and often unique combination gift sets, One gift I loved was the Baby Play Basket, a lined willow basket with toys specifically designed to stimulate and develop a whole range of skills in baby's

first year. I was also impressed by the Baby On The Go gift, which includes a fab Samsonite baby-changing rucksack, a pram blanket, four spoons in travel case, a feeding bowl, bibs, white muslins and a 'Baby on Board' car sign – all really useful stuff. You can, of course, also buy individual baby gifts.

> **Baby Celebrate T· 01477 571 158
> W· babycelebrate.co.uk**

BYE BYE EEYORE, HELLO DIOR

> If you love your designers, then pop down to Baby Dior where you can buy a pacifier in silver, blue or pink with Dior across the mouthpiece (they come in a cute case), or one of their Dior baby bottles (from £20.00). They have a few select pieces of jewellery that would make perfect christening presents. I fell in love with a very delicate gold chain with a minute diamond in the middle, although I actually wanted to wear it myself! In the end I purchased a very cute soft toy rattle as a gift and they packaged it in a lovely box with ribbon. Had my son still been a baby, I definitely would have bought one of the lovely Dior blankets. There are goodies for girls and boys, from newborn up to 12 years, and although it's quite a small selection we're talking quality, quality, quality.

> **Baby Dior: 6 Harriet Street,
> London SW1X 9JW
> T· 020 7823 2039 W· Dior.com**

BOXING UP BABY

> Featured on ITV's list of top ten baby gifts, The Baby Gift Box specialise in stylish, high-quality gifts for the newborn, christenings, baby showers and pregnancy. They have great combinations of gift sets and although some of you may think they're slightly pricey, you could club together at work or with friends to buy something special. The Proud New Parents box is fab, with soft fleece blanket, T-shirt, lullaby CD, soft-toy rattle,

a copy of *Junior* magazine, a disposable camera, a baby-on-board sign and 52 tips for new parents (illustrated cards), all presented in a luxury handmade gift box tied with polka-dot ribbon (£90.00). They have shipped presents as far afield as Brazil and Vietnam, and to many a celebrity (although their lips are sealed on who). If you can't find the perfect gift amongst their selection, they're more than happy to create your own special gift box.

> **The Baby Gift Box Co. London
> T· 020 8767 3004 W· babygiftbox.co.uk**

CUTER BY THE DOZEN

> They may look like the most beautiful bunch of flowers you've ever received, but on closer inspection you'll find that they're actually all practical gifts for a new baby simply presented as a stunning bouquet (you need to see the lovely photos on their website to really get the idea). They're delivered in a classic presentation box and can be sent to the home or maternity ward. The Bouncing Baby Bouquet (£37.00) is made up of a soft organic sleepsuit, the very handy muslin square, a bib, a face cloth, luxury soap and five pairs of cotton socks. This gift is available in sizes 0-3, 3-6 and 6-12 months. They also offer 'bouquets' for house warming, get well and other occasions.

> **bouquet bouquet T· 01489 790 562
> W· bouquetbouquet.co.uk**

SOFT AS A BABY'S... FIRST SWEATER

> Every baby should have at least one gorgeous cashmere item, whether it is cashmere clothes, cot blanket or a cuddly teddy. Mum will be especially delighted if you give her newborn a gift from Brora, who for a small charge will deliver their gorgeous goodies in their own handmade gift box tied with lovely ribbon.

> **Brora T· 020 7736 9944 W· brora.co.uk**

A PLACE FOR EVERYONE

> I saw Little Folk at the Country Living Magazine Christmas Fair (*see page* 186) and was really taken with their personalised keepsake gifts decorated with characters that children adore, ranging from fairies and pirates to animals. They had placemats in various designs, including well-known nursery rhymes like *Incey Wincey Spider* and favourite children's songs like *How Much is that Doggy in the Window*... which you can personalise with the child's name – they looked really smart. You could also add to the placemat (or buy individually) bone china cups, and coasters. The rest of their range includes initial pictures, T-shirts, bags, quilts, clocks and patchwork cushions. They would all make lovely christening or newborn gifts that you can also personalise with a message or birth details.

> **Little Folk, The Studio, 43 Landcroft Lane, Sutton Bonington, Loughborough LE12 5RE T·01509 670 335 W·littlefolk.co.uk**

SOFT AS A BABY'S MUM!

> Lucky Me offers a lovely selection of children's wear which includes wool or cashmere co-ordinated knitwear, blankets, sheepskin slippers and booties for babies and children up to four years old. Most of the knitwear is hand-knitted in Scotland and would make a gorgeous present to give a new baby. They also offer the cuddliest jellycat soft toys including Teddy Bear, Peter Penguin, Sammy Seal and Westie Dog. What I love is that, for an additional charge, they will wrap the gift in their beautiful packaging – a white box with soft blue writing on the lid that says 'Lucky Me', lots of soft white tissue and gorgeous ribbon. I'm actually hankering after the cashmere scarf for myself! Overseas shipping is available for £10.00.

> **Lucky Me T·020 7738 8555 W·luckymeuk.com**

MAKING BIRTH INTO ART

> Treat a baby you love to a wonderful hand-painted watercolour, personalised name picture in one of three different designs, or beautiful hand-painted initials. Annie also offers Nursery Corner Pictures with either a doll's house or train station, with the design personalised with baby's name, weight, birth date and birthplace. Even the time of the birth is shown on the clock, and you can also add your own personal message. Annie puts a lot of care and love into all her work and she has just launched a new range of gift-wrap and stationery.

> **Annie Haak Designs, 72 Weycombe Road, Haslemere, Surrey GU27 1EQ T·01428 641 006 W·anniehaak.co.uk**

THE FUN DOESN'T STOP AT CONCEPTION

> Besides a good selection of maternity, baby and children's wear, I love the gorgeous presents you can buy from La Conception to send to all your preggy girlfriends. The Congratulations On Your Pregnancy gift box is filled with heavenly goodies, such as a lavender-filled satin eye-mask, long (non-rising) vests, velvet neck pillow, and a vintage belt (or it can be personalised to your requirement) all presented in a lovely fabric box (£110.00). Also on offer are traditional gifts such as blankets, christening cups and a silver eggcup and spoon.

> **La Conception, 46 Webbs Road, London SW11 6SF T·020 7228 7498 W·laconception.co.uk**

FAMILY MEMORIES ARE MADE LIKE THIS

> Ruth makes adorable little personalised books with illustrations in watercolour or inks or a mixture of collage – from tiny, tiny accordion books like the one that folds out and says 'congratulations' with your personalised message added, to little A6-size books like the one-to-10 counting books with lovely pictures and a personalised message

to the child. She also makes unique framed family trees using handmade stamps, print and collage which are just lovely. In fact she can personalise and hand make just about anything! Accordion books from £25.00.

> **Ruth Martin T · 020 8692 7952**
  W · anythingbuttheruth.co.uk
  E · ruth.martin60@ntlworld.com

WHO KNEW CAKE COULD GET ANY BETTER?

> My friend Barb in the USA makes these for her friends – they're stunning and I wondered how long they would take to reach our shores. Well, thanks to a family-run business, The Nappy Cake Company, they have arrived. For a new mum and dad or for a baby shower, you can't go wrong with one of these fabulous gifts.

> The 'nappy cakes' are designed to look like a real tiered cake, but are actually made from disposable nappies and then decorated with useful items such as: bottles, manicure sets, blankets, champagne, muslin squares, hair brush, bibs, bodysuits, rattle, washcloths, teddy, scratch mitts and soft toys. The largest stands three-feet tall. Choose from the standard, themed or luxury ranges or you can tailor make any of the nappy cakes to suit your taste or budget, and you can add in additional organic baby and new-mum toiletries.

> They also offer a baby shower package which includes the nappy cake along with a party pack to get your party off to a blooming start. Can ship internationally – prices on application.

> **Samantha Terry, The Nappy Cake Company**
  T · 01277 365 922 / 0780 300 1535
  W · thenappycakeco.co.uk

A TIMELESS TOUCH OF CLASS

> This is a lovely gift idea for a newborn or christening present. I saw James from The Print Rescuer at one of the many fairs

I attend. His enchanting framed prints have been rescued from old classic children's books (which were beyond repair) and then restored. Some even have a little watercolour added to highlight the wonderful illustrations – and of course I just had to buy one!

> They sell their pictures at many fairs such as House & Garden – Olympia, Country Living Magazine Shows – Islington, and the Hampton Court Flower Show. They do not sell the prints through their website, but if you're very specific about what picture you may want, they do offer a mail-order service. So if you love the illustrations from the likes of Winnie The Pooh, Babar or Beatrix Potter, get in touch and they'll see what they can find for you.
Prices: framed prints from £18.00 to £60.00 for a first edition.

> **The Print Rescuer, Holly Cottage, Bourton, Dorset SP8 5BJ**
  T · 01747 840 032 W · theprintrescuer.co.uk

ONE VISIT MAY NOT BE ENOUGH

> Really lovely fine bone china christening mugs, bowls, money boxes, keepsake boxes, egg cups and cutlery. I love the two-handled bone china cups for easy grasp with their delightful illustrations, and the fact that for only a small charge they will personalise some of the nursery gifts. These beautiful pieces are designed and manufactured in Stoke on Trent, England by Gillian Naylor and Mark Faulkner of the award winning Repeat Repeat Design Company.

> **Repeat Repeat T · 01782 845 870**
  W · enfantcollection.co.uk

ADD A LITTLE GLAMOUR TO BABY'S BREAKFAST AT TIFFANY'S

> I don't know anyone who doesn't get excited when presented with the iconic blue Tiffany box. They make lovely newborn and christening presents, including silver spoons, porcelain plates, baby cups, teething rattles and silver

JUST A THOUGHT...

I passed my lovely rose-gold christening charm bracelet on to my goddaughter as an antique gift. If you have something like that which you can pass on with your love, it will certainly make for a unique gift.

Another time I went to the supermarket and did a week's worth of shopping, filling the bags with quick and easy things to cook, newborn-sized nappies, latest magazines, loads of fresh fruit and comfort food snacks. I then delivered the whole lot to my friend just after she had had her baby. Not to blow one's own trumpet, she said it was one of the best presents she received. If you don't live close enough to do the same, why not send your friend a week's worth of pre-cooked meals, which she will only need to heat up.

Model Catering (*page* 284) and Feed Me, Feed My Baby (*page* 284) both offer this wonderful service.

frames. My top choice would be the Elsa Peretti baby brush, guaranteed to top any new mum's list of favourite presents received.
> **Tiffany & Co W · tiffany.com**
> **London – 25 Old Bond Street, London W1S 4QB and 145 Sloane Street, London SW1X 9AY T · 020 7499 4577**
> **New York – Fifth Avenue at 57th Street, New York, NY 10022 0800 2000 1122 / +1 212 755 8000**
> **Check their website for stores in other countries**

SOMETHING OLD, SOMETHING NEW
> Caroline Zoob uses antique fabrics to make gorgeous, gorgeous things, which I try not to drool over! Beautiful embroidered pictures, divine-smelling embroidered lavender cushions, and handmade quilts. They would make a wonderful welcoming gift for a baby or just a reward for your own hard work – *see page* 194 for further details.

Why not present the doting new parents with a voucher for a photography session? It might not be top of the frazzled pair's 'to do' list, but there is nothing like having professional photos of your newborn. Here are two fantastic photographers who can come to your home or go on location:

PUT YOUR FAVOURITE NEWBORN IN THE FRAME
> I saw Esther at the Designer Wedding Show – she does wonderful wedding photographs – and by chance she had also brought her baby portfolio. They were fantastic! All portrait work is non-studio based and she will travel anywhere to shoot. The photographic session starts at £100.00 (depending on location), then photographs are extra. She can print them onto canvas, make a lovely bespoke album, or you can have them framed.
> **Esther Ling T · 01379 652 111 W · estherling.co.uk**

STRIKE A POSE
> The only real problem with babies as far as I can see, is that they grow up far too quickly. Despite the best of intentions, it can be hard to get organised and capture their true newborn beauty on film, to have as permanent keepsake and to share with all those distant but excited relatives.
> That's why it's best to call in the professionals. Stephen Swain (an award-winning wedding photographer, *see page* 60) shoots on location or in his clients' homes to create stunning family and baby portraits.

> Because he is set up to shoot on film or digitally, parents can buy the images as hand-printed pictures or high-res files, which he can print on canvas or paper. Stephen can also supply his portraits on CD or as a DVD set to music, or even make them available online for friends and family anywhere in the world to look at and order. An unforgettable (and time-saving) gift for any new parent.

> **Tiny People, Stephen Swain**
T·020 8371 8726 W·tinypeople.co.uk

THEY'VE GOT *BOTTLES* – BRING FOOD!

A RECIPE FOR HAPPINESS AND HEALTH

> Professional chef and Food/Training consultant Kathryn Heather, came up with the fab idea of sharing her knowledge and experience by offering an innovative, in-home catering service for busy families. She offers organic pre- and postnatal catering to parents who want to know that they and their children or new babies are having healthy, balanced meals and receiving the best possible nourishment. Meals can be cooked in your own home (or delivered), and Kathryn will prepare a week or one month's supply of delicious, organic, additive-free meals. She can also prepare baby food (from six months), and cater for naming or christening ceremonies or your next dinner party. Minimum booking of six hours. Book in advance as Kathryn leads a very busy life jiggling jobs, courses and cooking.

> **Feed Me, Feed My Baby T·07930 327 263 / 020 7511 1627**
W·feedmefeedmybaby.co.uk

TEMPT YOUR TODDLER WITH A LITTLE MASH BANG WALLOP

> The wonderful Angus and Shoo Oliphant produce proper, organic, home-made food for children over a year old. They use the best ingredients they can get their hands on, with no preservatives or artificial anythings, no colourings, GMOs or sweeteners. With more than 10 yummy meal choices, including the wonderfully-named Mash Bang Wallop, Treasure Island Chicken, Chilli Yum Yum and Jolly Spag Bolly, you'll soon have your kids begging for 'more please'. You can buy the frozen meals from various shops throughout the UK (see stockists online) or have it delivered either by **W·foodferry.com** in London (parts of) or nationwide by **W·olimia.com**. They even have a multi-buy box to save you from having to choose!

> Thankfully some restaurants have realised the benefit of serving the best stuff and are offering Miniscoff meals on their menus (refer online). I love their fun-to-read and very witty website. Have I mentioned they've won lots of awards? Bet you're not surprised.

> **Miniscoff T·01225 783 221**
W·miniscoff.co.uk

BOOK A WORRY-FREE WEEK OF WONDERFUL FOOD

> You can see their main entry on page 27, but I wanted to remind you here about Sophie's wonderful new service of Deli Delivery. This is a great present for a new mum and dad, as Model Catering will deliver seven days' worth of frozen meals – all mum needs to do is thaw and cook them. All dietary requirements are catered for, so phone for the menu that includes – amongst other tempting dishes – coq au vin, moroccan lamb tagine, beef carbonade, shepherd's pie, and cumberland sausages, mash and onion gravy. They also have wonderful desserts, vegetable dishes and baby foods from four months to toddlers. Delivery nationwide.

> **Sophie Gray, Model Catering**
T·020 8964 1712 W·modelcatering.com

WOW YOUR WAY THROUGH WEANING

> Besides distributing the marvellous Miniscoff meals, Olimia also offer nationwide delivery of their own award-winning Truuuly Scrumptious range of ready-made pots of frozen organic baby food (for 4 months +), which are delicious.

> **Olimia T·01737 223 355 W·olimia.com**

LABELS

MAKE IT A CASH PURCHASE

> If you like to get out your needle and thread, you can't go wrong with Cash's name tapes which have been sewn onto garments since the 1870s. They offer woven nametapes and designer labels, and printed iron-on nametapes and shoe/identity labels. You can choose the colour of the ribbon and the colour and font of the text. They also do a really useful personalised luggage strap that locks around your suitcase so you can easily spot your bag on the airport carousel — I've had many people ask me where I got mine.

> **Cash's T·02476 466 466 W·jjcash.co.uk**

BE FIRST TO THE TAPE

> When I used gblabels for their great, custom-ised occasion ribbon (**W·gblabels.co.uk**; *see page* 210), the lovely Peter sent it to me within two days, which was quite amazing (do usually allow up to seven days). On their other website they offer two-line, woven name tapes which can include your email address or phone number — very useful and can be dispatched within 24 hours. Naturally, they also offer the iron-on labels. Lovely, efficient, friendly service.

> **GB Nametapes T·01646 600 664 W·gbnametapes.co.uk**

I'LL NAME IT IN ONE

> Since I ordered some of these little clothes and stick-on labels a few years ago, the makers have expanded and do all sorts of funky stick-on labels, dot labels, bag tags, shoe labels, personalised note pads, wrist-bands and invitations. The iron-on labels are great. It takes a couple of seconds and puts an end to lost property forever. My son loves his labels with a little icon (over 50 to choose from). The stick-on vinyl labels for things like bottles and cups are waterproof, dishwasher and microwave safe and UV resistant. Great when you're out to lunch with a group of mums and babies and you all have the same blue drinking cup. (Why is that?!) Allow two to three weeks for delivery. Confession — I'm very tempted to order some for myself!

> **Stuck on You T·0845 456 0014 W·stuckonyou.biz**

NANNIES
AT
NIGHT TIME

FULFIL YOUR NIGHT-TIME FANTASY

> Yes, for most parents of newborns, that fantasy will be sleep. What a welcome service — a nanny agency that specialises in full overnight care for newborn babies and children. They will provide a fully-vetted night nanny from 9.00 p.m. until 7.00 a.m. (other hours available) to look after your child through the night while you catch up on that much-needed sleep (or have a great night out!). They can do night feeds, change nappies, settle the child, prepare and sterilise bottles, give help and advice, and help sort out any particular problem. One couple had rocked their child to sleep for three hours every night for a whole year; they hadn't been out as a couple in all that time, and now the baby couldn't get to sleep without being rocked. Anastasia sent round one of her super nannies who fixed the problem within two nights!

Prices: from £60.00 a night plus a 3 monthly registration fee of £150.00 (+ VAT). They have many regional offices nationwide, so if you are outside London look on their website for the number of your nearest office.
> **Night Nannies T · 020 7731 6168**
W · nightnannies.com

CHILDREN'S PARTIES

Party cakes, see pages 251-255 and 278

PARTY GOODS, PRESSIES AND PRIZES

WHY SETTLE FOR LESS THAN AMAZING?
> Looking for inspiration, go to the Amazingmoms site and click on 'parties'. You'll discover over 150 birthday-party themes, each listing ideas for activities and games and links to party suppliers who stock party-ware in relation to that theme. I couldn't check all the sites they recommended under the themes (as much as I wanted to), so some may not deliver outside the USA, but one that certainly does is W · celebrateexpress.com — one of the best party sites I've seen. They have party-ware in over 135 themes, with 50 exclusive to them. Allow 15 days for international shipping.
> **W · amazingmoms.com**

THINK BIG THIS BIRTHDAY
> You may not think they will go with your all-white interior design, but your child will be so chuffed if you get a Bannerama personalised banner for his/her party. You can personalise the name, age, colour and wording, and even add your own photo, or for a little bit extra you can commission a one-off design. The party banners range from 3 ft to 10 ft long, with prices starting from £19.95.
> **Bannerama T · 01473 210 269**
W · personalisedbanners.co.uk

CLICK ON CHARLIE IF YOU'RE FEELING FANCY
> If you couldn't sew a straight hem if your life depended on it, help is at hand. From a simple fireman's helmet, to costumes with a mythical, historical or Christmas theme, Charlie Crow has one of the best selections I've seen of quick and easy fancy-dress costumes (for ages 18 months to 11 years). They also stock jokes, make-up, magic tricks and accessories.
> **Charlie Crow T · 01782 417 133**
W · charliecrow.com

GAME FOR ANYTHING
> Cool Parties offer an array of party equipment and goodies. Anyone who has young children knows that sometimes they haven't quite learnt the art of sharing, so a great way to prevent party tantrums is to hire a large selection of fun games and equipment. Cool Parties rent out trikes, soft play packages, bouncy castles and slides, and fun games.
> You can also hire colourful tables and chairs, bubble machines and karaoke machines. We loved their inflatable disco dome with mini hi-fi music and lights, and their Spiderman inflatable castle. They can also help you with the food, entertainment, venue and general organisation of your child's special day.
> **Cool Parties T · 0844 450 0045**
W · cool-parties.co.uk

DO PICK YOUR NOSE!
> Some fun party products from the Fred party range from Cubic Products: Your children will love being told that for one time only they are allowed to pick their nose at the table. Pick Your Nose paper cups come with a photo-realistic nose. When you tip your head to take a drink — voilà! — you get an instant nose job. There are 24 cups in a pack (12 oz cups), with an equal number of male and female noses (£6.95). Another excellent product is their novelty ice cubes collection:

The Cool Jazz 'cubes' are miniature frozen guitars with the neck of the guitar making a useful twizzle stick. I also love the Cool Jewels – three-dimensional, diamond-shaped ice cubes (£6.95) – fill with water or any kind of juice and freeze. Bling it on!

> **Cubic Products, Kenbury Works, Kenbury Street, London SE5 9BS**
> **T·020 7095 9399 W·cubicuk.com**

EARN HUGE MUM CRED!

> Kids love the excitement of receiving a badge with their own picture and name on, and Russell at Digital Expression can make up party badges with whatever picture or words you want. Email him the pictures and/or text and you'll receive the 55-mm badges within three working days. The only guests they're not suitable for are those under three years of age, due to the non-safety pin type. These great badges cost £15.00 for ten plus a set-up charge, with a discount for larger numbers. And seeing as you've already got those photos sorted out, Russell can also put the child's photo on a ruler (£3.50 each) for the party bag. (He's currently the only one in the UK to offer this service.)

> **Russell Turner, Digital Expression, 21 Jasmine Avenue Chapel Park, Newcastle Upon Tyne NE5 1TL**
> **T·0191 264 3207 W·poshbadges.co.uk**

LITTLE PEOPLE NEED BIG IDEAS

> I love this site for their fantastic collection of themed party supplies. There are endless ideas for how to theme your little one's next do, and each theme comes with a wide range of products, including invitations, tableware, balloons, party bags and gifts.

> You can also buy party games, music and party books. I ordered all the supplies for my son's fourth birthday party from here and I received the order within two days.

> **Great Little Parties T·01908 266 080**
> **W·greatlittleparties.co.uk**

CARE FOR A LITTLE CADILLAC CUISINE?

> Forget the paper plates; serve up your party food in fire engines (which include box, scoop, napkin and cup), pick-up trucks, jungle jeeps, or even pink Cadillacs. Kids absolutely love this great selection of party boxes and themed tableware, and as they all receive individual portions, you can be sure they are given the healthy bits along with the not-so-healthy bits – although making them eat the healthy bits is another story... You could, of course, make it into a game, whereby the first child to eat up all their party food will be allowed to have first dip into the party sack full of prizes, which, of course, you have purchased for incredible value online. We went for the animal cubes, zoo magnets, tomato splat ball, finger football, bath sponge and the jungle bubbles. They also have a colourful selection of piñatas which make for a fun game. You may even be tempted to buy the animal-print notebooks! They offer quick delivery and good customer service and, if you order in time, they also offer personalised Christmas presents.

> **Party Pieces T·01635 201 844**
> **W·partypieces.co.uk**

ARE YOU A STAR BAG LADY?

> You may have already heard about the wonderful shop Semmalina, run by sisters Emma Forbes and Sarah Standing (*see page 294*). They now offer bespoke, handmade, party bags, wrapped in decorated cellophane and coloured ribbon and stuffed with unusual, age-appropriate, party-themed gifts and sweets. They supply them not only for children's parties, but also for weddings, bar- and batmitzvahs, hen nights, twenty-firsts and Valentine's. Their Star Bags were given to all the guests at a pre-wedding party for a very well known singer. They'll source whatever items you fancy, and you can spend as little or as much as you want. The wrapping, sweets, ribbon and cellophane cost

£2.00 per bag, then you choose your contents — either by phone, email or a personal consultation at the shop. They would like a week's notice, but for orders of less than 30 bags they can create them for you in 48 hours. Who wants an Oscar bag?

> **Semmalina, 225 Ebury Street, London SW1W 8UT**
> **T· 020 7730 9333 W· starbags.info**

These online stores have great party-bag fillers, prizes and accessories:

W· favouritz.com T· +41 79 682 0608
A lovely site from Switzerland that offers Party in A Box filled with everything you need to host a themed party for eight or twelve children. The wooden boxes include outfits, invitations, decoration, games and even a shopping list for the themed food — plus photos to guide you through the day. 6 themes to choose from: Hawaii, princess, pirate, wild animal, cowboy and indian.

W· hawkin.com T· 0870 429 4000 We had great fun with the game of Tipsy Topple and the mini table tennis kit — the kids loved it. Really good party-bag fillers and prizes.

W· partybox.co.uk T· 01483 486 000 Good selection of inflatables and decorations along with all the usual themes, tableware and party essentials.

W· partydelights.co.uk T· 0161 776 1133
Great selection of party-ware and little party-bag gifts including nice stationery and colouring books. They also have a good selection of piñatas

W· partytreasures.co.uk T· 01324 495 292
Wide selection of themed party goods; plain-coloured food boxes which you can have great fun decorating; party favours and piñatas.

PARTY IDEAS

Some of us stress big time when it comes to organising children's parties. If you're having trouble coming up with an idea that hasn't been done before (or at least recently!) in your neck of the woods, here are a few suggestions that you may find helpful...

BABY YOU CAN DRIVE THEIR CAR

> Haven't been able to test this one out yet as our son, Finn, is only five, but I think this is a fantastic idea for your child's party. Children 6-13 years can drive real mini cars (max speed 10 mph) and navigate a course, which includes bends, traffic lights and road signs. In a fun way, they learn all about road awareness skills, rules of the road, hazards on the road and being considerate to other road users including pedestrians.

> You'll have them driving in no time, sitting their test and even earning their driver's licence. Younger children can be passengers or can drive with the help of a carer or Jumicar staff member, and for the eco-friendly, all engines are powered by environmentally friendly engines. Some of the franchises can even come to you and set up everything at your home or party venue (phone for details).

> **Jumicar – Branches in Bristol (01454 250 219), Dorset (07940 931 531) and Nottinghamshire (0115 966 9000) W· ukjumicar.co.uk**

PARTY FEVER FOR YOUR LITTLE DIVA

> If you're fed up with your barely-out-of-nappies fashionista making a grab for your favourite lipstick, it's time to book Mini Makeovers to come over and run a fun and funky beauty party (for ages 5-15 years). All the make-up they use is hypo-allergenic and age-appropriate, and depending on the age of the girls they can offer a huge selection of nail colours, sparkly make-up, glittery lipstick,

fab hair styling, temporary tattoos, face jewels, hair accessories, pop magazines and disco lights. The girls can even learn the latest dance routines, take home a mounted photo, or hire the services of a limousine. Great fun is guaranteed to be had by all. They will travel within approximately 60 miles of London. The average cost is £150.00, with no limit to the number of girls at the party.

> Mini Makeovers T·020 8398 0107
  W·minimakeovers.com

NO MESS, MUCH MERRIMENT

> Complete bliss for party-phobic parents: you provide the children and they can provide the rest – entertainment, invitations, party bags, sit-down party tea, special Party Bus birthday cake and prizes for all. They park the Party Bus outside your home (or anywhere you want) and the kids pile on for a fun-filled party. The party and activity area is filled with play equipment, music and karaoke and colourful party lights.

> They can play traditional party games, be entertained by each other's karaoke singing, dance to the disco, and eat and drink till they burst. Just think, you won't even have to wash any dishes or vacuum up squashed sandwiches and crisps.

> For children of all ages (up to 14 years), with a maximum of 14-20 children (depending on age). Prices start from £185.00. Party Bus covers south-east London into North Kent and Surrey. They're also members of the National Playbus Association.

> Party Bus, 1 Ascot Road, Orpington, Kent BR5 2JE
  T·01689 858 664 W·kidspartybus.com

PUTTING THE SPECIAL IN HOLLYWOOD FX

> For my son's next birthday, I'm booking Gilly and her team to come and do one of her Hollywood Special FX parties (ages five and up). She starts by doing a demonstration (usually on the birthday boy/girl) using loads of different materials and creating realistic blood, cuts, scars, bruises and other special effects. Then it's the kids' turn – they all get their own little packs to create the effects on each other using wax, gelatine, and other techniques. It's a great idea for a party – boys especially love it. Gilly is a professional hair and make-up artist and has worked on *Bridget Jones – Edge of Reason*, *Alfie* and *Strictly Come Dancing*. From £200.00.

> Gilly Popham T·020 8579 0368 or 07961 428 188 E·hi@gillypopham.com

COVER YOURSELF IN PARENTAL GLORY

> With the same set of children (and therefore parents) going to the same 10-15 birthday parties a year, coming up with a new and unusual theme can be more than a little challenging. Most kids love fancy dress, but if you want your child's party to stand out from the crowd, why not give each child a fantastic memory to take home with them?

> Melanie is a freelance make up artist and photographer, and she and her team will come to your home or venue, give each child an amazing makeover and then take loads of individual and group shots. Back at her studio she'll make individual magazine front covers such as *Vogue Parties* or *Pirate Times*. Your birthday girl or boy and his or her friends will adore it as Melanie can make a separate magazine cover for each child's costume. You can even help title the covers with little in-jokes guaranteed to raise a giggle. I pity the parent who has to host the next party after that kind of excitement!

> Price is £300.00 for a maximum of 10 children, which includes a 10 x 8 portrait for every child attending. You need to book about four weeks in advance, especially at the weekend, and she'll travel anywhere within the M25.

> Melanie Winning T·0795 233 7389
  W·melsimage.com

Also see page 167 for a Top Shop to Go party

A NIGHT TO REMEMBER

A number of organisations offer hugely popular sleepover parties. I like:

EVERY PARTY NEEDS A VIKING
> If your birthday boy or girl feels that DVDs and popcorn are 'so-o-o-o 2006', why not let him or her and seven friends have a sleepover in the Egyptian Sculpture Gallery at the British Museum. There are, however, a number of criteria...
> Firstly, you have to have at least one adult guardian, so pull straws – you'll be sleeping on the floor! Secondly, one of the children must be a Young Friend of the British Museum. Join for £20.00 a year and he/she will receive *ReMus*, the Young Friends' magazine. In this publication they list the available dates for the sleepovers throughout the year (you can't just book any night in the year). And lastly, you have to bring your own bedding.
> Each sleepover is themed – the theme of the last one they held was Vikings, where actors in fancy dress entertained with stories and activities.
> The evening starts at 6.00 p.m. and consists of story-telling, activities, crafts and prize-giving. (No dinner is offered – you must provide your own snacks). Activities continue in the morning (breakfast is provided), and the party finishes around 11.00 a.m.
> They're extremely popular and book up very quickly.
> **The British Museum T·020 7323 8195 W·thebritishmuseum.ac.uk/friends**

PARTY ON WITH THE PIRATES
> A reproduction of Sir Francis Drake's ship, *The Golden Hinde*, moored on the Thames, will host an amazing Jolly Roger party for you, where the lucky young guests can hunt for treasure, hoist the anchor and listen to wild stories.

> You'd better start saving, as it's £352.50 for 15 children, plus £10.00 per additional child.
> We loved the on-board sleepover option, giving children a taste of life as a 16th-century sailor (£39.00 per person). Period dress and meals are included in the cost. Children (aged six or over) must be accompanied by an adult and with a minimum group booking of 20. The fun starts at 5.00 p.m. and finishes at 9.30 a.m. the following day.
> **The Golden Hinde T·020 7403 0123 W·goldenhinde.org**

BECOME THE STAR OF THE JUNIOR PARTY CIRCUIT
> Find out how you can whisper across a crowded room, send a rocket to Mars, make a Science Night huggy or meet Phil the stunt frog. And then after your educational and fun evening, camp overnight in the Science Museum. The museum holds activity-filled sleepovers for children aged 8-11 years old. You'll need a group of at least five children and one adult. Bring your sleeping bag, wash bag and a packed evening snack. Some of the activities offered have included: Mission to Mars; Feel the Force; and Make it Move. It costs £30.00 per person and includes materials for workshops, staff on hand to make sure it all runs smoothly, overnight stay, breakfast and IMAX movie.
> Places fill up well in advance, so do book early to save disappointment (and figuring out what else you could do!).
> **Science Museum sleepover T·020 7942 4747 W·sciencemuseum.org.uk**

SOME GREAT
FACE PAINTERS

MAGICAL TRANSFORMATIONS
> We were in a very boisterous restaurant
packed with young families, when we saw a
rather large queue forming for Julie Clark
who was painting all the kids' faces with
fantastically realistic animals and images.
They all looked superb. If your child would
like to look like a flower, princess, bird,
butterfly, ladybird, panda or any other kind
of land animal or marine life, now you know
whom to call. Julie only uses hypo-allergenic,
professional theatrical make-up suitable for
children. She is based in north-west London,
but will travel further afield. She charges
£100.00 for two hours for up to 25 children.
> **Julie Clark, Majic Faces T·020 8205 5268
/ 07930 370 829 E·majicfaces@aol.com**

A WILD SUCCESS WITH THE KIDS
> Rena was amazing at our son's fourth
birthday party. What a talent! She painted all
the children's faces (except our son who told
us 'I've changed my mind') and they looked
stunning. It was lovely to see all the butterflies, monsters, pirates, dogs, mermaids,
batman and tigers sitting at the party table.
Rena has been painting faces for more than
five years and has over 30 different designs
to suit every occasion. She can even do
special effects like scars, bruises and bullet
holes. She uses child-friendly approved
paints and glitters from Snazaroo and
Charles Fox of Covent Garden, and also has
full insurance cover. In two hours she painted
about 16 faces, for which she charged
£70.00, great value for a gang of happy,
happy party-goers.
> **Rena Marchant T·020 7652 5505 /
07810 415 679**

> Also look at **W·snazaroo.com** which supplies
body and face paints, has a fab section in the
Gallery showing you step by step guides on
face painting ideas and a very comprehensive
directory of face painters in 15 countries.

PARTY PLANNERS

WHEN ONLY THE BEST WILL DO
> You've heard of society weddings, what about
society children's parties? Well, the woman
they all want is Marina at Kasimira, who
organises the most amazing bespoke parties
with such vitality and enthusiasm she gets as
excited as the children! Marina and her team
meet you for an initial consultation, then
come up with a bespoke idea depending on
your budget and the age of the children.
They have many high profile clients, but
won't reveal names (one three-hour party
they designed cost £70,000.00!)
> They absolutely love doing family parties,
where the adults have just as much fun
delicately tasting a spoonful of caviar taken
from the mouth of a large lion ice-sculpture,
as the kids do eating organic mini-burgers at
the mini food stalls. Their parties have
included one with a *Chitty Chitty Bang Bang*
theme with the real original car from the
movie, and one with a Victorian fairground
and Victorian games – the children were
given task cards which when completed were
rewarded with a visit to the scrumptious
sweet shop – you even had to dodge the
child catcher!
Prices: Parties start from £3,000.00
> **Kasimira T·020 7581 8313
W·kasimira.com**

*See page 199 for Michele Gudino, who offers
very creative party planning.*

*See pages 11-16 for caterers who also offer a
party-planning service*

PARTY FOOD
& REFRESHMENTS

LAUGH, I NEARLY STARTED

> You remember the ones – *Where do horses go when they're ill? The Horse-pital!* and *Man: Doctor, Doctor. My wife thinks she's a clock. Doctor: Well, stop winding her up then.* – that had you in hysterics when you were young(er). Well, Click the Cookie sell a great Giggle Tube for children with 30 cookies, each with 'an hilarious, side-splitting joke', individually wrapped in gold foil. At £12.99, it's a great idea for a party (click on Children's Fortune Cookies).

> **Click The Cookie T·01279 793 090
> W·clickthecookie.co.uk**

THE ICE VAN COMETH

> For an extra cool event, how about your own refurbished 1970s ice-cream van serving up scrummy flavours like gin and tonic sorbet (perhaps for the parents only), roasted pumpkin ice-cream or Valhrona chocolate sorbet with a brandy snap?

> You can now hire Lola's ice-cream van, with ice-creams and sorbets that are restaurant-made daily, contain no GM ingredients and are mostly organic. It costs £200.00 for up to two hours within London; £300.00 within a 40-mile radius of London, plus £3.00 per ice-cream. They can also deliver one-litre tubs for dinner parties, so you won't feel left out if you're entertaining on a smaller scale.

> **Lola's on Ice T·07871 797 260
> W·lolasonice.com**

THEMED FOR SUCCESS

> Anyone who has spent most of their child's long-awaited birthday in the kitchen producing dinky sandwiches, mini pizzas and cupcakes, not to mention all the canapés and drinks for the adults, will be very relieved to hear about Sparkles Parties. They can theme the cake and party food to reflect a favourite character,

hobby or interest, and what's more, everything is home-made and they can cater for any food intolerances and allergies, or supply all-organic goodies (at extra cost).

> Biscuits have been cut into the shape of Thomas the Tank Engine, The Incredibles and even the odd football or two. Fairy Cakes have been decorated with popular characters and even meringues have had the celebrity treatment. For the savoury food, Dinny Standen is happy to shape cheese biscuits but tends to leave the delicious sandwiches alone!

> Dinny also offers great cake designs for weddings and birthdays. Allow around two weeks' notice. Minimum charge: £9.00 for each food box (seven items plus drink) for a minimum of 15 children. Delivery is usually within M25 (delivery charge extra), but she will consider going further afield.

> **Sparkles Parties T·020 8549 2561 /
> 07050 114 047 W·sparklesparties.co.uk**

See pages 11-16 for top caterers who are often called on to cater for children's parties.

GREAT SWEETS
FOR PARTY BAGS

PIC'N'MIX A FEW SWEET MEMORIES

> Nothing takes us back to our childhood quicker than reminiscing with friends about what our favourite sweets used to be (and the huge bag full you could buy for your 10p pocket money!). I'll never forget the Black Jacks, gobstoppers, and flying saucers I used to look forward to all week and buy on a Friday on the way home from school. If you want to redevelop a taste for those early delights, these sites will fill your party bags with them. They even offer sugar-free selections, which is great.

> **W·aquarterof.co.uk T·01254 262 160
> W·sweetsforu.co.uk T·01257 400 780**

WORDS TO SAVOUR

> We received one of these personalised chocolates from a three-year-old as a 'thank you for my birthday present'. Eat Your Words produces a great selection of wrapped chocolate goodies for birthdays, Christmas or other special occasions. Just add your own message, or create your own design and message, which they will reproduce for the wrapping on the chocolate bar.
> **Eat Your Words T·01244 851 232 W·eat-your-words.co.uk**

GUILT-FREE TREATS

> I tried these sugar-free sweets thinking they wouldn't really taste any good, but I was very surprised. Then I gave Finn, my 5 year old son some and he scoffed the lot. Their Jelly Bears and Fruit Jellies have added vitamin C, natural colours, are sugar free and low carb. Available at selected Coffee Republic stores, Harvey Nichols' Food Hall, Selfridges and Fresh & Wild.
> **W·skinnycandy.com**

CHILDREN'S PHOTOGRAPHY

NATURALLY TALENTED

> Andrew is renowned for his wedding photography, as his website will attest, but he also has a knack for capturing children in a very natural way.
> **Andrew Florides T·01502 714 007 / 07710 496 070 W·andrewflorides.com**

FRAME YOUR FAMILY

> Lena Proudlock takes the most amazing photographs of children and families. The session costs from £295.00 and after the shoot she gives you a DVD of all the shots so you can make your choice. (*See also page* 131.)
> **Lena Proudlock, Berkeley House, 4 The Chipping, Tetbury, Gloucestershire GL8 8ET T·01666 500 051 W·lenaproudlock.co.uk**

For another two great photographers who take stunning child portraits, see page 283.

GREAT SHOPS TO VISIT

It's taken a while, but finally businesses are realising that shopaholics aren't cured of their addiction when they produce children – they just have more people to buy for! These places have everything you could ever need, and more:

A FAIRYTALE FIND

> This is the kind of shop you dream about as a child. It has shelves and tables filled to the brim with beautiful wooden toys, wonderful books, fancy dress, games, kites, boats, musical instruments and lovely baby toys. I couldn't resist the wooden swinging jester and the multi-picture block puzzles. The owners wanted to give children a good choice of quality toys all under one roof. They source from artisan makers and small companies in Britain and across Europe to find the stunningly crafted wooden cars and sailing boats, and soft, soft cuddly toys, many of which are handmade.
> With things like traditional elastic band-powered cars and pedal cars, you won't even need to stock up on costly batteries. Children (and the occasional adult) have to be dragged out by their ears!
> **Bramble Corner, The Square, Lewes Road, Forest Row, East Sussex RH18 5HD T·01342 826 800 W·bramblecorner.com**

GET SHACKED UP

> Maria and Gary are always travelling to source amazing accessories and gift ideas for their lovely shop, Chic Shack. They offer a great mix of painted furniture inspired by French and Swedish 18th-century designs, and contemporary children's and baby furniture. They also offer a made-to-order service

making furniture that can be disassembled if you move home – a great idea as there's nothing worse than having beautiful furniture made which you then have to leave behind. Their accessories, glassware, bed linen and stationery are great for newborn and christening gifts. And there are so many things for grown-ups that you might forget why you went in there in the first place!

> **Chic Shack, 77 Lower Richmond Road, Putney, London SW15 1ET**
> **T·020 8785 7777 W·chicshack.net**

BUYER BEWARE – THIS STORE COULD MAKE YOU POOR!

> Situated in the yummy-mummy area of Primrose Hill, this shop is bound to go down a storm. When it first opened I popped into Elias & Grace just to see if it was 'worthy' and spent a fortune – you wouldn't believe how worthy it was! Lovely gifts for newborns and children, from money-boxes and baby blankets, to colourful hand-knitted toys made by Blabla, a women's co-operative in Peru. Downstairs they stock fashion suitable for pregnancy – I drooled over a Matthew Williamson beaded cashmere coat and had to be dragged back upstairs.

> They also sell 100 per cent natural health and beauty products, including the wonderful NZ beauty range, **Hema**. The cleansing oil should be in everyone's bathroom, it's absolutely divine. You can book an appointment out of shop hours, which is very useful if you're on a hectic schedule.

> **Elias & Grace, 158 Regents Park Road, Primrose Hill, London NW1 8XN**
> **T·020 7449 0574 W·eliasandgrace.com**

A WARM WELCOME GUARANTEED

> Much needed in Islington, Igloo offers a friendly and fun haven, selling an eclectic range of clothes, shoes, toys, gifts, books, party stuff and more, for newborns to 12-year-olds. Their aim is to strive to do that bit more for their customers, for example they've introduced special services including on-site haircuts. We purchased the amazing Trunki here, a great sit-on/pull-along suitcase for young travellers (*see page* 297).

> **Igloo, 300 Upper Street, Islington, London N1 2TU**
> **T·020 7354 7300 W·iglookids.co.uk**

POP IN TO THE ONE-STOP HAPPY SHOP

> Visit, even if it's just to lie on their sofa for a cup of coffee – we bet you won't leave empty-handed. Semmalina is a prime destination and offers all sorts of wonderful treats, from one-off presents to hard-to-find, exclusive children's wear.

> For parties they offer their amazing StarBags party bags for any occasion (*see page* 287), fancy dress costumes and a made-to-order pass-the-parcel service. We love their unique Grab 'n Go bag with everything a parent and child needs for travelling – especially on long-haul plane trips. All bags can be tailored to your needs and include fantastic goodies. They also offer a great newborn pressie of a nappy bag full of useful and fun things.

> Semmalina is owned by sisters Emma Forbes and Sarah Standing who love to shop for unique, vintage furniture for kids, exclusive fashion and other amazing presents, so every time you go in there is something different.

> **Semmalina, 225 Ebury Street, London SW1W 8UT**
> **T·020 7730 9333 W·starbags.info**

IT'S IN THE MAIL...
ONLINE SHOPPING

If I hadn't received a fantastic car bed, with matching petrol-pump bookcase, from my dear friend Nina when she left the UK, then I would have decorated our son's room with lovely things purchased from these great mail order companies:

QUALITY THAT DELIVERS

> Aspace produces a range of cots, beds, bedding, wonderful sleepover solutions and fab furniture. Their aim is to '*produce terrific furniture especially for children that will look great and do its job without fuss for years to come.*' They also deliver when convenient to you – none of that annoying 'sometime between 8.00 a.m. and 6.00 p.m.' nonsense.

> **Aspace T·0845 872 2400 W·aspaceuk.com**

FAMILY FUN FOR YEARS TO COME

> From the practical, to the fun, to the educa-tional, the Great Little Trading Company has some fantastic things for children. Order their catalogue and we bet you'll spend ages marking the pages for the absolute 'have to buy' items. There's a great selection of furniture, playtime furniture, toy storage, bookcases, lockers, bed linen, toys, costumes, clothes and practical bits. We had to buy the bunny alarm clock for our son Finn who kept coming into our room at 5.30 a.m. It's great for children who can't tell the time – you set the alarm and the bunny's eyes open and ears pop up when it's okay for them to get out of bed. The kids' car organiser is also a must, along with some fabulous personalised Christmas gifts.

> **Great Little Trading Company T·0870 850 6000 W·gltc.co.uk**

BOX OF DELIGHTS

> Another innovative company where our friends buy lovely goodies. You can search the presents by age range, which is very handy – I never used to know what a seven year old boy would like for his birthday!

> They've great toys and personalised presents, especially the write your own book which comes back wire-bound after the child has written and illustrated the pages.

> **Letterbox T·0870 6007878 W·letterbox.co.uk**

SHOPPING SERVICES

DO YOUR WHOLE 'TO DO' LIST TODAY...

> First babies bring a lot more 'firsts' – first cot, pushchair, steriliser, bottles, nappies – the list goes on and on. It's not easy choosing the right ones among the endless products, equipment, clothing and furniture on offer. Should I get the three-wheeler buggy or the one that's easier to take on a bus? Should I buy the plastic milk bottles or the glass? Should I go with cloth nappies or disposables?

> Visit Babylist and you'll have all those questions answered. Having been in business for over 10 years and also being the first nursery advice service in the UK, these guys really speak from experience. They offer a truly unbiased consultation service and do not sell from stock but order specifically for each client.

> They offer all the best baby equipment and advice under one roof, with everything having been tried and tested by independent researchers. You'll find all the best-known brands, as well as some exclusive discoveries.

> If you pop into their London showroom, for a one-off membership fee you'll receive a private consultation, and you can see and test from the extensive products on offer.

> Once chosen, all goods are delivered two weeks before your due date, with no delivery charge, at a time to suit you, and they will even unpack and assemble – definitely worth it!

> Actually, talking of due date, they had a client whose twins arrived two months early, very unexpectedly. They got a panic call from the husband – help! And although not expecting to deliver for another month, they got every-thing to them the very next day – now that's fantastic, personal, flexible service. They say: 'You deliver the baby – we deliver the rest.'

> **Babylist, The Broomhouse, 50 Sulivan Road, London SW6 3DX T·020 7371 5145 W·babylist.com**

TRAVELLING WITH CHILDREN

Also see page 122 in Travel.

HELP IS CLOSE AT HAND

> The four most-hated words heard on a long car journey are 'Are we there yet?' and the next must be 'That will be £7.99', when you order one cooked breakfast which has seen better days at the service station. The ingenious Peter Keep has come to our aid: He has set up 5minutesaway, a directory of services and facilities available for motorists at or near each motorway junction. It provides information on pubs, hotels, petrol, restaurants and places of interest within three miles (or five minutes) of a motorway junction, not to mention shopping! He also includes clear directions on exactly how to get there, and other traffic and weather information. A useful site – pop it in your favourites.

> **W·5minutesaway.co.uk**

GET THE INSIDE GOSS' ON FAMILY TRAVEL

> Well worth taking a look at, babygoes2 has many plaudits and has been developed and staffed by parents for parents travelling with babies and children. Up-to-date research provides you with child-friendly escapes around the world, with or without childcare. And due to the popularity of the site, they have been able to negotiate with top tour operators and individual service providers for special offers and discounts. They also offer useful information, tips, advice, essential shopping and location reports and features.

> **W·babygoes2.com**

LIGHTEN YOUR BABY LOAD

> I'll never forget the paraphernalia we had to take when we went to the USA with our young baby. His nappies, special food, non-perfumed wipes, organic sun-cream and so on took up over half of our weight allowance. Given the new restrictions on luggage these days, babiestravellite is fantastic with a capital F! Shop online for all your baby's essentials and they will deliver to your holiday destination in the USA, from $5.00. They can also deliver worldwide, but due to international shipping restrictions, you may have to pay slightly more to cover import duty and taxes (see online for details).

> You can choose by individual brand or shop in bundles; they even have a special product request service and will try and source your exact requirements if you can't see exactly what you want in their extensive list of products. The website also has a handy travel-guide section with a baby travel forum, top USA hotels, resorts and spas, travel tips, airline policies, destinations and useful baby equipment rental services.

> Place your order at least 15 days prior to delivery – though they do offer a rush, urgent delivery service if you've left it to the last minute.

> **W·babiestravellite.com**

PAIN-FREE TODDLER TOTING

> Carrying my child when he was younger, for any length of time proved to be extremely difficult with my slightly dodgy back, so we were very interested in the Hippychick Child Hipseat, which was designed to alleviate backache caused by carrying children around. The Hipseat is a back-supporting belt with a padded foam shelf providing a firm shelf for your child to sit on, whilst supporting their weight from underneath. Instead of twisting the spine, the back stays straight.

> These are especially great for those long walks to the departure gates, when they have taken your buggy off you and you won't get it again until luggage collection (and the buggies are always the last luggage through!) CE tested to 30 kgs, and suitable for children

aged six months to three years.
Priced at £34.95.

> **Hippychick Limited, 1 Roberts Drive,
Taunton Road, Bridgwater, Somerset
TA6 6BH
T·01278 434 440 W·hippychick.com**

A SIMPLE STEP TOWARDS PEACE OF MIND

> Identifyme tell us that a staggering 80 per
cent of parents admit to losing their child at
some time before it's tenth birthday. If you've
ever worried about your little one wandering
off or being lost while shopping or in a crowd,
this is the perfect product for you. For peace
of mind, write your contact details, or your
hotel details if you're overseas, onto one of
these identity bracelets and strap it onto
your child. They are water and tear-proof
and are available in a range of European
languages. We used them when we travelled
to Singapore and New Zealand, and have also
given packs to friends who also loved them.

> They come in packs of three reusable
wristbands with an indelible pen for £5.00,
or a pack of 15 single-use wristbands for
£4.15. They also offer the Tomy Out and
About monitor (which looks fab), and allergy
and medical alert bands. Great idea, great
prices. Also available in Boots and
Mothercare stores.

> **T·0845 125 9539 W·identifyme.co.uk**

ARE YOU SITTING SAFELY?

> Our toddler was forever getting out of the
arm restraints on his car seat which made
for unsettling driving – and we were not
alone with this problem. Six out of eight
mums at my postnatal group had encoun-
tered the same thing. So we were all
delighted when Bev discovered the SnugSit
which fits neatly between your child and the
shoulder straps and secures them for great
child-proofing. It can also be used in a high
chair and pushchair.

> **Snugsit T·01394 386 725 W·raitzen.com**

ANYONE KNOW THE SPANISH FOR ORGANIC PRUNE PUREE?

> Just before we went to press I read
about tinytotsaway on **W·springwise.com**
(they always keep me abreast of fab ideas).
It's a service, similar to the one on page 296,
run by a British company, offering all your
child's necessities to be ordered online
and delivered to your holiday destination.
The range of goods is excellent, including
eco-friendly nappies and organic baby foods.
Nor more wasting hours of your holiday
trying to decipher or guess what products
you need in an under-stocked and over-
priced resort supermarket.

> Try to place your order 14 days prior to
travelling so you won't incur the admini-
stration charge. Costs are calculated
according to the country you are visiting
and the weight of the products ordered.
Weights are calculated in 12 kg increments,
and for non-EU countries a customs
clearance charge is also payable.

> **W·tinytotsaway.com T·01257 424 241**

DON'T LEAVE HOME WITHOUT IT

> This site has tons of helpful tips and
information for local and long-haul travel,
and many great products. I bought the
DermaHydra HandiKlenz (alcohol-free hand
sanitiser – £6.99), suitable for adults and
babies, and very useful when travelling
through locations where soap and (clean)
water are not readily available.

> **T·0845 2600 892
W·travellingwithchildren.co.uk**

TRUNKI HAS LANDED

> When I saw Trunki in *Junior* magazine I was
on the phone immediately to Magmatic to
find out where I could buy one locally before
heading off to New Zealand, via Singapore,
with our four-year-old son. I knew we were
going to be hanging round a lot of airports
on this trip, not to mention the long flights,

so this served two purposes at once. We filled it with all manner of treats to keep him occupied on the flight, and when we were at the airport he either pulled it himself or when he was tired we pulled him along on it (you can also carry it with the shoulder strap). It drew enormous attention and we were always being asked "Where did you buy that?".

> It is approved for hand luggage and is lightweight and durable. 10/10!
> Available in blue (Terrance) and pink (Trixie); suitable for children 3+ @ £24.99.
> **Trunki – Magmatic Ltd, PO Box 2604, Bristol BS8 9BH**
> **T·0870 626 0002 W·trunki.co.uk**

DID YOU KNOW...

Did you know that if you're a lone parent travelling with a small child, then the Skycaps porter service is free at Heathrow Airport?

T·020 8745 6011 W·skycaps.com

PETS

Couldn't forget pets, after all they are part of the family too!

TREATS & GOODIES

BUSY BAKERY TAKES THE BISCUIT

> The Alldog Hotel (*page* 301) started baking biscuits for the furry friends who stayed with them for day-care or at their dog hotel. They proved so popular they created London's Bakery for Dogs offering all-natural and organic ingredients, wherever possible, with no genetically modified elements, no added salt or sugar.
> All their freshly baked dog biscuits are tested by humans, and the range includes Savoury Slobbery Snacks and Sweet Treats. I love their Happy Christmas Biscuits, Christmas Stocking-Stuffers in the shape of stars, bells and candy-canes, and their Happy Birthday Biscuits, which spell out the dog's name and a birthday greeting. The snacks in a 200g bag cost £5.99.
> **T·020 7736 7806 W·alldog.co.uk**

EVERY CAT WANTS THE BEST SEAT IN THE HOUSE

> If I wasn't allergic to cats I would have one immediately just so I could buy it one of these simply divine cat beds. Christel and Otto Meyer design furniture for cats with a capital D for design. The one I would have to have is the Rondo which is available in two designs – wall-mounted or standing. The standing version is fantastic and your kitty cat can play with it, sharpen their claws on the special scratch cover, climb on it and go night night. I also fell in love with their Christmas edition. It has a bright red felt cover, printed with a luxurious gold design – every cat owner should have one!
> All the cat beds are available in felt, wicker or leather with a brushed stainless steel stand. The cushions come in four colours and are machine washable. Beds can be shipped worldwide.
> Prices: from €699
> **cat-interiors.de, Bahnhofstraße 5, 96215 Lichtenfels, Germany**
> **T·+49 (0)9571-94 00 117**
> **W·cat-interiors.de**

BEJEWELLED PAWS FOR THOUGHT

> I want a dog immediately so that I can buy him one of these wonderful Swarovski crystal collars and leads. The Gilded Paw offer a

great selection of dog and cat accessories from travel necessities to dinnerware, as well as collars, from black floral and beaded to imported croco-embossed leather with genuine Swarovski crystals. There are even ones for special occasions – love the pink faux fur collar with jewel heart (by Pawsitively Posh). They're happy to ship overseas so don't worry if your pooch isn't about to cross the pond.

> **The Gilded Paw, P.O. Box 2507, Westlawn, PA, 19609**
> **T· USA +1 888 509 8752**
> **W· thegildedpaw.com**

COLLAR COUTURE

> I love the story of how this business came about: Two gorgeous dogs, Holly & Lil met in the park and got on so well they decided to meet every week for long walks. Their owners Elaine and Sarah were discussing how they could never seem to buy fantastic dog collars, so made some for Holly and Lil themselves. Then their friends saw them and got horribly jealous and simply had to have one too, so Elaine and Sarah made some more. Then suddenly *everyone* wanted one (sounds like the latest IT bag!) and so began the business of Holly&Lil Collar Couture.

> Combining the British tradition of quality handmade leatherwork with some fantastic designs, these collars are fashionable and extremely hardwearing. There's such a great choice: collars with charms, boho dog collars, semi-precious with adornments – crystal pearls, moonstone and rose quartz; even limited-edition Harris tweed and a safari collection with the popular animal prints. Your dog will probably have trouble deciding which one it likes best!

> I love the 'Make Me One' option, where you can order your own bespoke collar. Their handmade collars are now being worn by dogs all over the world, and they also make funky calf-leather cat collars. You can visit

them at their studio Thursday-Saturday (please phone first for hours), or other days by appointment.
Prices: Collars from £45.00

> **Holly&Lil, 103 Bermondsey Street, London SE1 3XB**
> **T· 07811 715 452 / 07836 592 415**
> **W· hollyandlil.co.uk**

LILA PAWS

> Lila Paws offer the most fantastic, stylish dog beds and if I had a dog I would buy him the Park Life Snuggle Bed (£59.99) with removable base cover for easy washing. Then when we travelled I would have to buy the customised Bel-Air Global Gallivanter (£950.00).

> Faux black moleskin interior with lovely soft napa leather straps and a diamanté buckle. On the trunk lid there's a water bowl, bone cushion, pet passport holder and fixings to attach your collar and lead. Underneath the cushion you can place any pet garments or your doggies other 'must-not-travel-without' things. Each gallivanter is handcrafted with love and care and therefore you should allow six weeks for delivery. You can also design your own little mini sofa dog beds – look at their customer gallery online, it's quite adorable.

> **T· 020 8541 5877 / 07939 258 080**
> **W· lilapaws.co.uk**

DEM BONES, DEM BONES!

> Widely known for her lovely collection of pet collars, we love Mrs Bones for her pampering treats and toys, especially the plush, squeaky dog toys with hilarious names such as the Kate Sprayed Bag, Jimmy Chew, Manolo Barknik, Dolce and Grrrbana Shoes, a Chewy Vuiton bag and a Dog Perignon Champagne – just may stop him chewing on your own designer favourites!

> **Mrs Bones T· +1 877 767 1308 / +1 757 412 0500 W· mrsbones.com**

ARE YOU SOFT ABOUT YOUR PET?

> Chat, Cat, Chien, Dog, Grrr, Meow, Prrr, Woof – I love these pet cushions made by Cosima Pole from an assortment of patterned cotton, faux suede or fleece. You can custom-design your cushion by choosing from over 20 covers for the background fabric, then choosing the appliqué material and lastly one of the eight words. For a small extra charge, you can even have your pet's name sewn on the cover. Three sizes cater for little and large pets from £36.00.

> **Cosima Pole T · 0148 871 236
W · objects-of-design.com**

INDOOR CONVENIENCE

> I would think that this is the apartment/flat doggie-owner's dream invention. You get your very own indoor patch of real green grass (synthetic also available) with its own concealed plumbing system. You just have to remove the water pan that traps those 'cock the leg' moments. Naturally, you also have to water and mow the grass (with scissors), but this seems a small price to pay for Rover or Fifi to have their own personal lawn.

> **PETàPOTTY Showroom: 1026 S. Santa Fe Avenue, Suite 103, Los Angeles, CA 90021 T · +1 888 PET PAWS (738 7297)
W · petapotty.com**

GROOMING

ALL DOGS, ALL THE TIME

> We've mentioned Alldog elsewhere for their organic doggie biscuits (*page* 298), their Alldog Hotel (*page* 301) and their dog-walking services (*page* 303). Not surprisingly then, they also offer an excellent grooming service. They only use the finest shampoos and conditioners that keep coats soft, supple and tangle-free (including a special stain-removing shampoo for dogs with white or light coats), so your pooch will enjoy a wonderful grooming session. They also use a range of products for dogs with skin irritations or other sensitive skin conditions. Their range of treatments starts from £18.00 and they will pick up and drop-off your pooch for an extra £7.00 each way.

> **T · 020 7736 7806 W · alldog.co.uk**

DOGGIE BATHTIME MADE EASY

> Gone are the days of trying to get Rover into the bath with a ton of water spilling on the floor. Now you can sit back, relax and stay dry, as this family-run business visits your home or workplace to wash and groom your dog for you. They can even do it outside if you can run the electricity.

> As their name suggests, Mobile Dog Wash offers a full mobile dog-washing service, warm water spa-bath facility, turbo dryers (low heat and low noise), specialist shampoo and conditioners, and a grooming service. Prices: £10.00–£100.00 depending on the size of your dog and travel time. (Unfortunately they only cover the Kent area.)

> **Mobile Dog Wash T · 01622 843 658 / 07909 696 389
W · mobiledogwash.ukonline.co.uk**

DOG ABOUT TOWN

> Pet Pavilion was founded in Chelsea in 1995 as 'the ultimate place to indulge your pet'. They offer great services, from home delivery of pet products, to a delivery and collection service for grooming. Under the direction of Dan Thomas, who has been billed as the Nicky Clarke of pet hairdressing and has over 30 years' experience, your pooch will be given one of the best wash and blow-dries of his or her life. Dan has an excellent knowledge of show preparation and professional grooming, and your dog can have the full treatment, which includes a personal consultation, haircut, teeth, ear and gland check, and a manicure, or just a wash and dry choosing a tailor-made shampoo and treatment.

> As an added bonus, if your furry friend is suffering from abandonment issues and chewing up your best rug when you leave for work, or perhaps you're both battling for dominance over the comfiest armchair, Dan has also studied the psychology of dogs and can provide 'relationship therapy' to address any behavioural problems.

> They offer gastronomic delights, a fantastic selection of toys, treatments and accessories, even perfume and relaxing music. Due to popular demand, they also have a selection of party hats and party goodies for when clients throw Pugs from the Parks parties.

> Delivery/collection from £10.00; grooming prices vary so check online or phone. And remember, they are 'not simply retailers but masters in pet care'.

> **Pet Pavilion, Chelsea Farmers Market, 125 Sydney Street, London SW3 6NR T·020 7376 8800 W·petpavilion.co.uk**

> **or 174 Kensington Church Street, London W8 4DP T·020 7221 1888**

HOME
AWAY FROM HOME

RED CARPET TREATMENT FOR YOUR TOP DOG

> You may have already read about Alldog's organic doggie biscuits (*page* 298) and their dog-walking services (*page* 303). They offer two other great services for dog owners – day care or overnight stays at the Alldog Hotel. Run by Leila and Dinny Konig who've had a lifelong passion for dogs (their regular hotel guests call them their doggie 'god-parents'), their mission is '*to create a safe, healthy and happy environment for dogs. Whether it's for a day, a week or only a walk, we provide a place where your dog will receive lots of love and attention with our friendly and flexible services.*'

> If it's day care you require, they'll look after your dog in their private home, offering play with adults and other dogs. They have a large, gated outside garden, a spacious indoor lounge (with loads of beds and toys), and offer long walks in the park. We love it that if they pick your dog up s/he gets to listen to some great tunes, and they announce their arrival by beeping their 'woof woof' horn!

> It costs from £25.00 (8.00 a.m.-5.00 p.m.), plus £10.00 for pick-up and drop-off service, and they take a maximum of six dogs at a time. As they have limited spaces for day care, due to their regulars like Bud and Chester, Bartok & Bella, Mr Big and Scrabble, you need to book in advance.

> If you're off on hols or away for a couple of nights, then book your doggie into their Alldog Hotel with prices for an overnight stay from £25.00, or £35.00 per 24-hour period.

> **Alldog Hotel   T·020 7736 7806 W·alldog.co.uk**

THEY'LL BEG TO BE SENT TO THE DOG HOUSE

> Country walks, lots of play sessions, group runs, swimming in streams and ponds, occasional trips to the beach, plenty of food, toys and games, all within 350 acres of stunning woodland and meadows in Carmarthenshire, Wales. Sounds like a great holiday – but it's not for you, it's for your dog.

> But it's not a free-for-all; he also has to abide by The Dog House rules, which include no barging through doorways, jumping up or unsociable behaviour.

> The Dog House is billed as a state-of-the-art activity holiday and training facility designed for the education and enjoyment of dogs. Your dog will be given individual attention and the companionship of humans and other dogs, and return home fitter, healthier and not to mention, with great manners. Run by the lovely Gillian and Mark Thompson (Mark has a special way with dogs and is often referred to as one of the leading professional

dog trainers in the UK, although he's far to modest to say so himself!), The Dog House also offers residential training courses on puppy socialisation, general companion training, gun-dog training and individual consultancy so your dog will sit on command and won't beg, pee on the carpet or steal your roast dinner when your head's turned.

> They can pick up your dog from Fulham, London, or along the M4 to Wales in their state-of-the-art Hill's Mercedes Dog Bus (£35.00 each way). I loved the picture online of all the dogs sitting in front of a roaring fire watching TV – priceless!

Prices from £27.00 (plus VAT) per day.

> **The Dog House (UK) Ltd, Dinas Farm, Talog, Carmarthenshire SA33 6PD**
  T · 07000 364 364
  W · thedoghouseonline.net

PUT HIS NAME DOWN FOR PUPPY PARADISE

> The lovely John Burton and his family, Jenny, Mark and Julie-Ann, run the Elmwood Exclusive Hotel for Dogs where 'Dogs come first.' In business for over 30 years and the winners of many awards, your dog will be very lucky to have a stay here – that is if s/he passes for membership, and makes it to the top of the long waiting list. They only board 10 dogs at a time, and each dog has to pass a compulsory vetting system prior to being considered. Once accepted, the dog will have his own carpeted room equipped with his own bed, duvet or blankets, armchair and television. They like it to be a home away from home – that may even include playing the dog special songs on request or playing its favourite video.

> The canine guests have wonderful freedom and play with the other dogs in Pooch Park, with a large patio, shaded trees, bushes and a well-manicured lawn. At dinner time they head off to Pooch Palace, with a living and dining room where they can watch cartoons

on the TV – it seems that most of the dogs prefer *Tom & Jerry*!

> The longest resident stayed three years, while his well-known owner was working overseas. And when 'Elvis' comes to stay he has his own suitcase, collar, bags and towels inscribed with his name. With many clients from London, they offer a pick-up and drop-off service in their own jeep, although most dogs (many of whom are the beloved pets of celebrities and members of royal families) are chauffeur-driven to the Hotel. One client's dog is used to being fed beautifully cooked bones delivered by Harrods – they can't offer that, but what they do get is a service second to none. Okay, one dog has been given a tiny, tiny lick of champagne (but only at its owner's request). And for long-standing clients they're very happy to look after the dog in his old age. With acres of grounds and lovely walks in the countryside, the dogs often prefer living there to Belgravia – in fact, they have been known to sulk a bit when going home!

> **Elmwood Exclusive Hotel for Dogs, Elmwood, Swan Bottom, The Lee, Great Missenden, Buckinghamshire HP16 9NQ**
  T · 01494 837 420

INTRODUCE YOUR DOG TO THE LAP OF LUXURY

> This intimate boutique hotel, which has won awards for the Best Small Hotel in London, has views over Kensington Palace gardens and a wonderful service called the Milestone's Privileged Pooch Package.

> If you simply can't travel without Fido, they offer you and pooch a deluxe double or twin room and lots of treats. For doggie there are treats and toys, dinner, dog pillow and dog bowl. For you – a gift, an itinerary for dog-walking trips along with poo-poo bags for cleaning up, dinner for two and a full English breakfast. One night for two, plus dog, from £225.00.

> For longer stays of seven days or more, you could book one of their sumptuous, fully-serviced apartments. Or perhaps a suite, which includes 24-hour butler service and use of the hotel's Bentley for dashing off to the airport.

> **The Milestone Hotel & Apartments, 1 Kensington Court, London W8 5DL**
> **T·020 7917 1000 W·milestonehotel.com**

PET-SITTERS & DOG-WALKERS

DOOR-TO-DOOR SERVICE

> AllDog offers three walks per day during the weekdays and one walk per day on the weekends. Their early-bird walk is from approximately 7.30 a.m. till 9.00 a.m. and the afternoon walks from 2.30 p.m. till 4.00 p.m. while the day walk is slightly longer at about two hours from 11.00 a.m. till 1.00 p.m.

> They take a maximum of six dogs on the walks, with two on a leash at any time. (You need to book in advance due to the limited space.) They have a great run either in Hyde Park or on Wimbledon Common, get plenty of treats, bottled water and even practice the odd trick or two.
> Prices: from £15.00, including pick-up and drop-off in their custom-fitted van that announces itself with a 'woof woof' horn.

> Alldog's other services include Alldog grooming (*page* 300), and day care and the Alldog Hotel (*page* 301).

> **Alldog T·020 7736 7806 W·alldog.co.uk**

THE SERVICE YOU'VE BEEN PRAYING FOR

> A family-owned company established in 1992, and members of the NARP (National Association of Registered Pet-sitters), this acclaimed, self-employed team of pet-sitters offer their services throughout the UK. Recommended by the veterinary profession as an alternative to kennels and catteries,

Animal Angels provide professional house- and pet-sitters who move into your home while you're away on holiday or for business. With reputedly one of the most stringent methods of recruiting (all pet-sitters are fully insured and police checked), the pet-sitter will care for your house, aviaries, birds, cats, chickens, chinchillas, cows, dogs, donkeys, fish, gerbils, goats, guinea pigs, hamsters, horses, kittens, mice, parrots, pigs, puppies, ponies, rabbits, rats, sheep, tortoises or any other domestic animals. They've even been asked to look after a koala bear and a boa constrictor — not together, I don't think!

> The sitter is only allowed three hours per day away from your home and must be in during hours of darkness. They have long-standing clients of 12 years and are well-known sitters for the rich and famous. Prices: from £42.99 per day.

> **Sharman Dennis, Animal Angels,**
> **5 Aldridge House, Elms Road, Hook,**
> **Hampshire RG27 9DG**
> **T·0800 161 3242 W·animalangels.co.uk**

LEAVE YOUR FURRY FRIENDS IN SAFE HANDS

> Animal Aunts was created by the lovely Gillie McNicol in 1987 to provide animal care, home care and security. With over 70,000 bookings now completed, there isn't much they haven't been asked to do. Their latest booking is to look after three miniature Shetlands, 50 owls, six birds, five border collies, five Springer spaniels, four Cocker spaniels, one husky, four guinea pigs and four cats! And they even have someone on their books that can look after an elephant — not much call for that yet though!

> Gillie and her team of over 450 Animal Aunts have extensive experience in caring for animals, including horses, livestock and domestic animals. What makes them different from some of the others is that all of her pet-sitters are full-time. Their ages range from 21 to 82 years old, and she has pet-sitters who

have been dog-trainers, farmers and even vets, which would certainly calm your concerns as you head off on holiday.

> All sitters are interviewed personally and must provide impeccable references, as well as being police checked. They cover the whole of the UK and Europe, and will travel internationally. It's not only the feeling of leaving your pet/s in good hands, but also the peace of mind that your house is being looked after, your plants are being watered and your garden cared for. They even offer to take you to and collect you from the airport, and will stock your fridge prior to your return and can cook you a welcome home meal if you wish.

> If you don't require the full house-sitting service, they can provide daily visits to feed pets and/or exercise dogs, take your pet to the vet, post-operative care for your pets, and short-term care for a wedding or other event. Prices: from £43.00 per day.

> **Animal Aunts, Smugglers Cottage, Green Lane, Rogate, Petersfield, Hampshire GU31 5DA T · 01730 821 529 W · animalaunts.co.uk**

LET A PROFESSIONAL TAKE THE LEASH

> Established in 1999 by Hilary Parker, who had previously been offering pet-sitting and dog-walking to friends and family, this service proved so popular that she soon had to recruit other dog-walkers and pet-sitters. All of her employees go through a comprehensive vetting process, have been police checked and are fully insured. It's a real alternative to kennels and they can offer pet-sitting in your own home or the pet-sitter's home. The dog-walking service offers a half-an-hour or one-hour walk for your dog and they never walk more than four dogs at one time.

> **Dog Walkers UK, The Old Coach House, 69 South Road, Weston-super-Mare BS23 2LT T · 01934 424 273 / 07951 809 473 W · dogwalkersuk.com**

STRETCH THEIR IMAGINATION

> You may have seen the branded black cabs with Houndstretcher emblazoned across the side. You may not have known they offer a great dog walking-service on a regular or one-off basis. Doggie is collected from home, taken to a nearby park for a game of Frisbee, treasure hunts or fetch and, of course, gets that essential exercise which helps to relieve boredom and stress. They also offer day care, home boarding and training, dog portraits and paintings. Prices: from £15.00 per walk (fully insured).

> They also offer an English country 'dog' house hotel — Barking Bedgebury for a lovely countryside break for your dog. (**W · bestdoghotel.co.uk**)

> **Houndstretcher, Cadogan Street, London, SW3 2PR T · 07887 608 938 W · houndstretcher.com**

A HOME AWAY FROM HOME

> If the thought of your pooch being sent to a dog kennel while you head off on holiday brings you to tears, then contact Spoiled Rotten Pets. Carolyn Griffiths will introduce you to a dog-lover who will care for your dog in his or her home. The carer is only allowed one family dog at a time (unless more live together) and will shower it with all the love and attention it deserves. The carers all go through a rigorous selection process — Carolyn looks for the X factor in her carers, and believes your dog is a VIP family member and deserves nothing but the best. They regularly check the carer's homes and gardens, even the walks they will take the dogs on, and each carer signs up to Spoiled Rotten's Code of Practice. They also try to ensure that on future holidays your dog can go to the same carer who has already built up a loving relationship with your dog.

> Minimum booking is five days, although if you're a long-standing customer they may look at shorter stays. Currently Spoiled

Rotten's services are only available in Surrey, south-west London, North Hampshire, Middlesex and West Sussex, but they're growing quickly, so watch this space.
Prices: from £25.00 per day.
> **Spoiled Rotten Pets T·0845 230 8501**
W·spoiledrottenpets.co.uk

MORE THAN A PET SHOP

THE BEST REASON YET TO BUY A PET

> This shop is gorgeous, gorgeous and gorgeous, and even if you don't own a cat or a dog now, you soon will after popping in to see all the wonderful things you could buy for your pet. And just so you don't feel totally left out, Mungo & Maud do stock a few desirable pieces that just may tempt you anyway! Their dog beds are so attractive, for example, that one customer bought one for a cushion for her sitting room!

> This shop on the block is *the* dog and cat outfitters. Husband and wife team Michael and Nicola Sacher came up with the idea when trying to source suitable products for George, their English setter. He now gives his paw of approval to many of the products. Attention to detail is at the heart of everything, with handmade or uniquely sourced products that are exclusive to the boutique or website. Forget the latest handbag; the new must-have accessory is a small dog carrier, or a hand-stitched, woven leather bed. Perhaps you're after a vintage speckled cat bowl from the 1930s, or a covetable cashmere pet pullover. Their own linen drawstring bags with bone motif contains Mungo & Maud's own-recipe, organic carrot dog biscuits – woof woof.
> **Mungo & Maud, 79 Elizabeth Street, London SW1W 9PJ**
T·020 7952 4570 W·mungoandmaud.com

NOT ONLY IN AMERICA

> Calling all you style-conscious pet owners, head down to Pugs & Kisses, the luxury dog and cat boutique and spa. This pet palace was set up by American Candace Maher-Walsh, her two pugs Louie and Zucchini, and her cat Ollie, when she couldn't find any cool pet boutiques like the ones in New York. Now run with the help of Gemma Smallwood, who used to own Houndstretcher (pet-sitting and dog-walking business), they offer a fantastic range of pet beds, toys, carriers, eating accessories, health & beauty products and treats with a capital T. Many of the products are sourced from America as you can find the most fabulous products for pets there.

> They also offer a grooming spa with a full range of grooming services, from aroma-therapy baths to exfoliating treatments for dry coats and a Touch-Up service for walk-in appointments. Go on, treat your pet to a soothing paw rub!
Prices: walk-in treatments from £7.00; grooming from £35.00.
> **Pugs & Kisses, 183 New Kings Road, London SW6 4SW**
T·020 7731 0098 W·pugsandkisses.com
> **Or Bluewater Mall, Lower West Village, Dartford, DA9 9SE T·01322 427 089**

Pet Pavilion, see page 300

USEFUL SERVICES
FOR YOUR PETS

WELL-BRED DECISIONS

> If, like us, you're thinking of buying a dog, then you're probably also wondering about what breed you should go for. Approximately 59 per cent of dog owners buy a pedigree pooch, with a Labrador retriever being the top choice, followed by Yorkshire terrier, Border collie, Jack Russell and German shepherd.

> Breedadog.com was set up for professional breeders or caring owners, and has a Puppies for Sale register. The list of dog breeds is extensive, and they give you very useful breed profiles and helpful advice for the new puppy owner. If you want to contact them, use the email facility through their website.

> **Breedadog Ltd, Express Courtyard, Luke Lane, Brailsford, Ashbourne, Derbyshire DE6 3BY W·breedadog.com**

POOCHES WITH PASSPORTS

> These fantastic guides are currently written for US cities, but they're very useful if you want to take your dog with you when you travel, (or if you live there!). Each *City Dog* guidebook contains an informative and entertaining review on every imaginable type of dog-care on offer including: doggie day-care, pet-sitters, dog-trainers, dog boutiques, alternative therapies, pet-supply stores and boarding kennels. There are nine guides in print (6 are being bred) – Los Angeles, New York, Washington DC, San Francisco, Chicago, Atlanta, Boston, Detroit, and there is a general guide called *City Dog: The National Hotel & Resort Guide.*

> **W·citydog.net and Sellers Publishing, Inc W: rsvp.com**

ONLINE SEARCH PARTY

> Few things upset a family more than losing their dog. Luckily this great service, funded by donations, is here to help you in your time of need. Register online and Doglost will create a missing-dog poster that you can print off or email to friends. They also email the poster to all their helpers, and dog wardens, animal rescue centres, vets and pet shops within a 30-mile radius of where the dog went missing.

> The messages of support on the site to people who are looking for their dog are heart-warming and I guarantee that the Dogs Found and Reunited section will bring tears to your eyes.

> **Doglost T·01302 743 361 W·doglost.co.uk**

GRIN AND SHARE IT

> Now in its ninth year, PetSmiles offers an extensive directory for pet owners, with over 150,000 professional and non-professional, pet-related companies listed. It brings you up-to-date with the latest news, offers pet-owner advice and message boards. They have a great classified section where you can find a pet, dog-walker, pet-sitter, warning advice for scams relating to dog-walking/sitting positions, and much more. It seems a lot of pets needed rehoming due to unforeseen circumstances of current owners, so help out there if you can. One person was even offering up to 70 Russian hamsters – the perfect gift for that hard-to-buy-for person on your Christmas list!

> **W·petsmiles.com**

INDEX

INDEX

There are two indexes, one for subjects and one for names (see page 321).
Page numbers in *italic* indicate a Secret Service boxed entry.

335

NOTES